VISUAL ATTENTION
AND COGNITION

ADVANCES
IN
PSYCHOLOGY

116

Editors:

G. E. STELMACH
P. A. VROON

ELSEVIER
Amsterdam – Lausanne – New York – Oxford – Shannon – Tokyo

FOREWORD

Edwin Land, a master inventor, had a terrific fear of an artificial, robotic eye, one which could be made to move in all directions as efficiently and effectively as the human eye, or even a rabbit eye. Imagine, he repeatedly told me, the amount of noise it would make if ever it was half as efficient as the human eye; it would be quite unbearable. However that may be, those who work on eye movement have made a lot of fearsome noises, but usually restricted to their own circle, a somewhat esoteric one, given a special place in meetings and indeed commonly having meetings of their own, to the exclusion of many others who would find their endeavours interesting if they could but understand. This is something of a pity because, in a more general conceptual context, the work on eye movements provides us with some of the most compelling evidence that vision is an active process, rather than the passive one that so many, perhaps un-thinkingly have thought it to be.

There are many reasons why neurologists have for long regarded seeing as being an essentially passive process. The most compelling among these are: the orderly connections between retina and the primary visual cortex, which recreate a "map" of the visual field on the cortex; the consequences of lesions in the visual cortex, which is virtually total blindness; and the early maturity of the primary visual cortex, compared to the surrounding, associational, cortex which matures at different stages after birth, as if its maturation depended upon the acquisition of visual experience. The associational cortex thus seemed the perfect candidate for the vague role of "understanding" actively what the primary visual cortex had "seen" passively. That such views are only now becoming outmoded should not detract from the fact that they held sway for a very long time, perhaps for much too long. Any thoughtful reading of the literature on eye movements should have been instrumental in bringing about this demise but rarely have those concerned with eye movements addressed the more general consequences, theoretical and philosophical, of their findings.

It is perhaps unfortunate that eye movements have been treated more as an engineering problem than one that is intimately linked to a system whose function is the acquisition of knowledge. I am very happy that the present book goes a long way to redress this balance and give the enormously important work in eye movements the greater weighting that it deserves in the general field of conceptualising about vision as an epistemic system. It does so in an imaginative way, by bringing together different approaches. It is right that the opening chapter should be by Larry Stark and Yun Choi, for Stark and his colleagues have pioneered the scanpath theory and this first chapter thunders loudly and clearly the message of the book, that eye movements are controlled by internal models in "top down" fashion, but always servile to the primordial function of the visual brain — to obtain knowledge about the world. To me, it is also especially gratifying to find an emphasis placed on the human brain in general and on clinical material in particular. The latter aspect has often been neglected by the "hard" scientists for the very good reason, as they suppose, that brain lesions are opportunistic and rarely confined to a single locus;

evidence from such material usually does not, therefore, have the elegance and polish of the evidence derived from experimental material. Rarely have clinical scientists presented the elaborate and utterly bewildering diagrams that are common in papers on eye movement. But the nature of clinical evidence has changed beyond recognition in the past few years and the advent of imaging techniques now allows us to look at the brain in a way that seemed unimaginable only a few years ago. The consequence is that clinical scientists have begun to surface openly at scientific meetings, rather than disguise themselves as in the past. Of special general interest in this context is the very widespread distribution, in the human brain, of the cortical centres dealing with eye movements, as revealed in a recent imaging study by Chris Kennard and his colleagues. Such a widespread distribution, when compared to cortical centres that deal with particular attributes of vision like motion, tells us how very critical the eye movements system is in the operation of the visual brain. No doubt if Edwin Land had known about the extent of the system, cortical and sub-cortical, that is necessary to ensure the efficient movement of the eyes, he would have been even more terrified by the noise that a robotic simulator will make. I do very much hope that the chapters in this book will make plenty of noise of a different kind, by stimulating many to look more into the efficacy of the motor arm of an epistemic system.

S. Zeki

London,
December 1995

INTRODUCTION

W.H. Zangemeister[*‡], *H.S. Stiehl* [†‡], *C. Freksa* [†‡]

University of Hamburg
[*]Neurological Clinic
[†]Department of Computer Science
[‡]Doctoral Program in Cognitive Science

Vision plays a special role for the acquisition of human knowledge about the external world: what we see with our own eyes we take for granted to a much larger extent than what we hear. What we see also has a stronger impact on our "insights" than what we perceive with other senses — possibly with the exception of the olfactory sense. Our belief in our visual sense is so strong that frequently we do not consider its output as knowledge about the world subjected to errors, but simply as facts.

The nature and structure of "visual knowledge" has been investigated both in theoretical and empirical studies. The theoretical studies are based on empirical data and assumptions about anatomy, physiology, and functionality of visual systems. By combining such empirical data and assumptions with mathematical notations and computational structures, models of visual systems can be proposed, while infeasible assumptions, structures, and models can be refuted on a purely formal basis.

On the other hand, natural biological visual systems can be analyzed and their structures and functions can be explored under specifically controlled experimental conditions. Furthermore, artificial technical systems with visual capabilities can be synthesized to achieve specific functional properties. In both cases, working hypotheses are tested and possibly refuted to eliminate models inconsistent with the empirical data. Consequently, empirical investigations of natural vision systems provide interesting powerful data and structure/function hypotheses for the theoreticians to work with. The theoreticians, in turn, pose challenging questions to the empiricists who then will refine their empirical inquiry. This interdisciplinary theory-empiricism-cycle allows for zooming in on critical questions more quickly than when staying within the monodisciplinary approach. Synthesizing artificial systems on the basis of both theoretical models and empirical results adds additional power to the scientific discovery process. Constructing an artifact grounded on a computational model makes its designer aware of important issues which may not have arisen both in the theoretical and the empirical work. Furthermore, certain questions can be answered much more easily using an artifact than a natural system. Thus the synthesis of artifacts complements analysis of natural systems as empiricism complements theory.

The epistemological insight into visual systems serves as a clue for the need of active rather than passive vision. Since all perception and cognition is relative to the mechanisms and assumptions built into the system, no system will be able to reflect absolute truths about the world. Rather, visual recognition is organised by both externally and internally induced factors, including past experience, anticipation, beliefs, desires, emotions, etc., all of which influence the acquisition and interpretation of visual stimuli.

The performance of humans, animals, and robots with autonomous behaviour acting in complex environments relies on the efficiency of attentive mechanisms. Visual attention and its relation to cognitive processes is one of the keys to autonomous planning and acting. The question, to which parts of the environment attention should be directed, defines the problem of voluntary gaze control for recognizing objects, landmarks, or scenes. The cognitive model of what we expect to see evidently contributes to what we actually see.

Eye movements are an essential part of vision as they use (1) the fovea, a narrow retinal field of about 1/2 to 2 degrees with high resolution sensing, and (2) the periphery of the retina, an about 180 degrees wide field of low resolution sensing, sensitive particularly to motion and flicker. Eye movements carry the fovea to parts of a scene, a picture, or a reading matter to be processed with high resolution, eventually resulting in a discontinuous sampling in space and time. Despite this selective sampling of our environment, surprisingly enough vision provides us with a smooth and complete sensation.

The goal of this book is to put together some of the main interdisciplinary aspects that play a role in visual attention and cognition. This book is aimed at researchers and students with interdisciplinary interest. It grew out of an interdisciplinary colloquium on *Visual Attention and Cognition* organized by the Doctoral Program in Cognitive Science ("Graduiertenkolleg Kognitionswissenschaft", funded by the German Science Foundation) at the University of Hamburg, Germany, in June 1994. This cognitive science program at the University of Hamburg brings together researchers from artificial intelligence, linguistics, the neurosciences, philosophy, and psychology to work on open questions of cognition by exploiting synergetic effects of theories and methodologies of the various disciplines. After the colloquium, the contributions were exchanged among the participants, further experts were invited to contribute, and the resulting versions were reviewed by two independent referees.

The book is organised as follows. In the first chapter a general discussion of the influential scanpath theory and its implications for human and robot vision is presented. Subsequently four characteristic aspects of the general theme are dealt with in topical chapters, each of which presents some of the different viewpoints of the various disciplines involved. Hence the four chapter headings after the leading chapter cover neuropsychology, clinical neuroscience, modeling, and applications. Each of the chapters opens with a synopsis tying together the individual contributions. This structure is framed by a foreword by S. Zeki and a closing comment by V. Braitenberg. In the following a brief overview of the chapters is given.

Chapter 1 is devoted to the scanpath theory with respect to both human and robot vision. In this leading chapter *L.W. Stark* and *Y.S. Choi* compare as well as contrast human and robot scanpaths and, moreover, give a selected overview of own research on these two interwoven topics.

Chapter 2 is devoted to neuropsychological aspects. *G.W. Humphreys* elucidates in his synopsis some of the specific high level strategies with respect to neglect deficits of oculomotor behaviour and with respect to research on global versus local attention switching.

G.W. Humphreys, I. Gilchrist, and *L. Free* provide evidence that visual search procedures have direct access to intermediate level rather than to primitive level representations, where perceptual groups have already been coded and primitive information is re-interpreted. It is then shown that vision does compute detailed high level information, as local 3D relationships between image features, at a high speed even at the risk of decreased accuracy.

J. Findlay and *R. Walker* report new evidence for the distinction between a form of visual neglect characterised by an impairment of spatial attention and one characterised by an impairment of object-based attention. Since visual scanning usually is thought of as a process whereby different visual locations are successively sampled, the term "visual attention deployment" is often used to describe this process. The paper examines the mechanisms involved in the control of visual attention, presenting some results relevant to control in normal human subjects and also in patients with unilateral visual neglect, a condition often regarded as a disorder of visual attention (see *Humphreys* et al. and *Haeske-Dewick* et al. in this book).

H. Haeske-Dewick, A. Canavan, and *V. Hoemberg* discuss clinical as well as theoretical reasons for distinguishing between "motor neglect", where one side of the world is perceived — consciously or without awareness — but not responded to, and "perceptual neglect", in which one side of the world is neither perceived nor acted upon. In particular, the authors differentiate the transient clinical phenomena from subtle deficits that are only detectable with sensitive neuropsychological tests and may linger on indefinitely.

B. Velichkovsky, M. Pomplun, and *J. Rieser* investigate the integration of attention, language, and cognition in the process of communication. Several new paradigms of eye movements research are presented allowing to study communication, perception, and cognition as coordinated processes. The paper provides evidence for the perspective that different neurological levels of eye movement control have different functional specializations. The data on anticipatory management of attention reveal a strong interaction of cognitive and linguistic variables sensitive to the course of communication and problem solving processes.

Chapter 3 addresses clinical neuroscience aspects of visual attention and cognition. The synopsis by *W.H. Zangemeister* relates the neurophysiological, neuroimaging-related, and neurological interpretation of the following contributions.

M. Husain and *C. Kennard* emphasize the distributed network of the dorsolateral association areas of the human cortex involving the parietal and temporal lobes responsible for attention and orientation with respect to subsequent gaze re-orientation. In particular, express saccades and the disruption of patients' pursuit eye movements made against a structured background contribute to the clinical understanding of mechanisms of attention and orientation.

R. Seitz reviews the evidence provided by activation measurements using regional cerebral blood flow (rCBF) with positron emission tomography (PET). These techniques were used for mapping the human brain structures involved in information processing during motion, sensation, and particularly vision and cognition. This includes the occipito-temporal pathway involved in object identification, and the occipito-parietal pathway mediating the spatial relationships among objects. In addition, the paper reviews evidence indicating that visual information processing in the extrastriate areas that is mediated by an occipito-parieto-temporal network is strongly modulated by selective attention to a particular feature of the visual object .

W.H. Zangemeister and *U. Oechsner* demonstrate clinical neurological findings in patients suffering from neuro-visual deficits such as homonymous hemianopia. The ability of patients to optimize their short term adaptation of eye movement strategies already within six trials indicates a top-down control of search and scanpath in these patients.

Chapter 4 is devoted to modeling aspects. In his synopsis *H.S. Stiehl* expounds basic principles of as well as approaches to modeling visual perception and cognition from the information processing perspective.

A. Schierwagen addresses the problem of modeling the spatio-temporal dynamics of neural activity in the motor map of the superior colliculus, a brain structure being of fundamental importance for eye movement. He presents empirical data from electrophysiological, anatomical, as well as behavioural studies which eventually led to a non-feedback model. It is shown that the model is capable of resembling the neural motor map dynamics which in mammals triggers neurons controlling eye movement.

H. Schwegler reports on ongoing research on computational models of animal optomotor processes, specifically neural control of prey catching in tongue-projecting salamanders with binocular vision. In his work empirical data serves as a basis for mathematical models, particularly with respect to structure and function of retinotopic maps in the optic tectum. Both a tectum model and a network model called simulander are discussed in his contribution.

K. Pahlavan presents design principles and development issues with respect to an advanced binocular semiconductor-camera system resembling the prime biomechanics of the primate eye-neck-system. After a review of basics from biological systems, he thoroughly describes the electro-optico-mechanical features of this advanced experimental system which renders possible a large number of optical and mechanical degrees of freedom. Performance data recorded from experiments, e.g. saccade speed of up to 170 deg/sec, are also presented.

H. Janßen focuses on design and realisation of a computational architecture primarily modeling stimuli- as well as expectation-guided saccades. His working system is also part of an autonomous vehicle, called MARVIN, capable of basic visual behaviour. It blends a variety of biological principles such as foveal versus peripheral visual processes, vergence and smooth pursuit, expectation-driven gaze, selective attention, etc. He also reports on technical realisation issues and experimental results achieved under laboratory conditions.

R. Bajcsy sets the focus of her essayistic paper on active cooperation principles of autonomous agents (whether biological or artificial) distributed in space and time as well as interacting with a dynamically changing environment. She elaborates on fundamental interdisciplinary issues which are conceptually and theoretically related to active cooperation. Within the proposed cooperative framework, she stresses the utilisation of specific formal methods to cope with both dynamics of an agent and its dynamic interaction with the environment.

Chapter 5 addresses aspects of eye movement recording techniques and applications. In the synopsis by *A.H. Clarke* an overview of visuo-manual process control is given.

G. Gauthier, O. Guedon, R. Purtulis, and *J. Vercher* report on experimental results that could be used to design adaptive human-computer interfaces which support novice operators in learning teleoperation tasks more quickly. Human observers closely followed the motion of a visual target presented on a screen with a hand-driven cursor. The adaptive perturbation then consisted of a sudden increase in the hand motion detector sensitivity by 2.5 in either the horizontal or vertical, or concomitantly both directions, while the target trajectory was predictable. Adaptation was observed during open-loop and closed-loop tracking with a time course commonly observed in experiments involving optical alteration of the visuo-manual relationships through prisms or magnifying lenses.

A.H. Clarke covers the development and present state-of-the-art of high-resolution eye movement measurement techniques, with special reference to video-oculography. He also gives some exemplary clinical examples.

A. Fleischer and *G. Becker* present evidence that the contextual structure of a given task determines the uptake of specific visual information. The amount of visual workload is determined by their kinetics. With respect to the amount of information processed by the subject, characteristics of the scanpath are described on the basis of the state space. Herewith criteria are obtained which show that the analysis of eye movements provides an appropriate tool for the evaluation of visual workload during multiple task performance.

W.H.Z., H.S.S., and *C.F.*

Hamburg,
May 1996

Contents

CHAPTER 1

FROM EARLY SCANPATH THEORY
TO APPLICATION OF ROBOT VISION

Visual Attention and Cognition
W.H. Zangemeister, H.S. Stiehl and C. Freksa (Editors)
© 1996 Elsevier Science B.V. All rights reserved.

3

EXPERIMENTAL METAPHYSICS: THE SCANPATH AS AN EPISTEMOLOGICAL MECHANISM

Lawrence W. Stark and Yun S. Choi

Neurology and Telerobotics Units,
School of Optometry, University of California,
Berkeley 94720-2020

Abstract

Experimental metaphysics involves two experimental approaches, one to the philosophical fundamentals of epistemology, the theory of knowledge, and the other to ontology, the theory of reality. Our contribution to epistemology centers on the scanpath theory of vision: that internal cognitive models control active looking eye movements, perception, and active vision in a top-down fashion. Quantitative evidence about experimentally recorded scanpaths has recently been obtained in the form of string editing distances which measure the similarities and differences between scanpaths made by different human observers as they view a variety of pictures. A decisive new experiment documented that scanpaths during visual imagery tasks and those scanpaths formed while looking at actual pictures were the same. The subject's tasks during the imagery period was to imagine the previously viewed picture.

Our contribution to ontology stems from the new field, popularly known as "virtual reality". This "hype" name describes virtual environments formed by computer generated dynamic pictures projected on video screens and worn as head-mounted displays. Interaction, immersion, and interest provide routes to a sense of "telepresence," the compelling feeling that the human subject is acting and behaving in this distant artificial environment. This raises the ontological question, "Why does one feel present in the pupil of one's own dominant eye, here and now, in the so-called 'native reality'?" The answer is that normal vision, like virtual reality, is formed by illusions — of completeness and clarity, of space constancy, of continuity in time, of instantaneous action, of vivacity — and these illusions create our sense of presence.

Key Words: eye movements, scanpath, perception, string editing metrics, virtual reality, illusions, telepresence, robotic image processing, vision

1. INTRODUCTION

The mind in the brain is like the grasp in the hand. (Professor Warren McCulloch)

We owe our title to Professor Warren McCulloch, to whom we wish to dedicate this paper. Philosophers have long speculated that "we see in our mind's eye", but until the scanpath theory, little evidence had been brought forward in support of this conjecture. My own introduction to philosopy came at an early stage (16 to 17) when

I was immersed in the Humanities and Colloquium series of courses at Columbia College; to paraphrase Lewis Carroll, " . . . . the muscular strength that it gave to my awe has lasted the rest of my life." We have used eye movement (EM) measurement as a key to attempt to unravel processes of this 'mind's eye,' and thus to bring scientific evidence to bear on these philosophical questions.

Eye movements are an essential part of vision because of the dual nature of the visual system, which includes i) the fovea, a narrow field (about one-half to two degrees) of high resolution vision, and ii) the periphery, a very wide field (about 180 degrees) of low resolution vision, sensitive to motion and flicker. EMs must carry the fovea to each part of a scene or picture or to each word on a page of reading matter, so that these subparts, subfeatures or words can be visually processed with high resolution. This sparse sampling procedure cannot convey to our brain the scene's entire visual information; thus an alternative process providing the illusion of "clarity and completeness" must exist, permitting us to "see" the entire visual field with high resolution. The interrelationships between the research reported here and epistemology is presented in the *Discussion* section.

Our group has pursued several indirect methods of studying the brain's internal mechanisms for perception. One method includes scanpath EMs while persons are viewing or imagining various objects, figures and scenes. These studies have led to the scanpath theory of active perception. Because it is crucial to use careful quantitative measures even for such elusive phenomena as scanpaths, a major part of this chapter is devoted to a new quantitative measure, the string editing similarity measure. Our predecessors in EM studies of perception, including Yarbus (1967), raised some of these issues. It is likely our use of bioengineering techniques allowed us to foresee the consistency of dynamic patterns of EMs and to put forward the scanpath as an experimental fact.

We have pursued another direction in setting up autonomous visual-mechanical robot systems which, although primitive, are able to carry out a mimicry of these functions. Even at its present level of behavior, the robotic scheme is full of instructive examples -- top-down models, models with diffusely directed attention, and, especially, models with visual attention directed to *local* areas, allowing for active control of the bottom-up components of visual processing.

2. EMS AND THE SCANPATH THEORY

2.1. Early scanpath experiments

The scanpath was defined on the basis of experimental findings (Figure 1). It consists of sequences of alternating saccades and fixations that repeat themselves when a subject is viewing a picture, scene or object. Only ten percent of the duration of the scanpath is taken up by the collective durations of the saccadic EMs; the intervening fixations or foveations make up ninety percent of the total viewing period, providing an efficient mechanism for traveling over the scene or picture of interest (Bahill and Stark, 1979; Llewellyn-Thomas 1968; Stark et al., 1962, 1980a).

Scanpath sequences appeared spontaneously without special instructions to subjects (Figure 1) and were next discovered to be *repetitive* and *idiosyncratic* to a particular picture and to a particular subject (Figure 2) (Noton and Stark, 1971a, b, c). However, they could be shifted somewhat by different instructions or by implicitly assumed task conditions, confirming Yarbus' (1967) pioneering work using static displays of EMs (also Brandt 1940; Buswell 1935; Jeannerod et al., 1968; Pollack and Spence, 1968). This early evidence indicated that the scanpath was not only *idiosyncratic* to a particular subject but was also strongly related to the loci of important picture information in a particular picture or scene.. For example, note that despite the fact that the important subfeatures of a single figure like the totem (in Figure 2, left column) are few, and though all subjects visited and revisited them, the sequential pathway nonetheless provided for great variety and allowed the subjects' *idiosyncratic*, sequential behavior to be clearly visible.

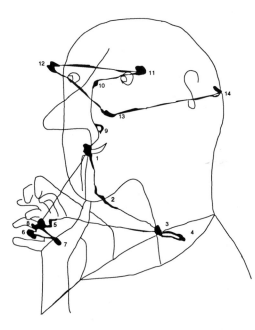

Figure 1. <u>Scanpath Sequence of EMs.</u> Irregular black lines indicate EMs made by a subject viewing for the first time a drawing adapted from Paul Klee's "Old Man Figuring." Numbers show the order of the subject's visual fixations (thick irregular dots caused by intra-fixational micro-EMs) on a picture during part of a 20-second viewing; lines between sequential fixations or foveations represent saccades, or rapid jumping, conjugate movements of eyes from one fixation to the next (modified from Noton and Stark, 1971a, b, c).

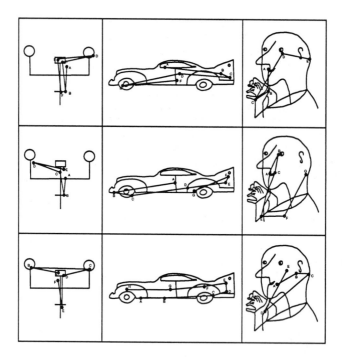

Figure 2. *Idiosyncratic* Scanpath. Variety in scanpaths is shown for three subjects and three pictures. Each horizontal row depicts the scanpaths of one subject for the three pictures. Examining the vertical rows, one sees how the scanpaths generated for any one picture also varied widely between the three subjects (modified from Noton and Stark, 1971a, b, c).

Markov matrices [M_1] capture part of the constraints of these sequences: even [M_0], or the probability of being in a particular fixation on one or another of the subfeatures, has much fewer visible constraints (Ellis and Stark, 1986; Hacisalihzade et al., 1992; Stark et al., 1979, Stark and Ellis, 1981).

When string editing similarity measures, "s"-indices (see Sections 3.2 and 3.7 below), are used to capture constrained sequential behavior, different causes of the sequential behavior can be parsed. The structure of the relevant information in the picture, including both the content and loci of the subfeatures, dictates *local* tactics. *Idiosyncratic* tactics are constrained by the standard approaches, if any, of a subject. For example, native English speakers might have a preference for starting from upper left, Hebrew speakers from the upper right. *Global* strategies, although not striking for pictures, are strongly manifest in reading text because of the standard structure of the printed page. The highest "s"-indices are, of course, for a single subject *repetitively* viewing a single picture under stationary, explicit and implicit task conditions (please refer to Section 3.7, where this subject is explicated).

2.2. Scanpath theory

These early experiments suggested to Noton and Stark that an internal cognitive model drove the EMs in the *repetitive* scanpath sequence. A more complete statement of the scanpath theory asserts that the internal cognitive model controls not only the active-looking scanpath EMs, but also the perceptual process itself, during which the foveations permit checking and confirming the sub-features of the cognitive model (Figure 3); thus, human visual perception is largely a top-down process (Noton and Stark, 1971a, b, c).

Philosophical approaches to perception from Plato to William James and Bertrand Russell suggested such a process, but until experimental scanpath studies were carried out, there was little scientific evidence to support these conjectures. Now, with rapid and precise functional magnetic resonance imaging (MRI) techniques being applied without danger to normal humans, more and diverse neurological support is expected.

The symbolic representations, or cognitive models, of a face and hands and of "this" face and hands, together with confirmation from the sparse sampling in time and space to which successive foveations contribute, provide the remarkably vivacious illusion of "clarity and completeness" characteristic of ordinary vision. The scanpath can be considered the sparse operational readout of the symbolic representation. Instructions for a scanpath include subfeatures and directions for travels from one subfeature to the next, yet even together they do not make up an iconic representation. In fact, as Professor Jerome Y. Lettvin has stated (1961, personal communication) perhaps the only iconic representation is the retinal image (O'Regan 1993)!

The contrary belief is that features of the external world control eye fixations and vision in a bottom-up mode by impinging upon the retina and sending signals to the brain. At the time of the publication of the scanpath theory, most visual neurophysiologists, psychologists, and computer vision scientists believed that events in the external world controlled EM. Their objections to the scanpath theory were reasonable.

However, an internal cognitive model must represent the external world fairly accurately or our species would have gone belly-up like the dinosaurs! But how would we be able to prove the assertion of the scanpath theory -- that an internal cognitive model and not the external world controls active-looking, scanpath EMs and the perceptual process?

SEARCHPATH THEORY: TOP DOWN COGNITIVE MODEL
CONTROLLING ACTIVE LOOKING AND PERCEPTION

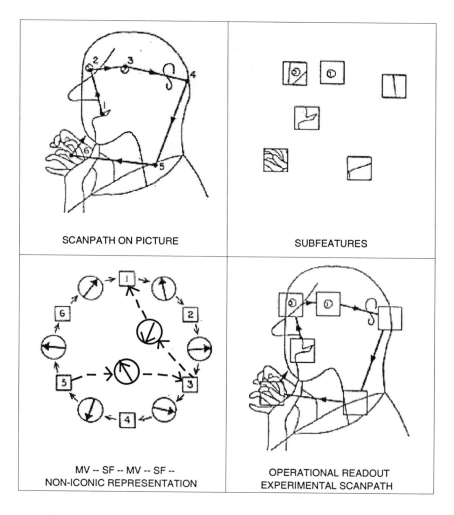

EXPERIMENTAL SCANPATH: OPERATIONAL READOUT FOR ACTIVE LOOKING

Figure 3. Scanpath Theory. Human visual perception is largely a top-down process, with a cognitive model actively driving foveated vision in a *repetitive* "scanpath" over subfeatures of the scene or picture of interest in order to check on and modify the working hypothesis or cognitive model (modified from Stark and Ellis, 1981).

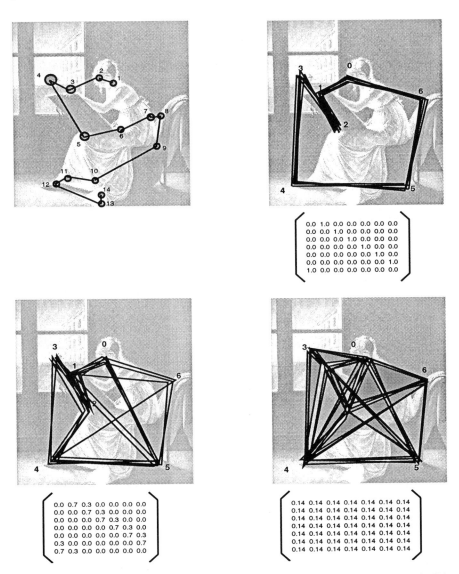

Figure 4 Markov Models for Generating Scanpaths. Simulation of scanpaths (solid lines superimposed on top of bleached pictures) from Markov matrices [M$_j$]. Coefficients listed under pictures of Madame Sevenin painted in 1807 by Madame Charpentiers of the School of David in Paris. Experimental scanpath (upper left), from Choi et al., 1995.

2.3. Ambiguous figures and Markov models

Answers to this question came from experiments with fragmented figures, ambiguous figures and necker cubes. These new results were able to show that as the mental images (representing the internal cognitive models) of an ambiguous figure changed, so the scanpath of the subjects changed (Ellis and Stark, 1978,1979; Stark and Ellis, 1981). This was true even though the physical picture in front of the subject, and thus the one imaged on the retina of the eye, was constant; strong evidence, indeed, for the scanpath theory. Recall that our problem was to experimentally separate the cognitive model and the external world for which the cognitive model was an adequate map (Brandt et al., 1989; Driels and Acosta, 1992; Ellis and Stark, 1978,1979, 1986; Flagg 1978; Singer et al., 1971).

At the same time, mathematical methods to quantitate the evidence for experimental scanpaths were developed. Experimentally determined Markov matrices of transition coefficients showed that scanpaths were neither deterministic nor equi-partitioned, but were considerably constrained by probabilistic coefficients. It was also possible to simulate quasi-scanpaths from Markov matrix coefficients[1] (Figure 4).

The deterministic matrix (Figure 4, upper right), with 1s in the superdiagonal, generates a deterministic sequential set of artificial saccades to seven selected fixation regions; these were selected by the experimenter to have relevant informational and spatial content and context and also to be coherent with several sets of experimental data. Numbers on pictures represent fixations at individual regions-of-interest (ROIs) with random location within a +/- one-half degree region; this level of scatter is likely enough in a real scanpath and useful in the simulations so that saccades do not exactly superimpose. The equipartitioned matrix (lower right) generates random scanpaths. Note that refixations from coefficients in the main diagonal are difficult to see in the figure.

The constrained probabilistic matrix (lower left), with 0.7 coefficient values in the superdiagonal and 0.3 values in the next diagonal, generates constrained, apparently scanpath-like patterns. A sample human scanpath (upper left) has numbers that represent successive fixations in a five-second period of viewing.

3. RECENT SCANPATH EXPERIMENTS AND STRING EDITING MEASURES

New experiments on reading (Figures 5, 6, and 7), searchpath EMs (Figures 8 and 9), totem scanpaths (Figures 10 and 11), and, importantly, visual imagery (Figures 12 and 13), now further support the scanpath theory. In addition, these new experiments have been subjected to string editing (Figures 6, 7, 9, 11, 13, and 14), which provides excellent quantitative evidence susceptible to statistical analysis.

---

[1] See Mandler and Whiteside, 1976; Meystel et al., 1992, 1993; Prokowski, 1971; Rybak et al., 1991a, b, 1992a, b, 1993; Schifferli, 1953; Senders, 1964, Senders et al., 1978; Stark et al., 1979, Stark and Ellis, 1981; Yeshurun and Schwartz, 1989; Zavalishin, 1968 .

Note that all regionalizations have been performed in an *a priori* manner on the text or picture presented. The difficulties of *a posteriori* regionalizations are set out in Figure 5 and in the related text below.

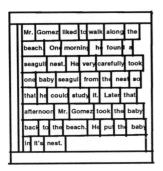

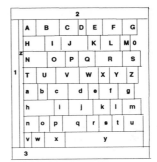

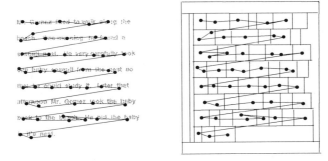

ABCEFHHIKLLNONPRRSTTUV ....   ABCDEFGHIJLMNNNOPOQRSSTU ....

Figure 5. <u>Reading EMs</u>. Page of reading text (upper left). Note straightforward *a priori* regionalization with one word per bin. These bins can be labeled with alphabetic symbols A,B,C . . . . (upper right). Fixations (heavy dots) and saccadic EMs as vectors, overprinted on reading text (lower left) and on bins (lower right); strings of alphabetic characters (bottom) representing these sequences of EM fixations (from Choi et al., 1995).

3.1. Reading EMs

It is quite straightforward to carry out *a priori* regionalization with one word per bin for a page of reading text (Figure 5) since each word makes for a natural region. The bins are labeled with alphabetic symbols (A,B,C . . . .), then fixations and vectors representing saccadic EMs from fixation to fixation are overprinted onto the reading text.   Experiments on reading EMs are ideal for illustrating the basic behavior of human EMs as well as the string editing analysis methods introduced in this text.

Experimental procedures also involved repeated calibrations, linearization and fixational definition; those algorithms will be illustrated below in Section 3.3 and have already been completed for the EM recording[2] (Figure 5, bottom left).

3.2. String editing

Fixations overprinted on bins formed from text (Figure 5, lower right) provide a means for forming a sequence of EM fixation sequences as "strings" of alphabetic characters (Figure 5, bottom line). Note that the first string is of the data shown; the second string is of another subject reading the same text.[3]

For example, twenty string editing sequences were obtained from reading text experiments on two subjects with two texts and with five presentations each (Figure 6).   The "Y-matrix" places string similarities, "s"-indices, from the experiment illustrated, into an array. The leftmost triangle encloses 45 "s"-indices representing string similarities from subject one for her ten repeated readings; the lower right triangle contains results for the second subject. The upper right square contains 100 "s"-indices for comparison of the results of the two subjects.

The *global* similarity of 0.35 documents the very strong constraint of reading text on EM fixation locations; we all have been taught that text should be read from upper left to lower right and with words ranging from left to right along each line. Further evidence for this strong constraint is that the random similarity of strings of length 44 and for 52 bins was only 0.07 (Figure 7). The larger value of 0.55 for *repetitive* represents the increase in constraint on actual locations of doubly-fixated words and of skipped words found in a single subject's similar repeated readings of the same text.

---

[2] See Abrams and Zuber, 1972; Baddeley, 1966; Carpenter and Just, 1976; Chomsky, 1957; Remond et al., 1957; Tsuda et al., 1992; Wickelgren, 1966.
[3] See Apostolico, 1988; Atallah, 1993; Bertossi, 1990; Brandt et al., 1989; Eigen et al., 1988; Hacisalihzade et al., 1992; Karp et al., 1977; Kruskal, 1983; Louchard and Szpankowski, 1992, 1993; Nussinov, 1989; Petrovic and Golic, 1993; Rabiner et al., 1978; Scinto and Barnette, 1986; Stark et al., 1992b; Wagner and Fischer, 1974; Wang and Pavlides, 1990; Wu and Manber, 1992.

```
string[1]=  DEFFGHGIJLMOPQRTTUWVXXXXYZbcdefghikkmopqrstut   size [1] = 45
string[2]=  FABCDEFGHIHJJLLPPRRUTUWWXXXUYZbcddgghjkkjnnoqrttu  size [2] = 49
string[3]=  ABCDEFFGHIIKLOPQRTUWWXXYZbcdfgghikkooprrttt  size [3] = 43
string[4]=  BCDEFGHIJKLOPQRSTUWWXXYZYZabcdfghikkmopqrstu  size [4] = 44
string[5]=  BDEEDDFGGHJILNPPQRTUWXYYZabcddfghiklopqrstu  size [5] = 43
string[6]=  AABCDEFGHIJLLNOPQRTUWVWXYZabcddgghjkkmoqrrst  size [6] = 44
string[7]=  ABCDEFFGHIJLOPPQRRTTUWXUYZbbcddeghjknoqqrst  size [7] = 43
string[8]=  ABCDEFGHJLLOPQRUTUWWXYZbccdegghjkkmnopqrstu  size [8] = 43
string[9]=  BCDEEAFGHIJLMOPQ0TTUWXYZbbccddegghikknoqrrstu  size [9] = 45
string[10]= ABCDEFGHIJIJLNOPQQRUSTUVWXXYZabcddfghikkooqrrttu  size [10] = 48
string[11]= ABCCDFFFGGGIJKLFNPPPQQRSSUUVWYZabcefghhijklmnoqqrsize [11] = 50
string[12]= ABCCDFFFGHIJLLMNPQSUVWYabdefghhjklmnprsstu  size [12] = 42
string[13]= ABCDFFFGHGHJKKLMNPQQRSSSUVWYabddefghhjlmnprstu  size [13] = 46
string[14]= ABCDEFFGHHJJKLMNPPQQSSUVVWYZbdcefghhhjjkklmmnpqrsstsize [14] = 52
string[15]= AACDFFGHHJKLMNPQQRSTUVWYZaceffghhiklmnpqrsttu  size [15] = 45
string[16]= CEFFFFFHJKLMNPQQRSUVZaddefghjknprstu  size [16] = 36
string[17]= BBCCDFFFGHGKLMUPQPRTVWYZcdfhhjklmmqrssssstu  size [17] = 43
string[18]= ABCDFFFGGGIJJKLMNPOQQRRSUVVXZacdefghhhhikllnoqrssu  size [18] = 50
string[19]= BCDFGHHIJKNPPQQSSUVVWYZacdeffghjjillmmoqqrsstu  size [19] = 46
string[20]= BCCDEFFFGHIJKLMNPPPQSSUTUVWZadefghnrqsstu  size [20] = 41
```

	1	2	3	4	5	6	7	8	9	10	11	12	13	14	15	16	17	18	19	20
1		43	63	73	56	57	59	61	60	54	29	39	43	34	49	31	35	34	45	32
2			52	50	40	57	56	56	43	61	33	29	33	41	36	14	17	35	31	27
3				73	54	66	61	68	56	61	35	48	38	38	52	23	42	33	35	32
4					61	66	61	68	57	66	35	41	41	35	57	23	35	30	48	37
5						54	59	54	52	54	35	41	35	33	54	31	45	28	42	35
6							63	70	66	69	41	48	41	41	53	25	38	37	48	37
7								66	68	61	38	41	40	42	49	25	42	35	42	37
8									63	54	24	50	40	35	56	28	40	28	42	32
9										56	25	34	36	34	45	25	33	27	38	37
10											46	36	50	42	52	20	26	46	46	40
11												48	61	62	54	25	33	62	44	57
12													62	48	60	48	60	43	41	57
13														61	65	45	40	57	48	49
14															52	39	31	62	53	57
15																45	49	49	58	49
16																	39	42	37	48
17																		28	31	42
18																			44	49
19																				44
20																				

<u>Figure 6</u> Y-Matrix of String Editing "s"-indices. String editing sequences [1 through 20] (upper) obtained (as in Figure 5) from reading text. The "Y-matrix" places string similarities, "s"-indices, in an array (lower), from Choi et al., 1995.

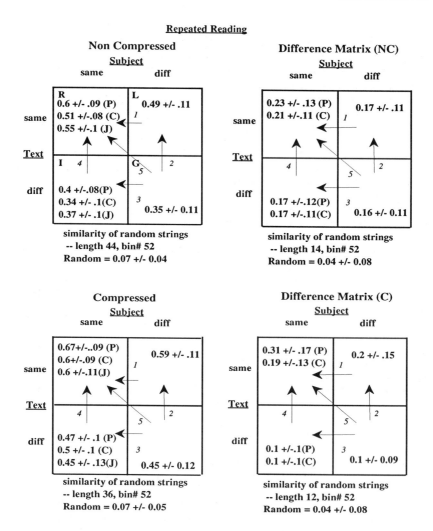

Figure 7. <u>String Similarities of Reading EMs</u>. *Repetitive* "s"-index with a value of 0.55 (in upper left box of upper left panel) indicates that when the same subject read the same text, on average 55% of the string sequences were identical. *Global* "s"-index with a value of 0.35 (in the lower right box of upper left panel) indicates that when different subjects read different texts, the string similarity was about 35%. Two types of strings were studied, compressed (lower) and non-compressed (upper). The difference matrix describes the behavior of normal subjects as compared to that of a reading robot, which fixates once on each word in sequence (from Choi et al., 1995).

Two types of strings were studied: compressed (lower) and non-compressed (upper). Our term "compressed" denotes that refixations in the same region are treated as one fixation, equivalent to setting diagonal coefficients of the $[M_1]$ matrix to zero. The similarity between the parsing of compressed and non-compressed strings enabled us to demonstrate the robustness of string editing "s"-indices. Dr. Yong Yu is working with us to compare string editing to other quantitative measures such as higher order Markov matrices (see also Ellis and Stark, 1986; Hacisalihzade et al., 1992) and linear programming, as suggested by Dr. Astley of the University of Manchester.

Parsing: For those considering the use of string editing and our parsing calculations, the numbered arrows (Figure 7) indicate the successive constraints captured by the "s"-index. Arrow 1 shows a quite modest increase in similarity when the individual subject's *repetitive* "s"-index is considered with respect to both subjects reading the same text. Arrow 2 documents the increase in the "s"-index produced by adding *local* structure, the same text page, and its resulting tactics, to the *global* strategy. Likewise, Arrow 4 shows a large increase for a single subject vs. multiple subjects; Arrow 5 indicates the largest increase from the *global* to the *repetitive* "s"-index value, again mostly due to *local* tactics. Arrow 3 shows the weak effect of a single subject's *idiosyncratic* tactics over the *global* strategies of all subjects. The difference matrix distinguishes the behavior of normal subjects from that of a reading robot, which fixates once on each word in sequence.

As might be expected, the *global* strategy component (0.35) of the "s"-index for reading is high because of the standard format of the printed page; the *local* tactical constraints of a particular page of text are also large since all subjects are constrained by the semantic and syntactical structure of a particular text even if, as is likely, this structure is enforced and control is generated by top-down models. A school of reading scholars has collected experimental evidence to the effect that present and recent information, such as word size and launching sites, have much to do with landing sites and words skipped.

Even though a whole page of text appears clear to a viewer, such illusory clarity does not correctly represent the true resolution which characterizes the eyes' ability to receive information from a page of text. In order for information transfer to take place, it is necessary for each word to be "big-R Read," that is, to be foveated during an EM fixation. In normal reading only about 60% of words are "R-Read," though the remaining 40% of unread words are counted in the nominal 300 word per minute definition of reading speed by educators; we call this "small-r reading." These numbers have been studied by reading EM researchers for over a century.[4]

---

[4]Please see McConkie et al., 1994, O'Regan et al., 1994 and Rayner, 1994 for details beyond the scope of this paper.

Visual search is a classical and important topic for eye movement and perception research. We include a number of important papers: Abernathy, 1990; Ahlswede and Wegner, 1989; Baeza-Yates and Gonnet, 1992; Brogan, 1990, Brogan et al., 1992; Choi et al., 1995; Chudnovsky and Chudnovsky, 1989; Engel, 1976; Enoch, 1959; Gal, 1980; Hilsenrath, 1990; Kiryati and Buckstein, 1990; Koopman, 1956a, b, 1957; Stark et al., 1992a, b; Stone, 1975; Waldman and Hobson, 1990; White and Ford, 1960; Yamashita, 1990.

3.3. EMs in visual search

Eye movement data were recorded for human subjects performing a visual search task in a stereoscopic, computer-generated, three dimensional scene.   Each experimental run consisted of six presentations; three different object placements on a common background (a quasi-natural scene) were used, and one of the placements was repeated three additional times.

Yamashita (1990) and Stark et al. (1992a) used head movements and windows driven by computer mouse movement to define searchpaths and employed only introductory level string editing measures. Thus a major contribution of this present paper is to extend the searchpaths to subjects making EMs over the scene without artificial apparatus such as head mounted display or windows driven by a mouse. Furthermore, the use of string editing has been expanded to quantify the *repetitive* nature of the searchpaths (Choi et al., 1995; also see footnote 4).

Defining the Searchpath The searchpath is defined as the *repetitive* sequence of saccades and fixations *idiosyncratic* to a particular subject and to a particular target pattern of loci. Searchpaths are believed to be generated and controlled by spatial models, while scanpaths are generated and controlled by the rich and compacted structures of the cognitive model.

An interesting control value is the 0.18 "s"-index for randomly constructed strings. This number is very similar to that of the "s"-index for the dissimilar searchpaths. The approximate equality of *global* and random string similarity indicates that little if any spatial modeling of the scene itself was identical or even similar among different subjects.

String editing appears remarkably useful for defining similarity and dissimilarity between EM patterns such as searchpaths and scanpaths. It is amenable to statistical analysis and robust to exact configuration size and placement of lines for regions-of-interest. Compressed strings are equivalent to sequences of fixations with the refixations removed. Although the importance of the refixations cannot be discounted, we find similar results with uncompressed and compressed strings. This similarity further demonstrates the robustness of the string editing measures.

As with most experiments, the present one has raised many questions. Can we distinguish experimentally between searchpath and scanpath?   Would a quasi-natural scene, but only a two-dimensional display, allow equally well for searchpaths? Is it possible to develop further quantitative studies able to distinguish among the various components of the spatial model and its consequences, the *repetitive* searchpath? Our computer graphic scene is designed to be quasi-natural; for example, cars, trucks and vans are depicted on roads or in parking lots. It is not clear how much the "3D-ness" of the search scene contributes to its "quasi-naturalness" (Figure 8a, upper), but these studies do provide an opportunity to demonstrate to the reader the careful methodology necessary in EM studies.

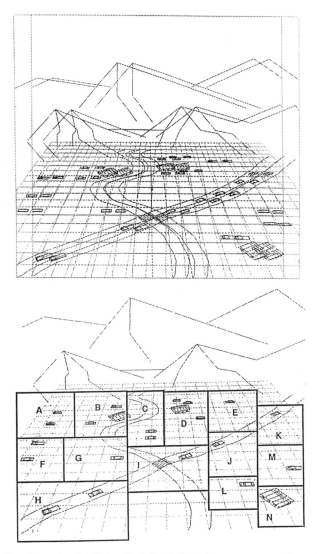

Figure 8a. <u>Searchpath EMs: Detail of 3D stereo presentation.</u> Two 2D scenes presented simultaneously (as far as the eye and brain are concerned) but actually successively (as far as the alternating LCD crystal glasses are concerned). It is not clear how much the "3D-ness" of the search scene contributes to its "quasi-naturalness" (from Choi et al., 1995).

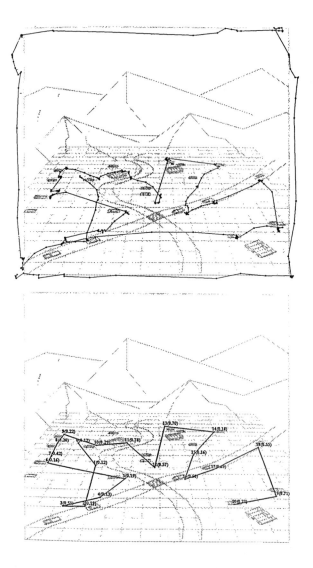

Figure 8b. <u>Searchpath EMs; Details of Experiment.</u>   With careful calibration, linearization of non-linearities in measurements of EMs can be achieved (upper). After the fixation algorithm has identified sequential fixations, the plot is redrawn (lower) with inter-fixational vectors substituted for the original, somewhat curved saccadic trajectories (modified from Choi et al., 1995).

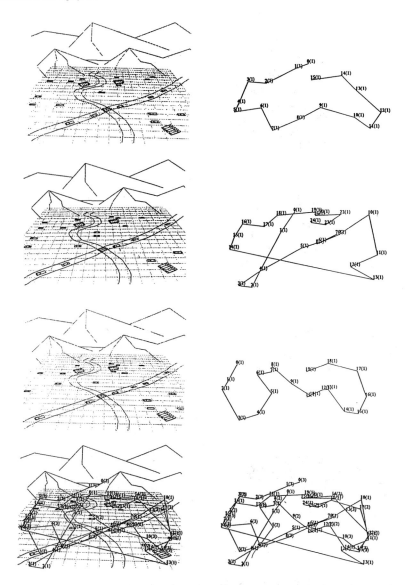

Figure 8c. <u>Searchpath EMs: Different Searchpath for Different Loci of Targets.</u> 2D pictures of a 3D visual search scene (left panels); searchpath movements of a single subject for each of the three different target loci shown on left (right panels). Superposition of all three searchpaths (lower right) and onto the search scene (lower left), from Choi et al., 1995; modified from Stark et al., 1992b.

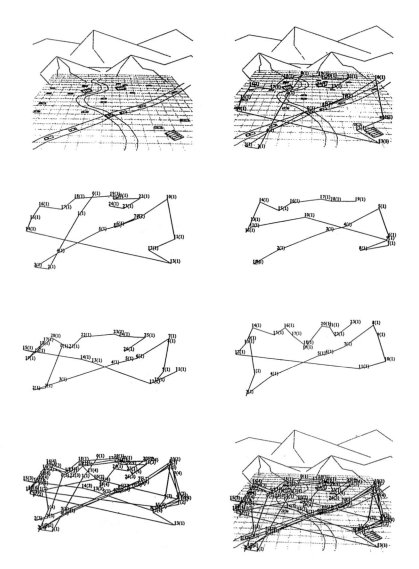

Figure 8d. <u>Searchpath EMs: Similar Searchpaths for Identical Target Loci</u>. Search scenes (upper left); searchpath superimposed on scene (upper right). Similar searchpaths for each of four identical presentations of target loci in the search scene (four middle panels); superposition of searchpaths qualitatively indicating strong similarity (lower left and right), modified from Choi et al., 1995 and from Stark et al., 1992.

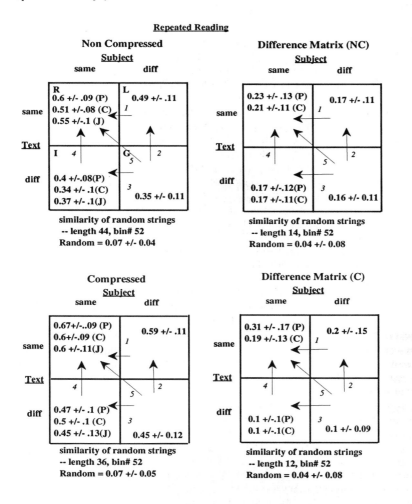

Figure 9. <u>String Similarities of Searchpath EMs</u>. *Repetitive* "s"-index value 0.49 (upper left box of the upper left panel) indicates that when the same subject repeated the searchpath looking for targets at the same loci, the *repetitive* string similarity was about 49%; quantitative evidence confirming the qualitative similarities can be seen in the lower panels of Figure 8d; "c" is compressed, "nc" is non-compressed (see text); note even though placement of target loci changed, the overall scene remained constant (from Choi et al., 1995).

Regionalization, or binning, is a difficult problem in mapping EM fixations back to an operational scanpath sequence driven by a conjectured cognitive model. Here we have divided the pictures into bins in two different ways, in ten larger regions and 15 smaller regions (Figure 8a, lower). Both sets of bins are arranged according to relevant information in the scene with emphasis on target loci over the wide set of different loci.

Calibration is crucial for accuracy in EM measurement devices of every type, in this case TV cameras. With calibration, linearization of non-linearities in the measurement can be carried out quickly with on-line computers (Stark et al., 1962); note also the final maneuver of having the subject fixate briefly on the corners of the display in order to determine that last minute drift had not occurred. After the fixation algorithm has identified sequential fixations, the plot is redrawn (lower, Figure 8b) with inter-fixational vectors substituted for the original curved saccadic trajectories (Bahill and Stark, 1979).Obtaining searchpath EMs of a single subject for each of the three different target loci on the same 3D visual search scene was a component of the experimental design (Figure 8c). The task for the subject, whose EMs are monitored, is to search and find five to seven trucks; vans and cars act as decoys. Superposition of these three searchpaths onto the search scene reveals fairly dissimilar trajectories.

Similar searchpaths were found (Figure 8d) for repeated search scene presentations (upper left) with identical loci of targets (B1 to 4); the experimental protocol consisted of three sets of loci (A, B and C) that were presented in fixed order (A, B1, B2, B3, C, and B4) (Yamashita, 1990). Searchpaths for each of four identical target loci presentations were superimposed, qualitatively indicating a strong similarity. EMs superimposed on scene B1 (upper right, Figure 8d), show correspondence of fixations with target loci. Foveations were necessary to "see" and to recognize targets in order to avoid errors.

Again, we first tested the robustness of the string editing "s"-index measure and used two different binnings, one with ten larger regions and one with 15 smaller regions. The robustness of our measure is confirmed by the similar values of "s"-indices for both larger and smaller bins and for compressed and non-compressed strings (Figure 9). We have repeatedly tested for robustness of our "s"-index. Other studies have compared the constraints in [M_1] Markov matrices and string editing distances (Ellis and Stark, 1986; Hacisalihzade et al., 1992).

The *repetitive* value of 0.49 in the upper left box of the upper left panel (Figure 9) indicates that when the same subject repeated the searchpath while looking for targets at the same loci, the *repetitive* string similarity was about 49%; quantitative evidence confirming the qualitative similarities has already been presented (lower panels, Figure 8d). For this particular task, the lack of *global* constraint of the fixations of the EMs and *global* strategies for EMs as linkages between fixations is confirmed by the low value of 0.18 for the *global* similarity of different subjects' searchpaths for targets with different loci. Indeed, the 18% value is similar to the random similarity of 24% for a simulation for strings of length 23 and for 15 bins.

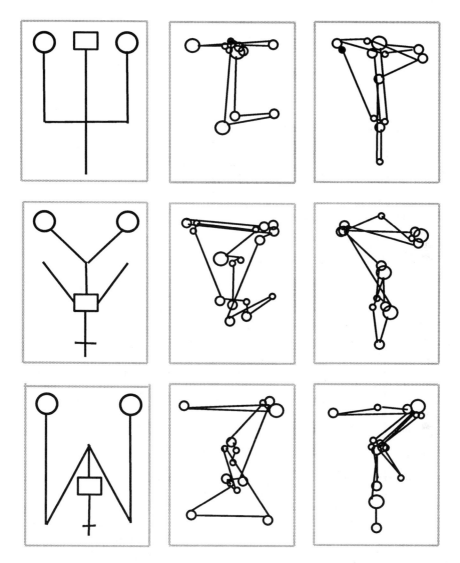

Figure 10. <u>Totem Scanpaths</u>. Three figures presented for viewing (left panel). Scanpaths for two subjects are visible as sequences of fixations (middle and right panels). Note: *idiosyncratic* and *local* differences and similar repeated scanpaths (*repetitive*) made during the seven second viewing period (from Choi et al., 1995).

Scanpath(Totem)

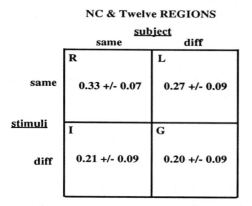

NC & Twelve REGIONS

Random (length 20, bin # 12) = 0.16 +/- 0.06

# of subjects: 2

# of stimui: 3

# of repeats: 4

Total N = 24

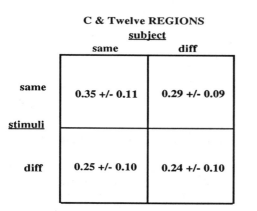

C & Twelve REGIONS

Random (length 13, bin # 12) = 0.18 +/- 0.07

Figure 11. <u>String Similarities of Scanpath EMs</u>. *Repetitive* "s"-index value 0.33 (upper left box of the upper left panel) indicates that when the same subject repetitively viewed the same totems, the *repetitive* string similarity was about 33% (from Choi et al., 1995).

3.4. Recent scanpath experiments: Totems

Three different totem figures were presented to two subjects for viewing. Their scanpaths are visible in the sequences of fixations superimposed on the totems (Figure 10). An important discovery that resulted from the early scanpath experiments was that the scanpath of a subject is *repetitive*. This can also be seen qualitatively in this figure since there was often enough time for two successive scanpaths.

For one five second viewing period and with three fixations per second, there were about 15 fixations. Another basic finding, that there are large *idiosyncratic* differences between subjects, is again visible in the sequences of fixations [M1]. Additionally, the loci of fixations, [M0], are similarly appropriate to the picture information in each totem. These three experimental findings led to the 1971 publication of the top-down active vision, active-looking scanpath theory, to which we can now add further supporting experiments and quantitative measures.

The string editing similarity measure, or "s"-index, adds crucial quantitative evidence (Figure 11). The "s"-index *repetitive* value of 0.33 (upper left box of the upper left panel, Figure 11) indicates that when the same subject repeated the scanpath looking at the same totems, the *repetitive* string similarity was about 33%, with quantitative evidence confirming the qualitative similarities seen (middle and right panels, Figure 10). The low value 0.20 of the *global* similarity for different subjects' scanpaths for different totem figures documents the lack of *global* constraint of the fixations of the EMs and the lack of *global* strategies for EMs as linkages between fixations.   Indeed, the random similarity calculated in a simulation for strings of length 20 and for 12 bins was 16%. Thus, free viewing of pictures, controlled by a very wide variety of different cognitive models, contrasts with the disciplined similarity of a reading page that provides strong *global* constraints for EMs during the reading task. When we test the robustness of the string editing "s"-index measure we find similar relationships between the average similarities of compressed and non-compressed strings.

3.5. Recent scanpath experiments: Visual imagery -- the Brandt experiment

The next experiments on visual imagery provide the strongest and clearest support for the scanpath theory. Subjects were allowed to look at and view each picture in an exploratory manner for 20 seconds and then for seven seconds (Figure 12); they were then asked to visualize or imagine the pattern for seven seconds while looking at a blank screen (showing only an empty grid). Three quite different patterns of Xs were used. They were then asked to draw the pattern of Xs on a blank grid. Calibrations, an important part of any experiment involving EMs, were made before the second period of looking and after the visualization period.

Eye movements that occurred while looking were superimposed onto patterns of Xs

(Figure 12), while EMs that occurred while visualizing or imagining the pattern were superimposed onto a blank screen. Circles here represent fixations (the size of the circle represents duration of fixation and a solid circle represents initial fixation).

The considerable qualitative agreement between the paired responses is of great significance. Note that no external world existed to guide the EMs during visualization. Only the internal cognitive model could be the source of control, providing strong support for the scanpath theory, revealing that the top-down cognitive model controls active-looking vision and perception, and that scanpath sequences are the operational readout of this top-down process (Brandt, 1989).

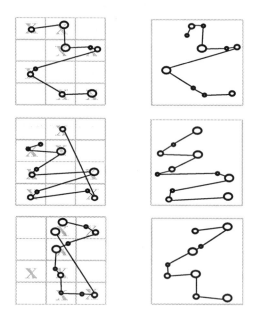

Figure 12. <u>Visual Imagery Scanpath Experiment</u>.   EMs while looking (shown superimposed onto patterns of Xs, left panel); EMs while visualizing or imagining the pattern (superimposed onto a blank screen, right panel). Note scanpaths similar to viewing scanpaths even during internal visualization when no external world image is available to guide EMs. This provides strong evidence for the scanpath theory (from Choi et al., 1995, after an unpublished experiment by Brandt and Stark, 1985-1992; see also Brandt et al., 1989).

Imagery

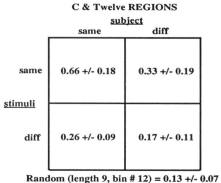

NC & Twelve REGIONS

	subject	
	same	diff
same stimuli	R 0.49 +/- 0.18	L 0.25 +/- 0.17
diff	I 0.22 +/- 0.09	G 0.15 +/- 0.10

Random (length 13, bin # 12) = 0.18 +/- 0.07
Picture vs. Immediate Imagery = 0.54 +/- 0.13

C & Twelve REGIONS

	subject	
	same	diff
same stimuli	0.66 +/- 0.18	0.33 +/- 0.19
diff	0.26 +/- 0.09	0.17 +/- 0.11

Random (length 9, bin # 12) = 0.13 +/- 0.07
Picture vs. Immediate Imagery = 0.66 +/- 0.13

Figure 13. <u>String Similarities of Scanpath EMs in Visual Imagery Experiments.</u> *Repetitive* "s"-index value 0.49 (upper left box of the upper left panel) defines the scanpath similarity when the same subject repeated the task while looking at or imagining the same picture pattern; quantitative evidence confirming the qualitative similarities can be seen between the left and right panels of Figure 12. Note also the high similarity value of 0.54 for the immediate imagery scanpath as compared to the preceding looking scanpath; this is a major finding (from Choi et al., 1995).

Several other factors were controlled. For example, after-images (AIs) have been suggested as a possible short-term memory factor; however, for AIs to play a transfer role, the eyes would have to be stationary while observing the pattern of Xs. Recall that EMs were continually in progress and thus no adequate AI could have formed.

Instructions to the subjects, most particularly the request that they draw the remembered pattern, led them to pay careful attention to the (randomly generated) pattern of Xs. Naive subjects were told that the pupils of their eyes were being studied for signs of effort in performing the task, a true "red herring" made believable by the magnified views of the eye displayed on Sweveralk TV screens in the dimly-lit laboratory room.

Quantitative evidence for the similarity of scanpaths while looking and while imagining without any possible external shaping stimulus (as conjectured by external world theories), comes from string similarity measures. Of significance is the value 0.54 (Figure 13, upper panel, bottom line) for comparisons between the scanpaths when a subject was viewing a picture pattern and when the subject was immediately visualizing, imagining and recalling the pattern. This visual imagery experiment not only confirms the *repetitive* and *idiosyncratic* nature of the scanpath, essential aspects of its very definition, but, even more importantly, demonstrates that constrained scanpaths are generated from an internal cognitive model, since in these experiments there is no external world picture to drive or influence the EMs and their fixations.

The *repetitive* value of 0.49 (Figure 13, upper left box of upper left panel) defines the scanpath similarity when the same subject repeated the task while looking at or imagining the same picture pattern; quantitative evidence confirming the qualitative similarities can be seen between the left and right panels of Figure 12. The low value, 0.15, of the *global* similarity for different subjects' scanpaths for different picture patterns documents the lack of constraint on the fixations of the EMs and the lack of constraint on the linkages between fixations. Indeed, the random similarity calculated in a simulation for strings of length 13 and for 12 bins was 18% -- almost the same value. Again, we could show the robustness of the string editing "s"-index measure with the similar values for the "s"-indices for compressed and non-compressed strings. Apparently, limitations on constraints on double fixations somewhat reduced the similarity index for *repetitive* scanpaths.

3.6. Recent scanpath experiments: Regionalization

Most of the recent experiments described above used *a priori* regionalization. That is, the pictures were arranged so that we could set up ROIs and other regions (regions-not-of-interest) either using a rectangular grid or by some simple extrapolation form the picture. An example of the latter is the 15 (or 10) bins for the visual search experiment.

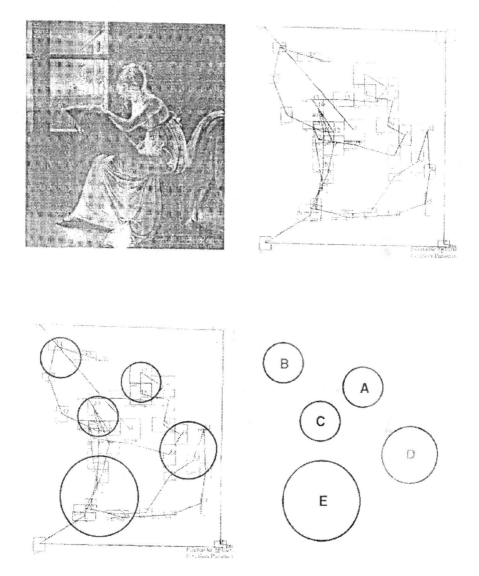

Figure 14. *A Posteriori* Regionalization. Copy of a painting by Mme. Charpentier (upper left) viewed by a subject for twelve seconds (upper right) with EM fixations; rectangular boxes indicate the range of micro-EMs during a fixation. Encircled ROIs chosen by the experimenter as appropriate to clusters of actual fixations (lower left) and with alphabetic indicators (lower right).

A posteriori regionalization is a more complex problem and requires either human editing or some much more sophisticated algorithm to ascertain where collections or clusters of fixations have occurred or are likely to occur. Indeed, together with Ulrich Oeschner, we have explored fuzzy clustering, both in simulations and for actual scanpath experiments (Oeschner, Choi and Stark, 1995, in preparation). An example of a posteriori regionalization (Figure 14) will help the reader gain insight into this problem.

Twelve seconds of viewing (Figure 14, upper right) reveals about 40 EM fixations; the last few are consequent to an instruction to the subject to fixate on the corners of the picture after a buzzer sounds. Rectangular boxes indicate micro-EMs during a fixation. Although biological EMs can be restricted to +/- 1/4 degree for point targets (St.Cyr and Fender, 1969; Stark et al., 1980b; Zuber et al., 1965) there is no requirement for such fixity of gaze while viewing pictures. Micro-saccades, micro-drifts, micro-smooth pursuit conjugate movements, micro-VOR, and small vergence EMs occur as well as the smallest micro-tremors (Zuber et al., 1965).

Encircled ROIs were chosen by the experimenter as appropriate for the clusters of actual fixations; he was also influenced by intuited relevant informational sites in the picture (lower left). Our recent research has used objective, fuzzy clustering algorithms for this procedure (Oeschner et al., 1995, in preparation). Regions-of-interest with alphabetic indicators provide for string sequencing studies (Figure 14, lower).

So a posteriori regionalization remains an open problem. As Yarbus (1967) discovered, subjects change their preferred fixation sequences with shifts in implicit self-ministered task instructions. During the viewing of ambiguous figures, scanpaths were found to change as the mental model changed (Stark and Ellis, 1981).

3.7. Parsing of String Editing Similarity Measure

Now that string editing can measure similarities and differences between successive scanpaths, it has become apparent that the similarities can be parsed among several different factors (Figure 15).

The panels in the previous four tables each represented four sets of constraints on the EMs: repetitive, idiosyncratic, local (artistic), and global. For each of the four experiments presented above, the full similarity produced by the repetitive nature of the scanpath (or searchpath, or reading EM pattern) is significantly greater than the global similarity. Indeed, only the reading EM pattern showed a global textual constraint that was significantly greater than the random values calculated (below).

Idiosyncratic constraints over and above the global constraints were most significantly present in the visual search experiments where the same subject had a somewhat similar searchpath for different target loci, although this was possibly due to the scene remaining the same during the experiment. Local constraint represents the similarity of strings of different subjects looking at the same picture. Often artists believe (without evidence) that the structure of their painting can control or influence

SIMILARITY INDICES

SUBJECT

	same	different
same	**REPETITIVE** T = 0.33 I = 0.49 VS = 0.49 Rdg = 0.55	**LOCAL (artistic)** T = 0.37 I = 0.25 VS = 0.18 Rdg = 0.49
diff	**IDIOSYNCRATIC** T = 0.28 I = 0.22 VS = 0.37 Rdg = 0.37	**GLOBAL** T = 0.28 I = 0.15 VS = 0.18 Rdg = 0.35

PICTURES LOCI TEXTS

	#Bins	Strg-Lngth	Random
Totem	12	13	T = 0.16
Imagery	10	23	I = 0.18
Visual Search	12	20	VS = 0.24
Reading	52	44	Rdg = 0.07

Figure 15. <u>String Similarity Experimental Results</u>. The ability to move from *global* to *repetitive* in steps via either *idiosyncratic* or additional *local* constraints allows us to "parse" the overall constraints leading to the high "s"-indices for *repetitive* scanpaths in these various experiments (see also Figure 7); from Choi et al., 1995.

the EMs of a viewer; a more likely source of the viewer's constraint is that informative details of a picture that require checking foveations are similar in different persons' mental images or cognitive models. The ability to move from *global* to *repetitive* in steps via additional *idiosyncratic* or *local* constraints allows us to "parse" the overall constraints leading to the high "s"-indices for *repetitive* scanpaths in these various experiments (Figure 7).

3.8 Definition of terms

Global: By this we mean any overall strategy for covering or attending to a display, scene, picture, etc. It is clear that the nature of the viewed matter and the spatial model for its general layout is important. For example, text is greater than search scene is greater than picture in determining a preplanned strategy. It is not likely that there is a specifiable "best strategy" for looking at a generalized road scene or generic display, nor that there is one road signers and display makers can exploit.

Repetitive: This is the essence of the definition of the scanpath, a *repetitive* sequence of saccades and fixations as a subject looks at a particular picture. The above definition is an experimental one; a deeper definition depends upon the generation of the scanpath as the operational phase of perception per se, controlled top-down by a cognitive or spatial model. This strong similarity due to repetition is in addition to the similarity due to *global* strategies and to the similarities due to *local* or *idiosyncratic* tactics.

Local: These *local*, artistic or loci tactics of control are the effect of the model corresponding to the important information and localization in a picture or a scene. While *local* tactics are independent of the particular viewing person, they are over and beyond the *global* strategic effect on similarity. An artist is presuming an ability to create *local* similarity when, with certain flows of line, she expects to be able to control the way people view her pictures. This belief, almost universally held by artists, is nonetheless unsupported by preliminary studies (Mme. Maryse LeRoy, University of Paris, 1989, personal communication).

It is possible that for each specific scenario or display there exists a particular tactic that could be exploited for maximum *local* similarity. This was the basis for Stark's suggestion (1981) in regard to TV broadcasting -- that by recording EMs of a small group of persons in the TV studio, moment-to-moment preferential regions-of-interest could be determined. These preferential loci, experimentally determined to be "relevant," information-rich regions-of-interest, could then be broadcast with higher resolution, at a cost of a lesser update rate of the rest of the picture.

Idiosyncratic: This is another tactical component of similarity that a single person may apply to all pictures and scenes; it is also in addition to any *global* strategy and in turn contributes to *repetitive* similarity. If it only shows up with same-scene experiments for the same viewing person, then it becomes identical to the *repetitive* similarity that in turn defines scanpath similarity. Thus, the *idiosyncratic* pattern of a single person must remain with that person as she looks at different scenes over and above any *global* similarity of all persons. These definitions and issues have been illustrated in the experimental results presented above and in Figure 7.

Random: This is the similarity of randomly generated strings as a function of the length of the strings and the number of possible bins. It also depends in a complex way upon the amount of similarity; the diverse ways the string editing program algorithm can find the least number of edits to make two strings identical become even more diverse as similarity decreases.

3.9. Summary
The expanded sets of experiments documented in this section together with the quantitative evidence from string editing similarity measures add solid support to the scanpath theory. While it was reasonable in 1971 to reject the early scanpath theory (as all such paradigm shifts should be rejected on the basis of insufficient evidence), it is no longer a conservative or viable stand, considering the weight of the evidence. While open problems remain and many further experiments need to be carried out, scanpath theory is now fully supported by considerable research data. This is especially clear with respect to the visual imagery experiments. Indeed, growing numbers of researchers from neurology, using functional MRI (Kosslyn, 1980; Posner and Raichle, 1994), and computer vision, exploring "active vision" (Aloimonos et al., 1991, 1992 a, b, c; Ballard et al., 1992, 1994), now believe in the predominance of the top-down processes envisioned in the scanpath theory.

4. ROBOTICS: TOP-DOWN SCANPATHS AS ACTIVE VISION

Buttressed by these new views of top-down human vision, we have applied the scanpath theory to robotic vision. Here we use our top-down knowledge of the complete and calibrated spatial layout of the robotic working environment, including position and orientation of the video cameras, the kinematic and dynamic nature of the robots, and the loci of work-pieces, to develop an exact computational "cognitive model" (Figures 16 through 22). This computer model then controls the image processing. On-the-scene visual enhancements (VEs) have been placed at critical locations on the robots and the workpieces to improve signal-to-noise ratios for processing the video images. ROIs are also generated from the cognitive model so that *local* image processing, such as *local* thresholding and centroid calculations, can be carried out efficiently and robustly (Miyata and Stark, 1992; Sutro and Lerman, 1973).

4.1 Telerobotic control: Robots and models
A scheme was developed for model control of robots and image processing using redundant control pathways and modes of operation (Figure 16). Lower 3D display shows the model in *local* regions close to the telerobotic working environment (TRWE). This model controls the actual robots, cameras and image processing. The numerical parameters defining the TRWE, abstracted by visual image processing (IP) algorithms working only within ROIs, are able to correct and update the 3D model. Thus the communication channel (COMM) can be narrow-band, since only sensed and control parameters are exchanged between the supervisor's upper 3D

display and the distant robotic model. The direct control human operator (HO) can view a display, partly controlled by him and partly by the upper 3D model. He can also manually control the robots and cameras by controlling the lower 3D model with immediate feedback, or he may give control to the supervisor. Supervisory control can produce a battery of operations, setting into motion emergency interruptions and reinitializing and recalibrating procedures, as well as the approval of suggested paths or task-segments. In the present study, we are interested in autonomous control based upon vision feedback; the visual information is in turn based upon scanpath concepts.

The laboratory bench contains a stationary m-robot with five degrees-of-freedom interacting with a mobile "toy" a-robot with mobility, three nonholonomic locomotory degrees-of-freedom and additional manipulator degrees-of-freedom including grippers (video camera oblique view, Figure 17). Three models display formats with increasing abstraction (Figure 17). The solid shape model shows the TRWE as a

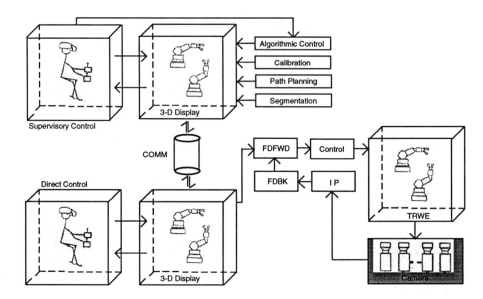

Figure 16. <u>Cooperative Control in Telerobotics</u>. Scheme for model control of robots and image processing. Note redundant control pathways and modes of operation (modified from Stark et al., 1987).

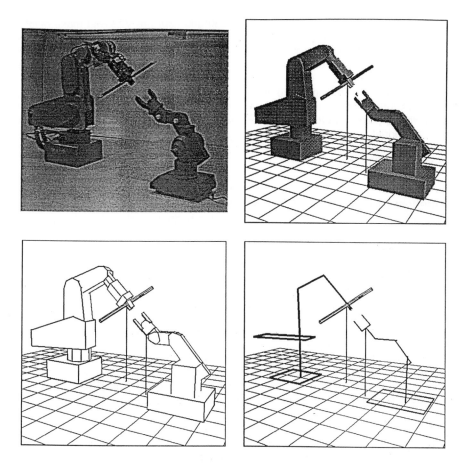

Figure 17. Robots and Robot Models, Oblique View. Video picture of robots (upper left); solid model (upper right); wire-frame format (lower left); skeletal model (lower right). Reference lines, grid floor and reflecting tape points are on-the-screen visual enhancements.

spatial box with a grid floor; reference lines and grid floor are VEs that make height easily visible for human supervisory or direct control. The wire frame format and the skeletal model also show the kinematic structure of the robot and thus convey the same essential information; note that the computer also has complete dynamic specifications for the robot.

Of course, these iconic models are not "in" the computer (or the computer's "brain"), but rather represent the computer's communication style to us humans! Likely, the models in the human brain are as diffuse and hard to localize or pin down as the computer model would be to a computer scientist. What is the meaning of iconic brain models in this context? Where do bottom-up sensory information flows meet top-down cognitive models?

4.2. Bottom-up image processing algorithm

Top-down control of image processing allows the bottom-up algorithms to be used efficiently (Figure 18). The ROI-predicted locations depend upon top-down knowledge of robot-commanded positions and the commanded position of the cameras. Thus, the 3D model knows where to expect the 2D projections of the VEs. This is one great advantage of top-down vision. Image processing can be directed to only the places where checking of location and identity in other contexts is required; no random or systematic visual search procedure needs to be employed. The fact that in the figure the VEs are located near the centers of the ROIs demonstrates that an excellent estimate had been made by the feedforward loop model.

The high contrast VEs had been produced by *local* adaptive thresholding -- a much more robust process than the screen-wide video image processing. In this example, the ROIs, controlled by the feedforward model, are excellent predictors of actual positions of the robot, as evidenced by contrasted VEs lying near the centers of the ROIs.

Centroid calculations, the black plusses within ROIs, are very rapid and enable feedback processing of the kinematic parameters of robots, showing accuracy in response to feedforward command. The ROI for the workpiece was not shown in this example since only the ROIs connected to the skeletal model of the m-robot were displayed (Figure 18).

The analogy between these computer image processes and human vision are meant to be strong, since they were indeed developed by modeling the scanpath concept of human vision. Top-down control sends the computer processing system to ROI after ROI in a serial fashion. In humans the serial operation is driven by the necessity of foveating ROIs with EMs, and in the computer by the absence of the parallel processing facilities. Once human or computer vision processing is restricted to the fovea or the ROI, then the high resolution portion of the eye and the visual brain, or the intense image processing portion of a computer's brain, can operate to compare the location and the identity of that portion of the picture, the subfeature within the fovea or the ROI. For our simple robotics example, identity is not a problem; however, the visual enhancements could conceivably consist of bar graphs requiring complex identification schemes (Figure 19). Implementation of such humanlike scanpath algorithms has recently been termed "active vision" or "model reference vision" in the computer vision community (Aloimonos and Rosenfeld, 1991, Aloimonos and Herve, 1992a, Aloimonos and Huang, 1992b, Aloimonos et al., 1992c; Bajcsy and Krotkov, 1993, Bajcsy et al., 1994, 1995; Ballard and Brown, 1992, Ballard et al., 1994).

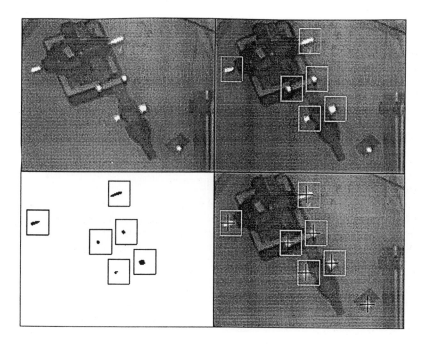

Figure 18. <u>Bottom-Up Image Processing Algorithms</u>. A dim video image of robots with superimposed high contrast on-the-scene visual enhancements (upper left). Again, dim picture of robots (upper right) with superimposed high contrast visual enhancements; now, however, ROIs are added from top-down knowledge models. High contrast visual enhancements (lower left, see also Figures 19 and 20). Results of centroid calculations indicated by black plusses within ROIs (lower right).

The function of the adaptive thresholding algorithm can best be seen in a pixel intensity plot that has pixel intensity as the vertical axis, as a function of the X and Y coordinates of the video picture (Figure 20). ROI outlines are indicated as edges of horizontal planes, cutting peaks representing VEs. ROI heights are proportional to adaptive thresholds, with each *local* region having a different threshold level. The advantage of *local* thresholds in the top down control of image processing is a very robust and autonomous scheme. The rectangular connection represents the feedforward robot model that has placed the ROIs correctly on the camera image plane.

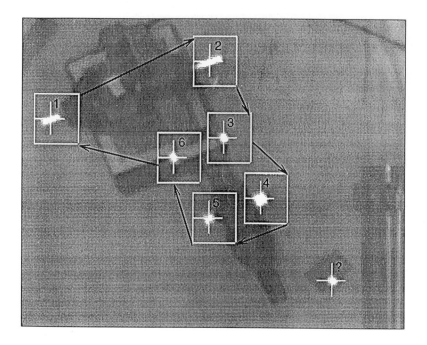

Figure 19. <u>Top-Down Scanpath Algorithm Operating on Robot Image</u>. Dim video pictures of robot with ROIs, superimposed and sequentially numbered for top-down computer active vision implementation of humanlike scanpath algorithms (from Yu and Stark, in preparation, 1995).

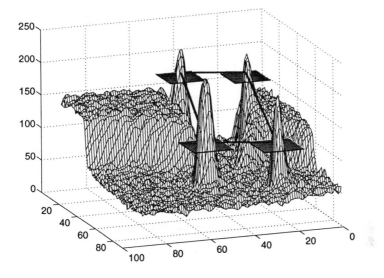

Figure 20. Adaptive Thresholding Algorithm. Oblique 3D view of pixel intensity plot. ROIs (horizontal squares) have heights proportional to adaptive thresholds; each *local* region may set a different threshold level. Note higher threshold where background pixels are more intense. ROI loci are placed on the basis of top-down control from the model; note heavy lines indicating model localization of ROIs (from Yu and Stark, in preparation, 1995; also adapted from A.H. Nguyen 1990; Zangemeister et al., 1989).

4.3. Control diagram showing feedforward and feedback paths:

The overview diagram (Figure 16) does not indicate the actual engineered control flows or block diagrams of defined control operations; these are further specified below in order to describe control processing and its active computer vision scheme and how they descended from the scanpath model (Figure 21).The control diagram comparator block (COMP) compares commanded movements in the segment queue with the measured feedback vector, Y-tilda, of key robotic positions. The control

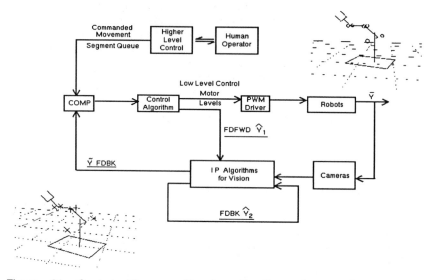

Figure 21. <u>Control Diagram Showing Feedforward and Feedback Paths</u>. Feedforward path extends from human operator (HO), to skeletal control model with circles for known positions of visual enhancements (upper right insert), to robot pose, Y-bar. The feedback path extends from cameras through vision system to feedback, Y-tilda. The feedback skeletal model with results of centroid calculation loci indicated as crosses (lower left insert). Note feedforward setting of ROI predicted positions, Y1-hat; alternatively, *local* feedback from previous position, Y2-hat, can be employed. Comparator obtains corrective error from difference of feedback, Y-tilda and commanded segment trajectory.

algorithm in the lower level control path sets motor levels for the pulse-width-modulation (PWM) driver. It also develops feedforward estimates, Y(1)-hat, which may be used to set ROI loci for image processing algorithms, the active robot vision. Cameras capture actual robot positions, Y-bar, for image processing of video pixels in the frame-grabber (Figures 18, 19, and 20). An alternate method of updating ROI loci is to use the previous position, Y(2)-hat. Tradeoffs between the use of Y(1)-hat and Y(2)-hat are an interesting subject for current research. Depending upon time limitations in image processing, redundancy of VEs can be a very useful tool for overcoming large amounts of controller and plant noise or image pixel noise. Note also that the supervisory human operator (HO) communicating with the higher level control algorithms, may generate commanded movements as complex sequences necessary to perform a useful task. These taskpaths are subsequently segmented into queues of linear segments for transmission to the lower level controller as the final condition of translation and of rotation for each segment.

A feedforward skeletal model, characterized by circles for 3D loci of visual enhancements and hence the ROIs, is placed near the higher level and lower level control elements (inset, upper right). A feedback model, characterized by crosses for 3D loci of the measured centroids of visual enhancements, is placed near the feedback path (inset, lower left). Differences between these models represent errors measured by the comparator that will be reduced in the control processes of this negative feedback system.

4.4. Summary of robot vision and robot performance

These models also enable the supervisor controller to preview and plan for movement segments and sequences of segments in developing complete task paths (Figure 22). As described above, simple rotational and/or linear translational segments are concatenated. Different model formats (Figure 17) can function for different roles -- solid models for initial condition (IC) and final condition (FC), skeletal models for intermediate steps in a segment trajectory. Graphics user interfaces (GUIs) are very helpful in these complex planning maneuvers, permitting easy control and previewing entire task paths. Color coding has been especially useful in designing human machine interfaces (HMIs) (Blackmon and Stark, 1995) .

Of course, this application to robotic vision and autonomous control of robotic motion does not prove that the scanpath theory is operative in man; the EM experiments reported above have provided that evidence. The use of the scanpath scheme in robotic vision does, however, explicate and make concrete the workings of this theory of active vision and its efficacy. Only those subfeatures essential for identification and control are processed, reducing the computational task greatly. The model not only controls, in a top-down fashion, the image processing, as in human vision in the scanpath mode, but can also control the robots, the cameras, and the displays for the supervisory human teleoperators. The model also serves to reduce communication bandwidth requirements, since only commanded (feedforward) and measured estimated (feedback) model parameters are transmitted. This top-down active visual scheme satisfies a visual feedback control system for robots.

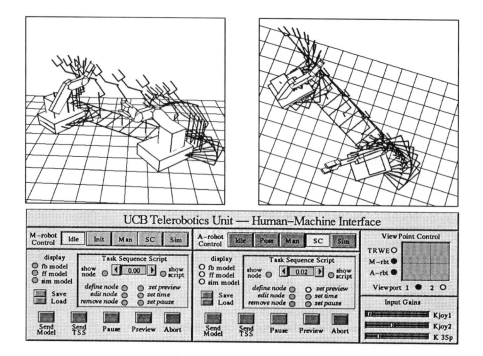

Figure 22. <u>Feedforward Model Previewing Dynamic Performance of Robot.</u>
Computer model of robot rotating, then translating, and then rotating again under
autonomous path-planning control. About ten successive frames document each
trajectory of these three movement segments selected from the total twelve segment
queue composing the complete task path; oblique and top views (upper). Note also
graphics user interface (GUI), created in laboratory (lower), (modified from Blackmon
and Stark, 1995).

5.   VISION

5.1. Visual processes
Three dichotomies are used in discussing vision. The oldest of these, called the duplicity theory, contrasts foveal and peripheral vision (neurophysiological parallels are X and Y cells, parvo and agnocellular, slow and fast dichotomies). Foveal vision supports high resolution recognition with its small field of view, approximately one-half degree, and very high resolution, approximately one-half arc-min (or 20/10 or 120 cycles/degree).

Color vision depends upon not only the trichromatic cones of Thomas Young, Maxwell, and Helmholtz, but also on the opponens processing that Hering, Jamison, Hurvich, and DeValois established. Opponens cells are a beautiful example of bottom-up organization of sense data (see Section 5.2. below).

Peripheral vision has a very wide field of view, approximately 120 to 180 degrees, but very low resolution. It is sensitive to motion and flickering lights.

Some time ago, the amount of information transmission capability of these two regions was estimated at about 40K bits/second for each aspect of vision. The foveal transmission rate is mainly just noticeable differences of luminance and color contrast for the 2500 foveal pixels. The comparable transmission rate for the periphery arises from the very large number of receptor fields in the wide periphery with perhaps only one bit of information per receptor field (Stark and Theodoridis, 1973). Given the requirement for foveation of any aspect of a picture for which high resolution analysis will occur, continual, very rapid saccadic EMs become an essential aspect of ordinary vision.

The second dichotomy comes from computer vision, where bottom-up and top-down are contrasted. The flow of sensory energy into the early stages of visual processing is bottom-up. The top-down aspects are central to the scanpath theory, and have to do with representational cognitive models. These control active-looking as scanpath EMs and have to with representational cognitive models.

The final dichotomy is one proposed by Kant (see Section 7.4 below) having to do with the internal categorization of sensory stimuli as functions of space and time. His *emfindung* is sensation without space and time, while his notion of perception includes organization in space and time, leaving open the locus for the addition of space-time to sensation.

As we shall see, there are bottom-up organizational processes that attach space and time dimensions to sensation. We prefer to still consider them sensory processing rather than perceptual processing for several reasons. One is that such processes seem to be accomplished by hard-wired networks of neurons that are innate in the various eyes and brains in which they have been studied. Of course, neurophysiologists have assumed bottom-up processing, so their experiments often do not adduce further evidence as to whether these processes are truly bottom-up or top-down. A second reason for placing these bottom-up organizational processes with sensation is that perception per se seems to be the place where top-down cognitive models are matched and compared with bottom-up information. The matrix for these comparisons seem to be strongly organized already in terms of space and time; for example, the shape from motion studies of Andersen (Andersen and Siegel, 1988, Andersen et al., 1991, 1995a, b).

Does dual vision provide a rationale for the central role of EMs? Understanding that visual processes can be bottom-up or top-down helps us to put in order our notions about vision. Keep in mind one of the most interesting questions for future neurophysiology, (especially aided by active imaging experiments, functional MRI and PET) is, "Where does bottom-up vision meet top-down vision?" A possible answer is in the loop interactions between layer four (bottom-up) and layer six (top-down) in the striate cortex; this site is more likely than loops between geniculate and cortex (Silito et al.,1994). Perhaps the "meeting" takes place even later, in the parietal cortex, so devoted to further visual processing, velocity, attention, and interactions with motor and motor planning cortical regions (Pribram, 1971; Assad and Maunsell, 1995) .

Higher level vision includes perception occurring in the "mind's eye." The cognitive model of a scene or a picture is the philosopher's "representation." Its operational phase is the active-looking scanpath. EMs are also driven in a top-down fashion so that critical ROIs determined from the cognitive model can be sampled with high resolution foveal vision.

5.2. Bottom-up with organization

The categories of bottom-up and top-down do not exactly coincide with Kant's separation of sensation, *emfindung,* from perception per se. Bottom-up physiology has to do with the reception of light in terms of intensity and, more importantly, as contrast -- both luminous and color contrast -- and also in terms of resolution. Perhaps it is also parallel to Descartes' idea of lux (Jay, 1993). Here we attempt to reserve Kant's distinction between sensation and perception for the interaction between top-down representation and bottom-up sensation, since we employ the scanpath as the operational mode of checking and confirming the top-down model in detail with each fixation. A series of bottom-up organizational processes, including Kant's space and time categories, are intermediate.

Wide angle peripheral vision, although low resolution, is ideally adapted for motion and flow field, and for pre-attentive "pop-up" parallel sensing (perhaps "pre-attentive" is not completely bottom-up). We emphasize that to assess velocity, the Kantian categories of time and space must be computed.

5.3. Bottom-up with organization: The frog's eye

A second and excellent example of such organizational processes comes from the great paper by Lettvin et al., "What the Frog's Eye Tells the Frog's Brain," (1959) where the investigators describe how they experimentally discovered that the frog's retina consists of multiple webs or retinas of receptor cells and neural processing elements able to abstract several distinct features from an image. For example, the "edge detector web" can detect edges in the visual field, especially those that move, and the "bug detector" can detect a small object moving in the visual field.

Each retinal detector is a component in a "rete" or web, a collection of receptors, processing bipolar cells, horizontal cells, and amacrine cells, all feeding into ganglion cells, whose axons form the optic nerve and transmit visual information bottom-up to the brain. Each of the five to eight detector webs carries out a sensory, bottom-up-with-organization function, eventually linked to an appropriate motor behavior. The frog can use the "edge detector" to jump away to avoid capture. He can also use the "bug detector" to predict the direction, distance and velocity of a fly, and then is able to flick his tongue out to catch his meal.

There is a double parallelism here: parallel nets or webs for each feature detected and parallel detection ongoing over multiple regions of the retina. The apparent top-down perceptual aspects of this system have arisen through evolutionary processes to accomplish the design of this elegant visual system. It took nature 350 million years of multi-cellular evolution to design the frog's eye; it took an additional 350 million years for evolution to produce McCulloch's brain so that he could discover "how universals are detected."

5.4. Bottom-up with organization: Psychophysics

Recently, psychophysicists have explored the possibility that bottom-up sensory organizational processes are at work in the detection of shape from motion (Andersen and Siegel, 1988, Andersen et al., 1991, 1995a, b) and in primate neurophysiology; discussion of these exciting experiments is beyond the scope of the present paper.

Gestalt psychologists used a concept that they called the Law of Pragnanz to account for the "filling in" of shapes in certain figures. The triangle illusion is a good example: here only the corners are defined, but this leads to a percept of the entire triangle. Underlying the Law of Pragnanz was an analogy between brain processes and physical fields, like gravitational fields. Indeed, the concept was more than a metaphor. Gestalt psychologists Koffka, Kohler and Wertheimer thought of these fields as spreading out and "filling in" neighboring regions. Believing that psychophysical "organization" was extremely refined in creating a "whole" or in "filling in," they actually tried to measure electromagnetic fields in the brain, alas to no avail (Kohler, 1929). Thus their attempt to grasp and explain what we call "the illusion of clarity and completeness" (see Section 8.2 below) was both unresolved and unsubstantiated by experiment.

There is a good deal of recent interest in attention shifts, especially when these are not accompanied by EMs, although, of course this is the most frequent occurrence. In our original discussion of scanpaths, Noton and I (1971a, b, c) took up this problem. We pointed out that for tachistoscopic presentations, and for small images that fall within the fovea, EMs are neither present nor necessary (except for microfixational EMs). We speculated that attention shifts would then play the same role as EMs. Since at that time EMs could be measured but attention shifts could not, it seemed better to turn our attention to EMs.

More recently, rapid serial visual presentation (RSVP), of text, or what we have called zero-eye-movement-reading, has been studied; with RSVP, people could read without EMs, but not faster nor more efficiently than with EMs (Stark and Krischer,

1988). Evidently, the evolutionary process, by linking perception and EMs, has forced cultural technology to present written information to humans in a manner consistent with visual processing and, indeed, not limited by EMs (Sun et al., 1985). Julesz (Krose and Julesz, 1989), Treisman (Treisman and Gordon, 1988, Treisman and Sato, 1990, Treisman, 1991, Treisman et al., 1992) and Enns (Enns and Rensink, 1991, 1993) have explored "pop-up" vision. Julesz proposed that primitive "textons" with up to second-order statistics were what we would call bottom-up, while higher order textons were top-down; he later disproved this brilliant hypothesis. Treisman emphasized that conjunctive properties of apparent primitives are clearly not pre-attentive, leaving open the question of the "bottom-up-ness" of primitive features (D.Aks, personal communication). In other, probing experiments, Kosslyn (1980) used reaction times to collect evidence that processing in visual imagery is similar to that for vision of actual scenes.

5.5. Neurology of vision
Brain Studies: Readers may be somewhat confused as to the overlap between neurology, neurophysiology, psychology, and philosophy. My own opinion as a neurologist is that neurophysiology deals with scattered, discrete and isolated information about part of the nervous system; neurophysiologists are especially happy when they are looking at a single neuron, one part in 10^{14} of the brain! When this information emerges as an overviewed schematic mechanism, it then becomes part of neurology.

Similarly, psychologists are very interested in the science of human behavior; many experimental psychologists are happy to move inside the brain and become neurophysiologists. Again, neurology is really intimately associated with the mechanisms of brain function. For example, in the specific area of central nervous system representations of external world scenes and objects, the new imaging techniques, such as functional MRI, are clearly neurological paradigms for the study of brain functions (Kosslyn, 1980; Posner and Raichle, 1994). Psychologists have moved to neurological research centers to use these new techniques.

6. SCANPATH

6.1. Summary of experimental results
One of the main objectives of this paper has been to present new experiments and especially new quantitative measures to evaluate and support the scanpath theory. The early evidence of the *repetitive* and *idiosyncratic* nature of the scanpath suggested, but did not prove, that an internal cognitive model controlled the scanpath EM sequences.

The new evidence extends these findings with objective statistical string editing similarity measures. In addition to older work showing that the scanpath changes with shifts in the subject's mental image, we now have evidence that the scanpath during visual imagery is quite similar to the scanpath while viewing. Without any external world, the internal cognitive model must be the source of the structure of the scanpath in these visual imagery experiments. The similarity measure, the "s"-index, produced by the string editing algorithm, provides enough information in our experiments to allow for parsing. By this we mean that we can assign different degrees of constraint onto the generating mechanism for the scanpath, dependent upon experimental conditions and the viewed picture.

Research on the scanpath is now in a very exciting phase. Many problems remain to be faced, such as *a posteriori* identification of regions-of-interest based upon the clustering of fixations around informationally significant features of a picture or scene.

Additional statistical studies that relate string editing similarity measures to hypothetical Markov models of different orders are now being undertaken. These Markov coefficients embed the different levels of sequence constraints defining the linkage mechanisms of the cognitive model.

6.2. History of the scanpath

Longstanding philosophical conjecture likely stimulated many of the issues that underlay the development of the scanpath theory. Hume had tried to reduce epistemology to psychological processes influenced by contiguity in time and space. But the bottom-up generation of Platonic ideals was not then, and has not been now, established (see Section 7.3 below). The philosophical conjectures that have dominated the history of thought -- Platonic ideals, Plato's "myth of the cave" and the matching of an internal concept to external bottom-up inflowing sensory data -- are central to our theme.

Neurological and neurophysiological research and thinking about perception were jolted by the great paper of Lettvin et al. (see Sections 5.3 and 7.2 on McCulloch above). The discovery of multiple networks of a few different types of ganglion cells was perhaps *the* major intellectual and experimental step in neurophysiology in our century. Not only did it explain sensory organizational mechanisms, but it also adduced motor behaviors responsive to each "universal." In our Kantian classification, this was, of course, bottom-up sensation with time and space organization. The Lettvin-McCulloch (1959) work suggests that evolution had selected the five types of ganglion cells and put them in hardware; that almost sufficed for frog behavior. Indeed, these and similar motor behaviors -- avoidance jumping to escape a predator, characterized by the "edge detector" network, and tongue aiming, informed by the "bug detector" to catch a fly on the wing -- were a demonstration of Descartes' automata in the animal world. More detailed neurophysiological studies of nerve information coding in a simple avoidance response of the crayfish showed that new patterns for motor control suddenly emerged from the brain, driven but not shaped by sensory input.

Computer vision was also developing during the fifties and sixties -- the age of cybernetics. The ideas of top-down and bottom-up, the division of visual processing into 2D, 3D and symbolic, have been handed to brain psychologists from computer vision. They provided us with excellent analogies to human visual and brain processes (Dr. Irwin Sobel, personal communication; see also Stark et al., 1979).

In the late 1950s and early 1960s, one of us (LWS) developed a self-organizing pattern-recognition scheme of multiple adaptive matched filters (MAMFs) (Okajima et al., 1963; Stark et al., 1962, 1963a). These filters were adapted and separated events into different distinguishable classes. An important aspect in the adaptation was to preserve information from random destruction by over-acceptance. The mathematics underlying this scheme is formally identical to artificial neural nets (ANNs), but the coefficients in the MAMFs have understandable values that enable understanding of the structure of the scheme as it develops (Stark, 1993a, 1994). At that time, most ANNs usually had a "teacher" to train them, rather than being self-organizing. Of course, for both MAMFs and ANNs, an enormous amount of top-down knowledge was introduced by the computer programmer in structuring many of the dimensions of the scheme and tightly organizing the input.

These pattern recognition systems could be closely compared with human pattern recognition (Wasui et al., 1964) especially when input reasons and output diagnoses were arranged in probability and cybernetic matrices; a physician's recollection of a specific case may be analogous to accessing a cluster of such matrix coefficients.

Throughout this period we were also studying neurological control systems; recall that Weiner et al. (1943) had thought feedback gave a teleology to artificial systems. These approaches were extended into planning notions for higher level control of motor behaviors (Pribram, 1971), which are demonstrated in robot control (see Section 4). This perhaps was the germ of the idea that bottom-up organization was not sufficient for complex behavior. It is likely that a top-down model might be flexibly constructed and govern not only motor behavior but also intentional perception (Searle, 1983).

Noton and the senior author started discussing artificial creatures such as Grey Walters' turtles. These had demonstrated apparent intelligent behavior using only fairly simple algorithms (Braitenberg, 1994; Paxson, 1953). We then got on to the serial nature of computer programs and of successive fixations carried by successive EMs from point to point. We realized that artificial computer vision schemes could provide for parallel processing, and this analogy led to the experiments that demonstrated the scanpath. The *repetitive* nature of the scanpath seemed surprising. One would have expected the fixations during a continued scan to shift to different sites to collect further, different information. This was, of course, naive bottom-up thinking. We soon switched to the top-down idea that an internal model possessed the information and was using the EMs and visual processes to check, confirm, or reject the model. The further *idiosyncratic* nature of the scanpath (Figure 2) supported this top-down view.

In a way this opposed the important work of McCulloch and Lettvin (see above) on the frog's eye. That paper raised issues of the evolution of complex organizational processes that are apparently bottom-up procedures yet contain Kant's time and space categories. Kant's categories are embedded in the anatomy that carries out the processing; the scanpath theory, on the other hand, interposes an essential level of intentioned (Searle, 1983) perceptions and behaviors that perhaps should be considered as "software" in comparison to sensory hardware. Representations apparently dominate in the human and likely are related to consciousness and other mysterious aspects of our brains. Here we have tried to briefly trace some of the origins of the idea of the scanpath.

6.3. Evolution: Searchpath

How are searchpaths different from scanpaths?   Searchpaths have a structure similar to scanpaths and are similarly defined as "*repetitive, idiosyncratic* sequences of saccades alternating with fixations." Their final, efficient (EMs, foveations and visual processes for recognition) and material (neurons, nerves, muscles, receptors) Aristotelian causes are the same.

How then are they different? A first answer is that they are generated and controlled by spatial models and not by the rich and compacted structure of the symbolic cognitive models that generate and control scanpaths; their formal causes are different. Thus our question now turns on the different properties of the spatial model versus those of the cognitive model.

Preliminary experiments suggest that spatial models represent the ability to remember positions of about six to seven loci, regions-of-interest containing objects or subfeatures of interest. When the number of loci goes much higher, to say 20, then the spatial model cannot handle this complexity and thus cannot accurately generate *repetitive* patterns from locus to locus. The only solution is to treat these large numbers of loci as a random search scene and to develop a "cover" algorithm so as not to miss portions of the search area (Stark et al., 1992b; Zhou et al., 1993).

However, if the loci are organized into an object, a pattern, or a series of subfeatures in a meaningful picture, then a cognitive model can be addressed, if it already exists, or a new one can be constructed by analogic reasoning. With this cognitive model, the brain can operate in the recognition arena, generate a scanpath and confirm a percept at one and the same time.

6.4. Information distribution in components of cognitive-spatial models

These components are the overall linkage and the multiple subfeatures. Under various task conditions the amount of information or knowledge represented by the overall model that includes implicit non-pictorial information can vary. Similarly, the information in the geometrical part or linkage of a cognitive-spatial model is a function of many factors as is the amount of information or knowledge represented by each of the subfeatures of a cognitive-spatial model. The relative distribution of information and knowledge between these two parts of the model can shift with time and task. This is true both for natural top-down models such as the scanpath or the searchpath and for artificial top-down models such as those used in robotics.

The cognitive model for the scanpath includes the linkage for the subfeatures; this linkage itself has embedded within it a good deal of information or knowledge. However, we estimate that the sum total of the sub-features, the small, high-informative regions-of-interest, such as the eyes on a face, or the figures in a landscape, is much richer in information. A factor arguing for this is the "vivacity" of ordinary vision with the active wide-field illusions of clarity, completeness, continuity, and constancy. The confirmation of top-down information from the cognitive model likely underlies the illusion of vivacity (see Section 8.2).

The spatial model for the searchpath includes the geometry of the target loci as its main information content. The spatial model is contrasted with a cognitive model, with cognitive implying some sort of symbolic representation. The subfeatures of a searchpath model are identical and require a single matched filter or some equivalent for the set of 7 +/- 2 identical targets in the different loci. These are rich subfeatures indeed, since search requires detection, recognition and identification. However,the information they contribute is less than the linkage information, and is identical for each class of target and decoy.

Another set of conditions exists for the top-down model for telerobotics. The overall non-pictorial model has full information on the kinematics and dynamics of the robot, the positions and lens-settings for the cameras, and the positions of any objects in the the the telerobotic working environment. The 2D projections of these positions onto the camera plan institute the linkage information per se. When we consider that the kinematics and dynamics of the robots include link lengths, joints, non-holonomic constraints, inertias, viscosities, dead spaces, and elasticities, we see how much information must be present in the overall model.

The subfeatures consist only of pictures of the visual enhancements that are placed onto the robot to make the image processing more robust; the overall model has already arranged the ROIs to surround each visual enhancement in its predicted locus. The *local* image processes, which include adaptive thresholding and centroid calculations, need produce only two numbers (X,Y) to locate the observed visual enhancement loci at the camera plane. It would be possible to expand on this minute information within the visual enhancements by using bar codes, for example. This would shift more information into the subfeature level, but at a cost of overloading the rather slow image processing system in our current technological embodiment.

Recently Ballard (Ballard and Brown, 1992, Ballard et al., 1994) coined a name, "deictic binding," for the contribution of the "working memory" of these linkages. He argues, and we agree, that they make central contributions to cognition. The discussion above plays with different cognitive and spatial memory structures to show how the balance among overall models and their linkages and sub-features can be different under different circumstances (Mackworth, 1978; Stark et al., 1962).

6.4. Is cognitive spatial vision possible without a model?

The simplest vision experiment is perhaps to present a flash of light to the peripheral retina in a dark room, and then to measure the EM the subject directs to that location. To the naive realist, this appears to be a clear-cut case of the external world controlling EMs, and a clear counter-example to the scanpath.

Two different considerations demonstrate that this simple view is not likely to be true. If one puts lenses or prisms on the subject's eyes, the subject will make errors in fixating the flashed locus and will then have to adapt his ocular-motor-spatial model or frame-of-reference (Gauthier et al., 1979). This is telling evidence that such a spatial model or frame-of-reference must exist for the initial simple experiment. In programming robotic vision, similar mapping of coordinate spaces is necessary, and, of course, was utilized in our robotic vision experiments (Section 4).

Another anecdotal example may be pertinent. Many people watch Sunday afternoon football on color TV with great zest and considerable understanding of the "plays," the standings of the teams, and the characteristics of individual players. One viewer may share his excitement about a particular "play" with a companion. "Did you see that great end run?" However, it may be that the companion has no knowledge of the game of football, no comprehension of the "plays," and has not followed the season's games with its outstanding players. That person, with likely 20/20 vision, may only have seen a jumble of colors moving over the screen. Without cognitive models of the game and its "plays," the companion can only say "Sorry, I didn't 'see' that play."

7. EXPERIMENTAL METAPHYSICS: EPISTEMOLOGY

Metaphysics includes the first principles of knowledge underlying all philosophical quests; for example, metamathematics has to do with first principles, the logic and consistency of proofs, formulas and equations underlying the structures of mathematics. The dictionary definition[5] of metaphysics is that branch of philosophy examining the theoretical or the first principles of reality and knowledge; from the title of Aristotle's treatise on first principles, so called because it followed ("meta" = after) his work on physics ("of nature"). Metaphysics includes epistemology and ontology. Epistemology is that branch of philosophy that studies the nature of knowledge, its presuppositions and foundations, and its extent and validity; from the Greek "epistasthai," to understand, and "logy," words or speech.

Ontology is that branch of metaphysics dealing with the nature of being and reality; from the Greek word for existence or being. An important branch of ontology that has departed philosophy and moved to astronomy (!) is the field of cosmology, the astrophysical study of the genesis, structure and constituent dynamics of the universe.

7.1. Introduction

My own knowledge of philosophy is limited, and rather than following in McCulloch's footsteps directly, I have instead taken my cue from a phrase of Bertrand Russell's (1945) which appears in his discussion of the logical refutations of Leibnitz by Kant: "The argument does not, to a modern mind, seem very convincing, but it is easier to feel convinced that it must be fallacious than it is to find out precisely where the fallacy lies."

---

[5] The following definitions relating to metaphysics, epistemology and ontology are paraphrased from the American Heritage Dictionary of the English Language, third edition, 1992, Houghton Mifflin Co., New York.

7.2. McCulloch

Many years ago, the philosopher David Hume positioned the basis of epistemology into the field of neurology or psychology by pointing out that introspective study of the human mind led him to substitute "contiguity" for an impossible-to-demonstrate philosophical cause and effect. Warren McCulloch[6], the most brilliant neurophysiologist of our century, wrote an article, "A Historical Introduction to the Postulational Foundations of Experimental Epistemology," in 1964, and had earlier, in 1948, given a lecture entitled, "Through the Den of the Metaphysician," on the same theme. He and the group of brilliant students around him, including Jerome Lettvin, Walter Pitts, and Patrick Wall, used his work on the formal neuron, on neural networks, on the functional organization of the cerebral cortex, and on the frog's eye (see Section 5.3), to elucidate a general plan for the ability of the human brain to obtain knowledge (McCulloch, 1988a, b).

7.3. The internal cognitive model

How are internal cognitive models constructed? Several theories have been proposed:

Platonic theory states that infants are born with a complete set of perfect ideals; these are awakened by experience or by Socratic anamnesis; for example, an "ideal" of a table is awakened by an actual experienced table and is thus recognized and can be named. Modern science probably holds that some models, e.g., a mother's face, may already be present at a child's birth. Hering's (1977) demonstration that conjugacy of saccades is present at birth, before any visual experience could coordinate the two eyes, and Coghill's (1929) demonstration that salamanders, kept under anesthesia until testing, had appropriate motor coordination for their developmental age, are arguments for further non-experiential innate motor mechanisms.

The internal experience theory asserts that propositional construction or analogic reasoning enables construction of internal cognitive models. These are then tested against experience, and, if found wanting, new models, also internally constructed, are again tested. The theory presumes that the human brain is a fantastic machine for generating and evaluating a wide variety of such internal cognitive models.

The external experience theory conjectures that, somehow, external experience flows inward and results in the development of internal cognitive models. An example in signal processing might be the development of multiple adaptive matched filters in a "self-organizing" system that can later be used to recognize new occurrences of the adapting set of events (Stark et al., 1962b). Aristotle thought that our "ideal" table was constructed at the center of a cluster in feature space, made up of all the different tables one has seen.

---

[6] In 1951, I had the pleasure of meeting Professor McCulloch and his entourage for an exciting week of discussions in Chicago. Some years later, in 1967, when I was a professor at the University of Illinois in Chicago, where much of his seminal work had been done in the 40s and 50s, I had the pleasure of seeing him awarded an honorary degree. I also enjoyed visits to the McCulloch Farm in Old Lyme, Connecticut when I was a young professor of neurology at Yale, and shared many happy years with Professor McCulloch at MIT.

Construction of cognitive models by internal experience appears to suit my approach to epistemology. A point to keep in mind is that influences from experience can occur repeatedly over many generations. By blind evolutionary mechanisms, any inheritable mechanism may be selected and may resemble a sequence of steps appropriate to a reasoning process; examples include the instinctual behaviors of insects or birds.

7.4. Kant's four stages of perception

Immanuel Kant (1950,1977) divided the overall perceptual setting into four aspects: appearance, sensation, perception, and representation (Figure 18). "Appearance" (*Erscheinung*) is the external chaotic world of Plato. Our term for this is "stuff"; it is important to realize that once the external world of appearances has been divided up into "things," a good deal of top-down analysis has already occurred. "Sensation" (*Empfindung*) represents "bottom-up physiology without space and time." Mueller's doctrine held that specific nerve energies were filtering mechanisms, for example, to allow optic fibers to transmit light information and auditory fibers to transmit sound information. We now know nerves to be remarkably homogenous in their conduction properties; modern neuroanatomy has shown that where nerves arise and where they terminate their connectivity determines what signal information they carry. Sensation also appears to have a level of bottom-up processing of organization that incorporates the space and time categories of Kant (see Sections 5.3 and 5.4 on Bottom-Up Organization).

We turn now to "Representation" (*Vorstellung*), the last of Kant's four stages of perception. Of course, philosophers have long been interested in these brain representations -- Leibnitz called them "noumenon," Plato, "ideals," and Berkeley, after whom my University is named, "notions." In Kantian philosophy, noumena are "objects reached by intellectual intuition without the aid of the senses" (Kant, 1950, 1977); I represent them as "files" in my office file case, where I keep as much of my knowledge as possible. Our term for brain representations is "top-down cognitive models."

Now, armed with top-down models, we can proceed downward to "perception per se" (*Anschauung*), where we meet bottom-up information carried by sensory mechanisms. Our definition for the "active-looking scanpath" in this phase of "perception per se," agrees with the "An" of *Anschauung* in treating it as a more planned, forceful and determined activity.   This is the function that our new quantitative scanpath evidence illuminates.   The scanpath is put forward as the active operational phase of perception per se. Each fixation in sequence checks out the representational model in a deliberate, intentional (Searle, 1983), active procedure.

PERCEPTUAL PROCESSES

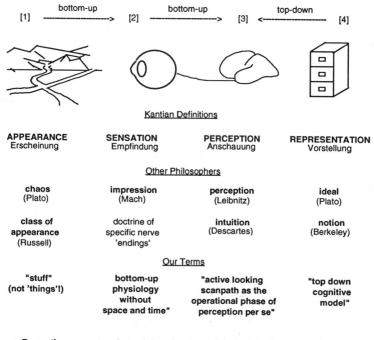

Perception as a more planned, forceful, determined activity. The top-down active-looking scanpath is mirrored by top-down active computer vision.

4/9/95

Figure 23. <u>Philosophical Definition of the Perceptual Setting.</u> Where does bottom-up meet top-down? Perhaps perception should be placed at the meeting, based upon recent neurological and functional MRI studies, of i) bottom-up automatic organization of the sensory inflow, much as the frog's retina can compute by using different ganglion cell networks, and ii) top-down processing using a cognitive model and the scanpath for checking subfeatures where expected. This scheme might work with feedback loops between different layers of cortical cells, e. g., layers four and six. See text (adapted from Stark et al., 1986, with thanks for discussions with Professor Wolfgang H. Zangemeister).

7.5. Models and hypotheses

Our philosophical quest has begun with the experimental evidence for the scanpath. New quantitative methods have been developed to parse the strength of cognitive model linkages for constraints represented by our *repetitive, idiosyncratic, local,* and *global* string-editing similarity measures. These, of course, vary dependent upon the picture, search scene or reading text the human subject is viewing. The informational distribution among the overall model, the linkage mechanism and the subfeatures that are being linked is itself quite variable for different types of top-down models, as we have discussed above. Of special interest are pure spatial models which may have provided the evolutionary structure on which to build cognitive models.

However, models can lead us astray; how cognitive models are constructed is a new and interesting area for brain research, perhaps approachable by modern techniques of functional MRI views of the active brain. The illusion of "virtual reality" and, indeed, of "reality," depends upon the visual illusions of "clarity and completeness, of continuity and of constancy"; of course, for other sensory pathways, similar illusions are at work. It also seems clear that computer image processing scientists will not quickly develop bottom-up computer vision schemes able to attain the knowledge of the physics of the world which seems to guide human vision. If the fish were to study the universe, perhaps the last thing they would discover would be the sea; we hope our recent awareness of the illusions of "clarity and completeness" and of "vivacity" is not the end of our studies of vision.

Doing much to extend earlier work by Brandt (1940) and Buswell (1935), Professor Alfred Yarbus (1967) carried out pioneering studies of EMs of subjects looking at pictures. The original Russian edition of his book (which he sent to me as a gift) features on its cover a designer's simplification of one of Yarbus' figures, showing EMs superimposed onto the bust of Queen Nefertiti. The designer had placed all of the fixations and joining saccadic paths within the silhouette of the figure; evidently, he followed an incorrect theory that EMs stay within such a boundary. This theory is disproven by the actual picture shown by Yarbus within the text of his book. I often show both the designer's simplification and the accurate experimental EMs side-by-side to warn myself not to let my theories allow me to disregard or distort my experimental data.

Another word of warning I take to heart -- as Laurence Sterne (1781) observed in *The Life and Opinions of Tristram Shandy, Gentleman,* "It is in the nature of a hypothesis when once a man has conceived it, that it assimilates everything to itself, as proper nourishment, and from the first moment of your begetting it, it generally grows stronger by everything you see, hear or understand."

8. EXPERIMENTAL METAPHYSICS: ONTOLOGY

8.1. Experimental ontology and virtual reality

Recently, the technology of computer displays has developed with extraordinary rapidity. The field of "virtual reality" is becoming more and more important, not only in entertainment, but in the workplace and even in modes of observation of scientific data.

Our contribution to ontology exploits the new field popularly known as "virtual reality." This "hype" name describes virtual environments formed by computer generated dynamic pictures projected on video screens and worn as head-mounted displays. Coordinated interaction between the subject and her environment immerses her in an artificial world of color and changing scenes; movement of the subject's head is instantly matched by a newly oriented binocular display congruent to the new egocentric direction, as movement of the subject's hand -- controlling a pictured robot, arm, hand, or vehicle -- is instantly matched by movement of the depicted object. Besides providing intuitive surroundings for achieving skill in the performances of various tasks and games, the virtual environment yields a sense of "telepresence," the compelling feeling that the human subject is acting and behaving in this distant artificial environment. This raises the ontological question, "Why does one feel present in the pupil of one's own dominant eye, here and now, in the so-called 'naive reality'?" The answer, directly from these studies, is that normal vision, like virtual reality, is formed by illusions -- of completeness and clarity, of space constancy, of continuity in time, of instantaneous action, of vivacity -- and these illusions create our sense of presence.

Virtual reality (VR) is the "hype" name for virtual environments, but hype and public relations alone do not drive the field of VR. So we ask ourselves: why do displays work so well? The answer, additional development of which is beyond the scope of the present paper, is that seeing is composed of illusions -- the illusions of clarity, completeness, constancy, and continuity -- which hide the actual processes of vision. These illusions work equally well in the world of VR and in the so-called "real" world; thus, the field of ontology is itself becoming amenable to experimental study.

8.2. Virtual reality and vivacity

In normal vision, we must be living and viewing within our internal visual model. We cannot possibly see the world with known visual mechanisms. Foveal sampling of the world, although continual and active, is a sparse sampling process (only two to four samples per second, with only one-half to one degree of the highest resolution vision at the fovea). Of course, sampling does not imply random sampling or even external-scene-directed sampling. Most likely, the eye sampling depends upon regions-of-interest expected from *a priori* reasoning or from an internal cognitive model; perhaps these phrases offer two ways of describing the same process (Stark, 1993a).

The powerful illusions of "clarity and completeness" enable us to "see" in our "mind's eye." We are not aware of the decreased resolution of peripheral vision away from the fovea. We are not aware of the decreased vision during saccadic EMs, or indeed, during blinks, which occur about once a second. We are not aware of the jumping of the retinal image with each saccadic EM; rather, we are assured of space constancy if the predicted motion of the eye, carried by corollary discharge, and the actual motion of the retinal image, are congruent within a fairly wide margin of error called saccadic suppression of image displacement.

Adapted from the Kant figure (Figure 23), Figure 24 shows the central role of active-looking EMs and the visual brain. The scene in the world (upper left) shows the glimpses of the world obtained during fixational pauses. This sparsely sampled visual information is certainly not sufficient to construct our vision of the world; thus the richness, clarity, completeness, and vivacity must be a visual illusion (upper right). This is equally true for a virtual world (lower left) seen by a subject wearing a head-mounted display. The virtual world is thus neither less nor more "real" than the "real" world; the same visual illusions of clarity, completeness and vivacity are felt.

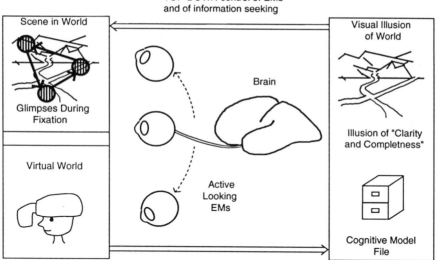

Figure 24. <u>Virtual Reality and Vision</u>. Multiple visual processes of perception operating in a similar fashion for virtual reality and for ordinary (so-called "real") vision. Why does virtual reality work? Because reality is virtual!

Telepresence is the feeling of being present in a distant world where one is controlling vehicles or robots or utilizing manual-ocular congruent reference frames, and where head movements result in almost immediate updating of the visual scene in the egocentric direction. The more the subject is immersed in the artificial display, the more he can interact with the artificial display and the more the compelling interest in the game or the work-task pulls him into activity in the virtual world, the more strongly he will feel telepresence. When I experienced telepresence in my own laboratory, carrying out a trivial robot manipulation, a pick and place task, I could no longer deny this illusory feeling.

Why then, do I feel present, in the pupil of my dominant eye, in the "real" world? It is because when I turn my head, those snatches of the world within the foveated areas or the regions-of-interest are updated instantly in the direction in which I am looking. When I move my hand in front of my eyes, my ocular-manual frames of reference are congruent, or at least have adapted to apparent congruence.

Finally, we can see two directions of information flow, the top-down control of EMs, directing the successive foveations (upper), and the feedback for vivacity (lower). When the bottom-up information confirms a sub-feature of the cognitive model, in the location hypothesized and controlled by the scanpath EMs, how reassured and happy is the brain, and our consciousness is rewarded with the illusion of vivacity (Scarry, 1988). When we are in the presence of a scene or picture, it is vivid; when we imagine it, most times, it is dim, vague, amorphous, and thus lacking in vivacity.

There is, however, a phenomenon contrary to this vivacity of actual ongoing vision, a maneuver to obstruct vivacity. If we fix our eyes on a small target in the scene and keep it there, the surrounding world gradually becomes much less "present" (K. Ezumi, personal communication). As soon as we start to saccade about the scene, the entire scene becomes vivid again, even if adequate sampling of the space has not been completed; the vivacity appears to be a consequence of free motions of the eye. Similarly, while we believe that we are able to see everything in a scene continuously and with high resolution, the brain is much more conservative. It continually directs EMs to explore and revisit key features of the scene expected from *a priori* reasoning or from an internal cognitive model, if indeed these are different processes.

8.3. Noiseless feedback

We would like to embed our top-down active vision scanpath theory into the matrix of information theory, but how to do this? Shannon's noiseless feedback theorem states that even if one were to have noiseless feedback from receiver to sender, channel capacity would not be increased! What advantage would noiseless feedback provide? Schalwijk and Kailath (1966) have provided a specific situation as an example.

A satellite orbits Jupiter and sends back to Earth pictures of Jupiter's surface; it has limited power and antenna size, and thus signal strength is weak. The channel between Jupiter and Earth has noise consisting of cosmic rays and solar wind. The

Earth antenna is large and power is essentially unlimited; this is the noiseless feedback. Although noiseless feedback cannot increase channel capacity, it can reduce the complexity of the code that achieves capacity. In this way, perhaps by sending back the received picture to be checked against the uncorrupted sent picture, the satellite need only send a few bits of information to correct errors of transmission. Thus more correct pictures can be received per unit time over the same channel.

How could top-down vision act in a similar manner to improve our visual awareness of our environment? Let us suppose that Adam Sillito's (1993) recent neurophysiological observations of a feedback interaction between levels four and six of the visual cortex provide such a potential mechanism. Incoming bottom-up visual information is very limited and noisy; the fovea has only 2,500 pixels and the photon carried information is immersed in a bath of photon noise.

Following Hecht (1938) we assume almost all the noise in bottom-up visual processing to be photon noise. But the top-down cognitive model need only confirm or reject specific expected subfeatures at particular loci sequenced rapidly on the scanpath made up of EMs. Recent studies in our lab (Hacisalihzade, 1992) have found rather inexact reconstituted matrix coefficients from generated strings in in extensive simulations. Yet when the inexact matrices were put into a TSD forced-choice situation, they often matched and selected the correct matrix and thus the appropriate cognitive model! The top-down process allows the sparse, inexact bottom-up scanpath to be used in a powerful manner!

8.4. Social arguments

The naive realist thus has these illusions of space constancy, continuity of time, and clarity and completeness to convince him of the reality of the external world. Second, he is reassured by the feedback loop that confines the accuracy of prediction from his model. This feedback is reinforced by the illusion of vivacity. Social interactions further support this dynamic; we are able to communicate and share our illusions. Shakespeare's *A Midsummer Night's Dream* provides a rich example:

Hippolita: 'Tis strange, my Thesus, that these lovers speak of.
Thesus: More strange than true: I never may believe
These antique fables, nor these fairy toys.
Lovers and madmen have such seething brains,
Such shaping fantasies, that apprehend
more than cool reason ever comprehends.
The lunatic, the lover and the poet
Are of imagination all compact:
One sees more devils than vast hell can hold,
That is: the madman, the lover, all as frantic
Sees Helen's beauty in a brow of Egypt:
The poet's eye in a fine frenzy rolling,
Doth glance from heaven to earth, from earth to heaven;

And as imagination bodes forth
The form of things unknown, the poet's pen
Turns them to shapes, and gives to airy nothing
A local habitation and a name.
Such tricks hath strong imagination,
That, if it would but apprehend some joy,
It comprehends some bringer of that joy:
Or in the night, imagining some fear,
How easy is a bush supposed a bear.
Hippolita: But all the story of the night told over,
And all their minds transfigured so together,
More witnesseth than fancy's images,
And grows to something of great constancy;
But howsoever, strange and admirable.
-Act V, scene 1

8.5. Problems with illusions

But, hark, are the fairies of Shakespeare "real" in an ontological sense? Perhaps the passage helps explain the unease we feel when viewing (and not sharing) the mass hysteria of strongly held beliefs -- patriotism, race, religion and other such cults that we as the "missing link" (between post savage ape and future civilized human beings) so frequently hold.

Also, when we consider society and its myths in broad contexts, we realize how much of what we here call our cognitive models exist in other forums, themes or theories of consciousness and of religion, permeating our interpretation of events. The impressionist artist, Berthe Morisot, mused ". . . . life is a dream and the dream is more true than reality -- there one is oneself, really oneself. If one has a soul, that is where it is to be found." Dr. Elaine Pagles, professor of religious studies at Princeton University has said about the Bible, "These stories, whether you believe them literally or not, are shadow images, the mental architecture we live in, and they are pervasive . . . . I began to see and become aware of the extent to which I perceive things through this idea of a universe of good and evil . . . . What I'm interested in is how these images and stories relate to the way we live. How do we interpret our own lives and understand ourselves through them? How does that imaginative process affect our dreams, how does it appear in our metaphors? How does our imagination of the invisible relate to the way we act and feel and think?"[7]

And yet we cannot get away from cognitive models, "We tell ourselves stories in order to live" (Didion, 1968); likely, the need for stories, illusions and the reification of nouns, are all part-and-parcel of human intellectual function. The scanpath is an exciting link connecting scientific studies of vision and these encompassing higher level mental processes.

---

7 See Remnick, 1995.

ACKNOWLEDGEMENT

We are especially grateful to our many colleagues for their discussions and help throughout the years. Professors Christian Freksa and Wolfgang Zangemeister, both of the University of Hamburg, should be given special recognition. While a student at Berkeley some years ago, Professor Freksa arranged for excellent programs for calibrations and analysis of scanpath EMs (Stark et al., 1979) and also educated the senior author (LWS) in the then current work in computer vision (Stark and Ellis, 1981). About ten years ago, Professor Zangemeister began (with the senior author) a series of scanpath experiments on subjects viewing artistic works (Stark et al., 1989; Zangemeister et al., 1995) and also engaged us in discussions of the philosophical concomitants of the scanpath theory (Stark et al., 1986).
The figures of the autonomous active robot vision system were prepared recently by T. Blackmon, Y. Ho and Y. Yu, and were based on work over the years by members of our Robotics Unit, including T. Blackmon, A. Hachenburg, M. Hirose, Y. Ho, W. Kim, A. Liu, A. Nguyen, F. Tendick, G. Tharp, and Y. Yu; the authors of the present article wish to thank these brilliant engineering scientists and helpful colleagues.
This research has been supported in part by USA, TRADOC, White Sands, New Mexico (Drs. Dixon and Payan, Technical Monitors) and by NCC-2-86, NASA-Ames Research Center (Dr. Stephen Ellis, Technical Monitor).
We also wish to thank Tina Choi, Inge Nordstrom, Jill Strohn, Jenny Tong, and Frozan Wahaj for their careful editorial help.

REFERENCES

Abernathy, B.,1990, Perception **19**, 63-77.

Abrams, S.G., and B.L. Zuber,1972, Reading Research Quarterly **8**, 40-51.

Ahlswede, R., and I. Wegner, 1989, Search Problems (John Wiley and Sons, Chichester).

Aloimonos, Y. and J.Y. Herve, 1992a, Exploratory active vision: theory, Proc. IEEE Computer Soc. Conf. on Comp. Vision and Pattern Recognition, Los Alamitos, Ca., 1992 (IEEE Computer Society Press, Los Alamitos) pp.10-15.

Aloimonos, Y., and L. Huang,1992b, The geometry of visual interception, Proc. IEEE Computer Soc. Conf. on Comp. Vision and Pattern Recognition, Los Alamitos, Ca., 1992 (IEEE Computer Society Press) pp. 741-743.

Aloimonos, Y. , E. Rivlin, and A. Rosenfeld,1992c, Object recognition by a robotic agent: the purposive approach, Proc. 11th IAPR International Conference on Pattern Recognition, Conf. A: Computer Vision and Applications, Los Alamitos, CA., **1** (IEEE Computer Society Press, Los Alamitos) pp. 712-715.

Aloimonos, Y. and A. Rosenfeld, 1991, Computer vision, Science **253**, 1249-1254.

Andersen, R. A., 1995a, Coordinate transformations and motor planning in posterior parietal cortex, in: The cognitive neurosciences, ed. M. S. Gazzaniga (MIT Press, Cambridge, Ma.) pp. 519-532.

Andersen, R. A., and R.M. Siegel, 1988a, Perception of three-dimensional structurefrom motion in monkey and man, Nature **331**, 259-261.

Andersen, R. A., E. C. Hildreth, H. Ando, and S. Treue, 1995b, Recovering three-dimensional structure from motion with surface reconstruction, Vision Research **35**, 117-137.

Andersen, R. A., S. Treue, and M. Husain, 1991, Human perception of structure from motion, Vision Research **31**, 59-75.

Apostolico, A., 1988, Efficient parallel algorithms for string editing and related problems, RIACS technical report TR 88-26; NASA contractor report NASA CR-185410 (Moffet Field: Research Institute for Advanced Computer Science, NASA Ames Research Center).

Assad J.A., and J.H. Maunsell, 1995, Neuronal correlates of inferred motion in primate posterior parietal cortex., Nature **373**, 518-521.

Atallah, M.J., 1993, A faster parallel algorithm for a matrix searching problem, Algorithmica **9,**156-167.

Baddeley, A.D., 1966, The influence of semantic and acoustic similarity on long-term memory for word sequences, Quarterly J. of Exp. Psych. **8**, 302-304.

Baeza-Yates, R., and G.H. Gonnet, 1992, A new approach to text searching, Comm. of the ACM **35**, 74-82.

Bahill, T.A., and L. Stark, 1979, Trajectories of saccadic eye movements, Scientific American **240**, 84-93.

Bajcsy, R., and E. Krotkov,1993, Active vision for reliable ranging: cooperating focus, stereo, and vergence, Int. J. of Computer Vision **11**, 187-203.

Bajcsy, R., J. Kosecka, and H.I. Christensen, 1995, Discrete event modeling of visually guided behaviors, Int. J. of Computer Vision **14**, 179-91.

Bajcsy, R., J. Ponce, D. Metaxas, and T.O. Binford,1994, Object representation for object recognition, Proc. 1994 IEEE Computer Soc. Conf. on Computer Vision and Pattern Recognition. Los Alamitos, Ca: IEEE, 1994 (Comput. Soc. Press) p.147-52.

Ballard, D.H. and Brown, C.M., 1992, Principles of animate vision, CVGIP: Image Understanding **56**, 3-21.

Ballard, D.H., M.M. Hayhoe, and J.B. Pelz, 1994, Visual representations in natural tasks, Proc. of the Workshop on Visual Behaviors,1994, Los Alamitos, Ca. (IEEE Computer Society Press) p. 1-9.

Bertossi, A.A., 1990, A VLSI system for string matching, Integration, The VLSI J., **9,**129-39.

Blackmon, T. and L.W. Stark, 1995, Model-based supervisory control in telerobotics, Presence, in press.

Braitenberg, V., 1994, Vehicles, experiments in synthetic psychology (MIT Press, Cambridge, MA).

Brandt, H.F.,1940, Ocular patterns and their psychological implications, American J. of Psych. **53**, 260-268.

Brandt, S.A., L.W. Stark, S. Hacisalihzade, and J. Allen, 1989, Experimental evidence for scanpath eye movements during visual imagery, in: Images of the Twenty-First Century. Proceedings of the Annual International Conference of the IEEE Engineering in Medicine and Biology Society, 1, eds. Y. Kim and F.A. Spelman (IEEE:New York) p. 278-279.

Bridgeman, B., and L. Stark, 1991, Ocular proprioception and efference copy in registering visual direction, Vision Research **31**, 1903-1913.

Brogan, D., 1990, Visual Search, Proceedings of the First International Conference on Visual Search (Taylor and Francis, London).

Brogan, D., A. Gale, and K. Carr, 1992, Visual Search: Proceedings of the Second International Conference on Visual Search (Taylor and Francis, Chicago).

Buswell, G.T., 1935, How people look at pictures (University of Chicago, Chicago).

Carpenter, P., and M. Just, 1976, Linguistic influences on picture scanning, in: Eye Movements and Psychological Processes, eds. R.A. Monty and J.W. Senders (Lawrence Erlbaum Assoc. , Hillsdale, NJ).

Choi, Y. S., A.D. Mosley and L.W. Stark, 1995, String editing analysis of human visual search, 'Starkfest' vision and clinic science special issue: Optometry and Vision Science **72**, 439-451.

Chomsky, N.,1957, Syntactic Structures (Mouton, The Hague).

Chudonovsky, D.V., and Chudonovsky, G.V.,1989, Search Theory (Maecel Dekker, Inc., New York).

Churchland, P.S.,1986, Neurophilosophy: Toward a Unified Science of the Mind-Brain (MIT Press, Cambridge).

Coghill, G.E., 1929, Anatomy and the Study of Behavior (Cambridge University Press, Cambridge).

Damasio, A.R., 1995, Descartes' Error: emotion, reason, and the human brain. (G.P. Putnam's Sons, New York).

de Valois, R. L., and K. K., de Valois, 1993, A multi-stage color model, Vision Research **33**, 1053-1065.

Didday, R.L., and M.A. Arbib, 1972, Eye movements and visual perception: A 'two visual system' model (COINS Technical Report 73C-9, University of Massachusetts).

Didion, J., 1968, Slouching towards Bethlehem (Farrar, Strauss & Giroux, New York).

Driels, M., and J. Acosta, 1992, The duality of haptic and visual search for object recognition, Proc. of the 1992 IEEE Int. Symp. on Intelligent Control (IEEE, New York) p. 255-260.

Eigen, M., R. Winkler-Oswatitisch, and A. Dress, 1988, Statistical geometry in sequence space: A method of quantitative comparative sequence analysis, Proc. of the Nat. Acad. of Sciences **85**, 5913-5917.

Ellis, S.R., and L. Stark, 1978, Eye movements while viewing Necker cubes, Perception **7**, 575-581.

Ellis, S.R., and L. Stark, 1979, Reply to Piggins, Perception **8**, 721-722.

Ellis, S.R., and L. Stark, 1986, Statistical dependency in visual scanning, Human Factors **28**, 421-438.

Engel, F.L., 1976, Visual conspicuity as an external determinant of eye movements and selective attention (Technische Hogeschool Eindhoven, Eindhoven, Netherlands).

Enns, J. T., and R.A. Rensink, 1991, Preattentive recovery of three-dimensional orientation from line drawings, Psych. Rev. **98**, 335-351.

Enns, J. T., and R.A. Rensink, 1993, A model for thee rapid interpretation of line drawings in early vision, in: Visual Search, eds. D. Brogan, A. Gale and K. Carr (Taylor and Francis, London).

Enoch, J.M., 1959, Effect of the size of a complex display upon visual search, J. of the Optical Soc. of America **49**, 280-286.

Fisher, G.H., 1971, Perception and art: Why do we see the world as we do?, Aspects of Education **13**, 63-90.

Fisher, D.F., R.A. Monty, and L.C. Perlmuter, 1978, Visual recognition memory for binary pictures: Another look, J. of Exp. Psych.: Human Learning and Memory **4**, 158-164.

Flagg, B.L., 1978, Children and television: Effect of stimulus repetition on eye activity, in: Eye movements and the Higher psychological processes, eds. J. Senders, D.F. Fisher, and R.A. Monty (Lawrence Erlbaum Associates, Hillsdale, NJ).

Gal, S., 1980, Search Games (Academic Press, New York).

Gauthier, G., J.-M. Hofferer, W.F. Hoyt, and Stark L., 1979, Visual-Motor Adaptation: Quantitative Demonstration in Patients with Posterior Fossa Involvement, Archives of Neurology **36**, 155-160.

Gould, J.D., 1967, Pattern recognition and eye-movement parameters, Perception and Psychophysics **2**, 399-407.

Gould, J.D., and A.B. Dill, 1969, Eye movement patterns and pattern discrimination, Perception and Psychophysics **6**, 311-320.

Groner, R., F. Walder, and M. Groen, 1984, Looking at faces: Local and global aspects of scanpaths, in: Theoretical and Applied Aspects of of Eye Movement Research, eds. A.G. Gale and F. Johnson (North Holland, Amsterdam, Netherlands) pp. 523-533.

Hacisalihzade, S.S., L.W. Stark, and J.S. Allen, 1992, Visual perception and sequences of eye movment fixations: A stochastic modeling approach, IEEE Trans. on Systems, Man, and Cybernetics **22**, 474-481.

Hecht, S., 1938, La base chimique et structurale de la vision (Hermann, Paris) (in French).

Hering, E., 1977, The Theory of Binocular Vision, trans. and eds., B. Bridgeman and L. Stark (Plenum Publishing, New York).

Hilsenrath, O. A., and Y. Y. Zeevi, 1990, Feature extraction and sensitivity matching in visual search in man and machine, in: Visual search, ed., D. Brogan (Taylor & Francis, London) pp. 225-235

Ishai, A. and D. Sagi, 1995, Common mechanisms of visual imagery and perception, Science **268**, 1772-1774.

Jameson, D., and L.M. Hurvich, 1989, Essay concerning color constancy, Annual Rev. of Psych. **40**, 1-22.

Jay, M., 1993, Downcast Eyes (University of California Press, Berkeley and Los Angeles).

Jeannerod, M., P. Gerin, and J. Pernier, 1968, Deplacements et fixation du regard dans l'exploration libre d'une scene visuelle, Vision Research **8**, 81-97 (in French).

Julesz, B., 1984a, A brief outline of the texton theory of human vision, Trends in Neurosciences, **7**, 41-45.

Julesz, B. , and T.V. Papathomas, 1984b, On spatial-frequency channels and attention, Perception & Psychophysics **36**, 398-399.

Kant, I., 1949, Prolegomena to Any Future Metaphysics, Bobbs-Merrill Company, Inc., New York).

Kant, I., 1977, The Philosophy of Kant, ed. C.J. Friedrich (Random House, New York).

Kaplan, I.T. and W. N. Schoenfeld, 1966, Ocularmotor patterns during viewing of visually-displayed anagrams, J. of Experimental Psychology **72**, 447-451.

Karp, R.M., 1977, Probabilistic analysis of partitioning algorithms for the traveling-salesman problem in the plane, Mathematics of Operations Research **2**, 209-224.

Kaufman, L., and W. Richards, 1969, Spontaneous fixation tendencies for visual forms, Perception and Psychophysics **5**, 85-88.

Kiryati, N., and A.M. Bruckstein, 1991, On optimal stopping of sparse search, in: Artificial Intelligence and Computer Vision, Proc. Seventh Israeli Conference, eds. Y.A. Feldman and A. Bruckstein (North-Holland, Amsterdam) pp. 71-80.

Kohler, W., 1929, Gestalt Psychology, (H. Liveright, New York).

Koopman, B.O., 1956a, The theory of search, Part I: Kinematic bases, Operations Research **4**, 324-346.

Koopman, B.O., 1956b, The theory of search, Part II: Target detection, Operations Research **4**, 503-531.

Koopman, B.O., 1957, The theory of search, Part III: The optimum distribution of searching effort, Operations Research **5**, 613-626.

Kosslyn, S.M., 1980, Image and Mind (Harvard University Press, Cambridge).

Krose, B. J., and B. Julesz, 1989, The control and speed of shifts of attention, Vision Research **29**, 1607-1619.

Kruskal, J.B., 1983, An overview of sequence comparison: Time warps, string edits, and macromolecules, SIAM Review **25**, 201-237.

Lai, D.C., 1975, Biocybernetic factors in human perception and memory, (Stanford University Center for Systems Research, Technical Report, Stanford, CA) pp. 6741-6745.

Lettvin, J.Y., H.R. Maturana, W.S. McCulloch, and W.H. Pitts, 1988,[1959], What the frog's eye tells the frog's brain, Proceedings of the IREE **47**, 1940-1959.

Llewellyn-Thomas, E., 1968, Movements of the eye, Sci. Am. **219**, 88-95.

Locher, P., and C. Nodine, 1973, The influence of visual symmetry on visual scanning patterns, Perception and Psychophysics **13**, 408-412.

Locher, P.J., and C.F. Nodine, 1974, The role of scanpaths in the recognition of random shapes, Perception and Psychophysics **15**, 308-314.

Louchard, G., and W. Szpankowski, 1992, Probabilistic analysis of a string edit problem (Le Chesnay, Inst. Nat. Recherche Inf. Autom. France).

Louchard, G., and W. Szpankowski, 1993, Analysis of a string edit problem in a probabilistic framework, in Combinatorial Pattern Matching, 4th Annual Symposium, CPM 1993 Proc., eds. A. Apostolico, M. Crochemore, Z. Galil and U. Manber (Springer-Verlag, Berlin) pp. 152-163.

Luria, S.M., and M.S. Strauss, 1975, Eye movements during search for coded and uncoded targets, Perception and Psychophysics **17**, 303-308.

Luria, S.M., and M.S. Strauss, 1978, Comparison of eye movements over faces in photographic positives and negatives, Perception **7**, 349-358.

Mackworth, N.H., and A.J. Morandi, 1967, The gaze selects informative details within picture, Perception and Psychophysics **2**, 547-552.

Mackworth, A.K., 1978, How to see a simple world: An exegesis of some computer programs for scene analysis, Machine Intelligence **8**, 510-537.

Mandler, M.B. and J.A. Whiteside, 1976, The role of scanpaths in recognition of random dot patterns, J. of Undergrad. Psych. Research **3**, 84-90.

McConkie, G.W., P. Kerr and B.P. Dyre, 1994, What are 'normal' eye movements during reading: Toward a mathematical description, in: Eye Movements in Reading, eds. J. Ygge and G. Lennerstrand (Pergamon/Elsevier, Oxford) pp. 315-328.

McCulloch, W.S., 1988a, A Historical Introduction to the Postulational Foundations of Experimental Epistemology, in: Embodiments of Mind (Massachusetts Institute of Technology, Cambridge, MA) pp. 359-372.

McCulloch, W. S., 1988b, Through the Den of the Metaphysician, in: Embodiments of Mind, (Massachusetts Institute of Technology, Cambridge, MA) pp. 142-156.

Meystel, A.M., I.A. Rybak, S. Bhasin and M.A. Meystel, 1992, Multiresolution stroke sketch adaptive representation and neural network processing system for gray-level image recognition, in: Intelligent Robots and Computer Vision XI: Biological, Neural Net and 3-D Methods, Proc. of the SPIE **1826**, 261-278.

Meystel, M.A., I.A. Rybak, S. Bhasin, and M.A. Meystel, 1993, Top-down/bottom-up algorithm for adaptive multiresolutional representation of gray-level images, in: The International Society for Optical Engineering, Proc. of the SPIE **1904**, 70-84.

Miyata, K. and L. Stark, 1992, Active camera control: seeing around obstacles, in: Power Electronics and Motion Control, Proc. of the 1992 International Conf. on Industrial Electronics, Control, Instrumentation, and Automation **2** (IEEE, New York) pp. 752-756.

Nguyen, A.H., and Stark, L., 1990, Model control of image processing: Pupillometry, computerized medical imaging and graphics **17**, 21-33.

Noton, D., and L. Stark, 1971a, Eye movements and visual perception, Sci. Am. **224**, 34-43.

Noton, D., and L. Stark, 1971b, Scanpaths in eye movements during pattern perception, Science **171** 308-311.

Noton, D., and L. Stark, 1971c, Scanpaths in saccadic eye movements while viewing and recognizing patterns, Vision Research **11**, 929-942.

Nussinov, R., 1989, The ordering of the nucleotides in DNA: computational problems in molecular biology, Computers in Biology and Medicine **19**, 269-281.

66   L.W. Stark and Y.S. Choi

O'Regan, J.K., 1992, Solving the 'real' mysteries of visual perception: The world as an outside memory, Canadian J. of Psych. **46**, 461-488.
O'Regan, J.K., F. Vitu, R. Radach and P.W. Kerr, 1994, Effects of local processing and ocularmotor factors in eye movement guidance in reading, in: Eye Movements in Reading, eds. J. Ygge and G. Lennerstrand (Pergamon/Elsevier, Oxford) pp. 329-348.
Parker, R.E., 1978, Picture processing during recognition, J. Exp. Psych.: Human Perception and Performance **4**, 284-293.
Paxson, E.W., and I. Barr, 1963, A neural net for consummatory behavior, Rand memorandum, RM-3393-PR.
Petrovic, S.V. and J.D. Golic, 1993, String editing under a combination of constraints, Information Sciences **74**, 151-163.
Pollack., I., and D. Spence, 1968, Subjective pictorial information and visual search, Perception and Psychophysics **3**, 41-44.
Posner, M.I. and M.E. Raichle, 1994, Images of Mind (Scientific American Library, New York).
Prokowski, F.J., 1971, A model for human eye movements during viewing of a general, two-dimensional, dynamic display, Unpublished doctoral dissertation, University of Connecticut.
Pribram, K.H., 1971, Languages of the Brain (Prentice-Hall, Englewood Cliffs, NJ).
Rabiner, L.R., A.E. Rosenberg and S.E. Levinson, 1978, Considerations in dynamic time warping algorithms for discrete word recognition, IEEE Trans ASSP **26**, 575-582.
Rayner, K., 1994, Eye Movements during skilled reading, in: Eye Movements in Reading, eds. J. Ygge and G. Lennerstrand (Pergamon/Elsevier, Oxford) pp. 205-218.
Remond, A., N. Lesevre and V. Gabersek, 1957, Approche d'une semiologie electrographique du regard, Revue Neurologique **96**, 536-546 (in French).
Remnick, D., 1995, States of mind: the devil problem, The New Yorker, April 3, 54-65.
Russell, B., 1945, A History of Western Philosophy (Simon and Schuster, New York).
Rybak, I.A., N.A. Shevtsova, L.N. Podladchikova, and A.V. Golovan, 1991a, A visual cortex domain model and its use for visual information processing, Neural Networks **4**, 3-13.
Rybak, I.A., N.A. Shevtsova and L.N. Podladchikova, 1991b, Modeling of local neural networks of the visual cortex and applications to image processing, in: The International Society for Optical Engineering, Applications of Artificial Neural Networks II, Proc. of the SPIE **1469**, 737-748.
Rybak, I.A., N.A. Shevtsova and V.M. Sandler, 1992a, The model of a neural network visual preprocessor, Neurocomputing **4**, 93-102.
Rybak, I.A., A.V. Golovan, V.I. Gusakova, L.N. Podladchikova et al., 1992b, A neural network system model for active perception and invariant recognition of grey-level images, in: Proc. IJCNN International Joint Conf. on Neural Networks **4** (IEEE, New York) pp. 1-6.
Rybak, I.A., A.V. Golovan and V.I. Gusakova, 1993, Behavioral model of visual perception and recognition, in: Human Vision, Visual Processing, and Digital Display IV, Proc. of the SPIE **1913**, 548-560.
St. Cyr, G.J., and D.H. Fender, 1969, The interplay of drifts and flicks in binocular fixation, Vision Research **9**, 245-265.
Scarry, E., ed., 1988, Literature and the Body: Essays on Populations and Persons (Johns Hopkins University Press, Baltimore) p. 220.
Schifferli, P., 1953, Etude par enregistrement photographique de le motricite oculaire dans l'exploration, dans la reconnaissance et dans la representation visuelles, Monatschrift fur Psychiatrie und Neurologie **126**, 65-118 (in French).
Scinto, L.F., and B.D. Barnette, 1986, An algorithm for determining clusters, pairs or singletons in eye-movement scan-path records, Behavior Research Methods, Instruments, & Computers **18**, 41-44.
Schalkwijk, J.P.M., 1966a, A coding scheme for additive noise channels with feedback - Part II: Band-limited signals, IEEE Transactions on Information Theory,vol. IT-**12:2**, 183-189.
Schalkwijk, J.P.M., and T. Kailath, 1966b, A coding scheme for additive noise channels with feedback, Part I: No bandwidth constraint, IEEE Transactions on Information Theory IT, **12**: 172-182.
Searle, J.R., 1983, Intentionality, an essay in the philosophy of mind (Cambridge University Press, Cambridge).

Senders, J.W., 1964, The human operator as a monitor and controller of multidegree of freedom systems, IEEE Transactions on Human Factors in Electronics **5**, 2-5.

Senders, J.W., D.F. Fisher and R.A. Monty, eds.,1978, Eye movements and the higher psychological processes (Lawrence Erlbaum Associates, Hillsdale, NJ).

Sillito, A.M.J., and K.L. Grieve, 1991, A re-appraisal of the role of layer VI of the visual cortex in the generation of cortical end inhibition, Exper. Brain Res. **87**, 521-529.

Sillito, A.M., H.E. Jones, G.L. Gerstein and D.C. West, 1994, Feature-linked synchronization of thalamic relay cell firing induced by feedback from the visual cortex, Nature **369**, 479-482.

Singer, J., S. Greenberg, and J. Antrobus, 1971, Looking at the mind's eye: Experimental studies of ocular motility during day dreaming, Transactions of the New York Acad. of Science **33**, 694-709.

Stark. L., 1973, Engineering Principles in Physiology, in: Information Theory in Physiology, vol. 1, eds. L. Stark and G. C. Theodoridis (Academic Press, New York) pp.13-32.

Stark, L.W., 1993, Top-down vision in humans and robots, Proc. of the International Society for Optical Engineering, Human Vision, Visual Processing, and Digital Display IV **1913**, 613-621.

Stark, L., 1993, Neural nets, random design and reverse engineering, Proc. of the IEEE International Conference on Neural Networks, San Francisco, CA.

Stark, L., 1994, ANNs and MAMFs: Transparency or Opacity?, Proc. of the European Neural Network Society, Sorrento, pp.123 - 129.

Stark, L., and J.F. Dickson, 1965, Mathematical Concepts of Central Nervous System Function, Neurosciences Research Program Bulletin **3**, 1-72.

Stark, L., and S. Ellis, 1981, Scanpaths revisited: Cognitive models direct active looking, in: Eye Movements: Cognition and Visual Perception, eds. Fisher, Monty and Senders (Erlbaum Press, New Jersey) pp.193-226.

Stark, L., and C.C. Krischer, 1988, Reading with and without Eye movements, in: Brain and Reading, eds. C. von Euler, I. Lundberg and G. Lennerstrand (Stockton Press, New York) pp. 345-355.

Stark, L., Vossius, G., and Young, L.R., 1962, Predictive control of eye tracking movements, IRE Transactions of Human Factors in Electronics **3**, 52-57.

Stark, L., M. Okajima, and G.H. Whipple, 1963a, Computer Pattern Recognition Techniques: Electrocardiographic Diagnosis, Communications of the Associationfor Computing Machinery **5**, 527-532.

Stark, L., M. Okajima, G. Whipple, and S. Yasui, 1963b, Computer Pattern Recognition Techniques: Some Results with Real Electrocardiographic Data, IEEE Transactions on Biomedical Electronics **10**, 106-114.

Stark, L., M. Okajima, G. Whipple, and S. Yasui, 1964, Comparison of Human and Computer Electrocardiographic Wave-Form Classification and Identification, American Heart J. **1968**, 236-242.

Stark, L., S.R. Ellis, H. Inoue, C.R. Freksa, and J. Zeevi, 1979, Cognitive models direct scanpath eye movements, Proc. of XII International Conf. on Medical and Biological Engineering, Jerusalem, Israel.

Stark, L., W. Hoyt, K. Cuiffreda, R. Kenyon, and F. Hsu, 1980a, Time optimal sacaddic trajectory model and voluntary nystagmus, in: Models of Oculomotor Behavior and Control, ed. B.L. Luber (CRC Press, West Palm Beach, FL).

Stark, L., R.V. Kenyon, and K.J. Ciuffreda, 1980b, An unexpected role for normal accommodative vergence in strabismus and amblyopia, Am. J. of Optometry and Physiological Optics **57**, 566-577.

Stark, L.W., W.H. Zangemeister, B. Hannaford, and K. Kunze, 1986, Use of models in brainstem reflexes for clinical research, in: Clinical Problems of Brainstem Disorders, eds. K. Kunze, W. H. Zangemeister, and A. Arlt (Thieme Medical Publishers, New York) pp.172-184.

Stark, L.W., K. Ezumi, T. Nguyen, R. Paul, G. Tharp, and H.I. Yamashita, 1992a, Visual Search in virtual environments, Proc. of SPIE Conference on Human Vision, Visual Processing, and Digital Display.

Stark, L.W., I. Yamashita, G. Tharp, and H. Ngo, 1992b, Searchpatterns and searchpaths in human visual search, Proc. of the Second International Conf. on Visual Search (Taylor and Francis, London).

Sterne, L., 1781, The Life and Opinions of Tristram Shandy, Gentleman (Harrison, London).

Stone, L.D., 1975, Theory of Optimal Search (Academic Press, New York).

Sun, F., M. Morita, and L. Stark, 1985, Comparative Patterns of Reading Eye Movement in Chinese and English, Perception and Psychophysics **37**, 502-506.

Sutro, L.L., and J.B. Lerman, 1973, Robot vision, in: Ist National Conference on Remote Manned Systems, ed. E. Heer (California Institute of Technology, Pasadena, CA) pp. 251-282.

Tootell, R.B., D. Malonek, and A. Grinvald, 1994a, Optical imaging reveals the functional architecture of neurons processing shape and motion in owl monkey area MT, Proc. of the Royal Society of London, Series B: Biological Sciences **258**, 109-119.

Tootell, R.B., D. Malonek, and R. Malach, 1994b, Relationship between orientation domains, cytochrome oxidase stripes, and intrinsic horizontal connections in squirrel monkey area V2, Cerebral Cortex **4**, 151-65.

Treisman, A., 1991, Search, similarity, and integration of features between and within dimensions, J. of Exp. Psych. **17**, 652-676.

Treisman, A. , and S. Gormican, 1988, Feature analysis in early vision: Evidence from search asymmetries, Psych. Rev. **95**, 15-48.

Treisman, A. , and S. Sato, 1990, Conjunction search revisited, J. of Exp. Psych. **16**, 459-478.

Treisman, A., A. Vieira, and A. Hayes, 1992, Automaticity and preattentive processing., Am. J. of Psych. **105**, 341-362.

Tsuda, K., M. Nakamura, and J. Aoe, 1992, A method of text reduction for text proofreading . systems, Proc. of the First Singapore Int. Conf. on Intelligent Systems, Singapore (Japan-Singapore A1 Centre, Singapore) pp. 537-542.

Wagner, R.A., 1983, On the complexity of the extended string-to-string correction problem, in: Time Warps, String Edits and Macromolecules: The Theory and Practice of Sequence Comparison, eds. D. Sankoff and J.B. Kruskal (Addison-Wesley, Reading, MA).

Wagner, R.A., and M.J. Fischer, 1974, The string-to-string correction problem, J. Assoc. for Computing Machine **21**, 168-173.

Waldman, W.J., and G. Hobson, 1991, Visual detection with search: An empirical model, IEEE Trans. on Sys. Man, and Cybernetics **21**, 596-606.

Walker-Smith, G.J., A.G. Gale, and J.M. Findlay, 1977, Eye movement strategies involved in face perceptions, Perception **6**, 313-326.

Wang, Y.P., and T. Pavlidis, 1990, Optimal correspondence of string subsequences, IEEE Transactions on Pattern Analysis and Machine Intelligence **12**, 1080-1087.

Weiner, N., A. Rosenbleuth, and J. Bigelow, 1943, Behavior, Purpose, and Teleology, Philos. Sci. **10**, 18-24.

Weiner, S., and H. Ehrlichman, 1976, Ocular motility and cognitive process, Cognition **4**, 31-43.

Weir, J., and R.H. Klein, 1970, The measurement and analysis of pilot scanning and control behavior during simulated instrument approaches, NASA CR-1535.

White, C.T., and A. Ford, 1960, Eye movements during simulated radar search, J. of the Optical Soc. of Am. **50**, 909-913.

Wickelgren, W.A., 1966, Acoustic similarity and intrusion errors in short term memory for English vowels, J. of the Acoustical Soc. of Am. **70**, 102-108.

Wu, S., and U. Manber, 1992, Fast text searching allowing errors, Comm. of the ACM **35**, 83-91.

Yamashita, H.I., 1990, Head scanning patterns in human visual search, Master's Thesis, UC Berkeley, Mechanical Engineering.

Yarbus, A.L., 1967, Eye Movements and Vision (Plenum Press, New York).

Yeshurun, Y., and E.L. Schwartz, 1989, Shape description with a space-variant sensor: algorithms for scan-path, fusion, and convergence over multiple scans, IEEE Transactions on Pattern Analysis and Machine Intelligence **11**, 1217-1222.

Zangemeister, W.H., K. Sherman, and L. Stark, 1989, Scanpath eye movements while viewing abstract images, in: ECEM V - Fifth European Conference on Eye Movements, eds. R. Scheind and D. Eaunberber (Pavia University Press, Pavia) pp. 261-265.

Zangemeister, W.H., K. Sherman, and L. Stark, 1995, Evidence for a Global Scanpath Strategy in Viewing Abstract Compared with Realistic Images, Nueropsychologia **33**, 1009-1025.

Zavalishin, N.V., 1968, Hypothesis concerning the distribution of eye fixation points during the examination of pictures, Automatic Remote Control **29**, 1944-1951.

Zhou, G., K. Ezumi, and L. Stark, 1993, Efficiency of Searchpatterns, Computers in Biology and Medicine **23**, 511-524.

Zuber, B.L., L. Stark, and G. Cook, 1965, Microsaccades and the velocity amplitude relationship for saccadic eye movement, Science **15**, 1459-1460.

Zusne, L., and K.M. Michels, 1964, Nonrepresentational shapes and eye movements, Perceptual and Motor Skill **18**, 1-20.

CHAPTER 2

NEUROPSYCHOLOGICAL ASPECTS

Visual Attention and Cognition
W.H. Zangemeister, H.S. Stiehl and C. Freksa (Editors)
73

NEUROPSYCHOLOGICAL ASPECTS OF VISUAL ATTENTION AND EYE MOVEMENTS - A SYNOPSIS

Glyn W. Humphreys

Cognitive Science Research Centre,
School of Psychology,
University of Birmingham,
Birmingham, B15 2TT, UK.

Abstract

I summarise the new work reported in this book on the neuropsychology of visual attention and eye movements. The work points to the multiplicity of brain mechanisms mediating visual attention and the direction of eye movements to seen objects. These mechanisms utilize different co-ordinate systems and likely link through to different response processes. The implications of this evidence for using measures of attention and eye movements in real-world situations is dicussed.

The visual world is highly complex, and typically contains many objects, only a few of which may be relevant for action. Hence it is important that biological visual systems employ processing mechanisms that enable relevant objects to be selected for action and irrelevant objects to be ignored. One obvious way that selection may be achieved would be to employ sesnory devices with built-in processing limitations; directing the sensory device at appropriate objects or locations in a scene would enable the objects to be selected and others to be ignored by default. In fact, this may well be one of the means by which human vision enables selection to take place. The eye is an extremely limited sensor, having poor spatial and tmeporal resolution that is inhomogeneous across the visual field. If the fovea of the retina is directed at an object, the object will be processed with high spatial resolution, but others parts of the image will not. Some form of selection will have been achieved. Of course, this analysis of selection in vision begs the question of how the eye can be directed to appropriate locations or objects in an image in the first place. What forms of visual processing are involved in selecting appropriate locations or objects for fixation? In addition, it also begs the question of whether other forms of selection also operate, but driven by internal processing limitations rather than more peripheral 'hardware' limitations (e.g., the limited resolution of the eye). Over the past 20 years, neuroscientists have been engaged in trying to delineate the mechanisms of so-called visual attention, by which the brain selects visual objects for action, and this work has led to an understanding of both the complexity of the problem, and the variety of processing mechanisms that appear to be employed. The papers reported in the section of this book on 'neuropsychological aspects' of visual attention and cognition provide useful summaries of current thinking on: the internal mechanisms that may be used to select objects (Humphreys, Gilchrist & Free), the mechanisms that direct eye movements to relevant objects and locations (Findlay & Walker), and the impairment of those mechanisms after selective brain lesion (Findlay & Walker, Haeske-Dewick & Canavan). In addition, the chapter by Velichkovsky, Pomplun and Rieser illustrates ways in which measures of eye movements and attention can be used in a variety of practical circumstances. Linking such measures to a better theoretical understanding of the mechanisms underlying eye movements and attention should enable us to optimise such practical developments.

2. MECHANISMS OF INTERNAL SELECTION.

It is clear that the eyes are not directed to visual locations in a 'blind' manner, so that relevant locations and objects are inspected purely by chance. It has long been known that the eyes tend to be directed initially, and to dwell on, objects of interest without necessary prior inspection of other locations and objects (Yarbus, 1967). There needs to be some internal processing mechanisms that direct the eye to such locations.

In their paper, Humphreys, Gilchrist and Free summarise evidence on the nature of these internal processing mechanisms. Much of this work has used visual search procedures in which observers are required to detect the presence of a particular target presented amongst multiple distractor items. Depending upon the relationship between the target and the distractors, search can vary from being extremely efficient and unaffected by the number of distractors in the field, to being inefficient and directly related to the number of distractors present. Both types of search can be observed even when observers do not make eye movements (e.g., Klein & Farrell, 1989), and so the differences reflect variations in the efficiency of internal mechanisms of selection. Typically when targets and distractors differ on the basis of some salient, simple feature (e.g., in colour or orientation), search is efficient. This suggests that such simple features can be computed and compared in parallel across the visual field. Such computations can be carried out prior to any selection of one part of the field. In contrast, when search is directly related to the number of distractors present, it may be that the differences between targets and distractors are not computed prior to selection but only afterwards (since distractors are then as likely to be selected as targets). By contrasting the types of stimulus information that support efficient search and those giving rise to inefficient search, investigators have tried to understand the means by which internal visual selection can be achieved; the information computed without selection may also serve to direct eye movements to relevant locations and objects in the visual field.

Humphreys et al. discuss recent evidence indicating that relatively complex forms of information can be computed prior to visual selection taking place. For instance, the information seems to include the grouping of elements into closed forms, and the relations between elements in 3D also seem to be computed. This recent work suggests that the visual system may use relatively rich, though perhaps somewhat noisy and error-prone, descriptions of the visual world to enable relevant objects and locations to be selected.

The mechanisms that underly the computation of the early description of the visual world (prior to selection operating) also seem to involve specific neurophysiological systems that can operate in a relatively independent manner. Humphreys et al. note evidence for separate grouping mechanisms, one involving edges computed from the image, the other involving surface properties of objects. The independent mechanisms may also be selectively damaged, giving rise to particular disorders of visual processing. Neuropsychological studies can thus help throw light on the nature of the underlying mechanisms.

3. NEUROPSYCHOLOGICAL STUDIES

Neuropsychological studies of visual attention have most frequently involved patients with unilateral visual neglect. In this syndrome, patients can fail to respond to stimuli presented on the side of space contralateral to their lesion. The performance of such patients can be improved by cueing them to attend to the affected side, and performance is also often modulated by the presence of stimuli on the unaffected side which can 'compete' for visual selection (neglect is exacerbated by the presence of such competing stimuli; see Riddoch & Humphreys, 1983; Robertson & Marshall, 1993). These last effects suggest that neglect can reflect a deficit in visual selection such that stimuli on the affected side of space tend to lose out when placed in competition for selection with other stimuli in the environment.

Haeske-Dewick and Canavan here describe evidence indicating that the various symptoms that characterise the neglect syndrome can dissociate. Some patients show neglect across a number of modalities (vision and touch, for example), others only within one modality. Some patients neglect stimuli present in the near environment but not those at a distance, other patients can show the opposite pattern. These dissociations are consistent with the existence of a number of different forms of spatial representation in the brain - some specific for a given inout modality, others for 'near' or for 'far' space etc. In addition, attentional selection may operate within each spatial representation, so that different patterns of neglect arise after brain lesion. Haeske-Dewick and Canavan report on the development of clinical tests that may in future help to distinguish between the different forms of neglect.

Findlay and Walker in their paper make a further distinction between the representation of space within visual objects relative to representations in which the spatial relations are coded between separate objects (see Humphreys & Riddoch, 1994). They note a patient who seemed primarily to neglect the space on one side of visual objects, even when those objects were presented on the side of 'non-neglected' side of space. This patient seemed to show neglect of space only within visual objects. Interestingly, this patient made eye movements to objects presented on either side of space relative to this body, but eye movements were made only to the unaffected side of single objects. This result suggests that the different forms of spatial representation also mediate eye movements as well as internal visual selection.

Findlay and Walker report other experiments indicating that eye movements are influenced by other occulomotor factors, independent of visual selection. For instance, eye movements to a target are facilitated if a gap is introduced between fixation and the target for the eye movement (Fischer, 1987). However, the magnitude of the gap effect does not increase when subjects can also pay attention to the forthcoming target location. The gap effect may then, at least in part, reflect release from ocular fixation. Patients with neglect can also show enhanced benefits from a gap between fixation and a target on the affected side. Findlay and Walker's work suggests that mechanisms that release ocular fixation can also be affected in the neglect syndrome, in addition to any effects on the attentional system.

Overall these results indicate that there is probably no single mechanism of selection in the brain; rather than are multiple mechanisms, determined in part by the stimulus modality, in part by the nature of the response, and in part by the form of spatial representation that may best support the mapping between stimuli and response.

4. APPLYING THE FRUITS OF BASIC RESEARCH

In their paper here, Velichkovsky et al. show how measures of eye movements and of attended locations can be used in applied settings. They document work in which people solving puzzles are provided with information about where their partners are looking. Performance was improved by giving people this extra information. In addition, pictures were pre-processed so as to reflect the distribution of eye movements in a set of independent observers performing different tasks. Interpretation of the pictures was biased by this extra information.

These studies show performance in a variety of circumstances could be improved by making explicit information about where other observers are looking or have looked. However, as the other papers here illustrate, people can attend selectively to visual stimuli without making eye movements. To generate a representation of likely locations for attention requires that an accurate theory of internal attentional operations be developed. Predictions from such a theory could also be built-in to a system that tracks explicit movements of attention (via eye movements), in order to minimize computation time when on-line feedback is required. Here it may be possible to inter-mesh theory with practice to provide optimal working solutions.

REFERENCES

1. B. Fischer, The preparation of visually-guided eye saccades. Review

of Physiology, Biochemistry and Pharmacology, 106 (1987) 1-55.
2. G.W. Humphreys and M.J. Riddoch, Attention to within-object and between-object spatial representations: Multiple sites for visual selection. Cognitive Neuropsychology, 11 (1994) 207-241.
3. R. Klein and M. Farrell, Search performance without eye movements. Perception & Psychophysics, 46 (1989) 476-482.
4. M.J. Riddoch and G.W. Humphreys, The effects of cueing on unilateral neglect. Neuropsychologia, 21 (1983) 589-599.
5. I. Robertson and J.C. Marshall, Unilateral neglect: Clinical and experimental studies, Hove, Lawrence Erlbaum.
6. A.L. Yarbus, Eye movements and vision, New York, Plenum Press.

Visual Attention and Cognition
W.H. Zangemeister, H.S. Stiehl and C. Freksa (Editors)
© 1996 Elsevier Science B.V. All rights reserved.

SEARCH AND SELECTION IN HUMAN VISION: PSYCHOLOGICAL EVIDENCE AND COMPUTATIONAL IMPLICATIONS

Glyn W. Humphreys, Iain Gilchrist and Linda Free

Cognitive Science Research Centre,
School of Psychology,
University of Birmingham,
Birmingham, B15 2TT, UK

Abstract

In this paper we review the evidence concerning internal mechanisms for selecting visual stimuli for action, and the inter-relations between the mechanisms of selection and mechanisms of perceptual grouping. We suggest that selection mechanisms in human vision operate on rapidly assembled visual descriptions coded in 3D.

1.   SELECTION IN VISION: FEATURES AND CONJUNCTIONS.
In order for vision to operate successfully in the world, there needs to be some form of selection mechanism. Computationally, selection is needed so that coherent actions can be addressed to a target object present amongst multiple distractors, given a limitation on the

number of actions that can be performed at a given time. The need for selection is also indicated by neurophysiological data. The cells that seem to be involved in coding high-level properties of the visual world, in the infero-temporal cortex, typically also have very large receptive fields (see Desimone & Ungerleider, 1989, for a review). The firing rate of such cells is often tuned to particular stimulus attributes (this can include something as specific as an individual face in one view; see Perrett, Oram, Hietanen & Benson, 1994, for a recent review). However, the firing rate will decrease when a non-preferred stimulus is simultaneously present in the receptive field. Some form of selection is needed in order to optimise the firing of the cell to the preferred stimulus (see Chelazzi, Miller, Duncan & Desimone, 1993; Moran & Desimone, 1985, for evidence).

Psychologists have long argued about the nature of visual coding that might take place before selection operates. "Early" selection theories stress that only simple visual properties, such as edges of particular spatial frequencies, colours and orientations, are coded prior to selection ("pre-attentively"; e.g., Treisman, 1988). Such properties may be registered rapidly by special purpose detectors, which operate in parallel across the visual field. However, higher-order representations of objects (e.g., specifying the relationships between simple image features) can only be computed more slowly, following selection, and perhaps even at just one location at a time. In contrast to such accounts, "late" selection theories hold that representations of complete objects may be encoded, and stored knowledge associated with these object representations activated, prior to selection taking place (e.g., Duncan & Humphreys, 1989).

In studies of vision, the question of which visual properties can be encoded prior to selection taking place is often addressed by means of visual search experiments. In a visual search task, the observer can be set to detect a particular target stimulus and to ignore varying numbers of distractor items. The efficiency of selecting a given target can be gauged by measuring the speed or accuracy of detection as a function of the number of distractors present. When there are relatively minor effects of the number of distractors present (e.g., if there is a search rate of under 10 msec/item), it can be argued that targets are detected on the basis of spatially parallel processing (e.g., it is likely to be difficult to realise a serial process in neural terms with a switch-rate of below 10 msec/item; see Crick, 1984). When there are large effects of the number of distractors present, when target-detection times increase linearly with the number of distractors, and when the search rates on present and absent trials are of the order of 1:2, it can be argued that search is spatially serial and self-terminating (the search rate on present trials is then half that on absent because, on average, only half the distractors will be searched when the target is present) (though see Humphreys & Muller, 1993; Townsend, 1972; for alternative accounts of such linear search functions).

In a series of classic experiments in the early 1980's, Treisman reported clear differences in search efficiency for targets defined by the presence of a single disjunctive feature (e.g., a red letter amongst blue letters, or an x amongst O's) and targets defined by the presence of a conjunction of the same features (e.g., a red X amongst blue X's and red O's) (e.g., Treisman & Gelade, 1980). These results suggested a clear difference between the kinds of visual information that can be computed prior to a serial stage of visual selection and the information computed following selection: simple disjunctive features are computed prior to selection (differences in shape, colour etc.), but they are only combined after subjects attend to the location where the attributes commonly fall.

Over the last 10 years or so, however, this picture has become somewhat more complex. For example, under particular circumstances relatively efficient search can be found even for targets defined by a conjunction of features. Thus if one of the dimensions defining the target is movement or stereo-depth, then conjunction targets can be detected with little effect of the number of distractors in the display (e.g., McLeod, Driver & Crisp, 1988; Nakayama & Silverman, 1986). With such displays, the distractors can be segmented into two planes, and targets can then be detected on the basis of a simple feature difference relative to the distractors falling within the same plane (e.g., for a moving X target presented amongst moving O's and static X's, the target can be detected by its difference in shape relative to the distractors in the plane defined by the moving items). With other dimensions this form of figure-ground segmentation seems more difficult (e.g., Treisman's classic example with colour and form), but even so efficient conjunction search can be achieved if the features defining targets and distractors are sufficiently discriminable (e.g., if there are salient colour and form differences between target attributes and distractor attributes) (see Quinlan & Humphreys, 1987; Wolfe, Cave & Franzel, 1989). Such results suggest that the simple distinction between "pre-attentive" coding of disjunctive visual features and "attentional" coding of feature conjunctions does not accurately capture the factors determining the ease of visual selection.

2.   GUIDED SEARCH

Some of these results, showing efficient conjunction search, can be accounted for if top-down control mechanisms can be used to "guide" visual search and selection. Wolfe (1994; Wolfe et al., 1989) has proposed that expectations for a particular target can be set up, involving the pre-activation of detection systems tuned to target features. An overall "saliency" map may then sum activity from the feature maps to signal the presence of a stimulus, though the attributes of the stimulus may only be encoded once the stimulus is selected. Conjunction targets can be detected efficiency if the maps for their component features are not activated by the features of some of the distractors. Top-down activation of the maps for the target features boosts the saliency of the elements that contain those features, and target selection benefits because only the target activates a common location in all the pre-activated maps (given that distractors do not activate both maps, for a 2-feature conjunction). Feature dimensions such as movement and stereo-depth may produce particularly efficient search because distractors not sharing the relevant target property generate little activity within the critical feature maps (e.g., in search for a moving target, static distractors produce minimal activation in maps for moving items).

Neurophysiological evidence for some form of top-down tuning of detection systems, to facilitate visual selection, has recently been reported by Chelazzi et al. (1993). They trained monkeys to make a saccade to one of a pair of complex stimuli, with the target to-be-selected being defined by a match-to-sample item (a selection cue) presented prior to the target display. They recorded the activity of cells in the inferotemporal cortex tuned to the features of the selection cue. They found that activity was maintained in these cells during the interval between the selection cue and the target displays, and, furthermore, that this "memory activity" facilitated activation generated by the relevant stimulus relative to the irrelevant stimulus in the target display. Consequently, there was more efficient selection of the relevant information.

3.   GROUPING AND SELECTION

Although the notion of top-down control of search and selection seems useful, other evidence suggests that selection does not operate solely on local features (or even on differences computed between such local features; cf. Wolfe, 1994). Perhaps the most relevant work here concerns the effects of grouping on visual search. Humphreys, Quinlan and Riddoch (1989) had subjects search for a target defined by a conjunction of local form elements. Distractors were either homogeneous (e.g., target ⊥ vs all ⊤ distractors) or heterogeneous (target ⊥ vs ⊤, ⊣ and ⊢ distractors). Search was little affected by the number of homogenous distractors, and it was strongly affected by the number of heterogeneous distractors (see also Duncan & Humphreys, 1989, for similar results). Also, responses were particularly fast on absent trials when the distractors were homogeneous. These results can be accounted for in terms of grouping between display members. Homogeneous distractors group together more strongly than they do to targets, enabling targets to be efficiently segmented and selected. Heterogeneous distractors can group as strongly (or indeed more strongly, depending on the attributes of the stimuli) with the target as with the other distractors. Targets that group with distractors are difficult to detect, since they are presented as parts on an emergent object description that may be difficult to map onto the original (pre-specified) description of the target. Search can then be inefficient, since several distractor groups may be selected before selection of the group containing the target (see Humphreys & Muller, 1993, for a formal simulation).

Such grouping effects in visual search, operating between stimuli defined by conjunctions of features, suggests that form conjunctions can be represented pre-attentively, in parallel across a visual display. Selection is affected by grouping between the form conjunctions. Even stronger evidence for this assertion comes from studies on the effects of redundant targets on search. Muller, Humphreys and Donnelly (1994) found that search for form conjunction targets was strongly facilitated when there were 2 relative to 1 such target present. Indeed, the probability of making fast reaction times (RTs) individually when 2 targets were present was more than twice the probability of making fast RTs to single targets when they were present; that is, there was an additional benefit when 2 targets were present over and above the benefits expected from independent processing of two single targets (cf. Miller, 1982). Mordkoff, Yantis and Egeth (1991) have reported similar evidence with colour- form conjunctions. These data are difficult to explain if conjunctions are not coded pre-attentively to be available to form groups.

Other evidence demonstrates that grouping between form conjunctions can be particularly effective when subjects have stored representations of the stimuli (e.g., if distractors are known letters; Wang, Cavanagh & Green, 1994), but that the conjunctions do not need to be identical for grouping to occur. Donnelly, Humphreys and Riddoch (1991) presented subjects with simple two-dimensional (2D) shapes, comprising different number of bracket elements (making squares, pentagons and hexagons). The task was to decide if all of the corners of the brackets faced away from a central fixation cross or whether one faced inwards. The target (the bracket facing in), when present, had exactly the same shape as at least one distractor in the display, and so the target could only be defined by the position of its features relative to fixation. Despite this, target detection was unaffected by the number of distractors present. However, one small change to the displays produced dramatic effects on search. When the bracket elements were rotated, so that the distractors now had corners facing inwards fixation and the target's corner face out, there were marked effects of the number of distractors on search efficiency. The differences between these displays cannot be attributed to simple changes in the features of the local elements (which were the same), but to changes in the grouping relations between the bracket elements. When the brackets face away from fixation, the terminators of the brackets are collinear and the elements, when grouped, form a closed shape (Figure 1a). When the brackets face in towards fixation, their terminators are no longer collinear and the elements do not form a closed shape (Figure 1b). Apparently there can be grouping between the corner junctions, even though they are not identical, on the basis of collinearity and closure.

These factors, of collinearity and closure, can also be separated experimentally. In recent studies we have found that, even with displays with "open" shapes, search can be efficient provided the brackets are sufficiently close (Figure 1c). With such stimuli, component lines in the corners are collinear and grouping can operate even though the individual lines are stopped by the corner junction. Note that this result runs counter to at least one recent computational account of grouping in early vision, which holds that grouping by collinearity cannot take place across corner junctions (Hummel & Biederman, 1992). We find that it can, provided the collinear lines are sufficiently close. Consistent with collinearity being important with such displays, rotating the corners to make the component lines non-collinear severely disrupts search even with small inter-element distances (see Figure 1d for an example display). However, with closed displays, inter-element distance has a less serious effect, and efficient search occurs even with elements spaced quite widely apart (as in Donnelly et al., 1991).

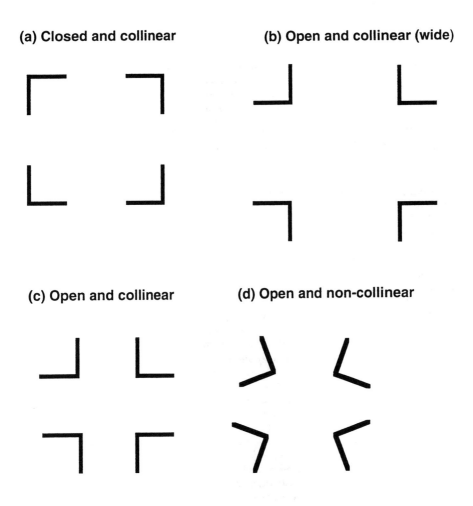

Figure 1.   (a) and (b) are example stimuli from Donnelly et al. (1991). (c) shows an "open" display with closed elements and (d) an "open" display with closed elements rotated to disrupt collinear grouping.

Overall, the data show that grouping can operate in a spatially parallel manner between form elements, and that grouping can involve information coded at different levels - between line elements (based on collinearity) and between corners (based on closure).

Duncan and Humphreys (1989, 1992) proposed an account of visual search in terms of grouping between the display elements. They argued that search efficiency can be described in terms of the inter-play between three factors: the similarity between the target and the distractors in the field, the similarity between the distractors, and the similarity of the distractors to the memory representation of the target. Inter-distractor similarity, and the similarity between the target and the distractors in the field, will determine the magnitude of grouping between display members, and the degree to which targets are segmented from or encoded into distractor groups. In addition to this, Duncan and Humphreys note that search will be slowed if distractors are similar to an expected target, even if the distractors are dissimilar to a particular target in the field. Selection involves matching segmented input representations against memory representations of targets (see above, for a discussion of Chelazzi et al.'s, 1993, neuropsychological data, which may indicate one means by which matching to the memory representation is achieved).

4.   AN INVESTIGATION OF GROUPING VIA SEARCH

We have seen that spatially parallel grouping operates, and that grouping between display members affects the efficiency of visual search (Section 3). Accordingly, it becomes possible to use measures of search efficiency as diagnostic of whether particular stimulus properties group in a spatially parallel manner. This in turn should constrain attempts to implement grouping procedures in computational vision systems.

We have used this logic to examine grouping as a function of 2 factors: the presence of collinear edges and the polarity of contrast of visual elements. Grouping could operate on the basis of several different visual properties, including collinear edges (see Section 3), image tokens that specify the polarity of contrast of the surface information, or image tokens based on shape but abstracted from surface details (cf. Marr, 1982). Also, edges may be coded in ways that preserve contrast polarity (e.g., if separate representations are coded for dark to light and light to dark edges; Watt, 1988), or edge information may be encoded in a more abstracted way, independent of contrast polarity (e.g., Grossberg & Mingolla, 1985). According to how grouping is implemented, different predictions can be made about search for displays containing image tokens that either have or do not have collinear edges, or that either do or not have the same contrast polarity.

To examine these issues, we have presented subjects with displays containing circles and squares which were either white or black against a grey background. Targets were defined on the basis of 2 of the stimuli forming a vertical group relative to pairs of distractors which formed horizontal groups. Since targets and distractors are defined by the grouping between local elements, search efficiency should vary directly as a function of how well elements group. Four primary conditions were examined. (1) Targets and distractors both contained bright circles. (2) Targets and distractors both contained bright squares. (3) Targets and distractors contained mixed polarity circles (one white and one black, relative to the grey background). (4) Targets and distractors contained mixed polarity squares. Figure 2 provides examples of the displays. Search efficiencies, measured in terms of the slope of the search functions (RTs relative to the number of distractors present) for the different displays, are shown in Table 1.

Table 1
Mean search slopes (msec/item) for search displays comprising items varying in their contrast polarity and the presence of edges (with square vs. circle components).

		Slope (msec/item)
(1)	Bright circles	16
(2)	Bright squares	11
(3)	Mixed contrast polarity circles	33
(4)	Mixed contrast polarity squares	12

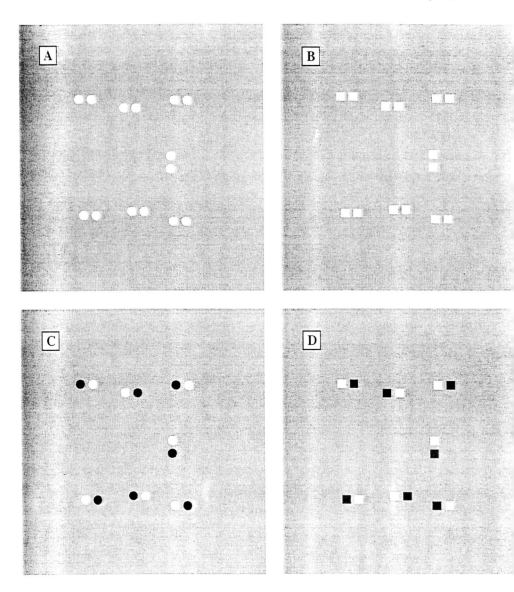

Figure 2.   Example displays containing targets and distractors varying in contrast polarity and edge information (squares vs. circles).

The findings were clear. Search was relatively efficient when the elements making up each target and distractor group had the same contrast polarity (with both circle and square elements), and with squares having opposite contrast polarities. In contrast, search was quite inefficient with opposite polarity circles. These results indicate the working of 2 grouping processes operating prior to selection. One involves grouping based on image tokens having the same contrast polarity. This form of grouping takes place even if the elements within the group are not connected by collinear edges (or indeed any other type of form information, such as closure). The other involves grouping based on collinear edges. This form of grouping is abstracted from information about the contrast polarity of the edges (cf. Grossberg & Mingolla, 1985). The evidence provides new insights into which grouping processes operate in parallel across visual images, and on the nature of the representations which enter into the grouping processes.

5.   THREE-DIMENSIONAL (3D) CONSTRAINTS ON SEARCH AND SELECTION

The evidence we have discussed so far has indicated that grouping between 2D features and form conjunctions influences the efficiency of visual search. Several other results demonstrate that grouping is not confined to 2D relationships but also involves 3D relationships between image elements. For example, Kleffner and Ramachandran (1992) used targets and distractors formed from patches with continuous levels of shading, each of which yielded the perception of a curved 3D surface (computer shape from shading). Targets had their lightest area at the top and darkest at the bottom (so they appeared lit from the top), distractors had their darkest area at the top and lightest at the bottom (and appeared lit from the bottom). They found relatively efficient search, with only small effects of the number of distractors on performance. In contrast, rotating the patches so that targets and distractors appeared to be lit respectively from the left and right led to inefficient search. The differences in search efficiency as a function of the apparent lighting position suggest that performance was not based on some simple local feature (present in targets but absent in distractors) but rather on the apparent change in the orientation of the target and distractor surfaces in 3D.

A similar argument for the role of 3D relations in visual search comes from the work of Enns and his colleagues (e.g., Enns & Rensink, 1990, 1992). They used box - like figures in which targets and distractors had the same 2D line orientations but differed in their 3D orientation (see Figure 3). Despite there being no 2D orientation differences, there were only relatively minor effects of the number of distractors on search efficiency. In contrast to this, there were large effects of the number of distractors in control displays where similar stimuli were used but which did not give rise to orientation differences between targets and distractors in 3D space. Apparently the inter-relations between the 2D line elements could be computed in a spatially parallel manner, to enable descriptions in 3D space to determine search.

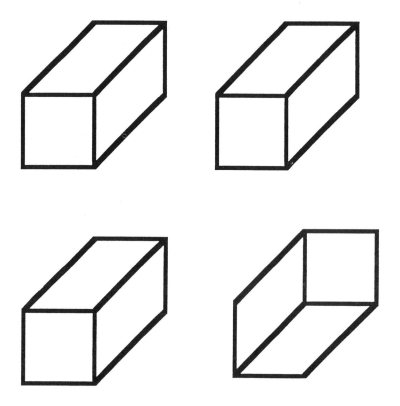

Figure 3.   Stimuli of the type used by Enns and Rensink (1990).

In our laboratory, we have demonstrated one other example of the effectiveness of 3D information on search. We examined search for cylindrical stimuli, with targets and distractors differing in size. The stimuli were depicted against local backgrounds that were either a set of lines in 2D (the control condition) or which gave the impression of a tunnel receding in depth. The perceived depth can generate a size illusion such that a cylinder of a given size appears relatively larger when shown at the back than at the front of the tunnel. We showed that search was affected by the perceived size of targets and distractors. When targets and distractors were placed so that their perceived size enhanced their real size differences, search was facilitated relative to the 2D control condition. When they were placed so that their perceived size difference was smaller than the real size difference, search was disrupted relative to the control condition (Humphreys, Keulers & Donnelly, 1994). These results occurred even when search in the control condition was relatively efficient, consistent with a parallel search process. The data indicate that estimates of the relative depths and sizes of the stimuli could be computed in parallel across the display, and that the estimates could be used to guide rapid search.

The work on 3D constraints on search suggests that, at the very least, there can be rapid, local estimates about 3D relationships between image features. Enns and Rensink (1992) argue that one of the goals of early vision is to rapidly encode the 3D world to guide locomotion and further visual analysis. To provide rapid encoding, accuracy may be sacrificed to some degree in order to compute important but complex relations in images. The data on 3D effects are certainly consistent with this picture. It would appear that search processes in vision depend on a number of distinct processing mechanisms, including some top-down "setting" of the systems, plus also processes that produce rapid grouping sensitive to 3D relations between image features. The complexity of these mechanisms defies simple attempts to distinguish "pre-attentive" from "attentional" processes in search. Perhaps instead what is needed is a fuller working - through of formal models of search and selection, in which the interactions between bottom-up and top-down processes are fully articulated.

Acknowledgements

This work was supported by grants from the Medical Research Council and the Joint Research Council Initiative in Cognitive Science, UK.

References

Chelazzi, C., Miller, E.K., Duncan, J. & Desimone, R. (1993) A neural basis for search in inferior temporal cortex. Nature, 363, 345-347.

Crick, F. (1984) Function of the thalamic reticular complex: The search light hypothesis. Proceedings of the National Academy of Sciences, 81, 4586-4590.

Desimone, R. & Ungerleidger, L.G. (1989) Neural mechanisms of visual processing in monkeys. In F. Boller & J. Grafman (Eds.), Handbook of Neuropsychology. Amsterdam: Elsevier Science.

Donnelly, N., Humphreys, G.W. & Riddoch, M.J. (1991) Parallel computational of primitive shape descriptions. Journal of Experimental Psychology: Human Perception and Performance, 17, 561-570.

Duncan, J. & Humphreys, G.W. (1989) Visual search and stimulus similarity. Psychological Review, 96, 433-458.

Duncan, J. & Humphreys, G.W. (1992) Beyond the search surface: Visual search and attentional engagement. Journal of Experimental Psychology: Human Perception and Performance, 18, 578-588.

Enns, J.T. & Rensink, R.A. (1990a) Influence of scene-based properties on visual search. Science, 247, 721-723.

Enns, J.T. & Rensink, R.A. (1992) A model for the rapid interpretation of line drawings in early vision. In D. Brogan (Ed.), Visual Search II. London: Taylor & Francis.

Grossberg, S. & Mingolla, E. (1985) Natural dynamics of perceptual grouping: Texture boundaries and emergent segmentations. Perception & Psychophysics, 38, 141-161.

Hummel, J. & Biederman, I. (1992) Dynamic binding in a neural network for shape recognition. Psychological Review, 99, 480-517.

Humphreys, G.W., Keulers, N. & Donnelly, N. (1994) Parallel visual coding in three dimensions. Perception, 23, 453-470.

Humphreys, G.W. & Muller, H.M. (1993) SEearch via Recursive Rejection (SERR): A connectionist model of visual search. Cognitive Psychology, 25, 43-110.

Humphreys, G.W., Quinlan, P.T. & Riddoch, M.J. (1989) Grouping processes in visual search: Effects with single- and combined-feature targets. Journal of Experimental Psychology: General, 118, 258-279.

Kleffner, D.A. & Ramachandran, V.S. (1992) On the perception of shape from shading. Perception & Psychophysics, 52, 18-36.

Marr, D. (1982) Vision. San Francisco: W.H. Freeman.

McLeod, P., Driver, J. & Crisp, J. (1988) Visual search for a conjunction of movement and form is parallel. Nature, 332, 154-155.

Miller, J. (1982) Divided attention: Evidence for coactivation with redundant signals. Cognitive Psychology, 14, 247-279.

Moran, J. & Desimone, R. (1985) Selective attention gates visual processing in the extrastriate cortex. Science, 229, 782-784.

Mordkoff, T.J., Yantis, S. & Egeth, H.E. (1990) Detecting conjunctions of color and form in parallel. Perception & Psychophysics, 48, 157-168.

Muller, H.J., Humphreys, G.W. & Donnelly, N. (1994) SEearch via Recursive Rejection (SERR): Visual search for single and dual form-conjunction targets. Journal of Experimental Psychology: Human Perception & Performance, 20, 235-258.

Nakayama, K. & Silverman, G.H. (1986) Serial and parallel processing of visual feature conjunctions. Nature, 320, 264-265.

Perrett, D.I., Oram, M.W., Hietanen, J.K. & Benson, P.J. (1994) Issues of representation in object vision. In M. Farah & G. Ratcliff (Eds.), The Neuropsychology of High-level Vision. Hillsdale, N.J.: Erlbaum.

Quinlan, P.T. & Humphreys, G.W. (1987) Visual search for targets defined by combinations of color, form, shape, and size: An examination of the task constraints on feature and conjunction searches. Perception & Psychophysics, 41, 455-472.

Townsend, J.T. (1972) Some results on the identifiability of parallel and serial processes. British Journal of Mathematical and Statistical Psychology, 25, 168-199.

Treisman, A. (1988) Features and objects: The fourteenth Bartlett memorial lecture. Quarterly Journal of Experimental Psychology, 40(A), 201-237.

Treisman, A. & Gelade, G. (1980) A feature integration theory of attention. Cognitive Psychology, 12, 97-136.

Wang, O., Cavanagh, P. & Green, M. (1994) Familiarity and pop-out in visual search. Perception & Psychophysics, 56, 495-500.

Watt, R.J. (1988) Visual Processing: Computational, Psychophysical and Cognitive Research. London: Erlbaum.

Wolfe, J.M. (1994) Guided search 2.0: A revised model of visual search. Psychonomic Bulletin & Review, 1, 202-238.

Wolfe, J.M., Cave, K.R. & Franzel, S.L. (1989) Guided Search: An alternative to the Feature Integration Model for visual search. Journal of Experimental Psychology: Human Perception and Performance, 15, 419-433.

Visual Attention and Cognition
W.H. Zangemeister, H.S. Stiehl and C. Freksa (Editors)

VISUAL ATTENTION AND SACCADIC EYE MOVEMENTS IN NORMAL HUMAN SUBJECTS AND IN PATIENTS WITH UNILATERAL NEGLECT

John M Findlay and Robin Walker

Department of Psychology, University of Durham,
South Road, Durham, DH1 3LE, England

ABSTRACT

Visual attention can be redirected either *overtly* by moving the eyes themselves to direct the visual axis to a new location or *covertly* by an internal mental process. This chapter reviews results concerning the two types of attentional orienting and their inter-relationship. Experimental results are then discussed which support a close connection between processes involved in covert and overt orienting respectively, but cast doubt on an assumption often made that attention is 'disengaged' from one location and moved to a new location. The results appear more consistent with models which propose a tight relationship between attentional orienting and saccade programming. Further experiments in which the eye movements made by patients with *unilateral visual neglect* are also reported. Patients with neglect are known to have problems in making saccades in the contralesional direction which have often been attributed to a deficit of 'attentional disengagement'. Our results question this view. Furthermore, the patients' ability to make saccadic eye movements was influenced by the form of neglect (spatial or object-based) that the patient shows. We conclude that dissociations in eye movement performance supports the view that attention cannot be regarded as a unitary concept.

Key Words: Visual attention, saccadic eye movements, human, unilateral neglect, global effect.

INTRODUCTION

Primate vision is characterised by active scanning movements of the eyes. These movements allow the high resolution foveal region to be directed to any desired location and thus control can be exercised over the wonderfully elaborate mechanisms which analyse the retinal image. The control may be used for many purposes. Exploratory scanning obtains information about the visual environment and seeks new sources of stimulation. Search scanning seeks a particular visual target. Ordered scanning can be deployed to explore a region in an efficient systematic way, an ability which perhaps reaches its apogee in human text reading. Scanning is a voluntary, or at least a centrally directed, process but its mechanisms may be affected by salient events in the visual field which elicit the scanning movements of orienting. It is customary to think of scanning as a process whereby different visual locations are successively sampled and to use the term 'visual attention deployment' as a convenient description for this process. The chapter will examine the mechanisms involved in the control of visual attention, presenting some results relevant to control in normal subjects and also in patients with unilateral visual neglect, a condition often regarded as a disorder of visual attention (Humphreys and Riddoch, 1993).

Visual exploration in general involves movements of the body, trunk, head and eyes, in some circumstances assisted by other muscles (e.g. the hands may be used to deal with visually occluded objects). Research on visual attention has, however, been almost exclusively concentrated on the situation in which a stationary observer with head immobile views a stationary environment. Under these circumstances, just two types of attention need to be considered, overt and covert attentional movements. In *overt* movements, the observer's eyes actually move to direct the visual axis to a new location. However, *covert* movements of attention may also be made when the eyes are held stationary. Many demonstrations have now confirmed the insight of Helmholtz (1866 trans. 1925) that movements of visual attention can also occur when the eyes remain fixed. In this introductory section, we shall briefly review the properties of the two types of attentional movement and then consider their relationship.

Overt and covert attentional orienting

Overt visual orienting refers to orienting by means of saccadic eye movements. The basic properties of these movements are well understood. Saccades are stereotyped movements which rotate the eyes quickly and efficiently (Carpenter, 1988). Following the movement, the eyes are brought to rest in a new stable position of gaze and it has recently been appreciated that the attainment of this post-saccadic stability involves a self-adaptive calibration process (Optican and Miles, 1985; Kapoula, Optican and Robinson, 1989). Although often thought to be conjugate movements with both eyes rotating equally, recent work has demonstrated that a substantial amount of disconjugacy can occur during a saccadic movement when re-orienting to a different depth plane (Enright, 1984; Findlay and Harris, 1993). Target-elicited saccades occur when a subject makes a saccadic orienting movement to a newly displayed target. Such saccades have been the subject of intensive study in an attempt to elucidate the motor programming involved (Becker and Jürgens, 1979; Becker, 1989; Findlay, 1983, 1992). A *target-elicited* saccade may be specified by its *latency* (the time between the target appearing and the start of the eye movement) and its *amplitude* (the angular rotation of the eye). The way in which these properties are controlled will be discussed in detail in a later section.

Covert visual orienting is studied most directly in experimental paradigms where subjects are instructed to keep their eye still while attention is directed to a location away from the fovea. Evidence of covert attention comes from findings of improved visual performance at the attended location accompanied by degraded performance at non-attended locations. This *cost-benefit* approach was spelt out particularly clearly by Posner (1980), who demonstrated that simple reaction times to targets at the attended location were shorter (the benefit) and those to targets appearing at an unattended location were longer (the cost) than those found in a neutral baseline condition. Similar results have been found with certain visual discrimination tasks (Müller and Findlay, 1987; Müller and Rabbitt, 1989). The redirection of attention may be achieved in two ways. In the first, variously termed *endogenous* (Posner, 1980), *voluntary* (Jonides, 1981; Müller and Rabbitt, 1989), or *centrally cued*, direction of attention, the subject is instructed to direct attention to a particular peripheral region, often by means of a centrally presented visual cue such as an arrow pointer. In the second, the redirection of attention is achieved by some form of stimulation at or close to the peripheral location, such as the brightening of a 'box' within which a target may occur. Such stimulation results in costs and benefits which appear very similar to those of centrally directed attention. This situation has been termed *exogenous* (Posner, 1980), *automatic* (Jonides, 1981), *reflexive* (Müller and Rabbitt, 1989), or *peripherally cued*. The first two terms acknowledge the fact that the second form of attention is much less under direct voluntary control.

Posner suggested that covert orienting could be thought of as a *spotlight*, enhancing processing in the area illuminated by the beam. This metaphor is easy to grasp and has proved popular, but a number of workers have pointed out the inadequacy of the spotlight idea to account for all data and have suggested various alternatives. The *zoom-lens* approach of Eriksen (Eriksen and St James, 1986) recognises that the size of the attended area can vary in different situations. Hughes and Zimba (1985, 1987) have emphasized the importance of inhibitory effects in non-attended regions. In their 1987 paper, they argued that attentional effects are restricted directionally and suggested that when attention is directed to one location, costs will be imposed for locations which involve an attentional crossing of either the horizontal or the vertical meridians. This third approach may be termed *hemifield inhibition*.

Yet another type of theory of covert attention is that of *oculomotor readiness*. The suggestion here is that the processes involved in covert attention are identical to those involved in preparing to move the eyes, but without the final release of the prepared eye movement. The predictions of this theory depend on the assumptions made about how eye movements are programmed. Rizzolatti, Riggio, Dascola and Umiltà (1987) assumed that selection of the direction of movement was an important time consuming stage. They supported their theory by demonstrating significantly greater attentional costs for invalid targets in the opposite direction to the cued target in comparison with invalid targets which were at a different location but in the same direction as the cued target. These *meridian crossing* effects are in practice similar to the predictions made by the hemifield inhibition theory of Hughes and Zimba (1987).

Support for the assumptions made by Rizzolatti et al. (1987) can be found in the literature on saccade programming. Becker and Jürgens carried out a study of saccadic tracking of a target which moved in two sequential steps along the horizontal axis (the double step task). This task requires a subject to modify a saccade in the course of preparation. When the two steps involved locations in opposite (left and right) directions, extra programming delays were apparent compared with two steps involving locations in the same direction. This suggests that the direction and amplitude of the movement are programmed separately, with considerable extra time incurred whenever a reprogramming of direction is required (Becker and Jürgens, 1979, see also Abrams and Jonides, 1988).

It must be cautioned that these findings come from studies involving only saccades along the primary axes (left-right or up-down). When more modest direction changes are involved in a double step task (for example from an upper right direction to an upper left direction), there is much less difference evident between the time required for direction re-programming and that for amplitude re-programming (Findlay and Harris, 1984; Aslin and Shea, 1989). It is now clear that different forms of coding are used at different stages in the programming of saccadic eye movements (Sparks and Mays, 1990). The superior colliculus is thought to be an important centre in this programming and one in which the signal for eye movements is coded in a spatially distributed way in a two-dimensional map. This signal is converted to a more co-ordinate based system (to match the axes of the oculomotor muscles) at a subsequent stage in the brain stem. If attentional effects operate as oculomotor readiness at the *collicular* level, for example if attentional orienting operated by facilitation of a local collicular region, then effects more resembling an attentional spotlight may be expected. Similar effects might also occur in cortical centres connected with saccade programming in which visual space is retinotopically mapped (Wurtz and Goldberg, 1989). Umiltà, Riggio, Dascola and Rizzolatti (1991) have also argued that the predictions of oculomotor readiness theory may extend beyond meridian crossing effects.

Early work testing oculomotor readiness theory did not consider these subtleties. The oculomotor readiness theories predict a tight relationship between overt and covert orienting and several experimental studies have looked for such a link in tasks which require both overt and covert orienting. Early work (Klein, 1980; Remington, 1980) required subjects to make a manual response to one type of target and a saccade to a second type of target. This introduces a further discrimination task however and results from these studies are difficult to interpret because the latencies of the saccades are much greater than are normally found and clearly show a dual task interference effect. Shepherd, Findlay and Hockey (1986) adopted a complementary approach and required their subjects to initiate a voluntary saccade, while at the same time carrying out a reaction time task to assess covert orienting. The critical condition was where a different location to the saccade target was designated (by instructions and by stimulus probability manipulation) as the locus for covert orienting. Under these circumstances, the shortest reaction times were associated with the location to which the saccade was directed, rather than that to which covert attention was directed. This result indicates that it is not possible to attend to one location and simultaneously move the eye to a different location.

The experiments showing a close relationship between attentional orienting and saccade programming have used *centrally* cued orienting. This was the form of orienting used by Shepherd et al. (1986) and more recent work using central cueing (Hodgson and Müller, 1995; Schneider and Deubel, 1995) has confirmed the tight link between the two forms of orienting. However, experiments using *peripheral cueing* (Crawford and Müller, 1992; Reuter-Lorenz and Fendrich, 1992) obtain different results from those using central cueing; notably these studies have failed to obtain a meridian crossing effect. This may be because of the problem involved in suppressing the saccadic response to the peripheral cue, as suggested by Umiltà et al. (1991).

A further suggestion bringing together work on both covert and overt attention was made first by Posner's group (Posner and Cohen, 1984; Posner, Walker, Friedrich and Rafal, 1984). They argued that any act of attentional orienting requires three sub-processes, *disengagement* of attention from the old location, *movement* of attention to the new location, and *re-engagement* of attention at the new location. Each of these sub-processes is time demanding. This division appears to offer an attractive explanation of a consistent and important finding in the control of overt attention. If a subject is required to move his or her eyes to a target, the mean latency of the saccades is substantially reduced if a prior visual fixation stimulus is removed a short time in advance of the appearance of the target. The effect is known as the *gap effect*, because of the presence of a temporal gap in which no stimulation is present. The speeding produced by the gap effect does not involve foreknowledge of the target location but does occur only for saccades made to the target location (Reuter-Lorenz, Hughes and Fendrich, 1991; Reuter-Lorenz, Oonk, Barnes, and Hughes, 1995). One explanation of the gap effect (Fischer, 1987; Fischer and Breitmeyer, 1987) suggests that the disappearance of the fixation stimulus promotes the disengagement of attention, thus shortening or eliminating one of the stages involved in attentional orienting.

It is thus apparent that a wide variety of theoretical positions exist concerning the way attentional influences occur. In the remainder of this chapter, we shall present some recent results of our own work which addresses the issues.

EXPERIMENTAL WORK WITH NORMAL SUBJECTS

In a recent article (Walker, Kentridge and Findlay, 1995), we have questioned the idea that the gap effect depends on attentional disengagement (see also Kingstone and Klein, 1993; Reuter-Lorenz, et al., 1995). We measured the latencies of target elicited saccades when subjects were given prior instructions to attend to a particular direction (right or left) in the visual periphery. Such instructions produce consistent effects on the latencies of saccades made to targets in the attended and unattended directions. If the target appeared in the non–attended direction, latencies were slower by about 30 ms than in a neutral condition with no attentional instructions. If the target appeared in the attended direction, latencies were on average a few milliseconds faster than in the neutral condition. We then combined such attentional instructions with the gap manipulation, reasoning that if the gap speeding worked through attentional disengagement, a prior attentional instruction should eliminate, or at least reduce, the gap speeding. Our results showed no such effect. The gap manipulation produced a consistent speeding of a magnitude which was independent of the attentional instructions. We conclude that two independent processes are involved. One generates the gap facilitation and the other is responsible for the latency changes produced by covert attentional orienting.

In our article we also explored a third factor which affects the latency of saccades. If a second target stimulus appears in a location in the opposite hemifield simultaneously with the saccade target, saccade latencies are slower (Lévy-Schoen, 1969, Findlay, 1983). This slowing appears to operate automatically because it is unaffected even when the subject is already prepared to make a saccade in the direction of the target. We showed this by comparing latencies of saccades to single targets and to bilaterally presented targets. This comparison was made under various attentional instructions including one in which all saccades were made in a predetermined direction. In all conditions, the same increase in latency resulted when a target was also presented in the bilateral location. We concluded that the three effects of *prior covert attentional orienting, gap facilitation* and *bilateral target slowing* all operate separately, since there were no interactions when they were combined factorially in our experiments.

We believe these three influences on the latency of target-elicited saccades provide clues about the physiological processes involved in programming saccadic eye movements. The gap effect shows that some preparatory processes involved in generating saccades can operate without knowledge of the spatial position of the saccade target. This supports the idea that saccade programming requires activation of both WHEN and WHERE mechanisms, the first concerned with the decision to make a saccade and the second with its spatial metrics (Becker and Jürgens, 1979; Van Gisbergen et al. 1981). In contrast to suggestions that the gap effect involves disengagement of attention, it seems best regarded as a manifestation affecting the WHEN system, which operates separately from the WHERE system involving the spatial component of attention. Munoz and Wurtz (1992, 1993) have recently shown that activation in the rostral pole of the superior colliculus exerts a general inhibitory effect on the initiation of saccades and thus forms a good candidate for the implementation of a WHEN system (see also Paré and Guitton, 1994).

In the following experiment, we attempted to test further the interactions between attentional instructions and saccade generation. Subjects viewed a screen in which targets could appear as shown in Figure 1 to the left and right of fixation at near (5.5⁰) and far (9.5⁰) eccentricity locations. The four target locations were designated A, B, C, D and the latency of saccades made to these locations measured. In the attention conditions a central letter cue (A, B, C, or D) appeared at the central fixation location and subjects were instructed to covertly orient their attention to that location prior to the onset of the saccade target. Targets appeared at cued locations on 70% of trials (valid trials) or equiprobably at one of the other three locations (invalid) on the remaining 30% of trials. Invalid saccade targets could thus appear in either the cued hemifield or the non-cued (opposite) hemifield. There was also a neutral condition with no prior cue.

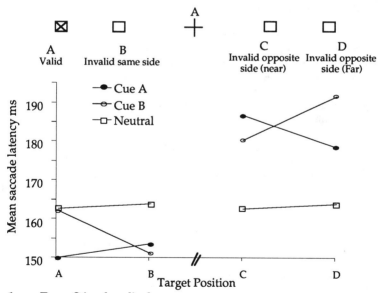

Figure 1. Top - Stimulus display.
   Bottom - Mean saccade latency obtained under neutral conditions and when attention was oriented covertly to the location indicated by the symbolic letter cue. The data for the cued condition have been collapsed over saccade direction.

Figure 1 shows the resulting saccade latencies. The latency of saccades made to targets at cued locations was found to be significantly reduced compared to the neutral condition. This shows that covertly orienting attention can produce a facilitation effect on saccade generation which is specific to the direction of the saccade. The latency of saccades made to targets in the non-cued hemifield were subject to a large significant increase. These meridian crossing effects are similar to those found by Walker, Kentridge and Findlay (1995) using a verbal pre-cue.

An interesting interaction effect was observed between the eccentricity of the saccade target and the eccentricity indicated by the cue. The latency of saccades obtained to the near target location (target at B) was found to be comparable following a cue to either the near or far eccentricity location (cue A or B). However, the latency of saccades made to targets at the far eccentricity location (target at A) was faster following a cue that indicated the far location (cue A) than when the cue indicated the near target location (cue B). This shows that when attention was covertly oriented away from fixation to the far location, the latency of saccades made to targets at intermediate locations was equally facilitated. However, when the saccade target appeared at a greater eccentricity than the attended location, the latency of saccades was not facilitated.

The effects of covert attentional orienting obtained on saccade latency in this experiment are similar to those shown in the results obtained by Rizzolatti et al. (1987) in their manual reaction time experiment. In both cases, the strongest effect is the meridian crossing effect. Rizzolatti et al. (1987) also found a smaller effect whereby a stimulus at the cued location elicited a faster responses than one at a non-cued location in the same hemifield (also found by McCormick and Klein, 1990). In our experiment, a somewhat different result emerged. If the near (5.5°) location was cued, targets at this location elicited a fast saccadic response while targets at the far location (9.5°) led to significantly slower responses, although still faster than to those in the opposite hemifield. This is the same pattern as Rizzolatti et al. observed with manual responses. However, when the far location was cued, responses to both far and near location were equally speeded. Such an asymmetry between the effects of cueing far and near targets was not observed in the manual reaction time experiments. The pattern we have found is the one which might be predicted by the zoom lens account of visual orienting.

In conclusion, we believe that the close similarities between experimental results on eye movements and on manual responses demonstrate considerable support for the oculomotor readiness account of attentional orienting. Furthermore we have shown that oculomotor readiness theory may share similarities with both the meridian crossing and the spotlight models of attention. Nevertheless, in our experiments, as in those of Hodgson and Müller (1995), there also appear to be some minor differences between the programming of oculomotor and of manual responses.

EXPERIMENTAL WORK WITH NEUROLOGICAL PATIENTS

Although much of the work on the human attentional system has involved experiments with normal subjects, insights have also been gained from investigating the performance of neurological patients. In particular, patients with a condition called *'unilateral visual neglect'* (or neglect for short) have been examined as their deficits appear to reflect a problem in attentional orienting (Posner, Walker, Friedrich and Rafal, 1984; 1987). Neglect occurs after cortical brain damage (usually a stroke) and patients fail to respond to stimuli located in the side of space opposite to the side of the lesion. Neglect is most typically associated with damage to the right hemisphere of the brain which results in left sided neglect. Patients with neglect following right brain damage appear to ignore, forget or turn away from the left (contralesional) side of space. For example, neglect patients may eat food from only the right side of their plate, shave only the right side of their face, draw the right side of an object omitting the left side and read words only from the right side of a page. Thus the patients omit the left sides of stimuli under many different situations.

Neglect patients are also found to have deficits in making saccades into the contralesional hemifield (Silberpfennig, 1941; Girotti, Casazza, Musicco, and Avanzini, 1983; Ishiai, Furukawa, and Tsukagoshi, 1987). Girotti et al. (1983) showed that patients with right parietal lobe damage and left sided neglect failed to make a saccade to a contralateral target on a quarter of all trials and many of these saccades were of small amplitude and long latency. This pattern of defective eye movements did not result from a contralateral visual field defect as one of the patients who had intact visual fields showed the same deficit.

We (Walker, Findlay, Young and Welch, 1991) examined the saccades made by a patient B.Q. who showed severe left sided neglect following a stroke in the region of the right parietal lobe. B.Q.'s ability to make left and right saccades was examined under fixation overlap and fixation gap conditions. The presence of a fixation gap produced a marked difference to her performance in comparison with that in the overlap condition. In the overlap condition B.Q. made left saccades on only 5% of trials. All of these saccades were of long latency and small amplitude. In the gap condition B.Q. made left saccades on 50% of trials. These saccades had normal latency and amplitude. Thus, the presence of the fixation gap greatly improved B.Q.'s ability to orient into her neglected hemifield and showed that she is still receiving contralateral sensory input. Our interpretation at the time of this finding was that the offset of a fixation cross facilitated attentional orienting into the neglected hemifield. However, it was also observed that B.Q. made more saccades to targets presented in the right (ipsilesional) hemifield in the gap condition than in the overlap condition.

The finding that under overlap conditions B.Q. rarely made saccades, or reported stimuli, presented in the neglected hemifield raises an interesting issue concerning the diagnosis of a visual field defect in patients with neglect. B.Q. had been reported as having a dense left hemianopia following perimetric field plotting using a consistently displayed fixation point. As B.Q. could overtly report and make saccades to left stimuli in the +100 ms gap condition it appears that she was 'neglecting' the left stimuli in the overlap condition and not failing to report them due to a field defect. Although the issue of such pseudohemianopia resulting from cortical brain damage has often been suggested (Poppelreuter, 1917; Silberpfennnig, 1941) the possibility that many neglect patients are misdiagnosed as being hemianopic is still ignored by many clinicians today.

B.Q.'s improvement in making left saccades in the gap condition appears to be consistent with the idea that a deficit of attentional disengagement is involved in neglect (Posner et al. 1984). In the gap condition the offset of fixation would automatically disengage attention and enable a contralesional saccade to be made. However, our work with normal subjects (see above) has questioned the idea that the gap effect is produced by attentional disengagement. We recently examined the eye movements made by a group of neglect patients under fixation gap conditions and overlap conditions (Walker and Findlay, in press). There was no increase in the numbers of contralesional saccades made in the gap condition for three neglect patients. One patient did make more contralesional saccades in the gap condition than in the overlap condition but he also made more ipsilesional saccades in the gap condition. It was concluded that their deficits in making contralesional saccades does not result form an inability to disengage attention. We are thus led to seek an alternative explanation for B.Q.'s improvement in making contralesional saccades in the gap condition. Recent work on the gap effect (Kingstone and Klein, 1993; Walker et al. 1995) has attributed the latency reduction to a combination of a warning signal like effect and an effect of ocular fixation release (Munoz and Wurtz, 1992). B.Q.'s greatly improved performance in the gap condition suggests that these factors may be particularly significant in neglect patients.

In further experiments (Walker and Findlay, in press) we have examined the effects of presenting saccade targets bilaterally and simultaneously in the left and right hemifields on the latency of saccades made by four patients with right hemisphere brain damage and left sided neglect. Two of the patients (R.R. and T.S.) had recovered to the extent that few overt symptoms of neglect were manifest. These patients made saccades to targets in the left visual field when presented alone. The two remaining patients failed to saccade to single targets in the left visual field. With bilateral targets, three patients made saccades exclusively to the right and only R.R., whose case will be considered in detail below, made any saccades to the left. A novel result emerged when a comparison was made between the latencies of rightward saccades made to single ipsilesional targets and rightward saccades made when bilateral targets were presented. In contrast to the results from normal subjects, the four patients with neglect did not show the normal increase in saccade latency with bilateral target presentation, which is about 30 ms (Findlay, 1983; Walker, Kentridge and Findlay, 1995). This failure to obtain a latency increase with bilateral targets cannot simply be attributed to a lack of a sensory input from the contralateral hemifield since the result appeared in patients with intact visual fields. Three of the patients appeared to be unaware of the contralesional target while patient R.R. both reported the presence of the left target on bilateral trials and occasionally saccaded towards it.

It appears likely that the increase in saccade latency observed with bilateral targets results from crossed inhibition between centres responsible for controlling orienting in the two hemifields. For instance, such crossed inhibition is known to occur in the superior colliculus (Rizzolatti, Camarda, Grupp, and Pisa, 1974). The absence of bilateral slowing in patients with neglect suggests that the effect is subject to modulation which depends on the parietal lobe (see: Walker and Findlay, in press). The parietal lobe has connections with the superior colliculus which as discussed is known to be involved in saccade generation.

Patient R.R. : A case of object-based neglect

One of the patients (R.R.) was obviously different from the other three patients in that he often made saccades to the contralesional bilateral target. These saccades had longer latencies than his saccades to single targets in the left field (although on the data available, the difference was not significant statistically). Moreover he was aware of the left target and thus did not show the phenomenon of *'visual extinction'*. Extinction is a common manifestation of neglect and occurs when two stimuli are simultaneously presented and the patient seems unaware of the leftmost stimulus. It is often believed that extinction is a mild form of neglect. However the absence of extinction in R.R. suggests a more complex relationship between extinction and neglect since, on some tasks, such as drawing - see Figure 2, R.R. shows clear evidence of left neglect.

R.R. shows left neglect which appears to be object-based. When asked to copy a simple line drawing (Gainotti, Messerli and Tissot, 1972), R.R. often omits the left side of individual objects while continuing to draw objects located laterally further to the left of these objects (see Figure 2ab). When shown 'chimaeric' stimuli in which left and right halves of different objects or faces are joined at the vertical midline (see Figure 3), R.R. often fails to report the object or face located on the left side.

Figure 2. a) Model scene b) Copy of the scene made by neglect patient R.R.

Figure 3 An example of a chimaeric object (face).

Humphreys and Riddoch (1994; see also Humphreys and Riddoch this volume) have distinguished between *'within-object'* and *'between-object'* forms of neglect and demonstrated that both forms can co-exist in a single patient. In within-object neglect, the material neglected is that on one side of the *object* which is currently attended whereas in between-object neglect, the material neglected is on one side of *visual space*. We believe that R.R. is a patient who shows a form of left side 'object-based' neglect, without showing spatial neglect. We have performed a detailed examination of R.R.'s ability to make saccades to arrays of objects and to single objects. When asked to scan a simple scene containing objects located to the left and right sides of midline, he made saccades to fixate on objects located to both the left and the right sides of the midline. However, his saccades and fixations made to *individual objects* were found to be restricted to the right sides of these objects (Walker, Findlay, Young, and Lincoln, submitted). The bilateral target paradigm involves two spatially separate targets which do not form an object and as R.R. shows object-based neglect he does not show visual extinction with such spatial targets. We speculate that only patients with spatial neglect would show evidence of extinction on the bilateral target task.

The global effect and neglect

We have also examined the effect of presenting two targets simultaneously in the ipsilesional hemifield of patients with neglect (Walker and Findlay, in press). Presenting two targets in the same hemifield is known to alter the landing position of saccades made by normal subjects and it is of interest to know if patients with neglect would show the same effect. When a normal subject makes a saccade to a single target presented away from fixation, the landing position of the saccade is found to fall slightly short of (undershoots) the exact target location.

However, when a normal subject makes a saccade when two targets are presented on the horizontal axis in the same hemifield, the saccade landing position shows a systematic overshoot to the near target position. If, for example, a subject makes a saccade to a single target at 2° eccentricity, the saccade will tend to fall short at approximately 1.8^o. However when two targets are presented at 2° and 4° eccentricity locations in the same hemifield, saccades tend to overshoot the first target position and land at a greater eccentricity (approximately 2.5^o). This overshoot has been termed the 'global effect' (Findlay, 1982). Normal subjects show an overshoot (global effect) of approximately 27% when two targets appear in the same hemifield (Barbur, Forsyth and Findlay, 1988). The magnitude of the global effect is affected by the relative physical characteristics of the stimuli (Findlay, 1982; Deubel, Wolf and Hauske, 1984). Cognitive factors show some influence (Findlay and Kapoula, 1992) but the effect appears to operate as a 'default option' for the saccadic system (Findlay, 1992).

We have investigated the global effect in two patients R.R. and T.S. R.R. shows evidence of visual neglect (without visual extinction) and T.S. shows evidence of visual extinction (without visual neglect).   The two patients were found to behave differently on the global effect task. R.R.'s mean saccade amplitude made to a single target positioned at 2° eccentricity was 2.3^o, but when made to the 2° target when a second target was positioned at 4° (global effect targets) his mean saccade amplitude increased to 2.9^o. Thus R.R. shows a global effect overshoot of 35% which is within the range found with normal subjects. However, T.S. was found to show a much greater global effect than is found in normal subjects. His mean saccade amplitude to a single target at 2° was 2.4^o, but when made to the global effect targets his mean saccade amplitude showed a large overshoot with a mean amplitude of 3.6^o and a global effect of 75%. This difference is illustrated in Figure 4.

We believe that the differential performance on the global effect task of R.R. and T.S. can be related to the different forms of attentional deficits that the two patients show. As discussed above, R.R. is a case of 'object-based' neglect. As a result he is not abnormally influenced by a second spatially separate saccade target, does not show 'visual extinction' with bilateral targets and shows a normal global effect. Patient T.S. is a case of spatially based neglect and has recovered in the months following his stroke to the point where the main manifestation is visual extinction. He is abnormally influenced by the presence of a second target presented in his ipsilesional visual field and shows a much greater global effect than is observed in normal subjects. It has been suggested that one of the components of neglect is an attentional bias to ipsilesional stimuli (Kinsbourne, 1987; Ládavas, Petronio, and Umiltà, 1990). We believe that our results show that this ipsilesional attentional bias could be dependent on the frame of reference of the stimuli that is presented. R.R. shows object-based neglect and appears to have an attentional bias to the ipsilesional side of an object regardless of the spatial position of the object (Walker et al. submitted). In contrast, T.S. shows a spatial form of neglect and his attention appears to be biased towards the stimulus located at the most ipsilesional spatial position.

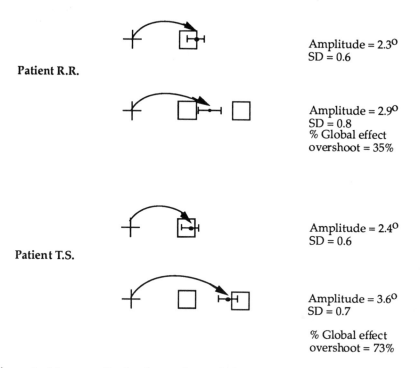

Figure 4   Mean amplitude of saccades made by neglect patients R.R. and T.S. in a global effect paradigm.

CONCLUSIONS

We believe that work on visual attention has made substantial progress in recent years. However the data now demand a move away from the conception of attention as a unitary process. For example, the view that attention is disengaged, moved, and re-engaged is popular. The gap effect, whereby saccade latencies are reduced by prior disappearance of a fixation point, is often used to support this position. Our analysis of the gap effect shows that this interpretation is flawed.

Fractionation of the attentional system seems necessary to account both for our data on saccade programming in normal subjects and also in the work with neglect patients. In our work with normal individuals, we demonstrate general support for the oculomotor readiness theory of covert attentional orienting. We believe covert attentional orienting affects oculomotor readiness in a way which is independent of the gap facilitation effect and the bilateral target slowing effect. Centrally cued attentional orienting operates to produce a pattern of costs and benefits which shows a strong meridian crossing effect but also a smaller zoom lens like component within the attended hemifield. Other workers have shown that a different pattern is characteristic of peripherally cued orienting.

The diverse patterns shown by patients with neglect also supports the position that attention is not a unitary construct. We show that characteristic differences in eye movement patterns, such as the absence of bilateral target slowing, differentiate neglect patients from normal individuals. There are also striking differences in the patterns shown by individual neglect patients. In particular we have obtained further support for the distinction between a form of visual neglect which is characterised by an impairment of spatial attention and one in which the impairment is characterised by an impairment of object-based attention.

REFERENCES

Abrams, R. A. and J. Jonides, 1988, Programming saccadic eye movements. J. Exp Psychol, Human Perception and Performance, 14, 428-443.

Aslin, R. N. and S. L. Shea, 1987, The amplitude and angle of saccades to double-step target displacements. Vision Research, 27, 1925-1942.

Barbur, J. L., Forsyth, P. M. and J. M. Findlay, 1988, Human saccadic eye movements in the absence of the geniculocalcarine projection. Brain, 111, 63-82.

Becker, W. 1989, Metrics. In: The Neurobiology of Saccadic Eye Movements, eds., R.H. Wurtz, and M.E. Goldberg (Elsevier, Amsterdam) pp 13-67.

Becker, W. and R. Jürgens, 1979, An analysis of the saccadic system by means of double step stimuli. Vision Research, 19, 967-983.

Carpenter, R. H. S. 1988. Movements of the eyes. (Pion Press, London).

Crawford, T. J. and H. J. Müller, 1992, Spatial and temporal effects of spatial attention on human saccadic eye movements. Vision Research, 32, 293-304.

Deubel, H., Wolf, W. and G. Hauske, 1984, The evaluation of oculomotor error signals. In: Theoretical and Applied Aspects of Oculomotor Research, eds., A. G. Gale and F.W. Johnson. (North-Holland, Amsterdam). pp 55-62

Eriksen, C. W. and J. D. St James, 1986, Visual attention within and around the field of focal attention: a zoom lens model. Perception and Psychophysics, 40, 225-240.

Enright, J. T. 1984, Changes in vergence mediated by saccades. J. of Physiology, 350, 9-31.

Findlay, J. M. 1982, Global processing for saccadic eye movements. Vision Research, 22, 1033–1045.

Findlay, J. M. 1983, Visual information for saccadic eye movements. In: Spatially Oriented Behavior, eds., A. Hein and M. Jeannerod (Springer-Verlag, New York) pp 281-303.

Findlay, J. M. and L. R. Harris, 1984, Small saccades to double stepped targets moving in two dimensions. In: Theoretical and Applied Aspects of Oculomotor Research, eds., A. G. Gale and F. W. Johnson (Elsevier, Amsterdam) pp 71-77.

Findlay, J. M. 1992, Programming of stimulus elicited saccadic eye movements, In: Eye Movements and Visual Cognition, ed., K. Rayner (Springer-Verlag, New York) pp 8-30.

Findlay, J. M. and L. R. Harris, 1993, Horizontal saccades to dichoptically presented targets of differing disparities. Vision Research, 33, 1001-1010.

Findlay, J. M. and Z. Kapoula, 1992, Scrutinization, spatial attention and the spatial properties of saccadic eye movements. Quart J. Exp Psychol, 45A, 633-647.

Fischer, B. 1987, The preparation of visually guided saccades. Review of Physiology, Biochemistry and Pharmacology, 106, 1-55.

Fischer, B. and B. G. Breitmeyer, 1987, Mechanisms of visual attention revealed by saccadic eye movements. Neuropsychologia, 25, 73-83.

Gainotti, G., Messerli, P. and R. Tissot, 1972, Qualitative analysis of unilateral spatial neglect in relation to laterality of cerebral lesions. J. Neurology, Neurosurgery and Psychiatry, 35, 545-550.

Girotti, F., Casazza, M., Musicco, M. and G. Avanzini, 1983, Oculomotor disorders in cortical lesions in man: The role of unilateral neglect. Neuropsychologia, 5, 543-553.

Helmholtz, H. von 1866 (Trans 1962), Treatise on Physiological Optics, Volume III (trans. 1925 from the third German edition), ed., J. P. C., Southall, (Dover, New York).

Hodgson, T. L. and H. J. Müller, 1995, Evidence relating to premotor theories of visuospatial attention. In: Eye Movement Research: Mechanisms, Processes and Applications, eds., J. M. Findlay R. Walker and R. W. Kentridge (North-Holland, Amsterdam) pp 305-316.

Hughes, H. C. and L. D. Zimba, 1985, Spatial maps of directed visual attention. J. Experimental Psychology: Human Perception and Performance, 11, 409-430.

Hughes, H. C. and L. D. Zimba, 1987, Natural boundaries for the spatial spread of visual attention. Neuropsychologia, 25, 5-18.

Humphreys, G. W. and M. J. Riddoch, 1993, Interactive attention systems and unilateral visual neglect. In: Unilateral Neglect: Clinical and Experimental Studies, eds., I. H. Roberston and J. C. Marshall (Lawrence Erlbaum Associates Ltd., Hove) pp 139-167.

Humphreys, G. W. and M. J. Riddoch, 1994, Attention to within-object and between-object spatial representations: Multiple sites for visual selection. Cognitive Neuropsychology, 11, 207-241.

Ishiai, S., Furukawa, T. and H. Tsukagoshi, 1987, Eye-fixation patterns in
    homonymous hemianopia and unilateral spatial neglect.
    Neuropsychologia, 25, 675-679.
Jonides, J. 1981, Voluntary versus automatic control over the mind's eye
    movements. In: Attention and Performance IX, eds., J. R. Long and A. D.
    Baddeley (Lawrence Erlbaum Associates, Hillsdale N J) pp 187-203.
Kapoula, Z., Optican, L. M. and D. A. Robinson, 1989, Visually induced plasticity
    of post saccadic ocular drift in normal humans. J. Neurophysiology, 61,
    879-891.
Kingstone, A. and R. M. Klein, 1993, Visual offsets facilitate saccade latency :
    does pre-disengagement of visuospatial attention mediate this gap effect ?,
    J. of Experimental Psychology, Human Perception and Performance, 19,
    1251-1265.
Kinsbourne, M. 1987, Mechanisms of unilateral neglect. In: Neurophysiological
    and Neuropsychological Aspects of Spatial Neglect, ed., M. Jeannerod
    (Elsevier Science Publishers B.V. North Holland, Amsterdam) pp 69-87.
Klein, R. 1980, Does oculomotor readiness mediate cognitive control of visual
    attention? In: Attention and Performance VIII, ed., R. S. Nickerson,
    (Lawrence Erlbaum Associates, Hillsdale N J) pp 259-276.
Ládavas, E., Petronio, A. and C. Umiltá, 1990, The deployment of visual
    attention in the intact field of hemineglect patients. Cortex, 26, 307-317.
Lévy-Schoen, A. 1969, Détermination et latence de la réponse oculomtrice à
    deux stimulus. L'Année Psychologique, 69, 373-392.
McCormick, P. A. and R. M. Klein, 1990, The spatial distribution of attention
    during covert visual orienting. Acta Psychologica, 75, 225-242.
Müller, H. J. and J. M. Findlay, 1987, Sensitivity and criterion effects in the
    spatial cuing of visual attention. Perception and Psychophysics, 42, 383-
    399.
Müller, H. J. and P. M. A. Rabbitt, 1989, Reflexive and voluntary orienting of
    visual attention : time course of activation and resistance to interruption.
    J. Exp Psychol, Human Perception and Performance, 15, 315-330.
Munoz, D. P. and R. H. Wurtz, 1992, Role of the rostral superior colliculus in
    active visual fixation and execution of express saccades. J.
    Neurophysiology, 67, 1000-1002.
Munoz, D. P. and R. H. Wurtz, 1993, Fixation cells in monkey superior
    colliculus. I. Characteristics of cell discharge. J. Neurophysiology, 70, 2,
    559-573
Optican, L. M. and F. A. Miles, 1985, Visually induced adaptive changes in
    primate saccadic oculomotor control signals. J. Neurophysiology, 54, 940-
    958.
Paré, M. and D. Guitton, 1994, The fixation area of cat superior colliculus : effects
    of electrical stimulation and direct connection with brainstem omnipause
    neurons, Exp Brain Research, 101, 109-122.
Poppelreuter, W. 1917. Die psychischen Schadigungen durch Kopfschuss im
    Kriege 1914/1916: 1. Die Storungen der Niederen und Hoheren
    Seeleistungen durch Verletzung des Okzipitalhirns. Leipzig: Voss.

Posner, M. I., 1980, Orienting of attention. Quart J. Exp Psychol, 32, 3-25.

Posner, M. I. and Y. Cohen, 1984, Components of visual orienting. In: Attention and Performance X, eds., H. Bouma and D. G. Bowhuis (Lawrence Erlbaum Associates, Hillsdale N J) pp 530-555.

Posner, M. I., Walker, J. A. Friedrich, F. J. and R. D. Rafal, 1984, Effects of parietal injury on covert orienting of attention. J. of Neuroscience, 4, 1863-1874.

Posner, M. I., Walker, J. A. Friedrich, F. A. and R. D. Rafal, 1987, How do the parietal lobes direct covert attention? Neuropsychologia, 25, 135-145.

Remington, R. W. 1980, Attention and saccadic eye movements. J. Experimental Psychology: Human Perception and Performance, 6, 726-744.

Reuter-Lorenz, P. A., Hughes, H. C. and R. Fendrich, 1991, The reduction of saccadic latency by prior offset of the fixation point: An analysis of the gap effect. Perception and Psychophysics, 49, 167-175.

Reuter-Lorenz, P. A. and R. Fendrich, 1992, Oculomotor readiness and covert orienting : differences between central and peripheral precues. Perception and Psychophysics, 52, 336-344.

Reuter-Lorenz, P. A., Oonk, H. M., Barnes, L. L., and H. C. Hughes, 1995, Effects of warning signals and fixation point offsets on the latencies of pro versus anti-saccades: Implications for an interpretation of the gap effect. Experimental Brain Research, 103(2), 287-293.

Rizzolatti, G., Camarda, R., Grupp, L. A. and M. Pisa, 1974, Inhibitory effects of remote visual stimuli on visual responses of cat superior colliculus : spatial and temporal factors. J. of Neurophysiology, 37, 1262-1275.

Rizzolatti, G., Riggio, L., Dascola, I. and C. Umiltá, 1987, Reorienting attention across the horizontal and vertical meridians: evidence in favour of a premotor theory of attention. Neuropsychologia, 25, 31-40.

Rizzolatti, G, Riggio, L, and B. M. Sheliga, 1994 Space and selective attention. In: Attention and performance XV. eds., C. Umiltà, and M. Moscovitch (MIT press: Cambridge, MA). 1994, pp 231-265.

Schneider, W. X. and H. Deubel, 1995, Visual attention and saccadic eye movements: evidence for obligatory and selective spatial coupling. In: Eye Movement Research: Mechanisms, Processes and Applications, eds., J. M. Findlay R. Walker and R. W. Kentridge (North-Holland, Amsterdam) pp 317-324.

Shepherd, M., Findlay, J. M. and G. R. J. Hockey, 1986, The relationship between eye movements and spatial attention. Quarterly J. Expt Psychol, 38A, 475-491.

Silberpfennig, J. 1941, Contributions to the problem of eye movements. III. Disturbances of ocular movements with psedohemianopsia in frontal lobe tumours. Confinia Neurologica, IV(1-2), 1-13.

Sparks, D. L. and L. E. Mays, 1990, Signal transformations required for the generation of saccadic eye movements. Annual Review of Neuroscience, 13, 309-336.

Umiltá, C., Riggio, L., Dascola, I. and G. Rizzolatti, 1991, Differential effects of central and peripheral cues on the reorienting of spatial attention. European J. Cognitive Psychology, 3, 247-267

Van Gisbergen, J. A. M., Gielen, S., Cox, H., Bruijns, J. and H. Kleine Schaars, 1981, Relation between metrics of saccades and stimulus trajectory in visual target tracking; implications for models of the saccadic system. In: Progress in Oculomotor Research, eds., A. F. Fuchs and W. Becker (Elsevier, North Holland, Amsterdam) pp 17-27.

Walker, R., Findlay, J. M., Young, A. W. and J. Welch, 1991, Disentangling neglect and hemianopia. Neuropsychologia, 29, 1019-1027.

Walker, R., Kentridge, R. W. and J. M. Findlay, 1995, Independent contributions of the orienting of attention, fixation offset and bilateral stimulation on human saccadic latencies. Experimental Brain Research, 103, 2, 294-310.

Walker, R., Findlay, J. M., Young, A. W. and N. Lincoln, Saccadic eye movements in object based neglect. (submitted) Cognitive Neuropsychology.

Wurtz, R. H. and M. E. Goldberg, eds., 1989, The Neurobiology of Saccadic Eye Movements. Reviews of Oculomotor Research Volume 3. (Elsevier, Amsterdam).

Visual Attention and Cognition
W.H. Zangemeister, H.S. Stiehl and C. Freksa (Editors)
© 1996 Elsevier Science B.V. All rights reserved.   115

NEW DEVELOPMENTS IN THE UNDERSTANDING

AND TREATMENT OF THE HEMISPATIAL NEGLECT SYNDROME[*]

Hilary C. Haeske-Dewick [a] , *Anthony G. M. Canavan* [a & b] *and Volker Hömberg* [a]

[a]Neurological Therapy Centre, Hohensandweg 37, D-40591 Düsseldorf, F.R.G.

[b]Institute for Health Services Research, 24 Crawley Green Road, Luton,
Bedfordshire, LU1 3LF, U.K.

ABSTRACT

Hemispatial neglect following brain injury is an important topic in both neuropsychological research and clinical practice. This term refers to a cluster of debilitating behaviours observed in patients, which is characterised by a failure to orientate or respond to stimuli in space contralateral to the side of the brain lesion. In the present paper, an overview of classical and more recent clinical and experimental findings are presented. In particular, one large multi-centre study (Pizzamiglio et al., 1992) is commented upon. This study arose as a result of research co-operation throughout Europe and, along with other work by this group, it broadens our understanding of hemispatial neglect phenomena. In addition, new treatment possibilities, arising from recent research, are discussed.

Key words: Parietal-lobe, Hemispatial-inattention, Symptoms, Assessment, Treatment.

1. INTRODUCTION

In the early days or weeks following a right sided parietal lesion, the patient may fail to respond completely to the left side of the world: It is as though everything left of the bodily midline has ceased to exist. In extreme cases the patient will fail to dress the left side of the body, shave the left side of the face or comb hair on the left side of the head. Food on the left side of the plate will be left uneaten, people in the left field of vision will be ignored, words will be only half read (e.g., "icecream" will be read as "cream", "football" as "ball"). When asked to draw in the numbers on an empty clock face, all twelve will be placed in the right hemicircle.

---

[*] The first author was supported by a Royal Society European Science Exchange Program fellowship. This work is a spin-off of the ESCAPE Non-Visual Neglect Study.

As will be shown below, such symptoms are for the most part fleeting phenomena, and can disappear completely even without therapeutic intervention. But more subtle deficits, detectible only with sensitive neuropsychological tests, may linger on indefinitely.

As will also be discussed below, a most important issue is to distinguish between *motor neglect*, in which one side of the world is perceived (either consciously or without awareness) but not responded to, versus *perceptual neglect*, in which half of the world is not acted upon because it fails to be perceived.

2. CLASSICAL FINDINGS

The hemispatial neglect syndrome is often a severe concomitant of right posterior cerebral brain lesions. Such lesions can occur as a result of cerebrovascular accident, tumour or head injury. Neglect is estimated to result in such patients with a frequency of 12% to 85% (see Pizzamiglio et al., 1992). Reasons for this rather uncertain estimate will be discussed below. Neglect has also been noted, if less often and less severely, following left-hemisphere damage (De Renzi, 1982). Individuals who suffer from supranuclear palsy (with lesions in the midbrain) and others with thalamic lesions are also found to show forms of neglect (Posner, 1991), although these shall not be discussed here.

Patients with neglect appear to be unable to process or respond to stimuli in the hemispace contralateral to the side of their lesion. They consequently *neglect* stimuli in one half of space, to the left or right of the body's midsagittal plane or line of sight. For patients with neglect symptoms, this means that they may bump into objects or fail to eat from one side of the plate, they may attend to only one side of the body or fail to read words on one side of a page.

Neglect is reported to be most severe in the first few weeks following a brain lesion, but it can also resolve within this time. Approximately one month post-lesion, the most striking forms of neglect have often improved. However, for many patients lasting neglect symptoms seriously impede the functional recovery and rehabilitation process.

At present, three main hypotheses seek to explain the neglect phenomena. The first suggests that neglect arises from some perturbation in the cognitive representation of space (Bisiach and Luzzatti, 1978). According to this hypothesis, stimuli on the patient's left side are *ignored* because central mechanisms fail to construct an internal representation of one side of space. The second hypothesis, and perhaps the most widely supported, proposes that neglect results from a failure to attend to stimuli in the contralesional hemispace, due perhaps to a difficulty in disengaging attention from ipsilateral targets (Posner et al., 1982). The proposal that left and right cerebral hemispheres have differential attentional capacities, with the right seemingly dominant for spatial attention (Bisiach and Vallar, 1988), is also important for the latter hypothesis. Finally, it is also suggested that hemispatial neglect can arise due to a motor-intentional problem (Heilman et al., 1987). In this instance it is proposed that neglect is caused by an inability to sustain a movement in or towards contralateral hemispace (*directional hypokinesia*).

Unilateral neglect is in fact thought of as a syndrome of deficits. While these deficits primarily involve a failure to respond to stimuli presented in the contralateral hemispace, the symptoms have been more closely defined. Heilman et al. (1985), for example, list five major behavioural manifestations of the neglect syndrome: Hemi-inattention, hemiakinesia, hemispatial neglect, extinction to simultaneous stimuli and allesthesia. The extinction phenomenon in particular may linger on in patients with no obvious neglect in daily life: Such patients can respond to stimuli on either side of the body when presented individually, but if two identical stimuli (e.g., patterns on a screen) are presented bilaterally and simultaneously, only one will be responded to, the one ipsilateral to the lesion. Allesthesia is the tendency to displace a stimulus presented on the contralateral side over to the ipsilateral side.

Visual neglect is the most commonly reported form of neglect. Clinically, visual neglect is manifested on tasks such as line bisection or line cancellation. For example, when a patient is asked to bisect a straight horizontal line in the middle, the centre of which is placed at his/her midline, bisection occurs too far to the right (as if most of the left half of the line were not present). Similarly, when asked to strike out multiple individual lines, the patient fails to strike out lines situated on the left. For clinical neuropsychologists the Behavioural Inattention Test (BIT) is a frequently used tool in the detection of unilateral visual neglect (Wilson et al., 1987). It consists of two sections: Six conventional sub-tests (e.g., line cancellation) and eight behavioural sub-tests (e.g., menu reading). Behavioural sub-tests are included to increase the BIT's everyday validity and thus aid in rehabilitation programs.

3. NEW DEVELOPMENTS IN THE UNDERSTANDING OF NEGLECT

3.1. Contralesional Neglect

It is becoming increasingly clear that neglect symptoms do not only occur in the visual modality. It is also perhaps worth remembering, that due to differences in the laterality of information processing in the brain for each sensory modality, it may not be possible to find true parallels to visual neglect. In this respect, the tactile modality is perhaps the closest parallel to the visual system and there have indeed been reports of tactile neglect in search tests following right hemisphere damage (Weintraub and Mesulam, 1988).

The possibility of detecting auditory neglect is more complex, since following right hemisphere damage the left hemisphere remains able to perceive sounds coming from within the left hemispace. This aside, one study has indicated that the right hemisphere does have a role in the deployment of attention to auditory stimuli, although this occurs not only in the contralateral but also in the ipsilateral space (De Renzi et al., 1989).

Furthermore, olfaction is primarily an ipsilaterally innervated sense. Since patients with right hemisphere lesions have been identified as failing to respond to their left nostril on stimulation of both, there has been some suggestion that these results support the notion of an *olfactory neglect* consistent with the representational hypothesis (Bellas et al., 1988).

In addition, neglect in mental imagery has been described (Bisiach and Luzzatti, 1978) as have distinctions between a perceptual and a premotor form of neglect (Tegner and Levander, 1991). The mental imagery task has become rather famous in the neuropsychological literature. Patients are asked to imagine themselves at one end of a well-known square (in fact, since much of this research was carried out in Italy, at one end of a famous Piazza such as the Piazza del Duomo in Milan). They are then asked to describe what they would see while walking to the other side of the square, where they have to imagine themselves turning around and walking back again, once again describing everything that they can see. In this situation, the patients show neglect in imagination, describing only buildings ipsilateral to the lesion in each direction, depending upon the perspective in imagery.

There are also reports that neglect in the left hemifield can exist in *near* but not *far* space in man (Halligan and Marshall, 1991). In this delightful single case study, the authors noted that their neglect patient was nevertheless a successful darts player (in this English pub-game, the player must throw small pointed darts at a target two metres away with an accuracy upon contact of a few centimetres). They therefore constructed a line bisection task based upon the darts principle, and found that their patient, who performed poorly on the standard paper and pencil version (*near* space), was accurate in *far* space.

Between 1990 and 1993 further research on hemineglect was carried out as part of "The Evaluation of the Efficacy of Technology in the Assessment and Rehabilitation of Brain-Damaged Patients" programme funded by the Commission of the European Community. This research involved collaboration between neurological research centres throughout Europe, and information about this and a wide range of similarly supported projects is reported in Stachowiak (1993).

In 1992, a report of the work completed by participating centres in the investigation of spatial neglect, principally visuo-spatial neglect, was published (Pizzamiglio et al., 1992). The researchers collaborating in this project were interested in the observation that although performance on neglect subtests, such as those of the BIT, were usually positively correlated, considerable individual variability between tests was usually evident. The authors therefore wondered whether neglect as an entity was a result of several independent mechanisms within visuo-spatial processing. In this paper, the contribution that both perceptual and motor skills make to the expression of neglect phenomena come under scrutiny.

On examination of the BIT sub-tests it is clear that for successful performance on individual tasks, different skills are required. First, while some tasks do not use distractors others do (e.g., in the star-cancellation sub-test the small stars to be crossed out on the page are intermingled with distracting large stars, letters and words) and may thus demand greater attentional capacity. Second, while some tasks primarily emphasize an overall perceptual judgement (e.g., line bisection), others require both complex perceptual and motor skills (e.g., drawing). The authors wondered whether it was these differing demands that underlay individual variability and stated:

"*It seemed important to empirically test* (sic) *whether differences between tasks convincingly rely on different processes or can be considered variations of a common operation which may be tapped at different degrees of complexity*" (p. 234).

To investigate this question further a total of 121 right brain-damaged patients with unilateral neglect drawn from seven European clinics was assessed. A positive diagnosis of neglect was made if it was identified on at least one of the eight tests used in the study. Most of these patients had experienced cerebrovascular accidents (87%), with brain damage in the other patients caused by head injury, neoplasia or other neurological conditions. At assessment, time since injury ranged very widely between patients, with a median duration of six months. Average age was 59 years and average years in education was 9 years.

The aforementioned tests included the six conventional sub-tests from the BIT (line crossing, letter cancellation, star cancellation, figure/shape copying, line bisection, representational drawing) and two additional neglect tests which are described in detail below.

In the first of these additional tests, the Wundt-Jastrow illusion test (Massironi et al., 1988), two partial ellipses of identical shape and size are presented, one above the other, on a card. This test is based on the finding that when the ellipses are shown to healthy subjects, a visuo-spatial illusion results, such that one ellipse is perceived to be longer than the other. In a sequence of 40 trials, the ellipses are shown in ten sizes (from 6 to 58 degrees), two orientations (curving upwards or downwards) and two directions (leftwards or rightwards) and subjects are required to identify which ellipse appears to be longer. In neglect, one would expect a considerable number of unusual responses (ie. those not corresponding to the illusion) when the ellipses fan out from a leftwards base. In fact, in this case, neglect patients may even perform *better* than healthy controls, by failing to fall for the illusion!

The second additional test was the semi-structured scale for the functional evaluation of personal neglect (Zoccolotti and Judica, 1992). Here, the patient is presented with three objects (comb, razor (for man)/ powder compact (for woman) and spectacles) and is asked to show how each is used. If there are no systematic asymmetries in exploration the patient scores 0. For slight asymmetries the patient scores 1, when there are clear omissions 2, and when only a reduced portion of contralateral space relative to ipsilateral exploration is used, they score 3. For individuals with personal neglect, one would expect high scores indicative of reduced awareness of the left side of the body.

The authors found considerable variability across tests in their sensitivity to detect pathological performance. To illustrate, less than 30% of patients were impaired on line crossing and even fewer showed pathological performance on the personal neglect test. On the other hand, more than 70% of patients scored below the cut-off point on star cancellation and figure/shape copying. Results such as these emphasize the reason for the great variability in estimating the incidence of unilateral neglect following brain damage: The method of assessment can influence the figures dramatically.

On the other hand, no correlation between performance and time since injury was found and the authors thus suggest a stability in neglect symptoms on these tests over time in non-acute patients. Furthermore there was little evidence to indicate any relationship between performance and age or education.

The authors also set out to look at the relationships between tests. With the exception of the semi-structured scale of personal neglect, all tests were significantly intercorrelated, apart from line crossing with representational drawing. Personal neglect correlated significantly with only star cancellation, line bisection and the Wundt-Jastrow illusion test. Consequently, the authors suggested that the lack of a relationship between the personal neglect test and other tests may be due to a distinction between functioning in personal and extrapersonal space.

Correlational analysis was followed by cluster analysis, a statistical process designed to search for unitary elements (*clusters*) that account for variability observed in the data. Rather than the emergence of clear clusters, this analysis revealed a *chaining effect* for the extrapersonal neglect tests. Three main links were identified, with each link appearing to represent a set of particular skills.

First, star and letter cancellation were seen to be associated. The authors attributed this linkage to a similarity in the response mechanism required to complete the two tests: Since both tests require sequential analysis of target stimuli in the presence of distractors, both tests therefore make demands upon selective attention. Second, line bisection and the Wundt-Jastrow illusion test were shown to be linked together. Both of these tests require processing of the whole stimulus and include only a simple motor component. The authors therefore classified them primarily as tests of perceptual neglect. The third link was identified between line crossing and figure/shape copying. This was felt to have come about because both tests are dependent upon perceptual *and* motor skills: They require the screening of a complex stimulus followed by the organization of a fine, sequential motor response.

The seventh extrapersonal neglect test, representational drawing, appeared to be relatively independent of the other tests, as did the personal neglect test.

Some of the above distinctions were further supported by inspection of individual patient performance. While all patients with perceptual neglect showed other difficulties, it was noted that three additional patients showed selective deficits only on the personal neglect scale and that three showed deficits on only cancellation tasks. Once again these results underlined the heterogeneity underlying the *neglect syndrome*, which is therefore probably better designated the *neglect syndromes*.

In summary, the results reported by Pizzamiglio et al. (1992) allow a number of conclusions to be drawn about spatial neglect. First, sensitivity in the detection of pathological performance is task dependent. Second, high estimates of neglect are present only in the case of tests in which performance loads highly on selective attention. Third, a segregation of test measures into those tapping personal versus those tapping extrapersonal neglect supports the hypothesis of separate coding of these kinds of space. Fourth, the lack of an association between test performance and either age or time since injury indicates that neglect can exist long-term, and need not necessarily disappear within a few days or weeks. Finally, the paper indicates that a diverse set of tasks are required to maximize the possibility of identifying neglect in clinical settings.

3.2. Ipsilesional Neglect

In the course of this European project, the interesting phenomenon of ipsilesional neglect, i.e. right neglect following right hemisphere damage, were also addressed (Robertson et al., 1994). Of a sample of 90 stroke cases showing visual inattention following right hemisphere brain damage, 17 cases could be identified who showed more inattention to the right rather than to the left side on some tests. After ruling out several other alternative hypotheses to clarify these effects, such as reliability of the tests used, task specificity, neglect severity or the occurrence of undetected left brain pathology, the most parsimonious interpretation for this *paradoxical* finding appeared to be compensatory scanning in the presence of a general attentional dysfunction pertaining to either side of visual space after a unilateral but sub-dominant hemisphere lesion.

This hypothesis is further corroborated by findings indiciating a right hemisphere dominance for vigilance and sustained attention (i.e. Pardo et al., 1991). These findings are of particular interest as they generate further hypotheses about the mechanisms of recovery from unilateral neglect which is certainly, in part, determined by learned compensatory scanning processes.

Further evidence for such a hypothesis is given in a study by Goodale et al. (1990): These authors performed a kinematic analysis of limb movements in nine right hemisphere lesioned patients at a mean time of 21 weeks after lesion onset. The majority of these patients had shown evidence of unilateral neglect early after the lesion, whereas by the time they were tested by the authors, clinically measurable neglect was no longer present. Two different tasks were used, one involving reaching out and touching one of a number of letter targets on a screen in front of the subject, and the other requiring line bisection between two specified targets on the screen. Whereas the reaching movements were performed normally, line bisection still showed evidence of left unilateral neglect. Further analysis of the trajectories of the reaching movements demonstrated that the patients made wide right-sided arcs into the final target position, thus crossing the ipsilesional space before entering into the target area in the contralesional space. This pattern of trajectories was never present in any of the controls. The data documented that functionally the reaching behaviour had been compensated by using a compensatory visual feedback system.

It is not entirely clear if subjects were really aware of this compensation or if it occurred spontaneously. Certainly further longitudinal single case studies are necessary to clarify the time course and the possible lack of awareness underlying such compensations. This is especially important as what is derived from these studies could help to marshal more reasonable rehabilitation strategies for neglect patients.

Present work by the collaborating team of European researchers, which has been ongoing since 1993, is concerned with the development of a non-visual neglect assessment battery and is once again funded by the European Commission. In the new battery, visual neglect is assessed by the use of a number of conventional visual sub-tests from the BIT combined with further line bisection measures. In addition, the battery includes assessment of auditory and tactile extinction, personal neglect and warned and unwarned reaction time as well as motor and functional questionnaire assessment measures. Now known as the *ESCAPE* (European Standardized Computerized Assessment Procedure for the Evaluation and Rehabilitation of Brain-Damaged Patients) hemineglect project, it aims to develop a coherent system for the assessment and rehabilitation of brain-damaged patients suffering from neglect. Their aim is to achieve this through the harmonization of methodology and the evaluation of new procedures and treatments, with the goal of developing an assessment battery and European standards.

4. NEW DEVELOPMENTS IN THE TREATMENT OF NEGLECT

For some while it has been known that vestibular and optokinetic stimulation may temporarily reduce the amount of visual neglect, indicating that convergence of polysensory information on the networks possibly constituting the structural basis for neglect, may reduce the severity of the neglect. Various vestibular, optokinetic or somatosensory stimulation techniques have been used to influence visual neglect such as caloric stimulation (Rubens, 1985;Vallar et al., 1993b), optokinetic stimulation (Pizzamiglio et al, 1990; Vallar et al., 1993a) or neck muscle vibration (Karnath et al., 1993) have been used. However, none of these methods could be used for long-term clinical application. Recently Vallar et al. (1995) showed that left visuospatial hemineglect could also be improved by mean of transcutaneous electrical stimulation (TENS). This method has already been widely used in i.e. pain control, is easily applicable and might also be appropriate for long-term usage. The TENS stimulation affects afferent nerve fibres by producing an additional somatosensory input to polymodal cortical areas. It is interesting to note that mulitiple modalities (vestibular, optokinetic, somatosensory) have the potential power to influence neglect. A possible explanation for this is given by the fact that in the monkey cortex, particularly in the parieto-insular "vestibular" cortex multiple modalities converge (Grüsser et al., 1990a, b). This may be the substrate for the observed reduction of neglect symptoms. Certainly further work has to be done to establish such polymodal input strategies as a definite treatment tool for neglect.

5. CONCLUSIONS

From early clinical descriptions of the *neglect syndrome*, emphasizing the usually temporary but complete loss of one half of the visual world, our understanding has now advanced to the level of being able to pinpoint certain symptoms and clusters of symptoms that may be longer lasting and be based on a heterogeneous assortment of underlying impairments. The term neglect itself needs to be questioned, implying as it does an active avoidance of stimuli that by definition must have been perceived. As has been shown above, deficits may in fact lie at the level of sensation and perception, at a higher level of cognitive representation, or in the response domain. Furthermore, it would now appear that neglect is not restricted to the visual modality. Future research will be further aimed at describing the symptoms in better detail, through the development of more sensitive tests and treatments, and in particular an attempt will be made to delineate the various neuropsychological processes contributing to the appearance of these many and varied symptoms to create better treatment strategies.

REFERENCES

Bellas, D. N., R. A. Novelly, B. Eskenazi, and J. Wasserstein, 1988, Neuropsychologia **26** (**1**), 45-52.

Bisiach, E. and G. Luzzatti, 1978, Cortex **14**, 129-133.

Bisiach, E. and G. Vallar, 1988, Hemineglect in Humans, in: Handbook of Neuropsychology (Vol. 1), eds. F. Bollar and J. Graffman (Elsevier, Amsterdam).

De Renzi, E., 1982, Disorders of Space Exploration and Cognition. (Wiley, London).

De Renzi, E., M. Gentilini and C. Barbieri, 1989, Journal of Neurology, Neurosurgery and Psychiatry **52**, 613-617.

Goodale, M. A., A. D. Milner, L. S. Jakobson and D. P. Carey, 1990, Canadian Journal of Psychology **44**, 180-195.

Grüsser, O-J, M. Pause and U. Schreiter, 1990a, J. Physiol. **430**, 537-557.

Grüsser, O-J, M. Pause and U. Schreiter, 1990b, J. Physiol. **430**, 559-583.

Halligan, P. W. and J. C. Marshall, 1991, Nature **350 (April)**, 498-500.

Heilman, K. M., D. Bowers, E. Valenstein and R. T. Watson, 1987, Hemispace and Hemispatial Neglect, in: Neurophysiological and Neuropsychological Aspects of Spatial Neglect. Advances in Psychology Vol. 45, ed. M. Jeannerod, (Elsevier Science Publishers, North Holland) p. 115-150.

Heilman, K. M., R. T. Watson and E. Valenstein, 1985, Neglect and Related Disorders, in: Clinical Neuropsychology, eds. K. M. Heilman and E. Valenstein, (Oxford University Press, New York) p. 243-293.

Karnath, H. O., K. Christ and W. Hartje, 1993, Brain **116**, 383-396.

Massironi, M., G. Antonucci, L. Pizzamiglio, M. V. Vitale and P. Zocolotti, 1988, Neuropsychologia **26**, 161-166.

Pardo, J. V., P. T. Fox and M. E. Raichle, 1991, Nature **349**, 61-64.

Pizzamiglio, L., C. Bergego, P. Halligan, V. Hömberg, I. Robertson, E. Weber, B. Wilson, P. Zoccolotti and G. Deloche, 1992, Behavioural Neurology **5**, 233-240.

Pizzamiglio, L., R. Frasca, C. Guariglia, C. Incoccia and G. Antonucci, 1990, Cortex **26**, 535-540.

Posner, M. I., 1991, Structures and Function of Selective Attention, in: Clinical Neurospychology and Brain Function: Research, Measurement and Practice, eds. T. Boll and B. K. Bryant (APA, USA) p. 169-202.

Posner, M. I., Y. Cohen and R. D. Rafal, 1982, Philosophical Transactions of the Royal Society London **B298**, 187-198.

Robertson, I. H., P. W. Halligan, C. Bergego, V. Hömberg, L. Pizzamiglio, E. Weber and B. A. Wilson, 1994, Cortex **30**, 199-213.

Rubens, A. B., 1985, Neurology **35**, 1019-1024.

Stachowiak, F. J., 1993, Developments in the Assessment and Rehabilitation of Brain-damaged Patients (Gunter Narr Verlag, Tübingen) p. 55-89.

Tegner, R. and M. Levander, 1991, Brain **114**, 1943-1951.

Vallar, G., G. Antonucci, C. Guariglia and L. Pizzamiglio, 1993a, Neuropsychologia **31**, 1191-1200.

Vallar, G., G. Bottini, M. L. Rusconi and R Sterzi, 1993b, Brain **116**, 71-86.

Vallar, G., M. L. Rusconi, S. Barozzi, B. Bernardini, D. Ovadia, C. Papagno and A. Cesarini, 1995, Neuropsychologia **33**, 73-82.

Weintraub, S. and M. M. Mesulam, 1988, Journal of Neurology, Neurosurgery and Psychiatry **51**, 1481-1488.

Wilson, B., J. Cockburn, and P. W. Halligan, 1987, Behavioural Inattention Test. (Thames Valley Test Company, England).

Zoccolotti, P., G. Antonucci and A. Judica, 1992, Neuropsychological Rehabilitation **2**, 179-192.

Visual Attention and Cognition
W.H. Zangemeister, H.S. Stiehl and C. Freksa (Editors)
125

ATTENTION AND COMMUNICATION: EYE-MOVEMENT-BASED RESEARCH PARADIGMS

Boris Velichkovsky[a], Marc Pomplun[b], and Johannes Rieser[c]

[a] Unit of Applied Cognitive Research, Dresden University of Technology
[b] Department of Neuroinformatics/SFB 360, University of Bielefeld
[c] Department of Linguistics/SFB 360, University of Bielefeld

ABSTRACT

Recent technological development makes it possible to investigate the integration of attention, language and cognition in the processes of communication. Three studies approaching this problem are reported. The first study investigated the solving of puzzle tasks by two partners who shared the same visual environment but whose knowledge of the situation and whose ability to change it were different. One of them knew the solution but had no means to act on the situation. The other could act, but without knowing about the solution. In some trials, in addition to verbal communication, the eye fixations of one of the partners were projected into the visual space of the other. This gaze-position transfer improved the performance and changed communication processes.

The second study analyzed the interaction between visual attention and the production of linguistic expressions. The instructor in this study had to advise the novice about the construction of a 3-D block structure. The data revealed a strong bi-directional interaction of these variables. In particular, an analogue of the "Eye-voice span" effect sensitive to the course of communication was discovered.

In the last study distributions of fixations over ambiguous pictures were used for processing these pictures in such a way that in regions attracting less attention the brightness of elements was lowered. Then these pre-processed pictures were shown to naïve subjects for an identification. The results demonstrated a shift of reports in the direction of interpretation that accompanied eye movement data used for the pre-processing of pictures.

KEY WORDS: eye-movements, focus, visual attention, ambiguous pictures, task-oriented communication

1. INTRODUCTION

More than 100 years ago Ewald Hering (1868/1977) stressed the use of eye movements in human communication. While obviously an important component of interpersonal interaction, eye movements still have not been analyzed in this respect. This lack of experimental evidence can be explained primarily via constraints imposed by traditional techniques of eye movement research (cf. Yarbus, 1967; Hallett, 1985). High-precision eye-tracking always implied severe restrictions of head mobility and, therefore, an impossibility to speak. However, recent technological development opened the way to a high-precision head-free eye-tracking. By the system used for the present investigation (see Stampe, 1993) we could overcome traditional drawbacks. The system called OMNITRACK is a prototype of a non-invasive imaging eye-tracker. It is based on the use of ISCAN pupil-tracking boards and two video cameras for inputs of information about the position of the head within the environment and the position of the pupil within the head. The system is characterized by the following attributes: 1. Fast calibration which is stable over the whole period of study and does not suffer from accidental blinks; 2. Free head with permitted deviations from the straight-ahead position up to $15°$, and a practically unrestricted field of view; 3. The possibility to run experiments under normal illumination. The average precision of the gaze-position measurement with the help of OMNITRACK lies within $0.5–0.7°$. Meanwhile, these parameters have been further improved by the use of a neural network interface for calibration. This interface allows a precise and extremely fast adjustment of coordinates even for subjects wearing spectacles (Pomplun, Velichkovsky, Ritter, 1994).

Modern cognitive science and neuroscience are another source of new research questions. One of the main problems in these studies is the coordination of quasi-autonomous mechanisms of mental functioning (Neisser, 1994; Velichkovsky, 1990; 1994). Integration of verbal and non-verbal activities in the processes of communication is of particular theoretical and practical interest (Velichkovsky, 1995b in press). Without doubt linguistic reference and allocation of attention are closely related. In the analysis of Tomasello (1995), an act of linguistic reference is an act in which one individual intends that another individual attend to some aspect of their shared environment. An act of attention is conceived of, following Gibson and Reder (1979), as an act of intentional perception. This translates into: A intends for B to intentionally perceive X. An act of predication extends this process as one individual first secures "joint attention" to some entity with the other individual and then expresses an intention that the other attend to one of many possible aspects of this entity.

2. GAZE-POSITION TRANSFER AND COOPERATION

Existing investigations concentrated on more traditional forms of verbal communication. For instance, Chapanis, Ochsman, Parrish and Weeks (1972) compared the effects of four modes of communication on the solving of "real world" problems in two-man teams: typewriting, handwriting, voice, and natural, unrestricted communication. The main result was a relative efficiency of the natural communication. In a follow-up study (Chapanis, Parrish, Ochsman, Weekset, 1977) the same authors concentrated on the analysis of verbal conversation again demonstrating numerous differences between these communication conditions. The majority of contemporary studies stress mutual symmetry of partners' contributions to the goal (Hutchins, 1991), even if asymmetric, i.e. "expert" and "novice" interaction, represents the more frequent and important case. In several recent studies (e.g., Clark, 1991) the asymmetric case was re-introduced again but only concerning the analysis of linguistic means of reference.

What are the most efficient ways to disambiguate verbal instructions? Can we make communication in the distributed problem solving situation as fluent as is the interaction among different functional brain systems of one person (provided he/she knows the solution and has all the means to reach it in praxis)? In this last case different levels seem to "communicate" with the help of top- down and bottom-up attentional mechanisms (Velichkovsky, 1990). The situation here is similar to the evolving pragmatics of mother-child interaction. The socialization of child's attention in the second part of the first year of life and the on-going coordination of the foci of attention – "joint attention" states as Bruner (1981) called them – are the main prerequisites for the development of full-scale linguistic interaction and cooperative activities (see also Neisser, 1994; Vygotsky, 1935/1962).

2.1. Gaze-position transfer from instructor to constructor

The specific problem is then to study, how "communication of attention" of the partners influences cooperative problem solving. Practically, this may be reformulated as the question on the transfer of gaze-position information, because eye movements are the most reliable (albeit not ideal) indices of the dynamics of the external focus of attention. In no previous study was the problem of mutual understanding and facilitation of the cooperative problem solving investigated with the use of such a natural source of reference as the gaze direction. The situation is hardly better even concerning manual pointing. An exception to that is only research on early language acquisition where the basic role of deictic means of reference is considered a well-established fact (Clark and Sengul, 1978).

In our first study reported in this chapter we (see also Velichkovsky, Reingold, Stampe, 1994) used a variant of a computer Puzzle game. We selected three concrete meaningful pictures as the goal states to be reconstructed. After a short exposition of an intact picture before every task solution, one of the pictures was presented as a random configuration of overlapping parts. The subjects had the instruction to reach the goal state together and as soon as possible. The pictures differed in their relative complexity as measured by the average duration of solution. Twenty subjects took part in this experiment. Four of them were Instructors (Insts) who had spent at least 6 hours over a period of two days in solving the tasks. The other 16 subjects were novices or Constructors (Consts). In their training sessions they were permitted to solve only one puzzle task different from those used in the main series.

The general layout of the experiment is shown in fig.1. Const and Inst sat without visual contact in front of their own color monitors. Inst's gaze direction and pupil size of the right eye were constantly recorded. The information about gaze position (or the movements of Inst's mouse) could be transferred to the monitor of Const's, where this position was highlighted as a half-transparent red spot. The changes in the configuration of the picture's pieces could be brought about only by Const's mouse. Illumination conditions were kept constant.

Three major independent variables were used. The first one was the condition of communication: "voice", "voice and mouse", "voice and gaze". In the "voice" condition subjects were able to converse freely. In the "voice and mouse" condition Inst was also able to show relevant pieces on both monitors with his/her mouse. In the "voice and

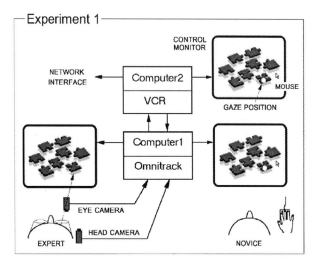

Figure 1: The general arrangement of Experiment 1

gaze" condition, instead of the mouse, Inst's gaze position was constantly visible at the corresponding location on Const's monitor. The second variable was learning phase: every Const solved all the tasks three times. The third variable was the complexity of the task which corresponded to the three different pictures used in the experiment. Two additional variables were the individual differences of Insts and Consts. These variables were nested: every Inst worked with four randomly chosen Consts. The order of all independent variables was counterbalanced. Solution time, conversation, the spatial distribution and duration of eye fixations as well as the average pupil size for every fixation were registered.

The results showed that all major independent variables of this experiment influenced solution time. The main effect of learning was especially strong, $F(2/117)=33.613$, $p<0.001$. The conditions of communication also strongly influenced performance, $F(2/117)=13.115$, $p<0.001$. Significant differences were present between the "voice" condition and either of the other conditions here. The difference between "voice and mouse" and "voice and gaze" conditions was non-significant. The third, relatively week main effect was that of task. There was also one nearly significant interaction connecting influences of learning and conditions of communication. The nature of this interaction is obvious from fig.2. It consists in a higher learning rate for "voice" condition in comparison to "voice and gaze" condition.

The corpus of verbal conversation presents the main challenge for an analysis of the results. First of all, Insts produced at least 5 times more words and sentences than Consts, who relatively rarely used clarification questions or just checked/confirmed understanding of advises. Secondly, there was a significant reduction of the number of words in conditions of direct reference, i.e. "voice and mouse", "voice and gaze" in comparison to the "voice" condition. Another correlated trend was a reduction in the variety of lexical items - indefi-

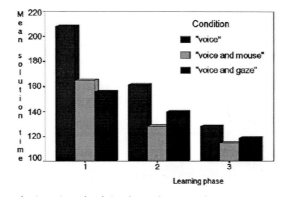

Figure 2: Mean solution time (sec) in dependence on learning phase and condition of communication in Experiment 1

nite articles, content words, spatial words - which were replaced by deictic demonstratives and definite referring expressions. For instance, a rich lexicon of spatial words became reduced to such indexicals as "the", "this", "here", "over here", "there", "over there", and "behind". The number of words and complete sentences declined in the course of learning (cf. Clark, 1991). Due to these changes, conversation in conditions of the manual or the gaze-mediated reference becomes by itself incomprehensible for any "third-party" observer.

The distribution of fixation lengths for the three communication conditions in Experiment 1 is shown in fig.3. This figure demonstrates a possible importance of fixations longer than 500 ms, which not only make almost 20% of all fixations but which also seem to be differently sensitive in the three communication conditions of the experiment. Indeed, the proportion of such fixations depended on the factor of communication condition, $F(2/117)=11.227$, $p<0.001$. The difference can be explained by the larger proportion of these fixations in the "voice and gaze" condition in comparison to both other conditions. No other major independent variables influenced the parameter of oculomotor behavior.

2.2. Gaze-position transfer from constructor to instructor

Twenty-one subjects took part in Experiment 2. Three of them were experts, who also participated as Insts in Experiment 1. The other 18 subjects were novices. The same three tasks were used. The main difference between this experiment and the previous one was that the transfer of gaze position was now realized in the opposite direction, from Const to Inst. Accordingly, there were only two levels of the first independent variable: the conditions of communication were either "voice" or "voice and gaze". As a consequence, there were only six trials, two at each of three learning phases for every Inst. The order of presentation of experimental tasks was additionally balanced across the subjects and phases of learning. In all other respects Experiment 2 was identical with Experiment 1.

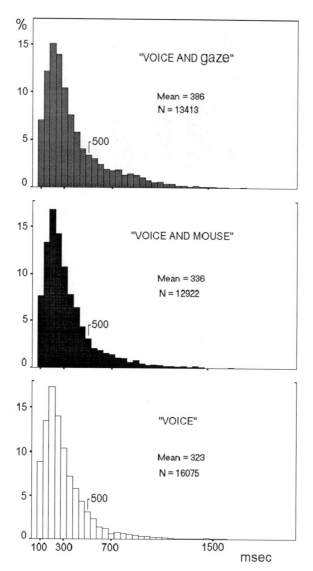

Figure 3: Distribution of fixation lengths for three communication conditions of Experiment 1

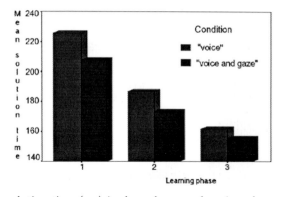

Figure 4: Mean solution time (sec) in dependence on learning phase and condition of communication in Experiment 2

In Experiment 2 all major factors influenced the performance. Again the strongest effect was that of learning, $F(2/90)=52.886$, $p<0.001$. The mode of communication contributed significantly, with the "voice and gaze" condition leading to faster puzzle solutions, $F(1/90)=6.968$, $p<0.01$. The task variable also influenced solution time. Of all possible interactions only the interaction of these three major variables was close to the minimal acceptable level of significance. The dependence of average solution time on communication mode and learning phase is shown in fig.4.

The distribution of fixation lengths in Experiment 2 is shown in fig.5. It demonstrates an even larger proportion of long fixations: about 27% of all fixations are longer than 500 ms. This is significantly more than in Experiment 1 (Kolmogorov-Smirnov Test, $Z=3.692$, $p<0.001$). However, there was no dependence of this parameter on the communication condition, $F(1/90)=1.310$, $p=0.255$. Influence of other major factors was also non-significant, with the exception of a weak second-order interaction of all three independent variables. This interaction can be reduced to a relatively larger proportion of long fixations at the beginning of learning for the "voice" condition and the most difficult task.

2.3. Discussion of the results

In both experiments one can see a beneficial effect of communication modes supporting a "joint attention" state. Particularly, the changes in conversation prove that reference by gaze as well as manual reference by mouse leads to the situation of direct physical co-presence for both participants (Clark, 1991). Because the gaze position transfer happened to be efficient in both cases, this can further mean that the optimal strategy for Insts is to support the actual self-initiated intentions of Const's, and not to constantly re-direct them by imposing their own course of action (cf. Tomasello and Farrar, 1986).

The question about possible differences in mouse versus gaze reference is of theoretical and practical relevance. Gaze direction is tied to attention, which is rarely the case in manual pointing. Both forms of pointing seem also to be different with respect to

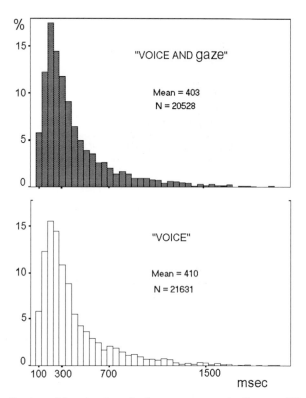

Figure 5: Distribution of fixation lengths for two communication conditions of Experiment 2

learning rate. The communication of gaze position is especially efficient as a support in situations with low redundancy: a relatively high complexity of tasks and a lack of repetition. Another difference is the divergent dependence on the visual feed-back. In the case of mouse-mediated pointing exactly such a feed-back is necessary. It seems, however, to disturb and slow-down Inst's activity in the gaze position transfer.

The gaze-mediated reference was quite natural for the subjects. This task obviously suits some preexisting mechanism (cf. Oram, Perrett, Hietanen, 1993). In particular, fixations with duration of more than 500 ms seem to play a communicative role. This is perhaps an apt solution: to split up the array of fixations and to use the longest of them for a specific interpersonal purpose. Such fixations, first, are easier to be detected and evaluated by the partners and, secondly, they can be better controlled by the producer. Indeed, in an independent study of eye movements as a response mode for operating with virtual keyboards (Stampe and Reingold, 1993) a filtering out of fixations with durations less than 400–500 ms clearly improved the reliability of the system.

In order to further clarify these relationships we turned to additional factors of individual differences of Insts and Consts. The analysis revealed rather divergent results for both experiments. In Experiment 1 the proportion of long fixations was dependent on the individual differences not only of Insts, $F(3/132)=40.370$, $p<0.001$, but also of Consts, $F(15/96)=21.123$, $p<0.001$, and their interactions with the conditions of communication: $F(6/132)=2.913$, $p<0.01$, and $F(30/96)=2.331$, $p<0.001$, respectively. At first sight this might be caused by the trivial fact of nesting these two variables in the experimental design. However, the comparison of residual components of the two ANOVAs ("Communication Conditions" versus "Individual Differences of Insts" and "Communication Conditions" versus "Individual Differences of Consts") shows something different: The long fixations of Insts are significantly better explained in the framework of individual differences of Consts than from the perspective of individual differences of the Insts themselves, $F(90/117)=1.784$, $p<0.01$. This corresponds to the known fact that communicative behavior is dependent on the vis-a-vis, not only on the producer (see Krauss and Fussel, 1991). In Experiment 2 no trace of such an "inter-subjectivity" was observed. The proportion of long fixations depended only on the main effect of individual differences of Consts.

This function of long fixations of Insts' is also quite clear from the correlation of their proportion with the time of solution. The correlation in Experiment 2 is positive: a higher proportion of long fixations is observed in the course of longer and, probably, more effortful solutions ($r=0.25$, $p<0.01$). One could expect this result on the basis of common knowledge about a positive relationship between duration of fixation and processing load (e.g., Nodine, Kungel, Toto, Krupinsky, 1992). In Experiment 1, however, an equally significant, but negative correlation was discovered between the same variables ($r=-0.28$, $p<0.001$). Indeed, the more longer fixations are produced by Insts the more comprehensive are their instructions for the Consts and the shorter is the path to the solution. This finally explains the lack of correlation between the length of fixation and the pupil size in Insts. The expected relationships between pupil size and length of corresponding fixation would be again that of a positive correlation (e.g. Kahneman, 1973). In fact this pattern was observed, but only in Experiment 2, i.e. in Consts ($r=0.13$, $p<0.001$). In Experiment 1 (Insts) there was only a small negative correlation ($r=-0.08$, $p<0.01$). The common interpretation of fixation times in terms of information processing load is inappropriate in such a communicative situation.

An even more interesting aspect of the pupillometric data is that the pattern of Insts as a whole differs from the analogous data of Consts in the sense of larger pupil sizes (fig.6). In Insts the activation seems to be more global and whole-task related: it began just after the start, and often persisted over the whole period of task solution until the moment when the goal picture clearly emerged out of the random distribution of pieces. In Consts the bursts of activation were more "molecular", they included several fixations within single problem solving episodes (cf. O'Donnel, Eggemeier, 1986). Insts also show more activation despite their better knowledge about the situation. The first explanation relies on a specific attitude of Insts to the task connected with their meta-cognitive and interpersonal role as advisers. Another explanation is based on the fact that only Insts - in contrast to novices - can build the image of the goal which extends its motivating influence over the whole period of problem solving.

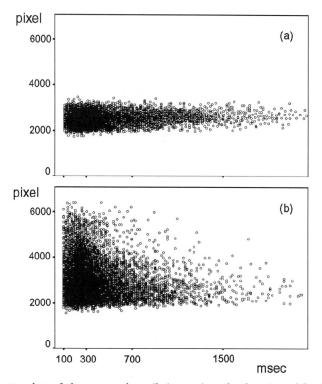

Figure 6: Scatterplots of the averaged pupil size against the duration of fixation in Constructors (a) and Instructors (b)

Both explanations are actually non-exclusive. The temporal extension of action and/or interpersonal attitudes usually demand a massive involvement of prefrontal structures. A relatively passive comprehension of advises and their sensorimotor realization relies rather on posterior cortical and subcortical mechanisms of control. Thus, different action units can correspond to different levels of activity control: strategic, meta-cognitive, and inter-subjective activity on the part of the Insts has to be differentiated from more tactical, cognitive and sensorimotor efforts on the part of the Consts. If attention is a kind of glue connecting the levels (Velichkovsky, 1990), then indeed the communication of attention is an important way to coordinate the partners' resources.

3. GAZE DIRECTION AND THE FOCUS OF LINGUISTIC REFERENCE

In a further series of experiments we (Clermont, Meier, Pomplun, Prestin, Rieser, Ritter, Velichkovsky, 1995) used the following setting: Again two subjects, Instructor

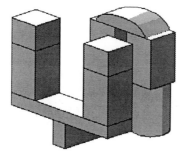

Figure 7: Instructor's blocks' world

(Inst) and Constructor (Const), participated in the study. They were separated by a screen. Inst had a block's assembly set before him (fig.7) and was instructed to describe it to Const. Const in turn was told to build up the same 3-D assembly according to the directives of Inst's. Both agents were allowed to converse freely during the task. The discourse produced by the agents consists of sequences of Inst's directives, usually paralleled by Const's assent/dissent, simultaneous actions and a concomitant ratification of these actions (cf. similarly, Clark, Wilkes-Gibbs, 1990; 1992). The latter was usually followed by a reply of Inst's. The following is an example of such a turn exchange:

Inst: "Well, on the ground stands a green longish rectangle upright";
Const: "Upright, yes."

The task setting, above all the distribution of roles (i.e. Inst versus Const, director versus builder), provides the partners with a series of goal-oriented moves like directives, check-backs, actions, etc. If Inst chooses a particular move, Const has different options to react. Both agents cooperatively determine the route the discourse will take (Herrmann, Grabowski, 1994; Schegloff, Jefferson, Sachs, 1977), however, due to the different roles of the agents, the communication situation is an asymmetrical one. As in the previous experiments, coordination and cooperation emerge on at least three different levels: the sensorimotor level (exact wording, elementary motor operations), the level of goals (intention, cognition, action), and on the so-called meta-cognitive level (intentions, beliefs, beliefs about beliefs, mutual beliefs).

We now turn to one of the most important preconditions for agents' cooperation in discourse, focus (see Bosch, van der Sandt, 1994; Grosz, 1981). Firstly, we investigated a technical notion of focus based on a computer-simulation of turn-exchange with a two-agent system called *SPEX* (Simulated Speech-Exchange System). In a second step we confronted this technical focus based on computer-simulation with an empirical focus provided by the data on sequences of foveal fixations. The eye movements were registered in the same way as in the earlier experiments.

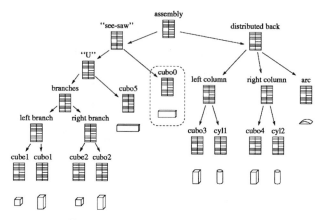

Figure 8: Data-structure for assembly

3.1. On the technical notion of focus

In a linguistic, particularly in a pragmatic context focus can be conceived as the information enabling Inst or Const to produce the next turn-relevant expression in a dialogue (Rieser, 1994). This notion of "focus" is more basic than the one usually used in linguistic, especially in phonologically oriented research. The source of focus-information is provided by perception and cognitive mechanisms such as the activation of constraints concerning, e.g. the shape of blocks. Hence, focus can be seen as a task-driven zooming or highlighting device. It operates on a dynamically up-dated data-structure, which, in the setting chosen, is determined by at least the following parameters:

- Inst's classification of the assembly,

- Inst's division of the assembly into parts (e.g. front, middle, back, upper and lower parts),

- Inst's perspective with respect to the assembly, its parts, and constituents,

- the position or orientation of parts in the assembly.

The data structure on which Inst's focus operates contains information about simple and complex objects. Figure 8 shows the data structure for the whole assembly used in the experiment without focus-information. Roughly, the assembly consists of a front, called "see-saw", and a "distributed" back. The front faces Inst. It has a top and a bottom, the bottom being a green cuboid (named cubo0), the top having the shape of a "U". Its bottom is a blue rectangular cuboid (cubo5), the top has a left branch and a right branch. In the rear we have two columns, consisting of cylinders cyl1 and cyl2. Each cylinder has a cuboid on top of it. The columns are bridged by a block named "arc" by the participants.

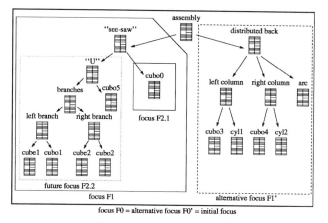

Figure 9: Embedded focus

Focus movements are important for assessing and categorizing the whole assembly and finding an optimal "entry" into the data-structure. The Inst can choose among various entrance points to the data structure, e.g. he/she can start from the front or the back. Applied to the data-structure of our block's assembly, focusing amounts to a succession of focus- frames, as shown in fig.9.

From fig.9 it can be seen that focus–movements usually proceed from the whole assembly to the deepest embedded non-supported block (i.e. to cubo0) of a non-supported sub-figure ("see-saw"). Thus we have a succession of the following type:

$$F_0 \searrow F_1 \searrow F_{2.1} \nearrow F_1 \searrow F_{2.2} \ .$$

Within F2.2, the focus will be first on cubo5, the blue block supported by green cubo0. The alternative focus-movement F1 embarks upon the distributed back and settles afterwards on the parallel cylinders cyl1 and cyl2.

3.2. Hypotheses on focus and clusters of fixations

From the previous discussion it should be clear that the role of the technical notion of focus is to yield a set of parameters needed for the semantic and the pragmatic interpretation of situated utterances. It must be able to handle changes of situated universes in discourse in order to achieve an interpretation of relational expressions like *long* and *in between*. The "history" of focus movements (cf. fig.9) serves as the basis for the interpretation of definite anaphoric noun-phrases like *the block* (a big red block), similar to devices used in discourse representation theory and other variants of dynamic semantics (cf. Kamp, Reyle, 1993). Linguistic arguments provide only one side of the coin, however. The other is whether this technical notion of focus can be used in psycholinguistic explanations. Ideally, one would like to develop a notion of focus covering linguistic as well as psycholinguistic data. The following initial hypotheses have been set up in the context of two projects: the investigation of transcripts and the simulation of planning activities and verbal actions of agents in SPEX. These hypotheses were taken to be empirically relevant, in the sense of being falsifiable or at least modifiable by the investigation of eye-movements.

Hypothesis 1: Global direction of focus-movement
> Focus-movement can have two main directions: from the front (basis of "see-saw") to the rear ("door") or vice versa.

Hypothesis 2: "History" of foci, "embedded focus"
> Focus-movement proceeds according to a principle of "focus- embedding", i.e. the sequence of events will be as follows:

> (a) initial focus on the whole assembly

> (b) subsequent focus on the integral part selected according to the direction chosen

> (c) within the integral part the focus is on the block which, non-supported, supports other blocks (i.e. the basis-block).

Hypothesis 3: Change of focus
> The move upwards from the basis-block to some next block is guided by the "support"-principle with respect to the integral part chosen.

Hypothesis 4: Focus and production of turn
> During turn-production the focus remains fixed on the object being the topic of the turn.

Hypothesis 5: Focus change, current and next turn
> Focus-movement and turn-production are related as follows:

> (a) Current focus determines the production of current turn.

> (b) Change of focus occurs between turns.

> (c) The next current focus determines the production of the next turn.

> (d) After a reply of Const's Inst will retain the old focus-position in order to match Const's utterance and his situation perceived.

Hypothesis 6: Test-actions
> In case of test-actions either an inverse focus-movement contrary to the direction of "support" is used or the agents go back to the basis-block thus initiating a new canonical focus movement.

Hypothesis 7: Privileged test-points
> Tests frequently occur, if the agents have just finished setting up an integral part of the whole assembly.

It is obvious, especially from hypotheses 2, 3, 4, and 5 that the whole list is based on the assumption of a rational, "recursively minded" instructor. Subsequent experiments were expected to test the technical notion of focus and to provide empirical data for a more adequate concept.

3.3. Discussion of the eye-movement data: Planning, search, and interactive focus-management

In order to test these hypotheses, an empirical study was carried out along the lines indicated above. 8 pairs of subjects participated in the experiments. Their conversations, actions and eye-movements were registered and analyzed off-line with the help of a special multimedia editor. Due to technical constraints only eye-movement data of Inst's could be taken into account.

While hypothesis 1, regarding the global direction of focus-movement, was confirmed by both the transcripts and the fixations, parts of the second hypothesis have to be modified in the face of the data. In contrast to predictions 2(a) and 2(b), Inst's focus neither encapsulates the whole figure, nor an integral part of it. It is only within integral parts of the figure that focus movements are governed by a stricter rule: The "support"-principle, formulated above in 2(c) to make Inst choose the basis-block as the starting point for the description, and in hypothesis 3 - to determine the next block to be focused within the selected part of the assembly, turns out to be suitable to explain the data obtained in the eye-tracking study. However, as the discussion of hypotheses 4 and 5 will show, this principle has to be considered as a default option: it can be flexibly changed according to emerging needs of the agents.

Hypotheses 4 and 5, which make up the core part of our expectations, contain predictions that are rather controversial. While from the perspective of computer simulation the postulated rigid relationship between focus and turn is a fruitful idea, from the point of view of psycho-linguistic explanation it is less convincing. Indeed, the high speed of speech production seems to require that the planning of each turn has to be rather independent of the actual utterance. Due to these considerations, we were especially interested in the empirical results regarding these hypotheses.

First of all, hypothesis 4, which in a way fixes the focus to the turn it determines, is disproved by the data, because the comparison of language and foveal fixations indicates powerful planning processes being at work. What we observe here is an analogue to the "Eye-voice span" phenomenon (Bouma, 1978; Buswell, 1920) which, as far as we know, has never been described outside reading research. The size of the span that could be clearly detected by our current method of editing speech and gaze-position records is slightly less than 500 msec. In the experiment we also observed spans which were longer. This new result provides an independent explanation for the fact that only fixations longer that 500 ms can be used for disambiguation of verbal reference (this chapter; Velichkovsky, 1995a in press) and for gaze- mediating pointing (Stampe, Reingold, 1993). One of our examples of the focus going ahead of speech is shown in figure 10. While describing the yellow and the red cuboids, Inst in this episode already focuses the two cubes, which (in accordance with the "support"- principle) he is going to refer to next.

However, although the focus preceding the respective turn has to be considered the default case, there are also some exceptions to this rule, which occur in connection with problems in syntactical search or lexical access. Figure 11 shows that when Inst is hesitant about which word to choose for an object, his focus remains static.

These findings do not only require hypothesis 4 to be reformulated, but they also affect the assumptions (a) – (c) stated in connection with the hypothesis 5, which have to be substantially changed.

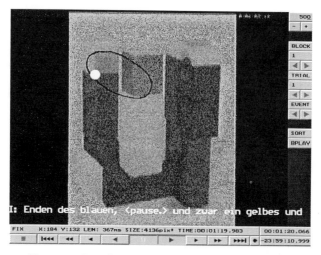

Figure 10: Inst: "namely a yellow one and a red one"

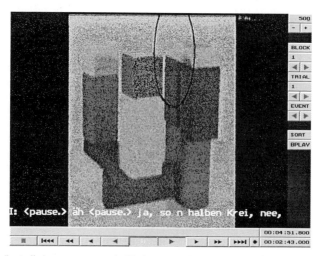

Figure 11: Inst: "uhm, yes, some half circ, no, it's not a circle, what are they called"

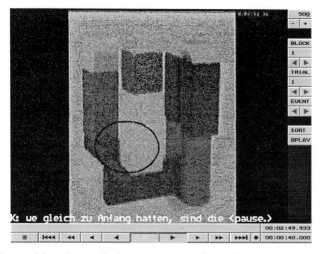

Figure 12: Const: "Are the mmh the green one and the blue one we had right at the beginning, are they..."

Prediction 5(d), however, introduces an aspect that has not yet been considered, for it allows Const to influence Inst's eye movements. This interactive aspect of the task, which plays a relatively minor role in the initial hypotheses, gains considerable weight with respect to the empirical results. In fact, there are several possibilities of Const's actively contributing to the establishment of Inst's foci. First of all, the rules of discourse require Const to adequately react to the instructions he receives. As long as this back-channel behavior merely contains some ratification, Inst's strategy remains unaffected. If, however, Inst is confronted with questions or Const's own proposals, the dynamics of the focus of attention starts to be determined by the partner's speech acts. This temporal reversal of the communicative roles is insofar a direct one, as Inst as a recipient of the utterance focuses the objects (or relations - see below) Const refers to. Fig.12 provides an illustration: While describing the red and the yellow cuboids, Inst is distracted by a question of Const's, who introduces the green and the blue block mentioned earlier again into the zone of "joint attention".

Compared to these new findings, the discussion of hypotheses 6 and 7 is less exciting. While the assumed directions of foci are confirmed, the existence of privileged test-points is not corroborated by our results. Both Inst and Const seemed to be rather reluctant to take the trouble to reconsider their achievements, at least as long as no obvious problems occurred. In the face of the typically human strategy to minimize efforts, these results are not too surprising.

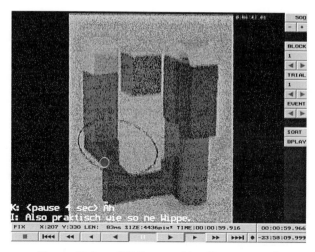

Figure 13: Inst: "Well, something like a see-saw"

3.4. Foveal fixations and focusing on properties and relations

The empirical material discussed here shows that not only objects as a whole can be in an agent's focus but also properties and relations of different sorts. This explains why sometimes visual fixations are localized not on objects, but, for instance, on regions of contact among them (in a partial refutation of Kurt Koffka's famous remark that "we perceive the objects and not spaces between them", see Koffka, 1935). Some further examples of property- and relation-oriented foci in the context of prototypical situations will be briefly discussed below. Although it is quite difficult to separate the different "contents" of foci, in most cases eye-movements data can serve as a tool to achieve such a separation.

(1) Focus yielding the basis for a comparison by metaphorical devices: Inst introduces the simile "see-saw" in order to characterize the front part of the assembly. Here clusters of foveal fixations concentrate on the block forming the characteristic beam of the "see-saw" (see fig.13). Focusing of a similar sort can be observed, if shapes or colors of different blocks are compared. (2) Focus on complex relations indicating positions: Inst has already introduced some block and describes the position of a new block to be placed on it. Here focus is on the area selected to support the new block. Focusing of this sort serves as a precondition for the production of verbs and prepositional phrases (e.g. *put something on something else*) or adverbs and adverbials indicating position (e.g. *left, right, in the middle*). (3) Focus on properties: If objects have already been introduced, focus can be on intrinsic properties of them, such as color. Similarly, intrinsic parts of objects, such as sides, bases or tops, often receive marking by focus.

Summing up, theoretical ideas about reference and focus in contemporary linguistics, cognitive philosophy, and AI – in order to be empirically interesting – have to be reformulated by taking into account three main results of our study. The first is that agents focus various regions of interest which directly influence speech production. The second result is the importance of anticipatory planning in language production that is manifested in the variant of the "Eye-voice span" phenomenon. The third is the evidence of the highly interactive character of focus-management in situated dialogue. Due to this interactive character of cooperation the size of the "Eye-voice span" can be flexibly reduced in the case of any cognitive or communicative problems by a convergence to the same area of common interest/efforts, i.e. to the zone of "joint attention".

4. TOWARDS COMMUNICATION OF PERSONAL VIEWS OF A SCENE

Both studies described above are related to disambiguation of reference in the processing of speech data. Objects, pictures and scenes are often extremely ambiguous, inducing different interpretations, depending on experience, mood, functional state and hundreds of other factors. For an efficient communication in real (as well as virtual) world these degrees of freedom of interpretation have to be bounded. In order to demonstrate the potential of eye-movement-based methods of attention-management in this domain of application we performed the following study using several notoriously ambiguous pictures, like Necker Cube, Escher's "Circlelimit IV" and "Earth" by Giuseppe Arcimboldo (Pomplun, Ritter, Velichkovsky, 1995 in press). There has been extensive research on ambiguous pictures throughout this century (Boring, 1942; Velichkovsky, Luria and Zinchenko, 1973; Rock, Hall and Davis, 1994). The question of interest is whether there are areas in every ambiguous picture that trigger particular interpretations when attended by the observer (cf. Gale, Findley, 1983, for earlier evidence). The first part of our experiment deals with this fundamental question.

In the second part of the study we made a further step: Based on the visual scanning pattern of several subjects, we processed the ambiguous pictures in a way that another subject, naïve to the scene, was directed towards a specific perceptive interpretation. The control of the subject's attention was achieved by highlighting those regions the former subjects preferred to fixate while having this specific perceptive interpretation.

4.1. Distribution of attention and interpretation of ambiguous pictures

We selected 6 ambiguous pictures as stimuli for our experiment. In this chapter, only one of these pictures, "Earth" by Giuseppe Arcimboldo (see fig.14), will be used as an example. It can be interpreted either as an assembly of various animals (interpretation A) or as a man's head facing the right side (interpretation B). Our intention was to record the fixations of a subject viewing this picture according to each of these interpretations.

One of the possible solutions of this problem is to prepare two unambiguous variants of the picture in such a way that they will support the interpretation A or B, respectively. These pictures can be shown separately and therefore separate fixation data can be recorded for each interpretation. The variant shown in fig.15 supports the perception of animals, because we had done minor changes on the original which made the shape of the head unrecognizable. The variant for interpretation B was achieved by a low-pass filtering of the initial picture to emphasize the global structure of the man's head (fig.16).

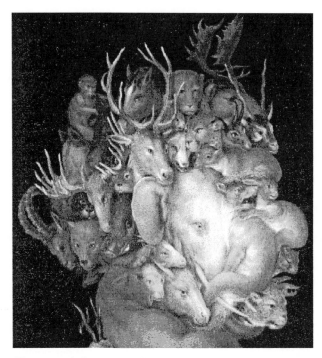

Figure 14: A fragment of "Earth" by Giuseppe Arcimboldo

However, in the case of using this method with unambiguous variants of the pictures we only receive gaze-position data with respect to static interpretations. It might be possible that there is a different distribution of fixations during the perception of the ambiguous picture. Therefore, we also recorded gaze-position data for each interpretation in a different way. While viewing the ambiguous picture our subjects got the task to press the left button of a computer mouse when perceiving variant A and the right button for variant B. According to these additional data, the fixations could be separated into two sets, one for each interpretation.

There were 6 subjects participating in the first part of the experiment. All 3 variants of the 6 pictures were successively shown to the subjects, the two unambiguous variants of a picture always preceding the ambiguous one. The unambiguous pictures were presented for 20 seconds, the ambiguous ones for 60 seconds. The order of presentation was counterbalanced across the subjects.

The presentation of the unambiguous pictures allowed us to record the fixation sets A and B, and the presentation of the ambiguous one the sets A' and B'. These later sets were obtained by dividing the fixation data in the way described above. In order to receive mathematical information concerning distributions of different fixation sets, we

Figure 15: In this variant of "Earth" the perception of animals is supported

defined a similarity measure yielding values in the range from 0 to 1. The similarities of fixation sets of different subjects recorded for the same picture and the same variant of interpretation were found to be in the interval from 0.75 to 0.90. Taking into account the specific measurement error of the eye-tracker, this result means that there were no significant differences in those fixation patterns. Hence, it was feasible to merge the 6 fixation sets for identical pictures into one larger set. Then we computed the similarity of every possible pairing of fixation sets A, B, A' and B' (as described above) for each picture. The results in case of "Earth" are shown in table 1. The comparisons of A with A' and B with B' yielded the highest similarity values with respect to most of the pictures. This fact shows that in these pictures there are specific regions to be attended while taking a specific perceptive interpretation. This does not depend on whether the interpretation is realized by a presentation of an ambiguous picture or its unambiguous variant.

The next step was to investigate the shape of these regions by visualizing them in the corresponding picture. Therefore we had to develop an adequate visualization method, which is the topic of the following section.

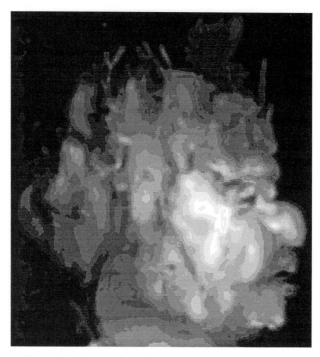

Figure 16: Here, only the structure of the head is visible

4.2. Different ways of gaze-dependent processing of pictures

During a very long period in measuring eye movements (e.g. Buswell, 1924; Yarbus, 1967, among many others) fixations were represented as sets of discrete points over a picture (fig.17a). Areas with a high density of fixations were interpreted as those which received most attention. However, attention is never directed to discrete mathematical points, but rather to more or less extended regions. The first method of deriving "areas of attention" from fixation points was based on cluster analysis (see Nodine, Kungel, Toto and Krupinski, 1992; Pillalamari, Barnette and Birkmire, 1993). One possible type of clustering is demonstrated in the previous section of this chapter, where clusters of fixations were marked by ellipses.

However, attention of a person is unlikely to be shaped like a set of ellipses with sharp boundaries (fig.17b). It is more realistic to define a smooth function as "attentional landscape" over the viewed picture. The higher the value of this function at a certain area of the picture is, the more attention is spent on it. In order to calculate a suitable function, we defined two-dimensional Gaussian distributions as "attentional components" centered at each fixation point and weighted for the duration of the corresponding fixation. The standard deviation of these distributions is set to one degree of the viewer's visual angle

comparison	similarity
A with B	41.0
A' with B'	70.8
A with A'	74.1
B with B'	84.2
A with B'	33.1
B with A'	60.4

Table 1: Similarities of fixation sets in %

according to the parameters of the idealized anatomic fovea. The "attentional landscape" can then be computed as the sum of these Gaussian distributions over the whole picture (fig.17c).

The visualization of this function can be achieved by processing every single pixel of the original picture. For instance, the initial brightness of each pixel can be multiplied by the value of the "attentional landscape" at its position. In the resulting picture the brightness of the regions which received higher attention is increased. For the observer this creates a "highlighting" effect in these areas (fig.17d).

4.3. Visualization and transfer of personal views of a picture

The second part of our experiment was based on the above-mentioned visualization of the "attentional landscape". For each of the 6 pictures we prepared two "highlighted" variants with respect to the fixation sets A' and B' for this picture. For the "Earth" picture these variants are shown in the next two figures, demonstrating significant differences in the attended regions between interpretations A and B. In Fig.18 the subjects had viewed various animals, so their attention was distributed rather homogeneously over the picture. But during perception of the "head" attention was strongly concentrated on the face region of the "man" as it is seen in fig.19.

We showed these 12 pre-processed and the 6 original pictures to 150 subjects who had not participated in the first part of the experiment. A counterbalanced subset of 6 pictures (two originals and four processed pictures), one for each thematic class of the pictures, was presented to every subject. The experimenter asked the subjects to describe the content of the pictures. Afterwards three experts agreed on which was the "first sight interpretation" (A or B) reported of each picture.

As concerns the original "Earth", 38 subjects found interpretation A ("animals") and 12 subjects interpretation B ("head"). When confronted with the picture processed according to interpretation A, all of the subjects selected interpretation A. In contrast, when the variant processed from the perspective of interpretation B was presented, only 8 subjects reported interpretation A, 42 subjects spontaneously chose interpretation B.

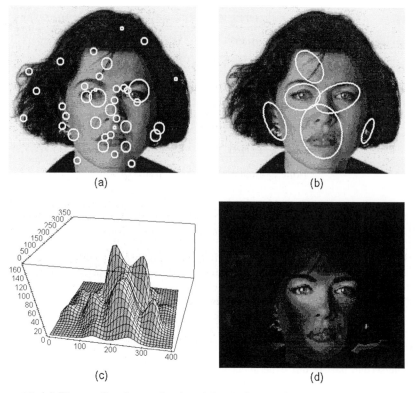

(a)   (b)

(c)   (d)

Figure 17: (a) Discrete fixations – the size of the circles signifies the duration of fixations, (b) ellipses as a result of a cluster analysis, (c) "attentional landscape" for the same data, (d) picture processed in terms of the "attentional landscape"

A statistical analysis (one-sided four fields χ^2-test: Lienert, 1973) of the data proves that the perception of the subjects has been significantly shifted in the predicted direction (uA = 3.87, p < 0.001; uB = 5.81, p < 0.001). This shift of interpretation was clearly found in most of the pictures with two exceptions - Necker Cube and Boring Figure. Both these pictures are black-and-white line drawings. One possible reason for the failure is that the modulation of brightness could not to be integrated into the main graphical theme of this class of pictures. On the whole however, the results of this study can be considered as a first successful step in communicative transfer of a person's subjective view of a complex scene.

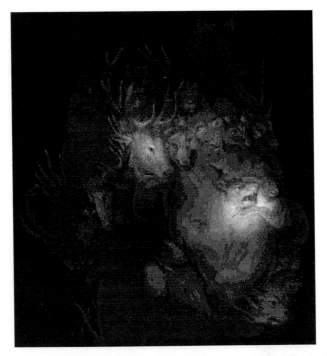

Figure 18: Picture processed according to the interpretation "animals"

5. CONCLUSIONS AND PERSPECTIVES

In this chapter we presented several new paradigms of eye movement research which allow to study communication, perception and cognition as coordinated processes, not separated among different "departments" of the brain's machinery. First of all, one can speak about a type of oculomotor behavior which does not serve visual information processing per se, but communication with others. Together with the discovery of express saccades (see Fischer, Weber, 1993), our data speak against the textbooks' wisdom of changing the fixation position "4-5 times" every second. This may well be the case in reading or in form perception, but not in other tasks. Especially in problem solving situations longer fixations and "dwell times" seem to be recognized as a rule (see Dick, 1980, among others). The emerging perspective is that different neurological levels of eye movement control have also different functional specializations. Eye movements in service of communication can be mediated by the evolutionary recent prefrontal fields (Bruce, Goldberg, 1984).

Another basic result is the first insight into the intricacy of cooperative behavior as it is seen in the analysis of partners' conversation, actions and eye movements. In particular,

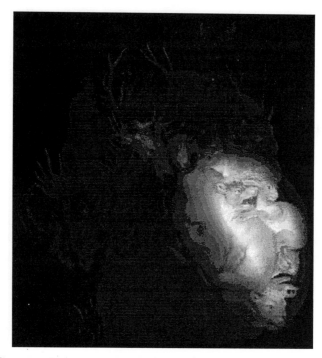

Figure 19: Picture processed according to the interpretation "head"

the data on the anticipatory management of attention, as in the discovered analogue to the classical "Eye-voice span" phenomenon, reveal a strong interaction of cognitive and linguistic variables sensitive to the course of communication and problem solving. The next step should be a description of the interaction within and outside of the zone of "joint attention". This task presupposes that simultaneous eye-tracking in both partners is possible.

The fast progress in eye-tracking and in digital image processing leaves no doubt that it will be soon possible to extend this research to more realistic 3-D situations. This appeals to the practical application of the methods. Several application domains are easily conceivable: 1. Support for physically disabled persons who are no longer in command of their limbs and speech mechanisms; 2. Interactive documentation and cooperative support, as in the case of a service engineer who – performing maintenance or repair work – might want to call up pertinent documentation without using hands or might want to describe the situation (to get advice) to an operator located at a remote site; 3. Enhancing low-bandwidth communication in such a way that the gaze position data will be used for the transmission at high resolution only of those areas of the image which are at the focus of attention; 4. Analysis and communication of tacit knowledge as, e.g. in sensorimotor skills or in some forms of visual medical expertise (cf. Norman, Coblentz, Brooks, Babcook, 1992).

Gaze-contingent image processing is of particular interest in this context. The explication of subjective views as well as person's immediate intentions can be the very missing link, which explains the well-documented priority of face-to-face communication to other, even most sophisticated forms of technologically mediated communication (Prieto, Acin, Zornoza, Peiro, 1995). Perhaps we are on the eve of a "subjective age" in the development of telematics. It will be characterized not only by the global orientation towards user's needs, but also by an orientation towards his/her immediate interests, efforts and intentions. As the only direct manifestation of attention, eye movements will be at the focus of this development.

Acknowledgements. We wish to thank Bruce Bridgeman, Theo Herrmann, Eyal Reingold, Helge Ritter, Dave Stampe and Mike Tomasello for their support in elaboration of this approach. Thomas Clermont, Clemens Meier, Peter Munsche, Elke Prestin and Karin Wagner greatly helped us in collecting and discussing the data. The study was supported by the German Science Foundation (DFG SFB 360) and in part by the Natural Sciences and Engineering Research Council of Canada.

REFERENCES

Boring, E.G., 1942, Sensation and perception in the history of experimental psychology. (Irvington, New York).

Bosch, P., and R. van der Sandt, eds., 1994, Focus and natural language Processing. 3 Vols. (IBM Institute for Logic and Linguistics, Heidelberg).

Bouma, H., 1978, Visual search and reading: Eye movements and functional visual field, in: Attention and Performance VII, ed. J. Requin (Lawrence Erlbaum, Hillsdale, NJ).

Bruce, C., and M. Goldberg, 1984, Physiology of the frontal eye field. Trends in Neuroscience **7**, 436.

Bruner, J., 1981, The pragmatics of acquisition, in: The child's construction of language, ed. W. Deutsch (Academic Press, New York).

Buswell, G.T., 1920, An experimental study of the Eye-Voice Span in reading. Supplementary Educational Monographs **17**, 2.

Chapanis, A., R.B. Ochsman, R.N. Parrish, and G.D. Weeks, 1972, Studies in interactive communication: 1. The effects of four communication modes on the behavior of teams during cooperative problem solving. Human Factors **14**, 487.

Chapanis, A., R.N. Parrish, R.B. Ochsman, and G.D. Weeks, 1977, Studies in interactive communication: 2. The effects of four communication modes on the linguistic performance of teams during cooperative problem solving. Human Factors **19**, 101.

Clark, E.V., and C.J. Sengul, 1978, Strategies in acquisition of deixis. Journal of Child Language **5**, 457.

Clark, H.H., 1991, Arenas of language use (The University of Chicago Press, Chicago).

Clark, H.H., and D. Wilkes-Gibbs, 1990, Referring as a collaborative process, in: Intentions in communication, eds. P.R. Cohen, J. Morgan, and M.E. Pollak (MIT Press, Cambridge, MA).

Clark, H.H., and D. Wilkes-Gibbs, 1992, Coordinating beliefs in conversation. Journal of Memory and Learning **31**, 183.

Dick, A.O., 1980, Instrument scanning and controlling: Using eye movement data to understand pilot behavior and strategies. Report No. NASA-CR-3306 (Langley Air Force Base, VA: National Aeronautics and Space Administration).

Fischer, B., and H. Weber, 1993, Express saccades and visual attention. Behavioral and Brain Sciences **16**, 553.

Gale, A.G., and J.M. Findley, 1983, Eye movement patterns in viewing ambiguous figures, in: Eye movements and psychological functions: International views, eds. R. Groner, C. Menz, D.F. Fisher, and R.A. Monty (Lawrence Erlbaum, Hillsdale, NJ).

Gibson, E., and N. Reder, 1979, Attention: The perceiver as performer, in: Attention and cognitive development, eds. G. Hale and M. Lewis (Plenum Press, New York).

Grosz, B.J., 1981, Focusing and description in natural language dialogues, in: Elements of discourse understanding, eds. A. Joshu, B. Webber, and I. Sag (Cambridge University Press, New York).

Hallett, P.E., 1985, Eye-movements, in: Handbook of perception and performance, Vol.1, eds. K.R. Boff, and L. Kaufman (John Wiley and Sons, New York).

Hering, E., 1977, The theory of binocular vision (Plenum Press, New York) (1st German edition 1868).

Herrmann, T., and J. Grabowski, 1994, Sprechen. Psychologie der Sprachproduktion (Spektrum, Heidelberg).

Hutchins, E., 1991, The social organization of distributed cognition, in: Perspectives on socially shared cognition, eds. L.B. Resnik, J.M. Levine, and S.D. Teasley (American Psychological Association, Washington, DC) p. 283.

Kahneman, D., 1973, Attention and effort (Prentice Hall, Englewood Hills).

Kamp, H., and U. Reyle, 1993, From discourse to logic (Kluwer, Dordrecht).

Koffka, K., 1935, Principles of Gestalt psychology (New York/London: Kegan Paul).

Krauss, R.M., and S.R. Fussel, 1991, Constructing shared communicative environments, in: Perspectives on socially shared cognition, eds. L.B. Resnik, J.M. Levine, and S.D. Teasley (American Psychological Association, Washington, DC) p. 172.

Lienert, G., 1973, Verteilungsfreie Methoden in der Biostatistik, 2. Auflage, Bd.1 (Verlag Anton Hain, Meisenheim/Glan).

Neisser, U., 1994, Multiple systems: A new approach to cognitive theory. European Journal of Cognitive Psychology **6**(3), 225.

Nodine, C.F., H.L. Kungel, L.C. Toto, and E.A. Krupinsky, 1992, Recording and analysing eye-position data using a microcomputer workstation. Behavioral Research Methods, Instruments, and Computers **24**(3), 475.

Norman, G.R., C.L. Coblentz, L.R.Brooks, and C.J. Babcook, 1992, Expertise in visual diagnostics: A review of the literature. Academic Medicine Rime Supplement **67**, 78.

Oram, M.W., D.I. Perrett, and J.K. Hietanen, 1993, Directional tuning of motion-sensitive cells in the anterior superior temporal polysensory area of the macaque. Experimental Brain Research **97**, 274.

Pillalamari, R.S., B.D. Barnette, and D. Birkmire, 1993, Cluster: A program for the identification of eye-fixation-cluster characteristics. Behavioral Research Methods, Instruments, and Computers **25**, 9.

Prieto, F., C. Avin, A. Zornoza, and H. Peiro, 1995, Telematic communication support to work group functioning, in: Proceedings of the 7th European Congress on Work and Organizational Psychology, Gyor, 19th–22nd of April.

Pomplun, M., B.M. Velichkovsky, and H. Ritter, 1994, An artificial neural network for high precision eye movement tracking, in: Lecture notes in artificial intelligence: AI-94 Proceedings, eds. B. Nebel and L. Dreschler-Fischer (Berlin: Springer Verlag).

Rieser, H., 1994, The role of focus in task oriented dialoge, in: Focus and Natural Language Processing, Vol.3, eds. P. Bosch and R. van der Sandt (IBM Institute for Logic and Linguistics, Heidelberg).

Rieser, H., and C. Meier, 1995, Modelling situated agents: "Reference shifts" in task-oriented dialogue (Report 95/12 of the SFB 360, University of Bielefeld).

Rock, I., S. Hall, and J. Davis, 1994, Why do ambiguous figures reverse? Acta Psychologica **87** 33.

Schegloff, E.A., G. Jefferson, and H. Sachs, 1977, The preference for self-correction in the organization of repair in conversation. Language **2**, 361.

Stampe, D.M., 1993, Heuristic filtering and reliable calibration methods for video-based pupil-tracking systems. Behavioral Research Methods, Instruments, and Computers **25**(2), 137.

Stampe, D.M., and E. Reingold, 1993, Eye movement as a response modality in psychological research, in: Proceedings of the 7th European Conference on Eye Movements, Durham, University of Durham, 31st of August – 3rd of September.

Tomasello, M., 1995, Joint attention as social cognition, in: Joint attention: Its origins and role in development, eds. C. Moore and P. Dunham (Hillsdale, NJ: Lawrence Erlbaum).

Tomasello, M., and M.J. Farrar, 1986, Joint attention and early language. Child Development **57**, 1454.

Velichkovsky, B.M., 1982, Visual cognition and its spatial-temporal context, in: Cognitive research in psychology, eds. F. Klix, J. Hoffman, and E.v.d.Meer (North Holland, Amsterdam).

Velichkovsky, B.M., 1990, The vertical dimension of mental functioning. Psychological Research **52**, 282.

Velichkovsky, B.M., 1994, The levels endeavour in psychology and cognitive science, in: Current advances in psychological science: Ongoing research, eds. P. Bertelson, P. Eelen, G. d'Ydewall (Lawrence Erlbaum, Hove, UK).

Velichkovsky, B.M., 1995a, Communication attention: Gaze-position transfer in cooperative problem solving. Pragmatics and Cognition **3**(2), 199.

Velichkovsky, B.M., 1995b in press, Language development at the crossroad of biological and cultural interactions, in: Human by nature: Origins and destiny of language, eds. B.M. Velichkovsky and D.M. Rumbaugh (Lawrence Erlbaum, Hillsdale, NJ).

Velichkovsky, B. M., E. Reingold, and D. Stampe, 1994, Communicative fixations: 'Joint attention' gain in cooperative problem solving, in: Proceedings of the 36th Meeting of experimentally-working psychologists, Ludwig-Maximilians-University, Munich, 28th–31st of March.

Velichkovsky, B.M., A.R. Luria, and V.P. Zinchenko, 1973, Psychology of perception (Moscow University Press, Moscow) (in Russian).

Vygotsky, L.S., 1962, Thought and language (MIT Press, Cambridge, MA) (1st Russian edition 1935).

Yarbus, A.L., 1967, Eye movements and vision (Plenum Press, New York) (1st Russian edition 1965).

CHAPTER 3

CLINICAL NEUROSCIENCE ASPECTS

Visual Attention and Cognition
W.H. Zangemeister, H.S. Stiehl and C. Freksa (Editors)

VISUAL ATTENTION AND COGNITION: A SYNOPSIS OF CLINICAL ASPECTS

Wolfgang H. Zangemeister

Neurological University Clinic, Hamburg
Martinistr.52, D 20251 Hamburg, FRG
e-mail: zangemeister@uke.uni-hamburg.de

Abstract

In this synopsis of chapter 3, an introduction and overview is given with regard to the functional anatomical and clinical neurophysiological aspects of visual attention and cognition.

Humans operate in a complex data rich world. Our visual system is constantly confronted with situations that require rapid processing and decision making. Yet, we are able to analyze almost effortlessly, information critical to the task at hand, while ignoring vast amounts of nonessential information. How is this done so effectively? Some have conjectured that top-down processes involving learning and semantic memory account for our ability to process information rapidly (Noton & Stark 1971; Homa et al. 1976; Friedman 1979; Julesz 1991). These processes form higher level associations among the components in a scene. Hence, efficiency in processing is gained by reducing the need for an element-by-element encoding of each item in the scene. How are these associations created? The associations among the components of a scene may be formed, for example, by using their spatial relations (Ullmann 1985), when performing a visual search. A simple example is that a schematic of a face is more readily perceived when the components of the eyes, nose and mouth are normally arranged as opposed to being scrambled. Another means of consolidating information is by its contextual significance based on the relation among the objects in a scene. Context in the natural environment plays an important role. This is because in a natural scene objects have powerful and complex relations, and the association of items in a scene provides the means for rapid and effective processing of visual information. The underlying association of this top-down contextual process with the bottom-up processes in early vision was recently investigated (Hung et al. 1995). It was demonstrated that better performance for simultaneous over sequentially presented items was a general phenomenon, independent of the kind of icons used. They suggested that both a parallel buffer and a serial retrieval mechanism linked to short term memory were involved in the early stages of visual processing. At the connectivity level of visual processing, contextual effects involved higher level processes that incorporated the complex relations among objects. The fact that these relations could be formed rapidly for briefly presented objects indicated that cortical neural connectivity may already be in place to facilitate these interactions.

Visual search has also been a subject of considerable study and interest in the neurosciences as well as operations research. Information as to how humans approach the search task is of great practical interest for applications ranging from air surveillance to manufacturing quality control inspections to search and rescue missions. The mathematical aspects of search theory go back to the probability of detection theory (Koopman 1956, 1957) that assumes that each glance or fixation is independent of the others. Most of these subsequent mathematical models have been based upon the effects of external environmental factors on search performance, ignoring or minimizing the effects of internal cognitive factors. Recent work includes psychophysical and human factors aspects of complex visual search and studies of eye movements during search. Storing and retrieving memories are important components of visual pattern recognition. Hence, the memory system of the brain must contain an internal representation of each pattern that is to be recognized. The process of constructing such representations is obscure. Recognition of a pattern may be viewed as the process of matching it with its stored internal representation. A non Gestalt view suggests that the internal model consists of component features that are matched step by step with the pattern during recognition. This serial recognition process is supported by the findings in several studies on object and pattern recognition that the eyes seem to visit the features of the object or items in the scene almost cyclically, following fairly stereotyped regular scanpaths or searchpaths rather than in random sequences. The scanpath was proposed to be the read-out of the internal representation of pictures, the so-called "cognitive model" (Noton & Stark 1971; Stark & Choi, this book).

Hochberg (1970) introduced the useful distinction between peripheral search guidance, in which the eye was drawn to move by information in the visual periphery and cognitive search guidance, in which the control of the eye was determined by some central plan as was suggested by the scanpath idea. It is difficult to develop these ideas at a general level because of the variety of forms that might be envisaged for such a central plan. However, the paradigm of visual search usefully constrains the subject's central plan to the task of locating a prespecified target. It is theoretically possible for eye movements during visual search to be totally controlled by cognitive guidance: for example by executing a predetermined systematic scan of the search area until the target is located in the fovea. However, it seems that more frequently, subjects attempt to extract some information from peripheral vision to direct the eyes to the target and thus the pattern of the eye movements during search appears much less systematic. Specification of the size of the object is much less effective and subjects show very little ability to direct their fixation to objects of a prespecified shape. These conclusions in many ways anticipated a current theme in visual search, the feature integration theory (Treisman 1980). This theory states that simple features can be searched for rapidly in parallel, whereas more complex features and combinations of features require a serial search process, involving either covert or overt attentional shifts. Feature integration theory has for the most part relied on indirect measures of attention and paid little attention to the detailed mechanisms of search such as oculomotor control.

The processes underlying shifting of attention from one item to another have recently been studied (Findlay; Seitz; Husain & Kennard, this book). Subjects were required to shift spatial attention in the right or left visual field along foveofugal or foveocentral directions. It was found that the superior parietal and superior lateral frontal cortex were more active when *shifting* attention compared to *maintaining* attention at the center of gaze. Further, the superior parietal region was active when peripheral locations were selected on the basis of cognitive or sensory cues, while the frontal region was active only when responses were made to stimuli at selected peripheral locations. These observations pointed to a more perceptive role of the parietal activations and motor related activation in the frontal lobe for shifts of attention. Interestingly, these areas of activation were present in both cerebral hemispheres for both visual hemifields in an almost overlapping manner. However, in the parietal lobe of the right hemisphere the visual hemifields were separated with a more posterior location of the right visual hemifield. Since the direction of the moving stimuli did not separate the activation areas, these rCBF increases in the parietal lobe did not simply reflect responses to spatial locations. Rather, they indicated a more widespread involvement of the right parietal lobe for shifting of attention. Raised attention during a first PET scan has been shown to specifically activate the prefrontal cortex, the superior parietal cortex, the cingulate, and the thalamus (Seitz & Roland 1992). Conversely, patients suffering from hemineglect revealed significant metabolic depressions in superior lateral frontal cortex, superior and inferior parietal, and cingulate cortex (von Giesen et al.1994). These areas included or were located in close neighbourhood to those specifically activated in active focussing and shifting of attention. These positive (activation) and negative (lesion) findings support the concept of a large-scale neuronal system underlying visual attention (Mesulam 1990).

Husain & Kennard start their review with the simple question: What happens during the saccadic reaction time? They review evidence which suggests focal attention normally engages a visual stimulus before a saccade is made to foveate it. Attention can be directed without making an eye movement and, under certain circumstances, in the direction opposite to an eye movement. So, the directing of focal attention does not automatically lead to the generation of a saccade and the two processes can be dissociated. Attention normally appears to shift to the target of a saccade before the eye movement is made. It therefore seems to be an important early step in preparing an eye movement. Exactly what this means in terms of neural operations or representations is yet unclear, but our understanding may improve with further analysis of the contributions of the posterior parietal cortex (PPC), pulvinar and superior colliculus.

The main function of the peripheral part of the retina is that of 'sentinels' which, when beams of light move over them, 'cry: "Who goes there?" and call the fovea to the spot,' remarked William James (1890). Husain & Kennard suggest, there is sufficient evidence to conclude that the parietal cortex, pulvinar and superior colliculus form part of the core neural architecture normally responsible for directing attention and gaze to visual targets. This group of structures serves the role of 'sentinel' in the primate visual system.

Visual search is influenced by multi-item boundary and surface groupings. These may indeed represent the perceptual representations on which the search process is based. The identification of a grouping that includes multiple items speeds search by reducing the total number of candidate visual regions that have serially to be investigated. Factors which influence boundary and surface grouping, such as featural contrast, item spacing, and spatial arrangement alter this number of visual regions to be explored, yielding variations in search time. If bottom-up mechanisms may drive the formation of these emergent perceptual units, then limits must exist on the capacity of semantic or even visual definitions of target items to exert top-down influence over preattentive grouping mechanisms. The ability of bottom-up processing to accurately distinguish ecological objects depends on a certain amount of autonomy or resistance to top-down interference. Otherwise, it would routinely result in perceptual illusions. Perceptual grouping indeed will often be guided by top-down processes (Stark et al.1992; Desimone 1993). However, some groupings may "emerge" from the structure of the scenic input without the help of top-down influences. Of course, the enforced bottom-up control of viewing is the main domain of our everyday modern life through movies, TV and visual public relation in particular. We learn and we apply these different kinds of top-down control of viewing during our whole life. However, diseases of the eyes, the optical pathways, the visual or motor cortex and its interconnections may cause, that at least one of the three parts of this control becomes disturbed: the sensory, the cognitive, or the motor connection that contribute to the proper functioning of these high levels of visual control.In case of deficiencies of one of these functional parts there is a need to recover from the given deficit, which may be feasible through certain strategies of adaptation. The typical, most frequent deficits that can be found clinically, — and may be simulated experimentally —, are: (1) Motor deficits of one or two eyes with deficits of coordinated eye-movements that may cause doublevision, or slowness and inaccuracy of eye fixation and eye movement; they can be overcome comparatively easily by moving only the healthy eye, and neglecting, i.e. suppressing the information of the eye with the movement deficits; or by helping interocular deficits through adaptive eye- and head- coordination, like in internuclear ophthalmoplegia. (2) More importantly, sensory deficits may disturb top-down control of vision by visual field defects of one eye, or both eyes in case of more centrally located disturbances as is the case in homonymous hemianopia. (3) Most variant difficulties and therefore a whole variety of adaptive strategies may occur with deficits of visual attention and cognition, like visual apraxia and hemineglect. Studies of these effects in hemianopic patients (Zangemeister & Oechsner, this book; Zangemeister et al.1982, 1985, 1995; Schoepf & Zangemeister 1993) demonstrate that it is feasible and quantifiable to observe short term adaptation as an effect of short term training in patients with hemianopic field defects who apply and optimize a high level, top-down visuo-motor strategy to search and scan for targets and sequences of targets in complex visual tasks. This strategy is also evident when patients use very small eye movements, i.e. mini saccades. Evidences for top-down versus bottom-up control are given from that study with respect to the paradox that top-down cognitive models prevail when we see, whereas local stair-steps of bottom-up control prevail, when we are blind. Also, the "complexity" of the picture - "attraction versus distraction"- influences the control of eye movement sequences of fixations in the case of homonymous hemianopia. Evidently, global viewing is the preferred strategy for the healthy subject, who tries to evaluate at the same time both the visual content and the complexity of the picture. Hemianopic patients however, are more busy with developing an optimal sequence of eye movements to detect the overall features of the picture when searching or scanning, since they have primarily to rely on more local and therefore limited picture evaluations that also include more bottom-up control than in the healthy subjects.

What is local scanning? Even though Noton & Stark (1971) and Stark & Ellis (1981) showed that peripheral information can be excluded as the immediate control for the scanpath, their results relate to local scanpaths. Groner et al. (1984) and also Finke (1983) support their top-down, cognitive model scanpath theory for a global scanpath, but argue in favour of an immediate peripheral bottom-up control of local scanning, although evidence for the latter is not conclusive at the present time. Jeannerod et al. (1968) has argued for an exchange between local and global scanning in free exploration. Evidently, the normal healthy viewer avoids this type of immediate bottom-up control in favour of the top-down controlled global scanpath, whereas the patient when viewing to the side of the blind hemifield relies strongly on such an exchange, that permits him to develop a more and more efficient strategy of searching and scanning with every repetition.

Whether the local scanpath is driven immediately by peripheral, bottom-up information or by small-scale cognitive models is unknown. Locher & Nodine (1987) have claimed immediate bottom up control in symmetry "that catches the eye". Mackworth & Morandi (1967) showed evidence for top-down active selection of informative details through "active looking". This detailed looking is apparently usually applied for realistic images, where anticipation of details may be balanced by a permanent exchange of bottom-up and top-down control (Zangemeister et al. 1995). Hemianopic patients carry this behaviour on to ambiguous and non-realistic images. Obviously with increasing complexity it is more difficult, to apply efficiently a bottom-up control as was shown earlier by Berlyne (1958; 1971), and this result applies also for the blind side of hemianopic patients.

Hemianopic patients may have lost one half of their central vision. But they are still capable, and often highly efficient, in integrating what the have "looked at": such that they may even "see" what is in their blind hemifield through applying preview control, prediction and closely connected visual integration. By far the most interesting examples of a failure of visual integration are to be found in patients with visual agnosia. Neurologists commonly speak of such patients as if they are 'form blind', suffering from object agnosia. But opinion on the subject has been divided, at least in part because the syndrome itself is complex and manifests itself with variations in different patients. Patients may be able to recognize some objects, but not others; they may not recognize an object at one examination and yet be able to do so at a subsequent one. Some may be able to read while others cannot. The lesions are commonly large, often associated with scotomas and some, but not all, patients suffer from problems of amnesia, aphasia and general mental deterioration.

All this makes it difficult to relate a specific impairment to a specific cerebral defect. Indeed, some neurologists have put forward the view that visual agnosia is nothing more than the consequence of a failing visual apparatus. Yet there exists a sufficient number of patients whose eyes are normal, who are not aphasic and who do not suffer from mental deterioration to testify to the fact that there is a syndrome in which patients can apparently see objects, or at least parts of objects, and yet be unable to recognize what the objects are. Since integration itself is a multistage process, one should not be surprised to find that there are degrees of agnosia, ranging from the severe effects of carbon monoxide poisoning, due to damage of Vl itself, to the relatively mild ones due to damage of more central visual areas. Of course, integration can also operate in the opposite direction, i.e. top-down, and patients as well as healthy people can be made to see things once they have understood them, but not until then. So, this is another way of looking at these defects, and the result of such an enquiry leads us to the view that seeing and understanding merge into one another, and are not discrete activities localizable to different parts of the cerebral cortex. Contrariwise, clinical evidence suggests that many examples of visual agnosia can be considered to be failures of the integrative mechanisms in the brain, leading the patient to both see and understand only in relation to the capabilities of the *intact* parts of the brain.

References

Berlyne, D.E. (1958), 'The influence of complexity and novelty in visual figures on orienting responses', *J.Exp.Psychol.* **55**, 289–296.

Berlyne, D.E., McDonnel, P. (1951), 'Effects of complexity and prechoice stimulation on exploratory choice', *Perception and Psychophysics* **10**, 241 – 246.

Finke,R.A. (1983), 'Directional scanning of remembered visual patterns', *J. Exp. Psychol.* **9**, 398 – 410.

Friedman, A. (1979), 'Framing pictures: the role of knowledge in automatized encoding and memory for gist'. *J. Exp. Psychol. Gen.* **108**, 316–355.

Groner, R., Walder, F., Groner, M. (1984), 'Looking at faces: Local versus global aspects of scanpaths', *in* A.G. Gale and F. Johnson, eds, 'Theoretical and Applied Aspects of Scanpaths', North Holland Publ. Company, Amsterdam, pp. 58 – 59.

Hochberg, J. (1968), 'In the Mind's Eye'. *in* R.N. Haber, ed, 'Contemporary Theory and Research in Visual Perception', Holt, Rinehart and Winston Publ., New York, pp. 309 – 312.

Hochberg J. (1970), 'Components of literacy: speculations and exploratory research', *in* H. Levin and J.P. Williams, eds, 'Basic studies on reading', New York, Basic Books.

Homa D., Haver B., Schwartz T. (1976), 'Perceptibility of schematic face stimuli: evidence for a perceptual gestalt', *Mem. Cognit.* **4**, 176–185.

Hung G.K., Wilder J., Curry R., Julesz B. (1995), 'Simultaneous better than sequential for brief presentations', *J. Opt. Soc. Am. A* **12**, 441–449.

James, W. (1890), 'The Principles of Psychology', New York, Holt.

Jeannerod, M., Gerin, P., Pernier, J. (1968), 'Deplacements et fixation du regard dans l'exploration libre d'une scene visuelle', *Vision Res.*, **8**, 81–97.

Julesz, B. (1991), 'Early vision and focal attention', *Rev. Modern Physics* **63**, 735–772.

Koopman, B.O. (1956), 'The theory of search Pt. I: Kinematic bases', *Oper. Res.* **4**, 324–246.

Koopman, B.O. (1956), 'The theory of search Pt. II: Target detection', *Oper. Res.* **4**, 503–531.

Koopman, B.O. (1957), 'The theory of search Pt. III: The optimum

distribution of searching effort', *Oper. Res.* **5**, 613–626.

Locher, P.J., Nodine, C.F. (1987), 'Symmetry catches the eye', *in* J.K. O'Reagan and A. Levy-Schoen, eds, 'From Physiology to Cognition', North Holland Publ. Company, Amsterdam, p. 353.

Mackworth, N.H., Morandi, A.Y. (1967), 'The gaze selects informative details within pictures', *Perception and Psychophysics* **2**, 547–552.

Mesulam, M.M. (1990), 'Large-scale neurocognitive networks and distributed processing for attention, language, and memory', *Ann. Neurol.* **28**, 597–613.

Noton, D., Stark, L. (1971), 'Scanpaths in eye movements during pattern perception', *Science* **171**, 308–311.

Schoepf D., Zangemeister, W.H. (1993), 'Correlation of Coordinated Gaze Strategies to the Status of Adaptation in Patients with Hemianopic Visual Field Defects', *Ann. N.Y. Acad. Sci.* **682**, 404–409.

Stark, L., Ellis, S. (1981), 'Scanpaths revisited: Cognitive Models in Active Looking', *in* B. Fisher, C. Monty and M. Sanders, eds, 'Eye Movements, Cognition and Visual Perception', Erlbaum Press, New Jersey, pp. 193–226.

Stark, L., Yamashita, I., Tharp, G., Ngo, H.X. (1992), 'Searchpatterns and searchpaths', *in* D. Brogan and K. Carr, eds, 'Visual Search II', Taylor & Francis, pp. 37–58.

Seitz, R.J., Roland, P.E. (1992), 'Variability of the rCBF measured with (11C)-fluoromethane and positron emission tomography (PET) in rest', *Comp. Med. Imaging. Graphics.* **5**, 311–322.

Treisman, A. (1980), 'A feature integration theory of attention', *Cognit. Psychol.* **12**, 97–136.

Ullman, S. (1985), 'Visual Cognition, Visual Routines', Cambridge, MA, MIT Press.

von Giesen, H.J., Schlaug, G., Steinmetz, H., Benecke, R., Freund, H.J., Seitz, R.J., 1994, Cerebral network underlying unilateral motor neglect: evidence from positron emission tomography. *J. Neurol. Sci.* **125**, 29–38.

Zangemeister, W.H., Meienberg, O., Stark, L., Hoyt, W.F. (1982), 'Eye-Head Coordination in Homonymous Hemianopia', *J. Neurol.* **225**, 243 – 254.

Zangemeister, W.H., Dannheim, F. (1985), 'Adaptation of Gaze to Eccentric Fixation in Homonymous Hemianopia', *in* E.L. Keller and D. Zee, eds, 'Adaptive Processes in Visual and Oculomotor Systems', *Adv. in Bio. Sci.* **57**, 247 – 252.

Zangemeister, W.H., Sherman, K., Stark, L. (1995), 'Evidence for global Scanpath strategy in viewing abstract compared to realistic images', *Neuropsychologia* **33**, 1009–1025.

Zeki, S., Shipp, S. (1988), 'The functional logic of cortical connections', *Nature* **335**, 311–317.

Visual Attention and Cognition
W.H. Zangemeister, H.S. Stiehl and C. Freksa (Editors)
165

THE ROLE OF ATTENTION IN HUMAN OCULOMOTOR CONTROL

Masud Husain and Christopher Kennard

Academic Unit of Neuroscience,
Charing Cross and Westminster Medical School
London, W6 8RF, United Kingdom

ABSTRACT

It has been proposed that saccadic eye movements to visual targets are preceded by covert shifts of attention to these locations. In this review, we discuss the evidence for this hypothesis and the role of brain regions in directing rapid shifts of attention and gaze. We suggest there is a common neural architecture mediating both these types of movement.

Keywords: Attention. Saccades. Posterior parietal cortex. Pulvinar. Superior colliculus.

The human visuomotor system is designed to explore the world *rapidly*. Peripheral vision serves to detect novel events and summons the fovea, responsible for high acuity vision, to scrutinize these more closely. The time between first detecting an object at the edge of the visual field and observing it with foveal vision is astoundingly short: just over 200 ms. But only a very small fraction of this is taken up with moving the eye. What happens during the rest of this period - the saccadic reaction time - has come to be the subject of great interest and debate. There is no argument that part of the saccadic reaction time is attributable to registering and localising the object of interest. There is also no doubt that part of the time must be devoted to activating the ocular motorneurone pool in the brainstem which is responsible for shifting the globe appropriately within the orbit. But does attention play any role in the events which occur in between? Why should anyone think it would?

1. COVERT SHIFTS OF ATTENTION

1.1. Posner paradigm
Consider first what happens when we notice a novel object in the periphery but make an effort *not* to move our eyes to inspect it more closely.

A number of studies have investigated what happens in this situation. When subjects fixate a central stimulus and are then cued to expect a novel event at a peripheral location by transiently illuminating that area, it has repeatedly been observed that manual reaction times to the onset of a stimulus at the cued locations are reduced compared to those occurring at uncued areas (Posner, 1980). In other words, there is a benefit in response time if the stimulus appears at the cued location. If, on occasions, the cue is invalid so the stimulus appears at a location other than that at the cued one, manual response times are increased.

The hypothesis has therefore been advanced that attention is spatially selective and may best be thought as a 'spotlight'. Posner (1980) has argued that when attention is cued to a location, the spotlight disengages from the fixation point and shifts to the cued area in anticipation of the stimulus. This is why short manual response times occur when the stimulus is flashed there. If the cue is invalid, however, the spotlight of attention has to shift quickly from the invalidly cued zone to the area where the stimulus is flashed. Hence, the cost in increased reaction time. If this interpretation is correct, attention can clearly be oriented covertly, without simultaneous movement of the eyes. But does it normally play a role in the generation of eye movements or overt shifts of attention?

1.2. Gap paradigm and express saccades

Saslow (1967) first demonstrated that saccadic reaction times are substantially shorter if the target which the eyes are fixating is extinguished before a novel target is presented, i.e. if there is a gap between these two events. In more recent years, Fischer and his colleagues have replicated and investigated this effect in more detail. They call these fast saccades, which have reaction times of ~100 ms, express saccades (see Fischer, 1987).

Fischer has proposed that express saccades tell us something about the normal role of attention in directing eye movements. He suggests that before a saccade can be made to a novel visual target, attention first needs covertly to disengage from the current fixation point, shift to the new target and engage it (Fischer, 1987; Fischer & Weber, 1993). This takes time and contributes to the duration of the normal saccadic reaction time. If, however, the fixation point is extinguished prior to target onset, attention is already disengaged when the target is flashed. So, the overall saccadic reaction time (measured from target onset) is reduced.

The parallels between Posner's model of covert attention and Fischer's theory of directed attention in saccadic eye movements are very apparent. Attention can clearly be directed without moving the eyes, but Fischer suggests a saccadic eye movement to a visual target first requires attention to move covertly and engage it. The idea is obviously appealing because it proposes a mechanism common to both the visual and oculomotor systems.

1.3. Why do express saccades occur?

A theory such as Fischer's is eminently testable, but unfortunately it still remains controversial. Many laboratories have failed to record saccades with express latency and a nagging worry has developed that express saccades may be anticipatory movements to predictable targets. In other words, they represent eye movements which are planned in anticipation, and not as a consequence, of target onset. Fischer has argued strongly against such an interpretation by demonstrating that express saccades may be recorded when target location and timing is unpredictable (Fischer & Weber, 1993).

Some laboratories have been successful in documenting express eye movements. However, the interpretation of why they occur varies. Reulen (1984) suggested that fixation stimulus offset leads to faster sensory processing of an eccentric visual target, i.e., it is easier to detect a target in a blank field than in the presence of a fixation point. Others have argued that fixation offset acts specifically to prepare the oculomotor system, so-called 'oculomotor readiness', because saccadic latencies are reduced in certain gap paradigms when manual response times are not (e.g., Reuter-Lorenz *et al.*, 1991; Reuter-Lorenz & Fendrich, 1992). This dissociation suggests the gap between fixation offset and target onset facilitates the saccadic system but not attention in general.

Perhaps the strongest evidence for an effect specific to motor systems comes from recent experiments conducted by Kingstone and Klein (1993). These investigators elegantly integrated into gap paradigms the cost-benefit analysis for manual response times Posner used to study covert attention. Using visual cues, they sought to shift attention covertly away from the fixation point and see if this had any effect on saccadic or manual reaction times. If attention is already disengaged from fixation and engaged on another stimulus, saccadic and manual reaction times should be reduced only when the attended stimulus is extinguished prior to target onset.

The results show that saccadic latencies, but not manual response times, are reduced when the fixation stimulus is extinguished prior to target onset *irrespective* of where attention is allocated. Offset of non-fixation stimuli which were covertly attended to had some, but significantly less, impact on reducing *both* saccadic and manual response times. But so did the offset of control unattended stimuli. Kingstone and Klein (1993) argue these results demonstrate two factors. First, offset of fixation stimuli reduces only saccadic reaction times so this appears to be an effect specific to the oculomotor system. Second, offset of other stimuli in the visual field reduces both saccadic and manual reaction times. This may represent an effect on motor preparation in general. Movements of covert attention, they argue, cannot explain their data.

Although this study is a remarkably careful assessment of the role of covert attention in the gap paradigm it has one shortcoming as an attack on the Fischer hypothesis: the mean latencies of the saccades were much longer than express movements. It could easily be argued that the brain events which occur in complex paradigms designed by Kingstone and Klein are fundamentally different from those which are responsible for generating express saccades. The alternative view is that express saccades tell us nothing useful about attention and only about the anticipatory capabilities of the human oculomotor system! Clearly, the gap paradigm is going to continue to be a rich source of investigation and controversy. But is there evidence from any other type of non-gap experiment that attention is first allocated to a peripheral visual target before the eyes move to engage it?

1.4. Do shifts of attention precede saccadic eye movements?

The first piece of evidence a cynic would wish to consider is whether saccadic latency is affected by directing attention to a point in space. Although some studies failed to demonstrate an effect, it is now clear that saccadic reaction times to cued locations can be significantly shorter than to uncued ones (e.g., Crawford and Muller, 1992; Shepherd et al, 1986). The differences are small - of the order of 20-30 ms - but cannot be accounted for by a fixation offset effect. Is there any other evidence that attention and saccadic eye movements are associated?

Nissen, Posner and Snyder (see Posner, 1980) asked subjects to make saccadic eye movements to a peripheral stimulus which appeared 7 degrees either to the left or right of fixation. In the same experiment, they measured manual reaction times to the onset of a probe stimulus which could be flashed at varying times either at the fixation point or near the saccade target. Mean saccadic reaction time was >200 ms. When the probe was presented at the same time as the saccade target, manual response times were the same irrespective of where the probe appeared. However, when the probe was presented >100 ms after the appearance of the saccade target, manual response times were significantly shorter if it appeared near the saccade target than at fixation.

Remington (1980) used a similar paradigm but asked his subjects to detect a 3 ms increment in luminance. Increased sensitivity to increments at the target location occurred within 100 ms after target onset, again well before eye movements occurred. These results suggest that attention moves covertly to a target before the eyes do. But must it? Can attention be dissociated from eye movement when a saccade is about to be made? One approach to answering this question is to direct attention away from the direction of an eye movement. At least three groups of experimenters have attempted to investigate this.

Shepherd and his colleagues measured manual response times to probe visual stimuli, either with the eyes remaining fixated or when saccades were made to visual targets (Shepherd et al, 1986). In one condition subjects were cued by a central arrow to shift attention toward a location which had only 20% probability of a probe appearing there subsequently. On 80% of trials the probe would appear at a point equidistant away from the fixation point but in contralateral space. Probes could appear at various times (stimulus onset asynchronies) after the onset of the cue. When subjects were asked to keep their eyes fixated it was found that manual responses to the probe stimuli were much faster if they appeared on the uncued side. In other words, subjects mentally reversed the direction of the cue arrow and appeared to shift attention to the uncued side which had the higher probability of probe appearance.

If subjects were instructed to make a saccadic eye movement to the cued location the pattern of manual response times was very different. In this condition, the eyes were instructed to move in the direction opposite to the likely position of the probe in 80% of trials. If attention can shift independently of the eyes, it ought still to be possible to allocate it to the uncued side whilst the eyes move toward the cued side. This does not appear to be the case because manual responses to probes appearing at the location of the saccade target were significantly shorter than those at the uncued side until well after the saccade had been completed. The interpretation of the investigators is that making a saccade *necessarily* requires attention to be allocated to the target position (Shepherd *et al*, 1986).

Quite the opposite conclusion has been advanced by Klein (1980) and Posner (1980) for the results of their own experiments which also required attention to be oriented away from the direction of eye movement. Using probe paradigms they found evidence to suggest attention could move in the direction opposite to eye movement. They therefore concluded that movements of attention *do not necessarily* have to precede eye movements to visual targets.

The problem with all these experiments is that they are complex and demanding of the observer. Perhaps the fairest summary of the evidence to date is that, under certain conditions, attention can be dissociated from eye movement when a saccade is about to be made *but* this is unlikely to occur normally in human visuomotor behaviour. Nevertheless, once it is accepted that movements of attention are not mandatory for eye movements it follows that neural mechanisms underlying these behaviours need not converge and may be completely separate. Our interpretation is not so extreme. There is ample evidence, we believe, that the neural systems involved in directing covert attention and eye movements to visual targets are normally not completely parallel (see also Rizzolatti *et al.*, 1985).

2. NEURAL ARCHITECTURE OF DIRECTED ATTENTION

2.1. Role of posterior parietal cortex

In order to find convergence of neural systems subserving attention and oculomotor control one has to consider whether there are brain regions which appear to be involved in both processes. It has long been suspected that the posterior parietal cortex (PPC) of man is somehow involved in perception, directing attention and motor control. Bálint (1907) first described a patient with bilateral infarcts of this area who experienced difficulty in noticing novel visual stimuli in the environment around him. On cursory examination the patient appeared to have a fixation of gaze but it soon became apparent that he did not have a gaze palsy; he simply did not notice visual objects which were not located in central vision. Even when he did notice them, the patient had great difficulty in shifting gaze from one object to another (see Husain & Stein, 1988).

Holmes (1918) described patients with lesions of the parietal lobes who had difficulty in maintaining fixation or moving gaze. Some of them also suffered from an impairment of visual localization, "groping ..... in a manner more or less like a man searching for a small object in the dark". Since these early investigations, a number of other syndromes - perceptual, attentional, motor, or a combination - have come to be associated with injury to the PPC (see DeRenzi, 1982; Husain, 1991). However, it has not been until relatively recently that the contribution of the PPC to directing attention and eye movements has been scrutinized in detail.

Posner and his colleagues studied how patients with unilateral parietal lobe injury perform on cueing tasks which require them covertly to shift attention. The patients performed reasonably well except on trials with invalid cues presented in the visual field ipsilateral to their lesions. On such occasions, subjects have to redirect attention from the ipsilaterally cued location to the contralateral field where the target appears. Patients appear to have trouble disengaging attention from ipsilateral locations and moving it in the opposite direction (Posner et al, 1984, 1987). Damage to the parietal cortex also leads to difficulties in directing attention if the visual field is diffusely illuminated transiently before a target for covert attention is presented (Petersen et al, 1989). Investigations of saccadic eye movements to visual targets after brain injury also suggest a special role for the parietal cortex in directing overt shifts of attention. Damage to this area produces significant increases in saccadic reaction time to visual targets (Pierrot-Deseilligny et al., 1991) and, interestingly, reduces the frequency of express saccades (Braun et al., 1992).

Many of these effects appear to be relatively specific to parietal lobe damage but clearly the PPC is not essential for these activities since they can be performed, albeit less swiftly or effectively, after it has been injured. Is there evidence from any other source that the parietal cortex is normally involved in shifting attention both covertly and overtly? In humans, scalp recordings have consistently demonstrated a negative potential over the parietal cortex which occurs ~100-200 ms after a visual event. The amplitude of this N-wave is enhanced when subjects attend to a location (e.g., Van Voorhis & Hillyard, 1977). There also appears to be activity over human parietal cortex prior to a visually-guided saccadic eye movement. A premotor positivity can be recorded 100-200 ms before the saccade and this appears to be maximal over the PPC (e.g., Kurtzberg & Vaughan, 1982; Thickbroom & Mastaglia, 1985).

Positron emission tomography (PET) has also been employed to image brain function whilst normal human subjects shift attention or their eyes to visual targets. Activation of the superior parietal and superior frontal cortices was observed when subjects covertly shift attention to peripheral locations (Corbetta et al.,1993). If they are requested to make eye movements to visual targets there is again activation of parietal and frontal regions (Fig.1) (e.g., Anderson et al.,1994).

Electrophysiological recordings from rhesus monkey PPC have also contributed to our understanding of neural systems underlying shifts of attention and eye movement to visual targets. 'Light-sensitive' cells in area 7a of the PPC have large receptive fields. They respond to the onset of novel visual stimulus and their firing is enhanced if the animal has to attend covertly to it (Bushnell et al., 1981; Mountcastle et al., 1981, 1984). The responses of these neurones is modulated by eye position and they may be involved in encoding the location of an attended visual stimulus in head- or body-centred coordinates (Andersen et al.,1985, 1993). 'Fixation' neurones discharge when an animal fixates upon a visual object of interest but their activity falls dramatically when a saccade is made (Yin & Mountcastle, 1978). They too are modulated by eye position (Sakata et al., 1980). The firing of cells in the adjacent lateral intraparietal area (LIP) appears more related to saccadic eye movements, i.e., overt shifts of attention to a visual target. On average this activity occurs ~10 ms before a saccade but some cells appear to discharge much earlier before the movement (Barash et al.,1991; Duhamel et al.,1992).

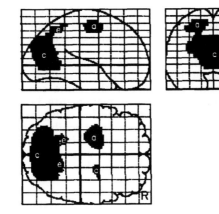

Figure. 1. Comparison of adjusted mean regional cerebral blood flow between 'reflexive' saccades to visual targets and fixation displayed as statistical parametric maps (SPM) in sagittal, coronal and transverse projections. a, Frontal eye field; c, peripheral striate and extra-striate cortex; e, area 7 of the posterior parietal cortex (see Anderson *et al.*, 1994).

This survey of the evidence from studies conducted in humans and monkeys demonstrates the involvement of the PPC in both directing attention and eye movements to visual targets. But what exactly is its contribution? Although the answer is not clearly established, it has been suggested the PPC is involved in several aspects of sensorimotor transformation: localizing objects in head- or body-centred coordinates, in directing focal attention across such representations of space and computing movement vectors between target position and current eye position (Andersen, 1987; Husain, 1991; Lynch, 1980; Mountcastle *et al.*, 1984). Whether these activities represent separate neural operations or the same one is not yet clear. Furthermore, some investigators remain hesitant to interpret their findings as 'premotor' activity within the PPC (e.g., Duhamel *et al.*, 1992).

2.2. Role of pulvinar
The pulvinar nucleus of the thalamus is another area of the brain which appears to demonstrate responses related to both the directing of attention and eye movements to visual stimuli. Electrophysiological recordings from this area in monkey have demonstrated responses to visual stimuli. As in the PPC, the firing of these neurones is enhanced when the animal covertly directs attention to such stimuli or moves its eyes to engage them (Petersen *et al.*, 1985). Furthermore, when muscimol, an analogue of the inhibitory neurotransmitter GABA, is injected into the pulvinar, monkeys have difficulty in shifting attention into the contralateral field (Petersen *et al.*, 1987). There is little data on the role of the pulvinar in humans. PET studies

have failed to demonstrate any activation of this area in cueing tasks (Corbetta et al., 1983), but patients with injury to this region appear to have difficulty in responding to visual targets in the contralateral field (Rafal et al.,1987).

Perhaps it is not surprising to find that the pulvinar and the PPC have very strong reciprocal connections. Clearly, the neural operations these regions perform are closely related, but the exact contribution of the pulvinar to directing attention or eye movements is even less well understood than that of the PPC. Posner and his collegues have suggested that it plays a role in engaging a visual target whilst the PPC serves to disengage attention from the current focus of interest. However, our analysis of the very scanty data does not allow us to say with certainty that these regions play such distinctively separate roles.

2.3. Role of superior colliculus

By contrast to the PPC and pulvinar, the superior colliculus appears not to have attention-related responses. Neurones in this region appear to respond to visual stimuli but show no enhancement when attention is covertly directed to them. They do, however, demonstrate activity prior to saccades to visual targets and appear to encode the motor error between current eye position and the eye position required to foveate a visual stimulus (Goldberg & Wurtz, 1972; Sparks, 1986; Wurtz & Mohler, 1974, 1976). Within the colliculus there are 'fixation' neurones with characteristics similar to the ones in area 7a of the PPC. Injection of muscimol into monkey superior colliculus impairs fixation and leads to an increase in the number of express saccades (Munoz & Wurtz, 1992).

The superior colliculus has strong connections with the PPC via the pulvinar. The layers of the colliculus which receive direct projections from the retina relay probably visual information to area LIP, whereas non retino-recipient layers project to area 7a perhaps updating spatial representations about saccadic eye movements (see Andersen, 1987). The retino-colliculo-pulvinar-parietal pathway may be a fast system involved in orienting attention and planning eye movements to a novel visual stimulus. The pathway from area LIP to the superior colliculus may be important in generating the saccadic eye movement required to engage it.

Because neurones within the colliculus are not influenced by covert attention, this region is not a site of convergence of mechanisms involved in directing attention and saccadic eye movements. It is now generally accepted that the superior colliculus is one important premotor output area for visually-guided saccades. The frontal eye fields is another such region. Ablations of either superior colliculus or frontal eye fields do not prevent saccades to visual stimuli, but injury to both renders animals incapable of making such movements (Schiller et al., 1980).

2.4. Summary of Neural Architecture

'The main function of the peripheral part of the retina is that of sentinels which, when beams of light move over them, cry: "Who goes there?" and calls the fovea to the spot,' remarked William James (1890). We suggest there is sufficient evidence to conclude that the PPC, pulvinar and superior colliculus form part of the core neural architecture normally responsible for directing attention and gaze to visual targets. This group of structures subserves the role of 'sentinel' in the primate visual system.

The PPC has 'light-sensitive' neurones with large receptive fields which respond to novel visual stimuli in the visual surround. These may be responsible for mapping space in non-retinotopic coordinates, e.g., in head- or body-centred frames of reference, and directing focal attention within such representations. 'Fixation' neurones within the parietal cortex and superior colliculus may be part of a system involved in holding attention on a visual stimulus once it has been engaged. Other cells, such as those in area LIP of monkey, may be involved in computing motor vectors in non-retinotopic frames of reference. These vectors may be passed on to the superior colliculus where further sensorimotor transformations occur before command signals are transmitted to brainstem eye movement generating structures.

The visual input to the PPC may be via extrastriate cortex but another important source of information appears to be the retino-collicular system. The contribution of the pulvinar, which is located between PPC and superior colliculus is less clear, but its connectivity to both structures and attention-related neural responses suggests it plays an important role in the 'sentinel' system. Saccades to visual targets can be made without this system but this requires visual information to be transmitted to the frontal eye fields. Neurones in this region of the brain do not show enhancement with covert attention but appear to have a more direct premotor role like the superior colliculus (Goldberg & Bushnell, 1982). Perhaps this parallel system through the frontal eye fields explains why the generation of visually-guided saccades is not completely abolished by lesions of the PPC or superior colliculus.

3. CONCLUSION

In this review he have concentrated on only saccadic eye movements. We started with a simple question: What happens during the saccadic reaction time? We have presented evidence which suggests focal attention normally engages a visual stimulus before a saccade is made to foveate it. Attention can be directed without making an eye movement and, under certain circumstances, in the direction opposite to an eye movement. So, the directing of focal attention does not automatically lead to the generation of a saccade and the two processes can be dissociated.

Nevertheless, attention normally appears to shift to the target of a saccade before the eye movement is made. It therefore seems to be an important early step in preparing an eye movement. Exactly what this means in terms of neural operations or representations is unclear but our understanding may improve with further analysis of the contributions of the posterior parietal cortex, pulvinar and superior colliculus. These areas of the brain appear to be part of a system which is normally involved in orienting attention and the fovea to novel visual stimuli. We suggest the computations performed within this 'sentinel' system - attentional, sensorimotor and motor - are likely to be responsible for part of the time required to generate a visually-guided saccade.

REFERENCES

Andersen, R.A., 1987, Inferior parietal lobule function in spatial perception and visuomotor integration, in: Handbook of Physiology Vol. V Part II, eds. Plum, F. and Mountcastle, V.B. (American Physiological Society, Rockville, MD) p. 483.

Andersen, R.A., G.K. Essick and R.M. Siegel, 1985, Science **230**, 456.

Andersen, R.A., L.H. Snyder, C-S Li and B. Stricanne, 1993, Current Opinion in Neurobiology **3**, 171.

Anderson, T.J., I.H. Jenkins, D.J. Brooks, M.B. Hawken, R.S.J. Frackowiak and C. Kennard, 1994, Brain **117**, 1073.

Bálint, R, 1907, Orvosi Hetilap **1**, 209 (in Hungarian).

Barash, S., R.M. Bracewell, L. Fogassi, J.W. Gnadt and R.A. Andersen, 1991, J. Neurophysiol. **66**, 1095.

Braun, D., H. Weber, T. Mergner and J. Schulte-Mönting, 1992, Brain **15**, 1359.

Bushnell, M.C., M.E. Goldberg and D.L. Robinson, 1981, J. Neurophysiol. **46**, 755.

Corbetta, M., F.M. Miezin, G.L. Shulman and S.L. Petersen, 1993, J. Neurosci. **13**, 1202.

Crawford, T.J. and H.J. Muller, 1992, Vision Res. **32**, 293.

De Renzi, E., 1982, Disorders of Space Exploration and Cognition (John Wiley, Chichester).

Duhamel, J-R., C.L. Colby and M.E. Goldberg, 1992, Science **255**, 90.

Fischer, B., 1987, Reviews of Biochemistry and Pharmacology **106**, 1.

Fischer, B. and H. Weber, 1993, Behav. Brain Sci. **16**, 553.

Goldberg, M.E. and M.C. Bushnell, 1982, J. Neurophysiol. **46**, 773.

Goldberg, M.E. and R.H. Wurtz, 1972, J. Neurophysiol. **35**, 560.

Holmes, G., 1918, Disorders of visual orientation. Br. J .Ophthalmol. **2**, 449 and 506.

Husain, M., 1991, Visuospatial and visuomotor functions of the posterior parietal lobe, in: Vision and Visual Dysfunction Vol. 13, ed. J.F. Stein (Macmillan, London), p. 12.

Husain, M. and J. Stein, 1988, Arch. Neurol. 45: 89-93.

James, W., 1890, The Principles of Psychology (Holt, New York).

Kingstone, A. and R.M. Klein, 1993, J. Exp. Psychol.: Human Perception and Performance **19**, 1251.

Klein, R.M., 1980, Does oculomotor readiness mediate mediate cognitive control of visual attention? in: Attention and Performance VII, ed. Nickerson, R.S. (Lawrence Erlbaum, Hillsdale, NJ) p. 259.

Kurtzberg, D. and H.G. Vaughan, 1982, Brain Res. **243**, 1.

Lynch, J.C., 1980, Behav. Brain Sci. **3**, 485.

Mountcastle, V.B., R.A. Andersen and B.C. Motter, 1981, J. Neurosci. 1: 1218.

Mountcastle, V.B., B.C. Motter, M.A. Steinmetz and C.J. Duffy, 1984, Looking and seeing: the visual functions of the parietal lobe, in: Dynamic aspects of neocortical function, eds. G.M. Edelman, W.E. Gall and W.M. Cowan (John Wiley, New York) p. 159.

Munoz, D.P. and R.H. Wurtz, 1992, J. Neurophysiol. **67**, 1000.

Petersen, S.L., D.L. Robinson and W. Keys, 1985, J. Neurophysiol. **54**, 867.

Petersen, S.L., D.L. Robinson and J.D. Morris, 1987, Neuropsychologia **25,** 97.

Petersen, S.L., D.L. Robinson and J.N. Currie, 1989, Exp. Brain Res. **76,** 267.

Pierrot-Deseilligny, C., S. Rivaud S, B. Gaymard B and Y. Agid, 1991, Brain **114,** 1473.

Posner, M.I., 1980, Q. J. of Exp. Psychol. **32,** 3.

Posner, M.I., J.A. Walker, F.J. Friedrich and R.D. Rafal, 1984, J. Neurosci. **4,** 1863.

Posner, M.I., J.A. Walker, F.J. Friedrich and R.D. Rafal, 1987, Neuropsychologia **25 (1A),** 135.

Rafal, R.D. and M.I. Posner, 1987, Proc. Natl. Acad. Sci. USA **84,** 7349.

Remington R.W., 1980, J. Exp. Psychol.: Human Perception and Performance **6,** 726.

Reulen, J.P.H.,1984, Biological Cybernetics **50,** 251.

Reuter-Lorenz, P.A., H.C. Hughes and R. Fendrich, 1991, Perception & Psychophysics **49,** 161.

Reuter-Lorenz, P.A. and R. Fendrich, 1992, Perception & Psychophysics **52,** 336.

Rizzolatti, G., Gentilucci M. and Matelli M., 1985, Selective spatial attention: One center, one circuit, or many circuits? in: Attention and Performance XI, eds. M.I. Posner and O.S.M. Marin (Lawrence Erlbaum, Hillsdale, NJ) p. 251.

Sakata, H., H. Shibutani and K. Kawano, 1980, J. Neurophysiol. **43,** 1654.

Saslow, M.G., 1967, J. Opt. Soc. America **57,** 1024.

Schiller, P.H., S.D. True and J.L. Conway, 1980, J. Neurophysiol. **44,** 1175.

Shepherd, M., J.M. Findlay and R.J. Hockey, 1986, Q. J. of Exp. Psychol. **38A,** 475.

Sparks, D.L., 1986, Physiol. Rev. **66,** 118.

Thickbroom, G.W. and P.L. Mastaglia, 1985, Electrenceph. clin. Neurophysiol. **62,** 277.

Wurtz, R.H. and C.W. Mohler, 1974, Brain Res. **71,** 209.

Wurtz, R.H. and C.W. Mohler, 1976, J. Neurophysiol. **39,** 745.

Yin, T.C.T. and V.B. Mountcastle, 1978, Fed. Proc. **37,** 2251.

Van Voorhis, S.T. and S.A. Hillyard, 1977, Perception and Psychophysics. **22,** 54.

Visual Attention and Cognition
W.H. Zangemeister, H.S. Stiehl and C. Freksa (Editors)
© 1996 Elsevier Science B.V. All rights reserved.

IMAGING OF VISUAL ATTENTION WITH POSITRON EMISSION TOMOGRAPHY

Rüdiger J. Seitz

Department of Neurology,
Heinrich-Heine-University Düsseldorf,
P.O.-Box 10 10 07, D-40001 Düsseldorf, FRG

ABSTRACT

Measurements of the regional cerebral blood flow with positron emission tomography (PET) provide a tool to map the human brain structures activated by information processing of motion, sensation, vision and cognition. The visual system has been demonstrated in subhuman primates to consist of a large number of interconnected striate and extrastriate cortical areas subserving different aspects of visual information processing. It is firmly established from animal experiments and PET studies in man that an occipito-temporal pathway is involved in object identification, while an occipito-parietal pathway mediates the appreciation of spatial relationships among objects. Other functions of visual information processing include discrimination and identification of disparity, colour, motion, face identity, and word processing and have been localized by use of PET activation studies in different subregions of the human extrastriate cortex. Further, it was demonstrated that visual information processing in the extrastriate cortical areas is strongly modulated by selective attention to a particular feature. This attentional system appears to be modulated by a distributed network including the cingulate gyrus.

1. Introduction

Living human beings are subjected second per second to a large number of external stimuli that are perceived by the visual, auditory, and somatosensory sense organs and transmitted by afferent nerve fiber tracts to their brains. Out of this wealth of incoming information they consciously perceive only few by sorting out those stimuli that are meaningful to them in a given situation. In the somatosensory system it is well established that gating mechanisms on the spinal, thalamic, and cortical level mediate this selection of information (Rushton et al. 19981, Chapman et al. 1988, Libet et al. 1991). Roland (1982) was the first to show that direction of attention to a certain sensory modality leads to specific patterns of increases of the regional cerebral blood flow (rCBF) in the human brain that differ between sensory modalities.

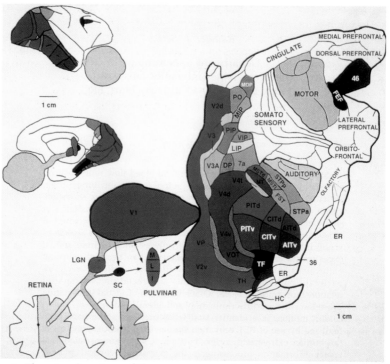

Figure 1. The visual system of the macaque monkey in a lateral view (upper left), mesial view (lower left), and after unfolding of the convoluted cortex in a 2-dimensional map (right). The projections from the retinal half field of both eyes to the striate cortex (V1) via the lateral geniculate (LGN) and to the peristriate cortex V2 via the superior colliculi (SC) and pulvinar of thalamus are demonstrated schematically. The sizes of the cortical areas reflect the amount of neural machinery of each structure. Visual areas are depicted in violet, the occipito-temporal pathway in greenish, and the occipito-parietal pathway in orange. The frontal eye field (FEF) and area 46 involved in memorizing saccadic eye movements (Funahashi et al. 1989) are drawn in black. Reprinted with permission from van Essen et al: Information processing in the primate visual system: an integrated systems perspective (1992), American Association for the advancement of Science.

In the visual domaine, stimuli of physiological relevance can be differentiated into a number of catagories such as disparity, shape, colour, spatial frequency, disparity, motion, and faces. Figure 1 demonstrates that the primate visual cortex has been parcellated into more than 30 cortical visual areas with dense and rich anatomical interconnections. The borders of these areas are not as distinct as in this unfolded map but show transitions and interindividual variabilities (van Essen, personal communication). Also, these areas are not fully interconnected but anatomical projections consisting of feed-forward and feed-backward interactions provide hierarchical levels of cortical visual processing. This network exceeds the borders of the occipital lobe communicating also with cortical centers that subserve motor control, other sensory modalities, and supramodal information processing. Recently, network analysis employing significant rCBF increases and interregional correlations has demonstrated the different strengths of intercortical interactions in human object vision and human spatial vision (McIntosh et al. 1994). Neural mechanisms of directing attention allow for channelling visual information processing within the visual system.

2. Behavioral aspects of focal attention

Primates and man can focus their attention to a certain visual object and even more to a single aspect of a visual stimulus. According to Mesulam (1990) direction of attention is mediated by a high-level neural network that enables simultaneous information processing in a parallel distributed manner. This network includes three major cortical nodes (Fig. 2): one in the premotor cortex around the frontal eye field and area 46 related to orienting and exploratory movements, one in the superior parietal lobule around the intraparietal sulcus related to sensory representation of the extrapersonal space, and one in the cingulate cortex related to the motivational control of attention. In addition, subcortical structures such a the superior colliculi, the thalamus, and the reticular activating structures are involved in the channeling of information to the cortical relay nodes. For a better understanding of the processes underlying the direction of attention let us assume two different behavioural conditions.

First, a person walking down-town manages his path through the crowd passing by at shop windows. It may occur that he or she all of a sudden will recognize a person acquainted with. Our propositus will recall where and when he has seen the face before. By associating circumstantial information he will decide whether simply to pass by, to greet formally, or to cordially cheer the person. Similarly, our propositus may all of a sudden recognize an item in a shop that attracts him by design or manufaction. It may be that he had been looking for it since some time or that he remembered that he had possessed it some time ago.

In a second situation, a person is entering a crowded hall. It is well known to the reader that one may not recognize well acquainted persons in such a situation even if they are seated in the first row. Conversely, one may figure out a certain person rapidly and with astonishing ease, if one knows for example that this particular person is wearing a red jacket. Similarly, it is possible to identify a searched person out of a large number of persons by looking for the way he moves or acts. Also, one can figure out his own car in a crowded parking place with no need to read its licence number. The type, colour, repair, and possibly the location of the car may facilitate the search.

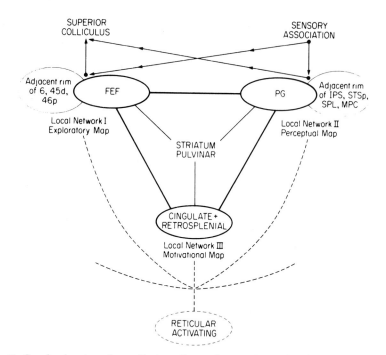

Figure 2. Cerebral network mediating directed attention. The three cortical nodes around the frontal eye field (FEF), around the intraparietal sulcus (IPS) in superior parietal lobule (cytoarchitectonic area PG in monkeys), and cingulate gyrus are interconnected reciprocally. Projections from other cerebral structures and subcortically to striatum and pulvinar of thalamus are also shown. Lesion to one relay site results in neglect behaviour. Taken from Mesulam et al. (1990) with permission.

These examples may illustrate different modes of visual perception. In the first situation, simple visual features are rapidly and continuously processed across the entire visual field. This has been termed the preattentive mode of information processing (Koch and Ullman 1985). In the second situation, the computation of basic representations leading to a certain visual perception has been attributed to selective attention (Koch and Ullman 1985). In the selective mode certain visual features can be processed preferentially for the goal of object recognition ("bottom-up"). Conversely, the above mentioned examples indicate that pre-knowledge facilitates object identification ("top-down"). It was shown experimentally (Miyashita 1988) and modelled as flow chart that object recognition involves retrieval of mental representations stored previously in long-term memory (Sakai and Miyashita 1994). In both latter situations, objects are recognized by routing selected target characteristics through the relay nodes involved in visual information processing (Ungerleider and Haxby 1994). Figure 3 illustrates a model for visual pattern recognition based on such a dynamic routing of visual information.

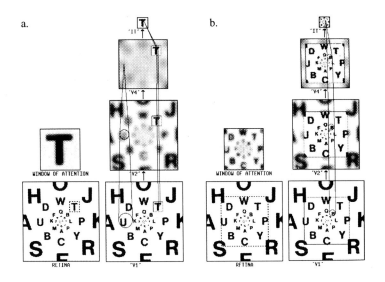

Figure 3. Dynamic routing of visual information in a computer simulation of simple attention. At the level of the retina the dashed line depicts the position and size of the window of attention. Through the visual areas V1, V2, and V4 the attended stimulus "T" is transferred to the infratemporal cortex IT for object recognition (a); the hypothetical receptive field has the highest resolution. This corresponds probably to a maximal local activation. For comparison, the non-attended "U" is blurred at the level IT. b) The focus of attention is so wide that in the receptive field of area IT no single item will be analyzed, because spatial resolution is sacrificed. Thus, the neuronal activity in IT is probably not enhanced. (Taken from Olshausen et al. 1993 with permission).

In this contribution, the neural substrates underlying basal visual information processing, selective visual attention, and shifting selective attention to visuospatial cues will be reviewed. For identification of these processes in the human brain measurements of rCBF by positron emission tomography (PET) have been used. First, we will provide methodological information concerning mapping of human brain function by neuroimaging techniques and then discuss neuroscientific findings on visual information processing.

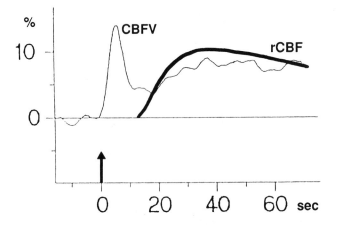

Figure 4. Time course of the cerebral hemodynamic response to physiological stimulation. The regional cerebral blood flow velocity (CBFV) in the large cerebral arteries rises within a few milliseconds after stimulation onset (arrow) and peaks after about 3 seconds. This immediate and transient increase of the CBFV represents a generalized unspecific arousal reaction (Sitzer et al. 1994). The ensuing and locally specific CBFV increase coincides with the count rate increase of the rCBF tracer in the specifically activated cortical region. The data were obtained in left middle cerebral artery (CBFV) and left sensorimotor cortex (rCBF) during voluntary right hand sequential finger movements.

3. Positron emission tomography

PET activation studies essentially rely on the tracer technology measuring the local task-specific cerebral accumulation of the rCBF tracer throughout the human brain (Raichle 1987). The rCBF is quantitatively related to neuronal energy consumption underlying synaptic activity (Sokoloff 1986). It has been demonstrated that the hemodynamic response to physiological stimulation occurs within a few milliseconds and peaks in the range of 2 to 5 seconds (Toga, personal communication, Fig. 4). In contrast, deoxygenation of blood as measured by functional magnetic resonance imaging (fMRI) has a slower time course culminating at approximately 10 seconds in motor cortex during voluntary finger movements (Bandettini et al. 1993) and between 20 and 30 seconds in visual cortex in checker-board activation (Kleinschmidt et al. 1994). With respect to the neuronal processes that evolve in the time frame of milliseconds, an inherent limitation of the rCBF techniques is, therefore, the long duration of the measuring time needed. Consequently, the temporal relation of task-induced neuronal activity changes that take place in different parts of the brain cannot be elucidated with PET measurements of rCBF nor with measurements of deoxyhemoglobin using functional magnetic resonance imaging (fMRI, Kwong et al. 1992, Frahm et al. 1993). This may be a considerable disadvantage for rCBF studies on visual processing, since flow of information "bottom-up" and regulation of the flow of information in a "top-down" fashion cannot be studied by rCBF measurements. Thus, refined task designs are required to isolate the anatomical structures involved in information processing.

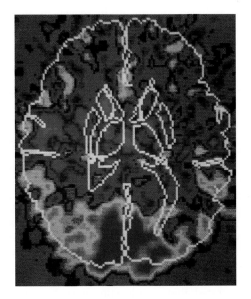

Figure 5. Increases of the mean rCBF in striate and extrastriate visual cortex during stimulation with geometric patterns compared to rest. The rCBF was measured using bolus inhalation of [18F]-fluoromethane as detailed by Roland et al. (1990). High rCBF increases in visual cortex are depicted in red (20 ml/100g/min), moderate rCBF increases in yellow (9 ml/100g/min), rCBF decreases in blue; green corresponds to zero. Transaxial slice with superimposition of the cerebral surface, lateral sulcus, thalamus, caudate nucleus, putamen, and ventricular system drawn in from a computerized brain atlas (Greitz et al. 1991). Right in the images corresponds to left in the 11 subjects examined.

PET image analysis utilizes pixel-by-pixel image subtraction and parametric statistics to demonstrate significant rCBF changes related to a specific activation state compared to an appropriate control condition (for review see Thatcher et al.

1994). Further, localization of rCBF changes to the underlying brain anatomy requires superimposition of external anatomical templates or coregistration with the individual's brain anatomy such as by magnetic resonance (MR) images (for review see Thatcher et al. 1994). These vigorous statistical methods result in a dramatic data reduction, since only rCBF changes common for a group of subjects or the maximal rCBF changes in an individual survive data processing (Seitz et al. 1996).

4. Visual information processing

Visual stimulation induced significant increases of the regional cerebral glucose metabolism and rCBF in the striate cortex (Fig. 5, Fox et al. 1988). The rCBF changes in the visual cortex have been shown to exhibit a retinotopic organization and a quantitative relation to the frequency of checker board stimulation until up to approximately 8 Hz (Fox et al. 1984, 1987). Recently, similar results were obtained by fMRI, however, with improved spatial resolution compared to PET scanning (Schneider et al. 1993). It should be mentioned that the deoxyhemoglobin technique of fMRI measures signal changes related to the relative oxygenation of the venous blood due to the stimulation-induced overshoot of local blood supply compared to the local oxygen consumption (Fox and Raichle 1986, Fox et al. 1988, Seitz and Roland 1992a, Marrett et al. 1993). If one used as reference state for visual activation a resting state with open eyes in darkness and as stimulus a simple white cross against black background, it becomes evident that significant rCBF increases occurred bilaterally in the extrastriate and parietal cortex, while the striate cortex itself did not exhibit significant rCBF increases (Fig. 6). These data resemble recent observations by Gulyas and Roland (1994) on binocular disparity discrimination demonstrating that visual information is processed at a number of cortical areas, even if the visual stimulus is simple in nature. That this is actually the case can be derived from a number of studies on different kinds of visual stimulation. These studies demonstrated that simple stimuli such as shape, colour, object motion, disparity, words, and faces induced significant rCBF increases in specific areas of the extrastriate cortex, the occipito-temporal cortex and the parietal lobe (Lueck et al. 1989, Petersen et al. 1990, Gulyas and Roland 1991, Zeki et al. 1991, Sergent et al. 1992, Watson et al. 1993). Such studies shed light on the organization of the human visual system indicating that it may parcellated in a similar way as was experimentally demonstrated in primates (Desimone et al. 1985, Zeki and Shipp 1988, Van Essen et al. 1992).

It should be pointed out, however, that significant rCBF increases in visual stimulation tasks were not restricted to the visual areas in the occipital, temporal and parietal lobe. Rather they also occurred in the frontal lobe and cingulate cortex depending on the given task design. For example, visual presentation of of words but not of non-words involved rCBF increases in the left prefrontal cortex that was related to inadvertent processing of the semantics of the stimuli (Petersen et al. 1990, Gevins et al. 1994). Similarly, Gulyas and Roland (1991, 1994) demonstrated that processing of binocular disparity, of visual forms and colour activated the parietal lobe, the prefrontal cortex, cingulate, and the cerebellum. The activations in frontal lobe were clearly different from rCBF increases in the frontal eye field induced by voluntary eye movements (Fox et al. 1985, Petit et al. 1993). Most recently, the specific activation of the frontal eye field by horizontal saccadic eye movements was demonstrated by fMRI (Fig. 7). This technique is based methodologically on echo-planar imaging and provides maps of cerebral tissue perfusion comparable to rCBF measurements with PET (Edelman et al. 1994). As outlined above, the frontal eye field is regarded as a cortical field related to orienting and exploratory activity (Mesulam 1990).

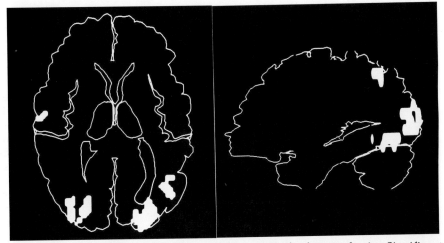

Figure 6. Simple visual information processing in the human brain. Significant mean rCBF increases induced by looking at a white cross compared to staying with open eyes in darkness in ten healthy volunteers. The rCBF was measured using intravenous bolus injection of [^{15}O]-butanol as detailed by Herzog et al. (1993). The significant rCBF increases represent those pixels in descriptive t-maps corresponding to $p < 0.05$ that occur in clusters of 12 and more pixels (corresponding to $p < 0.001$ corrected for image resolution).
a) Areas of activation occur bilaterally in the occipital visual association cortex. Note that there is no rCBF increase in the area of the calcarine. Transaxial slice through the calcarine, Sylvian fissure, thalamus, and lateral ventricles; right in the image corresponds to left in the subjects. b) A sagittal plane on a right paramedian level cutting through the lower part of the lateral ventricle shows an additional activation area in the superior parietal lobule; left corresponds to rostral in the subjects. The anatomical structures were drawn in from a computerized brain atlas (Greitz et al. 1991).

The widespread rCBF increases in extrastriatal and frontal areas induced by visual information processing appear to differ between young and old people. It was recently shown that young people had higher mean rCBF increases in the extrastriate cortex during face recognition and location matching, while older people showed in the same experiments a greater activation in the prefrontal cortex and the inferior and medial parietal cortex (Grady et al. 1994). Particularly, the slower reaction times during location matching in the older subjects suggested that processing of spatial vision was particularly impaired in the elderly. It was argued that the more widespread activation of the prefrontal cortex reflected a compensatory effect.

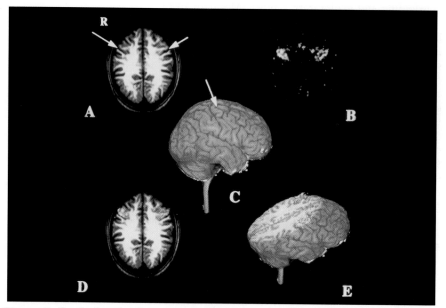

Figure 7. Cortical activation areas induced by visually guided eye movements. Transaxial plane (A) and lateral view of right cerebral surface (C) of T1-weighted anatomical MR images; arrows indicate central sulci. B: Activation areas obtained by echo-planar imaging after applying a spin-tagging radio-frequency pulse to proximal arterial blood and image subtraction. Superimposition of activation areas in transaxial plane (D) and reconstructed three-dimensional anatomical image (E). Note the additional activation areas in the frontomesial cortex corresponding to the supplementary motor area (Seitz et al. 1996). Taken from Edelman et al. (1994) with permission.

The finding that elderly activated a distributed cortical network during visual processing in a different way than young people suggests that personal life-time experience modulates the way of visual perception and thereby the degree of rCBF increases associated with vision. Supportive of this suggestion may be recent observation using measurements of deoxyhemoglobin by fMRI (Friston et al. 1994). In this study the authors correlated the visual input with the hemodynamic response function in the activated visual cortex showing that in simple photic stimulation the signal changes were more pronounced in the extrastriate than in the striate cortex. If this proves to be true it may represent support for "top-down" regulation of visual information processing mediated by focussed visual attention. A corresponding result was obtained by a PET activation study by Roland et al. (1990). In this experiment it was demonstrated that learning of geometric patterns resulted in a significant large mean rCBF increase in the visual cortex. Recall of the internal representations of these geometric patterns activated the limbic system and the medio-dorsal thalamus. In the striate cortex, however, there were only minor and non-significant rCBF increases in correspondence to more recent observations by LeBihan et al. (1993) using fMRI. In contrast, recognition of the geometric patterns in a series of similar geometric patterns induced significant, but minute rCBF increases in the calcarine that were of similar magnitude as the rCBF increases in the extrastriate cortex, the limbic system, and the thalamus (Roland et al. 1990). It should be emphasized that the presentation rate was higher in the recognition experiment than in the learning experiment. These observations demonstrated that focussing of attention to the visual domaine induced enhanced rCBF increases in the calcarine that may be related to optimal sampling of visual information. A similar finding was originally described by Roland (1981) for the somatosensory system and replicated later by Meyer et al. (1991). In contrast, pattern recognition demanded less effort and, thereby, less focussing of attention to the visual modality.

5. Selective visual attention

As discussed in the previous paragraph, focussing of attention to a sensory modality enhances the cerebral metabolism and thereby the rCBF in the corresponding primary sensory cortex. It may be asked whether focussing of vision to a selective characteristic of a visual stimulus may also raise the rCBF in those cortical areas specifically engaged for processing this information. One may hypothesize that selective visual attention will highlight certain areas that are located in the network of visual cortical areas. In activations tasks exploring selective visual attention, the attentional state has to be compared with the unattended presentation of the same stimulus. Corbetta et al. (1991) performed such a PET activation study employing selective and divided attention during visual discriminations. These authors proved the above mentioned hypothesis valid demonstrating that attention to speed activated a region in the left inferior parietal lobule, attention to colour a regions in the collateral sulcus and dorsolateral occipital cortex, and attention to shape activated the collateral sulcus, the fusiform and parahippocampal gyri, and the temporal cortex along the superior temporal sulcus. Recent evidence from animal single neuron recordings in macaque monkeys demonstrated that selective attention for colour increased neuronal activity in the extrastriate area V4 compared to the interference control state (Motter 1994a). It was demonstrated that the activity in V4 reflected a selection that was based on the cued feature and not simply on the physical colour of the receptive field neurons. In a further series of experiments Motter (1994b) observed that feature-selective processing occurring in area V4 could be sustained by the memory of a relevant cue. It was demonstrated that even after the selective processing had been established the activity of newly selected targets was enhanced, whereas deselected targets faded away to the background level of all other background objects. These experiments on selection of visual cues across the entire receptive fields of V4 neurons provide an alternative to earlier finding by Moran and Desimone (1985) who demonstrated a spatial restriction of focal attentive processes. On a systems-level it was modelled that reentry of recursive signals along ordered anatomical connections achieve integration by giving rise to constructive and correlative properties among feature maps (Tononi et al. 1992). These experimental results support the findings of the PET studies on selective attention proving the existence of a cellular equivalent to the "macroscopic "rCBF measurements in humans.

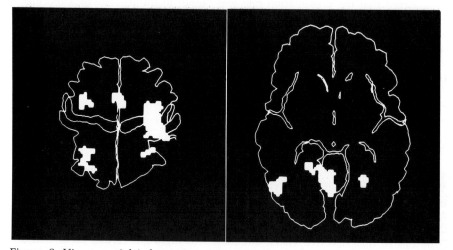

Figure 8. Visuo-spatial information processing in a visuomotor task. Significant mean rCBF increases induced by writing "r"s of different size under visual guidance. In the control condition the subjects held the pen motionless on the hand support. a) Accurate writing induced areas of activation in the left sensorimotor cortex, bilaterally in premotor cortex and supplementary motor area, and particularly in the right posterior parietal cortex. The cerebral surface and Brodmann's area 4 are displayed bilaterally. b) Fast writing induced areas of activation in the upper part of the cerebellar vermis, bilaterally in the visual cortex, and the right visual association area adjacent to the occipito-temporal sulcus. The cerebral surface, Sylvian fissures, and lateral ventricles are displayed. Transaxial slices with superimposition of anatomical structures drawn in from a computerized brain atlas (Greitz et al. 1991). Right in the images corresponds to left in the subjects.

The specific activation of visual association areas is not restricted to purely visual tasks but can also be demonstrated in visuomotor tasks. This shall be illustrated for different modes of hand writing under visual guidance (Seitz et al. 1994a). During accurate hand writing significant rCBF increases occurred in the posterior parietal cortex (Fig. 8a) that has been shown in animal experiments to code the spatial trajectories of movements (Kalaska et al. 1983, Caminiti and Johnson 1992). Furthermore, during fast hand writing rCBF increases were observed in the temporo-occipital region (Fig. 8b). This activation area was situated in close vicinity to the visual motion center as identified in humans by PET (Zeki et al. 1991, Watson et al. 1993). Also, it probably corresponds to the activation area present during movement observation (Decety et al. 1994).

These data demonstrate that the cortical areas of the visual information processing network may also be engaged when selective visual attention contributes to the successful performance of visuomotor tasks. In addition, selective attention induced rCBF increases also in limbic structures, the prefrontal cortex, and subcortical structures (Corbetta et al. 1991). Subcortically, the pulvinar has been demonstrated to be metabolically more active when attention was directed to an object in the visual field (LaBerge and Buchsbaum 1990). Therefore, it may be postulated that performance of a certain visual task involves those cortical areas that mediate the information processing of specific characteristics of visual stimuli. Other cortical areas, particularly in prefrontal and limbic locations, and the pulvinar of the thalamus are also activated as enabling bystanders. However, since their topographical distributions appear to depend on the attentional strategy actually employed, their physiological roles remain to be elucidated.

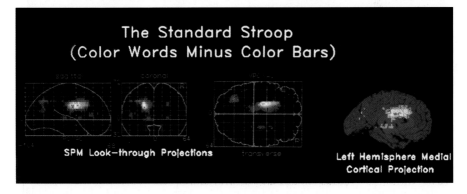

Figure 9. Significant mean rCBF increase in left midanterior cingulate during performance of the Stroop test. Shown are transparent projections in sagittal, coronal, and transverse planes of the stereotactic space and on a medial surface view as realized in the SPM-program (Friston et al. 1991). Taken from George et al. (1994) with permission.

6. Shifting of attention

The question concerning visual attention is related to the processes underlying the focussing of selective attention to a certain characteristic of a visual stimulus. This issue was examined using the Stroop interference task. In this task subjects were required to read words of colours silently but to name the colour of the letters aloud. It was demonstrated that the anterior and middle part of the cingulate was specifically activated (Pardo et al. 1990, George et al. 1994). Fig. 9 demonstrates that the area of activation was located in the left cingulate anterior to the anterior commissure. These data suggest that active focussing of attention to an intended aspect of task performance critically involves area 24 of the cingulate gyrus (Vogt et al. 1992).

Furthermore, the processes underlying shifting of attention from one item to another have been studied. Recently, Corbetta et al. (1993) published an intriguing paper on a closely related topic. In this study, subjects were required to shift spatial attention in the right or left visual field along foveofugal or foveocentral directions. It was found that the superior parietal and superior lateral frontal cortex were more active when shifting attention compared to maintaining attention at the center of gaze. Further, the superior parietal region was active when peripheral locations were selected on the basis of cognitive or sensory cues, while the frontal region was active only when responses were made to stimuli at selected peripheral locations. These observations pointed to a more perceptive role of the parietal activations and and motor related activation in the frontal lobe for shifts of attention. Interestingly, these areas of activation were present in both cerebral hemispheres for both visual hemifields in an almost overlapping manner. However, in the parietal lobe of the right hemisphere the visual hemifields were separated with a more posterior location of the right visual hemifield (Corbetta et al. 1993). Since the direction of the moving stimuli did not separate the activation areas, these rCBF increases in the parietal lobe did not simply reflect responses to spatial locations. Rather, they indicated a more widespread involvement of the right parietal lobe for shifting of attention.

In correspondence to these data, raised attention during a first PET scan has been shown to specifically activate the prefrontal cortex, the superior parietal cortex, the cingulate, and the thalamus (Seitz and Roland 1992b). Conversely, patients suffering from hemineglect revealed significant metabolic depressions in superior lateral frontal cortex, superior and inferior parietal cortex, and cingulate cortex (von Giesen et al. 1994). As apparent from Fig. 10 these areas included or were located in close neighbourhood to those specifically activated in active focussing and shifting of attention (Corbetta et al. 1993). Altogether, these positive (activation) and negative (lesion) findings support the concept of a large-scale neuronal system underlying visual attention (Mesulam 1990). It has been claimed that stimulus-dependent neuronal oscillations may represent the electrophysiological foundation for such a network (Gray et al. 1990). It will be a challenge to further parcellate the cortical areas and to uncover their relationships to visual imagination (Roland and Gulyas 1994). Furthermore, it may become possible to unreveal the temporal sequences of information processing in the different cortical and subcortical areas related to shifting and selecting of attention using combined information from functional neuroimaging studies and bioelectric and biomagnetic devices.

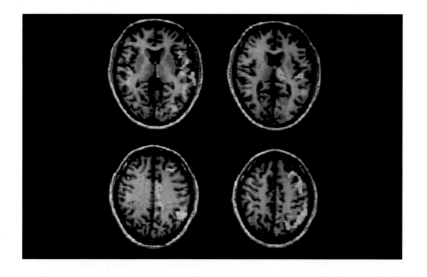

Figure 10. Significant mean depressions of regional cerebral glucose metabolism (rCMRGlu) in motor hemineglect compared to healthy controls. The rCMRGlu was measured as detailed in Seitz et al. (1994b). Significant rCMRGlu depressions occurred contralateral to the hemineglect in premotor and parietal, peri-insular, and cingulate cortex, and subcortically in thalamus. Note that the sensorimotor cortex around the central sulcus (arrow) is spared.

ACKNOWLEDGEMENTS

This work was supported by the Sonderforschungsbereich 194 of the Deutsche Forschungsgemeinschaft.

REFERENCES

Bandettini P.A., Jesmonowicz A., Wong E.C., Hyde J.S. (1993) Magnet Resonance Med 30, 161-173

Caminiti R, Johnson PB (1992) Cereb Cortex 2: 269-276

Chapman CE, Jiang W, Lamarre Y (1988) Exp Brain Res 72: 316-334

Corbetta M, Miezin FM, Dobmeyer S, Shulman GL, Petersen SE (1991) J Neurosci 11: 2383-2402

Corbetta M, Miezin FM, Shulman GL, Petersen SE (1993) J Neurosci 13: 1202-1226

Decety J, Perani D, Jeannerod M, Bettardi V, Tadardy B, Woods R, Mazziotta JC, Fazio F (1994) Nature 371: 600-602

Desimone R, Schein SJ, Moran J, Ungerleider LG (1985) Vision Res 25: 441-452

Edelman RR, Siewert B, Darby DG, Thangaraj V, Nobre AC, Mesulam MM, Warach S (1994) Radiology 192: 513-520

Fox PT, Raichle ME (1984) J Neurophysiol 51: 1109-1120

Fox PT, Fox JM, Raichle ME, Burde RM (1985) J Neurophysiol 54: 348-369

Fox PT, Miezin FM, Allman JM, van Essen DC, Raichle ME (1987) J Neurosci 7: 913-922

Fox PT, Raichle ME, Mintun MA, Dence C (1988) Science 241: 462-464

Frahm J, Merboldt K-D, Hänicke W (1993) Magnet Resonance Med 29: 139-144

Friston K, Frith CD, Liddle PF, Frackowiak RSJ (1991) J Cereb Blood Flow Metab 11: 690-699

Friston KJ, Jezzard P, Turner R (1994) Hum Brain Mapp 1: 153-171

Funahashi S, Bruce CJ, Goldman-Rakic PS (1989) J Neurophysiol 61: 331-349

George MS, Ketter TA, Parekh PI, Rosinsky N, Ring H, Casey BJ, Trimble MR, Horwitz B, Herscovitch P, Post RM (1994) Hum Brain Mapp 1: 194-209

Gevins A, Cutillo B, DuRousseau D, Le J, Leong H, Martin N, Smith ME, Bressler S, Brickett P, McLaughlin J, Barbero N, Laxer K (1994) Hum Brain Mapp 1: 101-116

Grady CL, Maisog JM, Horwitz B, Ungerleider L, Mentis MJ, Salerno JA, Pietrini P, Wagner E, Haxby JV (1994) J Neurosci 14: 1450-1462

Gray CM, Engel AK, König P, Singer W (1990) Eur J Neurosci 2: 607-619

Greitz T, Bohm C, Holte S, Erikson L (1991) J Comput Assist Tomogr 15: 26-38

Gulyas B, Roland PE (1991) Neuroreport 2: 585-588

Gulyas B, Roland PE (1994) Proc Natl Acad Sci USA 91: 1239-1243

Herzog H, Seitz RJ, Tellmann L, Rota Kops E, Schlaug G, Jülicher F, Jostes C, Nebeling B, Feinendegen L. Measurement of cerebral blood flow with PET and ^{15}O-butanol using a combined dynamic-single-scan approach. In: Uemura K, Lassen NA, Jones T, Kanno I (eds) Quantification of brain function. Tracer kinetics and image analysis in brain PET. Elsevier ICS 1030, 1993; 161-169

Kalaska JF, Caminiti R, Georgopoulos AP (1983) Exp Brain Res 51: 247-260

Kleinschmidt A, Merboldt K-D, Hänicke W, Steinmetz H, Frahm J (1994) J Cereb Blood Flow Metab 14: 952-957

Koch C, Ullman S (1985) Hum Neurobiol 4: 219-227

Kwong KK, Belliveau JW, Chesler DA, Goldberg IE, Weisskoff RM, Poncelet BP, Kennedy DN, Hoppel BE, Cohen MS, Turner R, Cheng H-M, Brady TJ, Rosen BR (1992) Proc Natl Acad Sci USA 89: 5675-5679

LaBerge D, Buchsbaum MS (1990) J Neurosci 10: 613-619

Le Bihan D, Turner R, Zeffiro TA, Cuénod CA, Jezzard P, Bonnerot V (1993) Proc Natl Acad Sci USA 90: 11802-11805

Libet B, Pearl DK, Morledge DE, Gleason CA, Hosobuchi Y, Barbaro NM (1991) Brain 114: 1731-1757

Lueck CJ, Zeki S, Friston KJ, Deiber M-P, Cope P, Cunningham VJ, Lammertsma AA, Kennard C, Frackowiak RSJ (1989) Nature 340: 386-389

Marrett S, Fujita H, Meyer E, Ribeiro L, Evans AC, Kuwabara H, Gjedde A (1993) Stimulus specific increase of oxidative metabolism in human visual cortex. In: Uemura K, Lassen NA, Jones T, Kanno I (eds) Quantification of brain function. Tracer kinetics and image analysis in brain PET. Elsevier ICS 1030, pp 217-228

McIntosh AR, Grady CL, Ungerleider LG, Haxby JV, Rapoport SI, Horwitz B (1994) J Neurosci 14: 655-666

Mesulam MM (1990) Ann Neurol 28: 597-613

Meyer E, Ferguson SG, Zatorre RJ, Alivisatos B, Marrett S, Evans AE, Hakim AM (1991) Ann Neurol 29: 440-443

Miyashita Y (1988) Nature 335: 817-820

Moran J, Desimone R (1985) Science 229: 782-784

Motter BC (1994a) J Neurosci 14: 2178-2189

Motter BC (1994b) J Neurosci 14: 2190-2199

Olshausen BA, Anderson CH, van Essen DC (1993) J Neurosci 13: 4700-4719

Pardo JV, Pardo PJ, Janer KW, Raichle ME (1990) Proc Natl Acad Sci USA 87: 256-259

Petersen SE, Fox PT, Snyder AZ, Raichle ME (1990) Science 249: 1041-249

Petit L, Orssaud C, Tzourio N, Salamon G, Mazoyer B, Berthoz A (1993) J Neurophysiol 69: 1009-1017

Raichle ME (1987) Circulatory and metabolic correlates of brain function in normal humans. In: Plum F (ed) Handb Physiol - The Nervous system V, Chapter 16: 643-674

Roland PE (1981) J Neurophysiol 46: 744-754

Roland PE (1982) J Neurophysiol 48: 1059-1078

Roland PE, Gulyas B, Seitz RJ, Bohm C, Stone-Elander S (1990) Neuroreport 1: 53-56

Roland PE, Gulyas B (1994) TINS 17: 281-287

Rushton DN, Rothwell JC, Craggs MD (1981) Brain 104: 465-491

Sakai K, Miyashita Y (1994) TINS 17: 287-289

Schneider W, Noll DC, Cohen JD (1993) Nature 365: 150-153

Seitz RJ, Roland PE (1992a) Acta Neurol Scand 86: 60-67

Seitz RJ, Roland PE (1992b) Comp Med Imaging Graphics 5: 311-322

Seitz RJ, Canavan AGM, Yaguez L, Herzog H, Tellmann L, Hömberg V (1994a) Neuroreport 5: 2541-2544

Seitz RJ, Schlaug G, Kleinschmidt A, Knorr U, Nebeling B, Wirrwar A, Steinmetz H, Benecke R, Freund H-J (1994b) Hum Brain Mapp 1: 81-100

Seitz RJ, Schlaug G, Knorr U, Steinmetz H, Tellmann L, Herzog H (1996) Neurophysiology of the human supplementary motor area: positron emission tomography. In Lueders O (ed) Adv Neurol 70, chapter 15, in press

Sergent J, Ohta S, MacDonald B (1992) Brain 115: 15-36

Sitzer M, Knorr U, Seitz RJ (1994) J Appl Physiol 77: 2804-2811

Sokoloff L (1986) Cerebral circulation, energy metabolism, and protein synthesis: general characteristics and principles of measurements. In: Phelps ME, Mazziotta JC, Schelbert HR (eds) Positron emission tomography and autoradiography. Principles and applications for the brain and heart. Raven Press, New York, pp 1-71

Thatcher RW, Hallett M, Zeffiro T, John ER, Huerta M (1994) Functional Neuroimaging: technical foundations. Academic Press, Orlando, Florida

Tononi G, Sporns O, Edelman GM (1992) Cereb Cortex 2: 310-335

Ungerleider LG, Haxby JV (1994) Curr Opinion Neurobiol 4: 157-165

Van Essen DC, Anderson CH, Felleman DJ (1992) Science 255: 419-423

Von Giesen HJ, Schlaug G, Steinmetz H, Benecke R, Freund H-J, Seitz RJ (1994) J Neurol Sci 125: 29-38

Vogt BA, Finch DM, Olson CR (1992) Cereb Cortex 2: 435-443

Watson JDG, Myers R, Frackowiak RSJ, Hajnal JV, Woods RP, Mazziotta JC, Shipp S, Zeki S (1993) Cereb Cortex 3: 79-94

Zeki S, Shipp S (1988) Nature 335: 311-317

Zeki S, Watson JDG, Lueck CJ, Friston KJ, Kennard C, Frackowiak RSJ (1991) J Neurosci 11: 641-649

Visual Attention and Cognition
W.H. Zangemeister, H.S. Stiehl and C. Freksa (Editors)

EVIDENCE FOR SCANPATHS IN HEMIANOPIC PATIENTS SHOWN THROUGH STRING EDITING METHODS

Wolfgang H. Zangemeister * *and Ulrich Oechsner* †

Department of Neurology
University of Hamburg, Germany

Abstract

In continuation of earlier studies, we recorded gaze movements in patients with hemianopic visual field defects primarily due to stroke. Use of high resolution infrared oculography enabled us to record and analyse a variety of tasks including paradigms of visual search, reading and scanpath eye movements. The tasks were recorded several times in sequential order. By applying string-editing methods to the problem of quantitatively analysing search- and scanpaths of the half-blind patients in comparison to healthy subjects, we were able to observe short term adaptation: I.e., training effects of eye movement strategies to improve the initially deficient result on the side of the blind hemifield with respect to the relative difficulty of the specific task. This quantitative and statistically confirmed finding adds new evidence for the top-down control of the human scanpath even in hemianopic patients.

Key Words: Homonymous Hemianopia, Scanpath eye movement, Short term adaptation, Functional Rehabilitation of Field Defect, Vector String Editing.

1   INTRODUCTION

How do we view pictures and scenes in our environment? Often, the eye movements are guided by catchy, visually interesting or seemingly important points of interest. Our eye may be guided directly to this spot of a picture by its special design, which accounts for detecting the arrangement of contrasts, border lines, colours, depth and special subfeatures especially with respect to the primary region of interest (ROI). This type of viewing strategy would correspond to a bottom-up control of viewing, where no cognitive model of the picture (i.e., perceptual hypothesis which has to be tested against sensory experience) is present and the eyes' movements and fixations are controlled by the features of the image.

Or we, that is "our mind's eye" might look around following an implicit cognitive plan, that guides us from here to there, and eventually to the destination we were originally looking for, or were somewhat anticipating: i.e., "we had the final target in mind". This corresponds to a searchpath, that applies to the so called top-down control (Noton & Stark

---

*M.D., Professor of Neurology
†M.Sc., Physicist

1971, Stark & Ellis 1981) of viewing, where the eyes' movements and fixations are driven by a cognitive model of the picture. In general, we apply a similar pattern of visual control when we read and scan pictures or scenes, which we then could call a readingpath and scanpath respectively (Noton & Stark 1971, Stark & Ellis 1981, Zangemeister, Sherman & Stark 1989, Stark, Yamashita, Tharp & Ngo 1992, Zangemeister, Sherman & Stark 1995).

Multi-item boundary and surface groupings influence visual search. They may indeed represent the perceptual components upon which the search process is based. The identification of a grouping that includes multiple items speeds up the search process by reducing the total number of candidate visual regions that have to be investigated serially. Factors which influence boundary and surface grouping, such as featural contrast, item spacing, and spatial arrangement alter the number of visual regions to be explored, yielding variations in search time.

If bottom-up mechanisms drive the formation of these emergent perceptual units, then limits must exist on the capacity of semantic or even visual definitions of target items to exert top-down influence over preattentive grouping mechanisms. The ability of bottom-up processing to distinguish ecological objects accurately depends on a certain amount of autonomy or resistance to top-down interference. Otherwise, it would routinely result in perceptual illusions. Of course, perceptual grouping indeed will often be guided by top-down processes (Zangemeister, Sherman & Stark 1995, Allman, Miezin & McGuinness 1985, Desimone 1993) . However, some groupings may "emerge" from the structure of the scene input without the help of top-down influences.

Of course, the enforced top-down control of viewing is the primary domain of our everyday modern life through movies, TV and visual public relation in particular. We learn and we apply these different kinds of top-down control of viewing during our whole life. However, diseases of the the eyes, the optical pathways, the visual or motor cortex and its interconnections may cause at least one of the three functional parts of the control to become disturbed: the sensory, the cognitive, or the motor connection that contribute to the proper functioning of the higher levels of visual control.

In the case of deficiencies in at least one of the three functional parts, there is a need to recover from the given deficit, which may be feasible through certain strategies of adaptation. The typical, most frequent deficits that can be found clinically, and may be simulated experimentally, are:

1. Motor deficits of one or both eyes involving coordinated eye-movements that may cause dipliopia as well as slowness and inaccuracy of eye movement and fixation. They can be overcome comparatively easily by moving only the healthy eye, and neglecting, i.e., suppressing, the information of the eye with the movement deficits, or by helping interocular deficits through adaptive eye and head-coordination, as found in internuclear ophthalmoplegia.

2. More importantly, sensory deficits may disturb top-down control of vision by producing visual field defects of one eye, or both eyes in the case of more centrally located disturbances such as found in homonymous hemianopia.

3. Most variant difficulties and therefore a whole variety of adaptive strategies may

occur with deficits of visual attention and cognition, like visual apraxia and hemineglect.

We put forward the following question, "What kind of adaptation may occur in a comparatively simple case, i.e., with a typical sensory visual deficit such as homonymous hemianopia, where the site of the lesion lies 'more peripheral' compared to the above noted higher visual functions ?"

When looking at the variant adaptive strategies that may be obtained, one has to consider the basic distinction between movements of the eyes only (Meienberg, Zangemeister, Rosenberg, Hoyt & Stark 1981) without any head- or body-movement, and, on the other hand coordinated eye- and head-movements in coordinated gaze (Zangemeister & Stark 1981, Zangemeister, Meienberg, Stark & Hoyt 1982, Zangemeister, Dannheim & Kunze 1986, Zangemeister & Stark 1989, Zangemeister 1991). This distinction is practically important, since the head as the moving platform of the eyes may be differentially used to increase the effective viewing angle for large objects of interest, like in large screen movies, searching around in natural environments, or reading of large scale advertisements.

It is theoretically important, since strategies may be different in the case of a retinal frame of reference with a fixed head, as compared to a head frame of reference. Often, the latter may be identical to the body frame of reference equalling position of gaze in space, like in case of a pilot or a car driver. Here, functional processing of coordinated gaze may be more flexible (Zangemeister & Stark 1982*b*) and therefore more efficient in terms of sophisticated performance; it may be, however, less efficient in terms of time, i.e., take much longer than the 250 msec of a typical saccade plus saccadic latency (Zangemeister & Stark 1982*a*, Gauthier, Mandelbrojt, Vercher, Marchetti & Obrecht 1985).

In 1971 Noton & Stark found patterns in the eye movements of subjects recognizing a familiar object, which they called scanpaths. Each subject seemed to have a typical scanpath for each object. During longer inspections of the object, the scanpath was repeated several times. This observation led Noton & Stark to the feature ring hypothesis which states that an object is represented in memory by its principal features and by the eye movements (saccades) which are necessary to proceed from one feature to the next. The stored features and saccades were proposed to be organized in a repetitive structure, which was called feature ring (Fig. 1).

Since 1971 the proposals of scanpath and feature ring were widely discussed. Because the hypothesis of Noton & Stark at first was based entirely on the subjective inspection of recorded eye movement patterns, there has been some effort to develop an objective method for the comparison of eye movements. Here, we shall report on the specific methods we have applied to quantita-

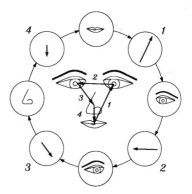

Figure 1: *Illustration of Noton & Stark's (1971) feature ring hypothesis. The internal representation of an object is supposed to consist of the principal features of the object and the eye movements (motor controls) necessary to get from one feature to the next. The features and motor controls are supposed to be organized in a repetitive structure.*

tively evaluate search- and scanpath eye movements as well as on the training results, i.e., the adaptive strategies of high level controlled eye-movements that hemianopic patients use, when the head and body is fixed (Zangemeister, Oechsner & Freksa 1995).

2 METHODS

2.1 Patients, experimental setup, conventional analyses

During the last three years we observed and recorded eye movements from patients with various visual field defects, the most important of which consisted of homonymous hemianopia. After checking the basic eye movement dynamics, we looked at the searchpath and scanpath eye movements in response to specific tasks. These included horizontal and diagonal searching of targets in pictures, the position of which was randomly varied on a large TV-screen; they also included scanpath recordings of viewings of abstract pictures of famous contemporary artists like *Ken Noland*, and one of the three coloured *Rorschach* pictures to test for symmetry perception. As a kind of intermediate test that included both qualities of a search and of a scanpath, we used ambiguous figures to test the ability to search for and scan two or three possible interpretations. Patients were also tested for reading capabilities without and with using free head movements, which has been published in part previously (Schoepf & Zangemeister 1992, Schoepf & Zangemeister 1993).

Subjects. We compared a group of normal healthy and full sighted subjects ($n = 10$) (mean age 35 ± 6 years) with a group of patients ($n = 10$) (mean age 52 ± 7) that had suffered from a stroke of the posterior cerebral artery of one side resulting in a pure homonymous hemianopia (HH) that was distinguished from hemineglect through a sequence of neuropsychological tests (Wilson, Cockburn & Halligan 1987). Visual hemifield defects with and without foveal sparing was quantified through high resolution computer perimetry (Octopus). Extension of the anatomical defect was quantified through cranial CT or MRT. Only patients with strokes dating back more than 3 months were tested, and this precondition permitted us to discard effects of spontaneous recovery from HH. All subjects had normal vision or corrected visual acuity and had no difficulty in adjusting to the apparatus.

Recording of eye movements. Measurement techniques for recording eye movements and eye blinks have been well described (Stark, Vossius & Young 1962, Zangemeister & Stark 1982a). Eye movements were measured using an infrared system (ASL210) that provided measurements of horizontal movements with a resolution of 0.05 degree over a range of ± 20 degree and of vertical measurements with a resolution of 0.1 degree over a range of ± 10 degree and permitted also detection of eyelid blinks. A calibration process, which assumed a nonlinear (polynomial) relationship between the eye movements and the output of the ASL210 did correct nonlinearities over this range. Overall system bandwidth was 0 to 100 Hz.

Low level visual stimuli. A white cross on a dark background which was predictively (in time and amplitude) alternating with an amplitude of 5 to 30 degrees was used as target for the measurement of saccadic time functions and main sequences (Bahill, Clark & Stark 1975) (i.e., the saccade peak velocity/amplitude relationship). The vertical and horizontal size of the target was 1 degree.

Higher level visual stimuli. Six pictures ranging from non-realistic search pictures to ambiguous pictures to more artful realistic and abstract pictures were chosen. The artful colour pictures were by Lane Terry "Deadeye" 1971, Ken Noland "Spring Cool" 1962. We also used a picture of the Necker Cube, a trivalent picture (i.e., an ambiguous picture with three possible interpretations, from Stark & Ellis (1981)), the largest of the three coloured Rorschach pictures, and the above noted diagonal and horizontal search sub-picture (see Fig. 10).

Experimental procedure. Subjects were seated comfortably in a ground-fixed dental chair that allowed a complete immobilization of the head through a tight head band and chin fixation firmly linked to the chair.

Protocol. Of importance were the different tasks defined by explicit instructions to our cooperative subjects. The basic task was to look carefully at the pictures to be able to remember the pictures and recall their specific features. Afterwards the subject had to describe the picture content and provide some details on request. The subjects were unaware that their eye movements were being recorded, as they were led to believe their pupil size and blink frequency were being measured. To create even more stable experimental conditions, the subjects received written instructions informing them about their task. Shortly after the run of the last group of pictures, an additional run was appended in which the patients had to imagine the pictures they just saw in the same sequence and within the same time. This provided us with some new data on imagined scanpaths in hemianopic patients.

Calibration runs were then performed to assure that eye movement and blink recordings were accurate. Presentations of the pictures were timed for 10 seconds with a one minute rest period between presentation groups. Six different pictures comprised a presentation group. A short rest period of 10 sec was requested between each picture within one presentation group. With a calibration run before and afterwards, and with intervening rest periods, the entire duration of the experiment was approximately 35 minutes. Presentation of pictures was done on a large VDT screen (21 inches diagonal). They were clearly viewed with high resolution under photopic vision. The screen was relatively large such that relatively large sized eye movements would be necessary to cover the material on the screen with a vertical and horizontal visual angle of 15 degree in each direction for the presented pictures. Room lighting was dim so as to focus the subject's attention on to the screen.

Data acquisition, analysis of the data. A number of menu-driven software programs operating both in an on-line and a follow-up mode were utilized. These presented the sequence of eye movements with saccades between fixation points. As is well known in the literature (Stark et al. 1962, Bahill et al. 1975, Bahill & Stark 1977, Viviani, Berthoz & Tracey 1977), saccadic eye movements often do not have a straight trajectory. We thus created a simplified presentation made of "interfixational vectors", that is a straight line vector going from one fixation point to the next. It is generally considered in studies of visual physiology that information of high resolution is not acquired to any great extent during the rapid saccadic eye movement. Therefore, for the present tasks, the exact path of the saccades is not important in itself; however, the location of each fixation lasting approximately 200 to 500 milliseconds, as well as the sequences of these fixations, was important. The analyzing software also counted the number of saccades in each of the fixed, 10 second picture presentations. Average fixation duration, which is inversely related to the number of saccades, was also calculated. Distributions of fixational durations were also plotted. Graphic displays were obtained which included "interfixational vectors" of eye movements and superimposed sequentially numbered fixations on the visual scene.

Eye blinks, which appeared in the original data as very rapid oblique jumps of the trace, have been removed by computer editing.

Global/local ratio. A particular pattern of eye movements occurred which differed according to the relative percentage of time the eye movements spent in making either a *global* or a *local* scan, using smaller eye movements in a particular region. We determined the ratio of global versus local viewing for each subject in each presentation from the statistics of saccadic sizes. The boundary between "local" and "global" eye movements was assumed to be 1 degree; that is, eye movements of the order of one degree of amplitude or less were considered local eye movements, whereas eye movements greater than 1.0 degree were considered global eye movements. This is in accordance with earlier reports on the range of micro-eye movements, particularly micro-saccades that range between 0.08 and 0.8 degree (see Brandt & Stark (1989) amongst others). If one changes this boundary from 1.6 to 4.6, 7.9, or 11 degrees, so that the definition of local becomes larger and larger, any discrimination provided by the global/local (g/l) ratio disappears (Zangemeister et al. 1989, Stark et al. 1992).

The statistical evaluation of differences between early and late presentations, pictures and conditions involved a non-parametric analysis of variance Winer (1971) . It was performed using the ANOVA software BMDP2, UC California, Los Angeles, analysis of variance and covariance with repeated measures, program version 1987.

2.2   Scanpath evaluation

Up to now Markov matrices and string editing have been used for quantification of the term "similarity of eye movements". Both methods work on sequences or "strings" of regions of interest (ROIs) which were visited by the eye during inspection of the object. At first the ROIs have to be defined a priori by the experimentator or a posteriori by clustering algorithms (regions that contain clusters of fixations are taken to be "of interest" to the patient). After defining, the regions are labeled by letters. Using the defined ROIs, the two-dimensional fixation-saccade sequence is then reduced to a one dimensional sequence of letters: if successive fixations are located in the ROIs "C", "D", "C", and "A", the resulting sequence of letters is "CDCA". Thus the task of comparing the eye movements of a subject or between subjects is reduced to the comparison of strings.

String editing was first used by programs for spelling correction (Morgan 1970, Wagner & Fischer 1974). Here it is necessary to find the words which are most similar to misspelled words. The distance of two words is defined as the minimum number of editing operations like deletion, insertion and substitution of a letter, which is necessary to transform one word into the other. Thus between "brown" and "town" the distance is 2 (deletion of b, substitution r → t). Transition probabilities between N states can be described by second order $N \times N$ Markov matrices (Kemeny & Snell 1983). The element (i, j) is the probability of state j following state i. Applied to the comparison of strings, each letter defines a state and the sequence of letters is understood as a sequence of transitions between states. To measure the difference between eye movement patterns with the help of Markov matrices, the transition probabilities of all letter combinations are computed for each pattern. The difference between the fixation strings is defined as the mean difference of the transition probabilities (Hacisalihzade, Stark & Allen 1992).

The objectivity of both string editing and the use of Markov matrices depends on the objectivity of the ROI-definition. A priori defined ROIs are completely subjective. The use of a posteriori defined ROIs is an objective method, but here analysis of different image viewings may result in different ROIs and thus the comparability is lost.

On the other hand, while evidence for scanpath and feature ring was found using string editing with different experimental paradigms like search tests (Allman et al. 1985) or visual imagery (Brandt & Stark 1989, Finke 1983), some authors (e.g., Groner, Walder & Groner 1984) doubted especially the storage of the motion controls (the saccades) in the internal representation of a familiar object as proposed by the feature ring hypothesis. The feature ring consists of two interwoven sequences (comp. Fig. 1): the sequence of features (ROIs) and the sequence of motor controls (saccades). We propose to use the latter for comparison of image viewings. The object features (or ROIs) are still supposed to be the important part of the feature ring, but they no longer have to be known (neither a priori nor a posteriori). By constructing a vocabulary of vectors and replacing each actual interfixational vector by the vector out of the vocabulary most similar to it, a "vector string" is obtained. String editing can then be used to compare different vector strings. This method we called "vector string editing".

2.3   Vector String Editing

String Editing can only be applied to a finite set of elements. The set of two dimensional vectors is not finite but can be approximated by a finite subset of vectors. We chose to divide both the possible directions (0 to 360 degree) and the possible lengths (0 to maximal extension of the field of vision) of an interfixational vector into 16 parts. The result is an alphabet or vocabulary of 256 vectors where each vector represents a certain interval of vector directions and lengths. The vectors in the alphabet are labeled by byte numbers. The low nibble contains the number of the direction interval, the high nibble the number of the length interval (see Fig. 2).

It is necessary to pay special attention to the first saccade. It is the step from the more or less random position of the eyes just before the presentation of the object to the first object feature which was found of interest by the patient, and thus a step into the feature ring. The interfixational vector corresponding to the first saccade was replaced by a vector from the center of the object to the position of the first fixation. This vector is no longer arbitrary (as the first interfixational vector due to the initial random position of the eyes), but always points to the first feature which was found of interest by the patient.

To make vector string editing invariant against scaling operations, the "maximal extension of field of vision" (which defines the length of the longest vectors in the vocabulary) was adapted to the size of the presented object.

In string editing different costs can be assigned to the editing operations insertion, deletion, and change. In a first approach to vector string editing we chose equal costs (i.e., unity) for each editing operation. In a second approach we chose costs which were dependent on the displacement in two dimensional space which was caused by the editing operation. That is, the cost of insertion or deletion of a vector was given by its length, the cost of replacing vector by vector was given by the length of the difference vector. This kind of vector string editing we called "weighted vector string editing". The vector string distances resulting from weighted vector string editing were renormalized to get results which were in the same order of magnitude as the distances from string editing with ROIs and vector string editing without weights.

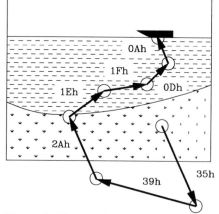

Figure 2: *Vector string editing. Each interfixational vector is classified by a byte number. The upper 4 bits encode the length, the lower 4 bits the direction. The vector string is the sequence of byte numbers, in the example (in hexadecimal notation) 35h, 39h, 2Ah, 1Eh, 1Fh, 0Dh, 0Ah.*

2.3.1   Numerical Simulations

We used numerical simulations to find the limits of vector string editing. In their 1992 paper Hacisalihzade et al. used a priori defined Markov matrices to generate sequences of fixations which were different realisations of the same Markov process. Application of string editing to groups of such sequences showed the ability of string editing to differentiate between different underlying processes.

In the first process (M_1) defined by Hacisalihzade et al. the transition probability from one state to the next was 90% and to the one after the next 10%. The other processes had increasing randomness (M_2: 70% from one state to the next, 30% to the one after the next, M_3: 50% from one state to the next, 10% to the one after the next, all other states equiprobable, M_4: all transitions are equiprobable). We chose M_1 and two matrices which were slightly different to M_1 (80% and 20% resp. 85% and 15% instead of 90% and 10%) to compare the discriminating abilities of string editing and vector string editing. These matrices are called $M(0.9, 0.1)$ ($= M_1$), $M(0.8, 0.15)$, and $M(0.8, 0.2)$ in the following. For four states they are given by

$$M(p_1, p_2) = \begin{pmatrix} 0 & p_1 & p_2 & 0 \\ 0 & 0 & p_1 & p_2 \\ p_2 & 0 & 0 & p_1 \\ p_1 & p_2 & 0 & 0 \end{pmatrix}.$$

The object chosen for the simulation of a scanpath was a 3×3 checker board (see Fig. 3). Each checker field was regarded as region of interest resulting in 9 possible states. For each Markov matrix 500 sequences with 30 elements were generated. String editing could be directly applied to these sequences (i.e., ROI-strings). For vector string editing we compared four different assumptions about the distribution of the fixations in each checker field (i.e. ROI) :

A_0 –   they were located exactly in the center of each checker field (Fig. 4a)

$A_{0.25}$ –   they were uniformally distributed in a centered square with $1/4$ of the area of one checker field (Fig. 4b)

$A_{0.5}$ –   they were uniformally distributed in a centered square with $1/2$ of the area of one checker field (Fig. 4c)

A_1 –   they were uniformally distributed across the whole checker field (Fig. 4d)

The simulation resulted in three distributions (there were three Markov matrices) of string distances obtained by string editing, and 12 distributions (there were three Markov matrices, and four assumptions) of vector string distances obtained by vector string editing and weighted vector string editing each. Subsequently we applied the Kolmogorov-Smirnov test to these distributions to get the probability of the assumption that all distributions had the same underlying Markov process.

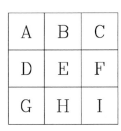

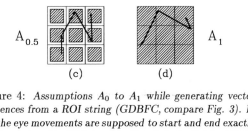

Figure 3: *Object used for simulation of eye movements. Each of the checker fields is a region of interest (ROI). The ROIs are labeled by the letters A to I.*

Figure 4: *Assumptions A_0 to A_1 while generating vector sequences from a ROI string (GDBFC, compare Fig. 3). In (a) the eye movements are supposed to start and end exactly in the center of a ROI (assumption A_0). In (b) to (d) the location of the start- and endpoints is getting increasingly uncertain (assumptions $A_{0.25}$ to $A_{1.0}$).*

2.3.2   Eye movement measurements

As a first test of (weighted and unweighted) vector string editing with data from eye movement measurements we used measurements with three hemianopic patients. The patients had to look for a small arrow in a coloured rectangle on a computer screen. The arrow systematically appeared on the diagonal of the rectangle, but the patients were not told where to look for it. We used string editing to show an adaptation effect : as the task and the object became more familiar, the string distances decreased.

String editing, vector string editing and weighted vector string editing were applied to two collection of strings. The first collection consisted of 16 strings from the pre-adaptation period, the second of 22 strings from the post-adaptation period. Again the Kolmogorov-Smirnov test was used to compare the resulting distribution of distances pre and post adaptation.

3   RESULTS

3.1   Results I: Vector String Editing versus String Editing

Numerical Simulations. Figure 5 shows the distributions which were calculated during simulation. The results of the Kolmogorov-Smirnov tests where we compared the distributions derived from the Markov matrices $M(0.9, 0.1)$, $M(0.85, 0.15)$, and $M(0.8, 0.2)$ are shown in Tab. 1. Here the logarithms of the probabilities of the distributions being the same are given. The distance between two distributions is taken to be significant if the probability p is less than 0.001 or $\log(p) < -3.0$.

As was to be expected, all distributions in Fig. 5 show increasing means with increasing uncertainty of the underlying process ($M(0.9, 0.1)$ to $M(0.8, 0.2)$. In case of vector string editing and weighted vector string editing the means are also increased if the positions of the start- and endpoints of the generated interfixation vectors are less certain (assumptions A_0 to A_1). Because of the greater number of elements in the vector alphabet, (unweighted) vector string editing soon reaches the maximum value of string and vector string distance, which is equal to the string length (30). As shown in Fig. 5 and Tab. 1, this results in very similar distributions for different Markov processes, which can no longer be discriminated by the Kolmogorov-Smirnov test. This is not the case for weighted vector string editing. Because of the weighting factors there is no fixed maximum distance and Tab. 1 shows significant differences for (almost) all comparisons of distributions. In case of assumption A_0 (all simulated fixations are located in the center of the ROI) weighted and unweighted vector string editing show almost equal discrimination properties. Surprisingly both methods are better than normal string editing. If the position of the simulated fixations in the ROIs is less certain (assumptions $A_{0.25}$, $A_{0.5}$, and A_1), normal string editing is always better than the vector methods. Unweighted vector string editing is not able to detect small differences in the underlying Markov processes if the fixations are uniformly distributed in at least half of the area of the ROI. Weighted vector string editing discriminates better but here the p-values also increase rapidly from assumption A_0 to A_1.

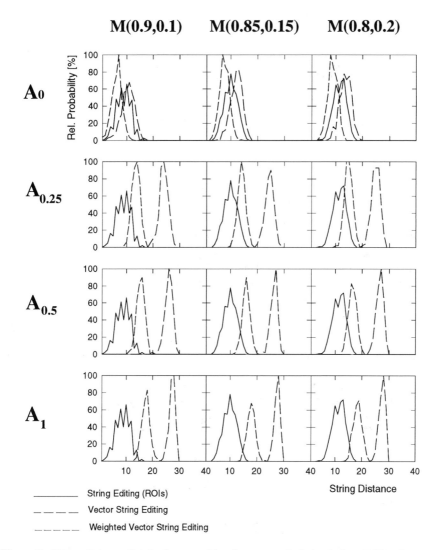

M(0.9,0.1)   M(0.85,0.15)   M(0.8,0.2)

Figure 5: *String distance distributions resulting from numerical simulation. ROI strings were generated using the Markov matrices $M(0.9, 0.1)$, $M(0.85, 0.15)$, and $M(0.8, 0.2)$. Using the model of a 3×3 checker board (Fig. 3) and the additional assumptions A_0 to A_1 (see Fig. 4) vector sequences were derived from the ROI strings. The figure gives the string distance distributions resulting from normal string editing (solid lines), vector string editing (short dashed lines), and weighted vector string editing (long dashed lines).*

		log(p) for		
		"$M(0.9, 0.1) =$ $M(0.85, 0.15)$"	"$M(0.85, 0.15) =$ $M(0.8, 0.2)$"	"$M(0.9, 0.1) =$ $M(0.8, 0.2)$"
String Editing (ROIs)		-6.7	-10.2	-28.2
Vector String Editing	A_0	-17.9	-12.2	< -32
	$A_{0.25}$	-3.1	-2.7	-10.6
	$A_{0.5}$	-2.0	-1.5	-5.3
	A_1	-1.0	-0.1	-0.9
Weighted Vector String Editing	A_0	-16.5	-13.9	< -32
	$A_{0.25}$	-5.3	-5.5	-18.5
	$A_{0.5}$	-3.8	-5.0	-13.1
	A_1	-2.9	-4.1	-15.0

Table 1: *Logarithms of the probability of two string distance distributions with different underlying Markov process being the same (as computed by use of the Kolmogorov-Smirnov test).*

Eye movement measurements. Figure 6 shows the distributions of string distances obtained by application of the three string editing methods to the eye movement measurements pre and post adaptation. Tab. 2 gives the results of the Kolmogorov-Smirnov test.

All string editing methods have been able to discriminate between the distributions pre and post adaptation. The best discrimination is obtained by using (unweighted) vector string editing, normal string editing is the second best. Weighted string editing is worse but ($\log(p) < -3$) still able to find a significant difference in the distributions.

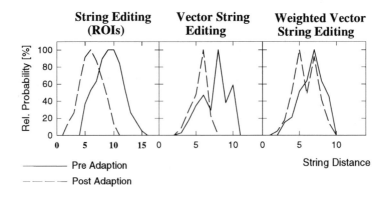

Figure 6: *Application of normal string editing (using ROIs), vector string editing and weighted vector string editing to actual eye movement data. Three hemianopic patients had to look for small arrows somewhere in a coloured rectangle on a computer screen. The string editing methods were used to look for differences between the string distance distributions before (solid lines) and after (dashed lines) adaptation of the patients to the given task.*

	String Editing (ROIs)	Vector String Editing	Weighted Vector String Editing
log(p) of "Pre Adaption = Post Adaption"	-18.0	-20.3	-3.2

Table 2: *The distributions of Fig. 6 corresponding to measurements before and after adaptation of the patients to the given task were compared using the Kolmogorov-Smirnov test. The table gives the logarithms of the probabilities of both distributions being the same.*

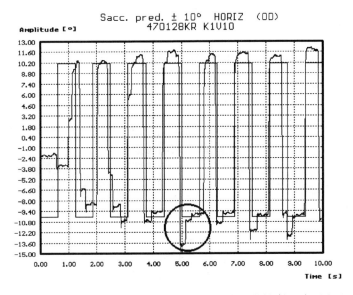

Figure 7: *Staircase pattern of saccades towards the blind hemifield (down) with time (sec) on abscissa and amplitude (deg) on ordinate, showing eye movements superimposed of a predictive step stimulus. Note the hypometric staircase saccades at the beginning and fast adaptation to this simple and anticipated stimulus within three repetitions with static overshooting or hypermetric saccades thereafter. The circle marks an early example for overshoot and successive fast glissades backwards to the target.*

3.2   Results II: Search- and scanpaths of hemianopic patients

Saccadic time functions and main sequences. Original recordings of responses
of hemianopic patients to low level visual stimuli, i.e. a predictively alternating target
of 5 to 30 degrees in amplitude demonstrate the characteristical eye movement pattern
(Meienberg et al. 1981, Zangemeister et al. 1982). Initial stair steps of small saccades
towards the blind hemifield were followed after two to four repetitions by overshooting
saccades (Fig. 7). These sometimes show fast glissades that move the fovea effectively
backwards to targets, and occur with increasing frequency when the hemianopic subject
has gone through many repetitions of predictive target presentations. An early example
of this is marked in Fig. 7.

Comparison of main sequences (i.e., the saccade peak velocity/amplitude relationship,
Bahill et al. (1975)) of these saccades with a large group of normal saccades demonstrated
that duration and dynamics of these saccades lie within the normal standard-deviation
(Fig. 8).

One way that global/local patterning could be ascertained was in terms of probability
density of saccadic amplitude. Plots of probability density of eye movement size and
of fixation duration have been calculated for each picture (Fig. 9). Fixation durations
did not discriminate between normal and hemianopic responses. However, size histograms
showed highly-peaked, exponential monotonic distributions for patient subjects indicating
large numbers of small saccades (which mostly occurred in the gaze direction to the blind

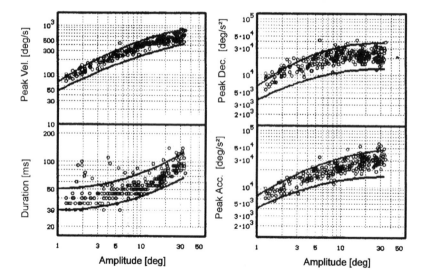

Figure 8: *Main Sequence double logarithmic plots of a typical patient's saccades. The two
thick curves enclose the 95 % confidence limit of our normal data base (n = 40). Abscissas
amplitude (deg), ordinates from left clockwise: peak velocity of saccade, peak deceleration,
peak acceleration, and duration. Note that the saccadic dynamics are within the normal range.*

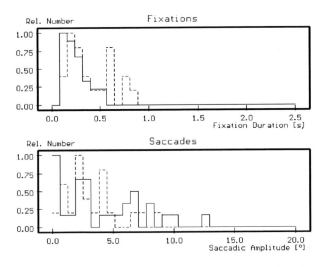

Figure 9: *Probability density curves of a normal subject's fixation durations and saccadic amplitudes during the scanpath (dashed lines) and of a hemianopic patient (solid lines). Note the relative high incidence of small saccades and shorter fixation durations in the patient. The ratio of global (> 1 deg) and local (≤ 1 deg) saccades is 3.8 for the patient and 20.0 for the normal subject.*

hemifield), i.e., a small global/local index. Conversely, histograms of eye movement size of normal healthy subjects showed a wider distribution with peaks at mid-sized saccades and reliance on larger saccades to overview the pictures, i.e., a large g/l index.

Visual search tasks. The search for a very small object on the hemianopic side of the patient's visual field was initially performed through a sequence of many small saccades that often erroneously clustered around the "wrong" side of the horizon (Fig. 10a). Whereas to the seeing hemifield, they resembled a normal pattern (Fig. 10b). After 10 repetitions on the hemianopic side, the sequence of saccades in search of this small target became almost normal (Fig. 10c) and mirrored the searchpath for targets in the seeing hemifield.

Markov as well as string editing analyses demonstrate here (as in most other hemianopic cases) a significant difference ($p < 0.01$) between the first and tenth response pattern. This suggests a very efficient short-term adaptation and optimization of the search paths in these patients.

With other visual stimuli, we obtained very similar behaviours. When looking for the "symmetry" of one of the three coloured Rorschach pictures (Fig. 11), in spite of this very specific task, the patients did not look towards the part of the picture that fell into the blind hemifield. After additional repetitions however, they changed their behaviour to a more symmetrical searchpath, so they were better able to compare the symmetries of the picture. It is noteworthy to recall that our patients were extensively tested for and did not show any signs of visual neglect. Again string editing, Markov analyses and statistics

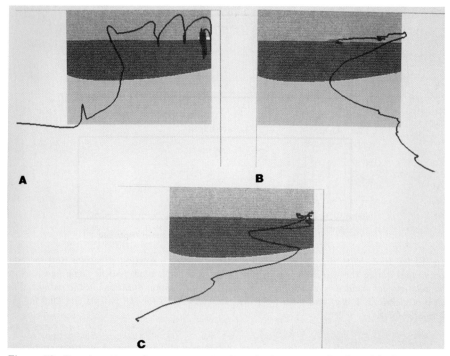

Figure 10: *Search pattern of eye movements when viewing a test stimulus with the target on the small dark target on the horizontal line on the right (side of the blind hemifield) and on the left (side of the seeing hemifield). A = first presentation on the blind side, B = first presentation on the seeing side, C = tenth presentation on the blind side (presentation duration: 3 sec, the pictures show about a 1/3 of the screen). Note: The searchpath to right (= blind hemifield side) after the tenth presentation resembles the searchpath to the left (= seeing hemifield side), i.e. shows short time adaptation.*

demonstrated significant differences and optimization in terms of time between first and last trial ($p < 0.01$ in all cases).

When the patients viewed a more realistic picture (Fig. 12), again they tended not to look at that part of the picture that fell within their blind hemifield. After some repetitions, however, they started to view the picture more symmetrically. This difference was again significant ($p < 0.01$).

In Fig. 13a and b, four examples of an enlarged view of eye movements during fixation are depicted of a sequence of eye movements of 0.1 to 1 degree. It appears that the sequences of small eye movements were also divided with respect to the blind hemifield, such that most fixations clustered around that part of the picture item that lies within the seeing hemifield. This is demonstrated for Figures 8 (Rorschach) and 9 (Pool Player) by the skewed distribution of eye movements as shown in Fig. 14. The tail of the curve resembles the small successive saccades towards the blind hemifield; the skewed peak of the curve reflects the higher probability of medium sized or larger saccades towards the

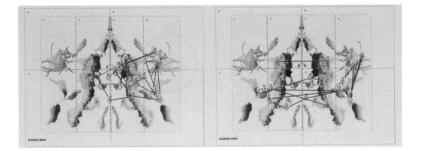

Figure 11: *Patient with hemianopia to left viewing the coloured Rorschach picture for 10 sec: left = first, right = sixth presentation. Fixations, which were defined by combined time/area/velocity criteria (the eye movements do not leave a circular area with radius 1deg for at least 200 msec, velocity < 5 deg/sec), are encircled. Eye movements are abstracted with lines connecting successive fixations that are also numbered.*

Figure 12: *Patient with hemianopia to left viewing a realistic picture. Same explanations as in Fig. 11.*

seeing hemifield. So far we have seen the effect only in patients with macular splitting (n=5).

Helmholtz & Southall (1962) found directional heterogeneously distributed saccadic and drift motions, where drift and saccadic motion were opposed to each other. Different subjects showed characteristical directional preferences. Nachmias (1959) found that the average saccade of a normal subject fixating one corner of an irregular stimulus pattern was directed away from the pattern. It is beyond the scope of this paper to decide if such an asymmetric visual field stimulation causes the asymmetrically distributed miniature eye movements, or, if it is the manifestation of an asymmetric micro scanpath in hemianopic patients.

The global/local ratios of search- and scanpath saccades of the HH patients, were generally low when looking towards their blind hemifield side, and high, when looking towards their seeing hemifield. The positive finding for normal healthy subjects, i.e. more global scans, and the negative finding for patients looking towards their blind hemifield, i.e. less global scans, was not only determined for the first viewing tasks but also for

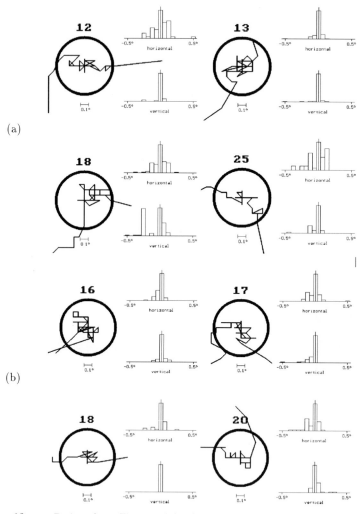

Figure 13: a. Patient from Fig. 11, left: four selected and numbered fixations with high resolution recording of miniature eye movements within the fixational area of ±1 deg (left). On right the statistical distribution of these movements, showing a "tail" in the blind hemifield, and a "skewness" towards the seeing hemifield. This suggests that most movements are made within the seeing hemifield. b. Patient from Fig. 12, left: four selected and numbered fixations with high resolution recording of miniature eye movements within the fixational area of ±1 deg (left). On right the statistical distribution of these movements, showing a "tail" in the blind hemifield, and a "skewness" towards the seeing hemifield.

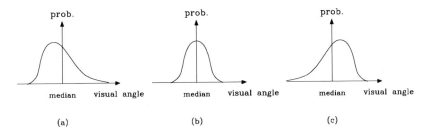

Figure 14: *Explanatory statistical figure, showing the expected skewness of miniature eye movements with respect to the seeing hemifield in comparison to a normal symmetrical distribution of these intra-fixational eye movements. a. Left sided skewness: patient with blind hemifield on the right. b. No skewness: normal subject. c. Right sided skewness: patient with blind hemifield on the left.*

the last viewing tasks, as shown by the overall high g/l ratios of healthy as compared to the low g/l ratios of hemianopic patients. Statistical evaluation demonstrated this size effect seen in the probability functions to be significant, i.e., the comparison of the most often occurring saccadic amplitudes of the two groups showed a significant ($p < 0.001$, Wilcoxon non-parametric test (Winer 1971)) difference.

4 DISCUSSION

Basic findings. Patients with hemianopic field defects exhibited a similar ocular motor strategy of sequences of eye fixations as healthy subjects, i.e., scan- and searchpath eye movements, in complex visual tasks. They also used short-term adaptation of their ocular motor strategy to overcome in a more optimal manner their hemifield blindness. The goal of this study was to compare exploratory eye movement strategies when looking at realistic, non-realistic and ambiguous pictures of a simple and complex structure and content between normal healthy subjects and HH patients with several repetitions. Eye movement recordings documented that scanpaths, i.e., repetitive sequences of saccadic eye movements having a sensory-motor-perceptual basis, occurred when they viewed such scenes. Global/local indices, string editing and Markov weighted measures of eye movement patterns were obtained by computer processing.

Vector String Editing: Discussion of Numerical Simulations. The simulation shows that vector string editing and especially weighted vector string editing can be of use for the comparison of eye movement sequences if the interfixational vectors or eye movement controls are not only movements from "somewhere" in ROI A to "somewhere" in ROI B, but well defined elements of the scanpath — as proposed by the feature ring hypothesis. If the motor controls are part of the internal representation of an object, the fluctuation between repeated object viewings should not be greater for vector strings than for ROI-strings (in the numerical simulation the vector strings were based on ROI-strings, additional uncertainties were added in the case of assumptions $A_{0.25}$, $A_{0.5}$, and A_1).

Thus the results of the numerical simulation imply that comparative use of string editing (based on ROIs) and vector string editing for the analysis of eye movement patterns could form a test for a part of the feature ring: the storage of the motor controls.

Vector String Editing: Discussion of Application to Eye Movement Measurements. Even if the comparison of p-values should not be taken too seriously ($\log(p) = -18$ is actually very similar to $\log(p) = -20$), the results in Tab. 2 imply that the sequence of interfixational vectors is as well defined as the sequence of ROIs and therefore support the "vector part" of the feature ring hypothesis.

The weighted vector string editing seems not to be well adapted to actual eye movement data. The cause may be that in weighted vector string editing more importance is placed on the larger saccades, while in human eye movements small saccades are much more abundant (and may be important) than big saccades. At present we are developing a vector alphabet with a nonlinear (logarithmic) partition of lengths.

Discussion of patients' results in scanning. These showed reduced local scanning by normal healthy viewers who relied on more global viewing, particularly in ambiguous and non-realistic pictures. HH patients did not show this difference; they exhibited their local scanpath patterns throughout the whole sequence of visual stimuli, particularly when they shifted gaze to the side of their blind hemifield. This suggests four conclusions. First, patients view pictures using the same top-down perceptual-cognitive processes that drive active looking or scanpaths in viewing ordinary realistic images, scenes and objects. Second, patients use primarily a low-level strategy that implies more local scanning and probably a bottom-up type of control particularly with respect to their blind hemifield. Third, patients as well as normal healthy subjects are able to improve their search and scanning performance within a short time during several alternating repetitions of different tasks: they change from a bottom-up to a top-down type of control to optimize the outcome of their search and scanning tasks.

And, fourth, patients demonstrate more difficulties to perceive complex and ambiguous or non-realistic images. Cognitive models control active viewing of realistic, ambiguous and non-realistic pictures in hemianopic patients. One main result of these experiments is that eye movement patterns of patients scanning complex images are similar to those of normal healthy subjects. Therefore, it can be concluded that both subjects and patients use a similar top-down approach to optimize their search and scan of pictures that were originally unknown and during the actual task sequences became more familiar. They viewed via a similar active perceptual process, utilizing cognitive schemas to drive their scanpath.

Similar to Gaarder (1960), Yarbus (1967) also believed in a high level "outflow" guidance of eye movements controlled through the viewer's mental image. Both Helmholtz and Yarbus suggested that changing the instructional task of their subjects altered their pattern of viewing.

The repetitive nature of the eye movement patterns for a subject continually viewing a picture was explained by Noton & Stark (1971) as a consequence of their "scanpath theory", in which eye movements are cognitively driven through an eye movement scanpath by a perceptual sensory and motor representation, to check if the picture agrees with what the observer imagings the object/scene really is. This representation was related to the "schematic diagram" of Hochberg (1968) . Noton and Stark used more realistic art, namely a figure of Klee's, while Stark & Ellis (1981) used realistic art and ambiguous figures, to provide further evidence that cognitive models , i.e., perceptual hypotheses, rather than peripheral vision, control the scanpath for active-looking perceptual processes. Brandt & Stark (1989) compared sequences of eye movements of subjects looking at a real visual stimulus and afterwards at its remembered mental image. Using string edit analyses (Hacisalihzade et al. 1992) , they were able to provide firm evidence for scanpath sequences of their subjects' eye movements in both conditions. Groner et al. (1984) have recently proposed that global scanpaths adhere to the Noton & Stark proposal, while smaller intermixed local scanpaths may be controlled peripherally.

Global versus local scanning. Since the underlying hypothesis for the scanpath theory is that an internalized cognitive model drives the eye movements, then from this observational evidence we inferred that in our experiments such models drive the eye movement patterns similarly for both healthy and patient subjects searching and scanning realistic, ambiguous and abstract pictures. Therefore the cognitive model should guide the eye movements in every condition, i.e. scanpath eye movements should occur also in searching and scanning towards the side of the blind hemifield. Indeed, a particular pattern of eye movements occurred according to the relative percentage of time the eye movements spent in making a global scan versus a local scan, using smaller eye movements in a particular region, depending if the subjects looked to the seeing or to the blind side of their hemifield. These observations were confirmed by the evaluation of the g/l ratio of each subject for each picture and task. A clear-cut difference was also demonstrated in the much higher g/l ratio of healthy as compared to the patient viewers when looking at abstract images especially in the search task.

Increased local scanning for patients as compared to healthy subjects. A second important result is the relatively high frequency of local scanning when patients viewed the complex visual test stimuli. Evidently, global viewing is the preferred strategy for the healthy subject that tries to evaluate both at the same time the visual content and the complexity of the picture. The patients however, were busier developing a more optimal sequence of eye movements to detect the overall features of the picture when searching or scanning, since they primarily had to rely on more local and therefore limited picture evaluations that also included more bottom-up control than in the healthy subjects.

What is local scanning? Although Noton & Stark (1971) and Stark & Ellis (1981) showed that peripheral information can be excluded as the immediate control for the scanpath, their results also relate to local scanpaths. Groner et al. (1984), and also Finke (1983), support their top-down, cognitive model scanpath theory for a global scanpath, but argue in favour of an immediate peripheral bottom-up control of local scanning as Allman et al. (1985) and Desimone (1993) does, although evidence for the latter is not conclusive at the present time. Although interesting, it is beyond the scope of the present paper to demonstrate conclusive evidence of a mini- or micro- search/scanpath as a special case of a local scanpath in hemianopic patients.

Jeannerod, Gerin & Pernier (1968) have argued for an exchange between local and global scanning in free exploration, as in the *Rorschach* task. Evidently, the normal healthy viewer avoids this type of immediate bottom-up control in favour of the top-down controlled global scanpath, whereas the patient when viewing to the side of the blind hemifield relies strongly on such an exchange, which permits him to develop a more efficient strategy of searching and scanning with almost every repetition. This change with repetition is gradual and progressive in patients, whereas we would expect it to be a brisk change (switch) in normal subjects with a digitally simulated hemianopic field defect.

In a previous study (Zangemeister et al. 1989, Zangemeister, Sherman & Stark 1995), our paradigms for viewing realistic and non-realistic images probably enforced this ability that was not present in the patient viewers. There, the naive subjects had equal global/local ratios for both realistic and abstract images. These ratios were similar to that of sophisticated subjects viewing realistic images. Whether the local scanpath is driven immediately by peripheral, bottom-up information or by small-scale cognitive models remains unknown. Mackworth & Morandi (1967) claimed immediate bottom up control in symmetry "that catches the eye"; Mackworth and Locher & Nodine (1977) showed evidence for top-down active selection of informative details through active gaze. In any case, this detailed looking is apparently usual for realistic images, where anticipation of details may be balanced by a permanent exchange of bottom-up and top-down control. The patients carry this behaviour to the ambiguous and non-realistic images. They use a more bottom-up like strategy when they first view pictures that extend also in their blind hemifield, which has also been described by Zihl & Wohlfart-Englert (1986). Only after many repetitions do they apply a more top-down like strategy that mirrors the one they use primarily when looking towards their seeing hemifield.

Realistic versus non-realistic and ambiguous pictures. Healthy subjects demonstrated more global scanning of the ambiguous and non-realistic images than they showed for their scanning of the realistic images, as was expected from earlier results (Zangemeister et al. 1989, Stark et al. 1992). These differences showed up not only in the significantly increased g/l ratios, but also directly in the scanpath patterns of the eye movements when fixation frequency, duration and interfixational saccadic amplitudes were compared. HH patients, however, first showed sequences of small amplitude fixational saccades as a local scanpath in both visual hemifields: i.e. they searched for some primarily relevant detail by use of which they could then generate a global scanpath. During this phase, their sequences of eye fixations appeared to be bottom-up influenced. Only after several repetitions were they able to change to the more efficient global scanpath while perceiving the different faces of the ambiguous figure, preferably on the side of the seeing hemifield, and rarely also on the side of the blind hemifield.

5 CONCLUSIONS

Evidences for top-down control and future lines of work. Our study demonstrates that it is feasible to observe and to quantify short-term adaptation as an effect of short-term training in patients with hemianopic field defects who apply and optimize a high level, top-down visuo-motor strategy to search and scan for targets and sequences of targets in complex visual tasks.

Regarding vector string editing, the experimental results presented here are preliminary. To further explore the feasibility of (weighted and unweighted) vector string editing to the comparison of eye movement data we are preparing experiments with paradigms like "recognition of familiar objects" and "visual imagery" (eye movement measurements during mental visualisation of a familiar object which is no longer visible, (compare Brandt & Stark 1989, Finke 1983).

Evidence for top-down versus bottom-up control from our study are given with respect to: First, seeing versus blind hemifield: the paradox that top-down cognitive models prevail when we see (seeing hemifield), whereas local (stair-)steps of bottom-up control prevail when we are blind (blind hemifield); Second, we find a strategy improvement with repetition. Third, the "complexity" of the picture (Berlyne 1958, Berlyne & McDonnel 1971) influences the control of eye movement sequences of fixations. Fourth, the task influence can induce more global top-down control. And, fifth, the size of the region that is viewed (ROI) highly influences the type of control that is applied: global versus local scanpath.

Future studies should try to simulate digitally a hemianopic field defect through the experimental setup using healthy subjects. Finally it should be possible to set up a neural network model that simulates the short-term adaptation that we have found in our patients.

References

Allman, J., Miezin, F. & McGuinness, E. (1985), 'Stimulus specific responses from beyond the classical receptive field: Neurophysiological mechanisms for local-global comparisons in visual neurons', *Ann. Rev. Neurosci.* **8**, 407–430.

Bahill, A. T., Clark, M. R. & Stark, L. (1975), 'The main sequence: A tool for studying human eye movements', *Math. Biosci.* **24**, 191–204.

Bahill, A. T. & Stark, L. (1977), 'Oblique saccadic eye movements: Independence of horizontal and vertical channels', *Arch. Ophthalmol.* **95**, 1258–1261.

Berlyne, D. E. (1958), 'The influence of complexity and novelty in visual figures on orienting responses', *J. Exp. Psychol.* **55**, 289–296.

Berlyne, D. E. & McDonnel, P. (1971), 'Effects of complexity and prechoice stimulation on exploratory choice', *Perception and Psychophysics* **10**, 241–246.

Brandt, S. & Stark, L. (1989), Experimental evidence for scanpath eye movements during visual imagery, IEEE Biomed. Engin. Proc. 11th Ann., Seattle, pp. A317–318.

Desimone, R. (1993), Neural circuits for visual attention in the primate brain, *in* G. Carpenter & S. Grossberg, eds, 'Neural networks for vision and image processing', MIT Press, Cambridge MA, pp. 343 – 364.

Finke, R. A. (1983), 'Directional scanning of remembered visual patterns', *J. Exp. Psychol.* **9**, 398–410.

Gaarder, K. (1960), 'Relating a component of physiological nystagmus to visual display', *Science* **132**, 471–472.

Gauthier, G., Mandelbrojt, P., Vercher, J., Marchetti, E. & Obrecht, G. (1985), Adaptation of the visuo-manual system to optical correction, *in* L. Stark & G. Obrecht, eds, 'Presbyopia - recent research', Fairchild Publ., N.Y., pp. 165 – 171.

Groner, R., Walder, F. & Groner, M. (1984), Looking at faces: Local versus global aspects of scanpaths, *in* A. G. Gale & F. Johnson, eds, 'Theoretical and Applied Aspects of Scanpaths', North Holland Publ. Company, Amsterdam, pp. 58–59.

Hacisalihzade, S. S., Stark, L. & Allen, J. S. (1992), 'Visual perception and sequences of eye movement fixations: A stochastic modeling approach', *IEEE Trans. Systems, Man, Cyb.* **22**, 474–481.

Helmholtz, H. v. & Southall, J. (1962), *Physiological Optics*, Dover Publ., New York. Transl. from orig. German version published in 1866.

Hochberg, J. (1968), In the mind's eye, *in* R. Haber, Hol & Rinehart, eds, 'Contemporary Theory and Research in Visual Perception', Winston Publ., N Y, pp. 309–331.

Jeannerod, M., Gerin, P. & Pernier, J. (1968), 'Deplacements et fixation du regard dans l'exploration libre d'une scene visuelle', *Vision Res.* **8**, 81–97.

Kemeny, J. G. & Snell, J. L. (1983), *Finite Markov Chains*, Springer, New York.

Locher, P. & Nodine, C. F. (1977), Symmetry catches the eye, *in* J. K. O'Reagan & A. Levy-Schoen, eds, 'From Physiology to Cognition', North Holland Publ. Company, Amsterdam, p. 353.

Mackworth, N. H. & Morandi, A. Y. (1967), 'The gaze selects informative details within pictures', *Perception and Psychophysics* **2**, 547–552.

Meienberg, O., Zangemeister, W. H., Rosenberg, M., Hoyt, W. F. & Stark, L. (1981), 'Saccadic eye movement strategies in patients with homonymous hemianopia', *Ann. Neurol.* **9**, 537–544.

Morgan, H. L. (1970), 'Spelling correction in system programs', *Comm. ACM* **13**, 90–94.

Nachmias, J. (1959), 'Two-dimensional motion of the retinal image during monocular fixation', *J. Opt. Soc. Am.* **49**, 901–908.

Noton, D. & Stark, L. (1971), 'Scanpaths in eye movements during pattern perception', *Science* **171**, 308–311.

Schoepf, D. & Zangemeister, W. H. (1992), Eye and head reading path in hemianopic patients, *in* S. F. Wright & R. Groner, eds, 'Facets of Dyslexia and its Remediation', Stud. Vis. Inform. Proc., Amsterdam - New York, pp. 267–291.

Schoepf, D. & Zangemeister, W. H. (1993), 'Correlation of coordinated gaze strategies to the status of adaptation in patients with hemianopic visual field defects', *Ann. NY Acad. Sci.* **682**, 404–409.

Stark, L. & Ellis, S. (1981), Scanpaths revisited: Cognitive models in active looking, *in* B. Fisher, C. Monty & M. Sanders, eds, 'Eye Movements, Cognition and Visual Perception', Erlbaum Press, New Jersey, pp. 193–226.

Stark, L., Vossius, G. & Young, L. R. (1962), 'Predictive control of eye tracking movements', *IEEE Trans. Hum. Fac. in Electronics* **HFE-3**, 52–67.

Stark, L., Yamashita, I., Tharp, G. & Ngo, H. (1992), Searchpatterns and searchpaths, *in* D. Brogan & K. Carr, eds, 'Visual Search II', Taylor & Francis, pp. 37–58.

Viviani, P., Berthoz, A. & Tracey, D. (1977), 'The curvature of oblique saccades', *Vision Res.* **17**, 661–664.

Wagner, R. A. & Fischer, M. J. (1974), 'The string-to-string correction problem', *J. ACM* **21**, 168–173.

Wilson, B., Cockburn, J. & Halligan, P. W. (1987), *Behavioural Inattention test*, Thames Valley Test Company, Titchfield, Hants.

Winer, B. J. (1971), *Statistical principles in experimental design*, McGraw Hill, London - Tokyo.

Yarbus, A. L. (1967), *Eye Movements and Vision*, Plenum Press, N Y.

Zangemeister, W. H. (1991), Voluntary influences on the stabilization of gaze during fast head movements, *in* S. R. Ellis, M. K. Kaiser & A. C. Grunwald, eds, 'Pictorial Communication of virtual and real Environments', London, New York, pp. 404 – 417.

Zangemeister, W. H., Dannheim, F. & Kunze, K. (1986), Adaptation of gaze to eccentric fixation in homonymous hemianopia, *in* E. L. Keller & D. Zee, eds, 'Adaptive Processes in Visual and Oculomotor Systems', Vol. 57 of *Adv. in Bio. Sci.*, pp. 247 –252.

Zangemeister, W. H., Meienberg, O., Stark, L. & Hoyt, W. F. (1982), 'Eye-head coordination in homonymous hemianopia', *J. Neurol.* **225**, 243 – 254.

Zangemeister, W. H., Oechsner, U. & Freksa, C. (1995), 'Short-term adaptation of eye movements in patients with visual hemifield defects indicates high level control of human scanpath', *Optom. Vis. Sci.* **72**, 467–477.

Zangemeister, W. H., Sherman, K. & Stark, L. (1995), 'Looking at abstract and realisticpictures: Evidence for global scanpath strategy in abstract pictures', *Neuropsychologia* p. in print.

Zangemeister, W. H. & Stark, L. (1981), 'Active head rotations and eye-head coordination', *Annals NY Acad. Sci* **374**, 540 – 559.

Zangemeister, W. H. & Stark, L. (1982*a*), 'Gaze latency: variable interactions of eye and head movements in gaze', *Exp Neurol* **75**, 389 – 406.

Zangemeister, W. H. & Stark, L. (1982*b*), 'Gaze types: interactions of eye and head movements in gaze', *Exp. Neurol.* **77**, 563 – 567.

Zangemeister, W. H. & Stark, L. (1989), 'Gaze movements: patterns linking latency and vor gain', *Neuro-ophthalmology* **9**, 299–308.

Zangemeister, W., Sherman, K. & Stark, L. (1989), Eye movements and abstract images, ECEM5, University of Pavia Press, Pavia, pp. 165–172.

Zihl, J. & Wohlfart-Englert, A. (1986), 'The influence of visual field disorders on visual identification tasks', *Eur. Arch. Psychiat. Neurol. Sci.* **236**, 61–64.

Acknowledgements

We should like to thank Prof. L. Stark, UC Berkeley, for his very helpful and lucid discussions through many years, and Dr. Hoekendorf from the Neurological Rehabilitation Center Soltau for the good cooperation. We are also very grateful to the Kuratorium ZNS, Bonn, which partially supported this study. Finally we should like to thank Prof. C. Freksa, Dieter Schoepf and Steffen Egner for their critical advice.

Mailing address :

Prof.Dr. W.H. Zangemeister
Neurological University Clinic
Martinistrasse 52
D 20251 HAMBURG, FRG
Fax : (+49) 40 4717-5086
e-mail: zangemeister@uke.uni-hamburg.de

CHAPTER 4

MODELING ASPECTS

Visual Attention and Cognition
W.H. Zangemeister, H.S. Stiehl and C. Freksa (Editors)
© 1996 Elsevier Science B.V. All rights reserved.

225

VISUAL PERCEPTION AND COGNITION:
A SYNOPSIS OF MODELING ASPECTS

H. Siegfried Stiehl

Universität Hamburg, FB Informatik, AB Kognitive Systeme,
Vogt-Kölln-Straße 30, D-22527 Hamburg, E.U.
`stiehl@informatik.uni-hamburg.de`

ABSTRACT

In this synopsis of Chapter 4, first a brief introduction as well as an overview is given taking basic principles of and approaches to the modeling of visual perception from the information processing perspective into regard. Particularly, the emerging nexus of computational vision and computational neuroscience will be stressed given the indispensable premise of interdisciplinarity. References to seminal research work as well as to state-of-the-art literature are also given to enable interdisciplinarily interested readers to zero in on the intricacy of modeling vision. Secondly, the individual contributions on exemplary research, which can be considered representative, are both summarised and related to the general context of this book.

KEY WORDS: Computational Models of Visual Perception and Cognition, Interdisciplinary Modeling, Computational Neuroscience, Computer Vision, Active Perception, Behavioural Vision.

1. THE COMPUTATIONAL PERSPECTIVE ON VISUAL PERCEPTION AND COGNITION: FROM RECONSTRUCTIVISM TO ACTIVE VISION AND VISUAL BEHAVIOUR

A variety of disciplines different in theory and methodology, e.g. neuroscience, psychophysics, cognitive psychology, ethology, philosophy, computer science, and mathematics, have been involved up to nowadays in vision research since the early works of the Greek philosophers and of the "Father of Optics" Ibn al-Haitham. Thus the range of research, as also reflected in Chapter 4, is remarkably broad (see Bruce and Green, 1992, for a worth reading introduction): Reaching from neuron response studies in electro-physiology via information processing (viz, computational) models in computer vision to mobile autonomous vehicles equipped with semiconductor cameras. In a critical review of contemporary computational vision research, Aloimonos and Rosenfeld (1991) pointed out:

"... researchers in different fields ask different questions about vision. Some ask *empirical* questions: How are existing biological visual systems actually designed? On the other hand, scientists and engineers try to answer theoretical and normative questions. The *theoretical* question is, What is the range of possible mechanisms underlying perceptual capabilities in vision systems? The *normative* question is, How should a particular class of vision systems (or robots) be designed so that they can efficiently perform a set of specific visual tasks? The three types of basic questions do not in general have the same answer."

Mainstream research can be hitherto characterised as more or less monodisciplinary within specific disciplines, but it is nevertheless successful in delivering an abundance of tantalising results. Particularly one cannot help but extolling the discovery of prime principles of structure and function of animal visual systems as well as of their tight coupling with behaviour (Spillmann and Werner, 1990; Zeki, 1993; Roth, 1994). As Orban (1991) put it:

> "The objection that the brain is poorly understood does not hold for vision. ... It is [therefore] likely that study of the visual system will not only help us understand vision as such but also the neuronal mechanism of higher cognitive functions such as perception, memory and learning which have important visual aspects."

However, one also has to concede that until now vision in toto has neither been completely understood nor completely been describable by a monolithic theory. Consequently, a fully-fledged conceptual and/or computational model with highly descriptive, explanatory, and predictive power is still not on the verge of creation. Some reasons are: i) the complexity and intricacy of vision even in so-called low animals, ii) the intrinsic limits of the experimental methods e.g. in electrophysiology, iii) the limits of the explanatory power of results from psychophysical experiments carried out in necessarily highly-constrained artificial laboratory environments as juxtaposed to vision in a complex natural environment, iv) the limits of mathematical formalisation of empirical data derived from scientific observations, v) the limits of prevailing reductionistic modeling, and lastly vi) the principal epistemological limits of science.

Given both the past monodisciplinary achievements and insights in these limits, the scientific community devoted to vision more and more adopts a cross-fertilising point of view. Consequently, researchers are appealed to contribute in a complementing manner such as to better jointly fathoming scientific principles (see, for instance, the early book by Beck, Hope, and Rosenfeld, 1983, as well as the actual anthology in Papathomas et al., 1995). Unraveling the conundrum of vision indisputably requires an interdisciplinary approach which is closely connected to modeling in the realm of the emerging paradigm of computational science (Levine, 1989). Since scientific disciplines face novel problems called "Grand Challenges" by Levine (1989), this rather new paradigm states that theory and experiment alone may not suffice for an utter understanding of phenomena, but will have to be complemented by computational models and hence by simulations on a digital computer. Supplementing the two classical cornerstones of science by computational models is particularly promising, not to say the ideal way, if experimental methods and techniques come up against limiting factors (see above for some main limits). In the general context of brain research, the computational neuroscience paradigm implies the derivation of biologically adequate computational models, provided mathematical tractability and formalisation, from the large body of empirical data (Schwartz, 1990; Churchland and Sejnowski, 1992). One of the prime reasons for learning from biology is that complex biological systems with their astounding performance, as brought forth in an evolutionary manner by mother nature, are an existence proof of its principal realisability. Clearly, in modeling the visual system many levels of abstraction exist and thus a varying degree of biological adequacy as well; moreover puristic engineering solutions to specific problems, e.g. in robot vision, may lie far off biological principles although they could well have been biologically inspired. Biological adequacy here means the incorporation of known structural and functional principles of a nervous system in the conceptual/formal model such as to eventually yield computational models with utmost descriptive, explanatory, as well as predictive power.

To be more specific, descriptive power of a model can be defined as the fidelity of resemblance of a model to structure and function of the biological system under consideration. Explanatory power can be related to the extent to which a minimal model can account for a maximal number of experimentally observable phenomena brought forth by the biological system. Predictive power, on the other hand, can be understood as the degree of the model's capability of deriving hypotheses, subsequently to be tested by the empirical disciplines, about structure and function from results of modeling and simulation. Moreover, results from simulations solely starting out from hypotheses about structure and function of the visual system (if, for instance, none, weak, or contradictory empirical evidence is available only) may also lead to the definition of specific experiments to be done by the experimental disciplines. In turn results of these experiments may contribute to the support or the falsification of both theories and computational models of visual perception. Given the once in a while sloppy and inflationary use of biological metaphors in non-biological disciplines, in computational neuroscience these three powers from above taken together could easily serve as a yardstick of biological adequacy of models, e.g. to rule out computer programs only superficially mimicking biological principles. Once powerful models have been implemented on digital computers for the purpose of simulating experimentally observable properties of e.g. the visual system, the degree of similarity between results from observational experiments, e.g. in visual psychophysics, and results from simulative experiments on a digital computer then has to be considered a final touchstone for biological adequacy.

Modeling has a long standing tradition in so-called structure sciences such as mathematics and computer science (by the way, computing science would be a more apt expression). Theoretical models of information processing machines as well as models of computation, both rooted in mathematics, were crucial for the advancement of the discipline of computer science. A key issue in computer science is the theory of computability of problems denoted in formal languages, which is - together with achievements in microelectronics - the very basis for computerisation of almost all facets of our modern life. No wonder that computer metaphors such as electronic brains were introduced right after the advent of computing machinery (e.g. von Neumann, 1958). Indeed even long before the availability of powerful digital computers, thoughts were given to potential similarities between brains and machines, ideas which led to the approaches of cybernetics (Wiener, 1948) and, as called today, artificial neural networks (McCulloch and Pitts, 1943). Both approaches intensively draw upon biological principles and generally have in common the concept of feedback (being ubiquitous in biological systems on arbitrary scales), which implies a mathematical formulation in terms of dynamical systems theory. In those days, however, the ever-increasing dominance of digital computers along with the primacy of symbol manipulation more or less solely fostered research on symbolic representations and associated processes (coined algorithms). Soon cognitive processes in the brain were declared to be symbol manipulations and transformations like in digital computers, a view put forward as the physical symbol systems hypothesis (Newell and Simon, 1976). Psychology capitalised on this hypothesis in a way that behaviourism has eventually been superseded by the information processing approach to perception and cognition in general. To put it bluntly, so-called box-and-arrow models have become en vogue since this approach allows both a conceptually simple "divide&conquer"-decomposition of complex problems in computable subproblems and a practically simple transformation of the subproblems into computer programs. In short, biological adequacy has mainly been replaced by the paradigm of functionalism thus putting emphasis on the successful replay of the observable function of a cognitive system through computer programs by largely ignoring biological details of structure, function, and behaviour (see also Brooks, 1991a, for a readable critique of early cognitivism).

It is this context of cognitivism in which the seminal work by Marr has to be placed, the first book (posthumously published) ever on a computational model of human vision ranging from retinal processes to object recognition (Marr, 1982). Depending on the reader's viewpoint, this treatise has been characterised as a computational theory of, a cognitivistic working hypothesis about, or an information processing approach to visual perception. In any case, Marr's work has established computer vision as a subdiscipline of Artificial Intelligence and substantially spurred computer vision research within the realm of reconstructivism. The hallmark of the reconstructionist approach is the recovery of a viewer-centred representation of depth cues from images of the world which subsequently is matched to stored symbolic-geometric world models for recognition and interpretation purposes. Marr's definition of visual perception as an information processing scheme implied bottom-up low-level processes for the derivation of a symbolic primal sketch of images and medium-level vision processes for quantitative depth cue (coined shape) recovery, the latter linked with top-down high-level processes resembling cognitive visual abilities. In the wake of this influential work, emphasis has been put on both theoretical grounding and mathematical tractability of the shape recovery paradigm which resulted in reformulating computational vision as a problem of inverse optics to be tackled with regularisation theory (Poggio et al., 1985). Conceptually, assumptions and prior knowledge about the physical world and the imaging process (e.g. optics, photometry, projective geometry) were considered as being crucial for reducing the potential visual ambiguity of a two-dimensional array of grey-values or, respectively, colours which human beings can easily perceive as an image of the world. Mathematically, formalisations of strong assumptions, being mainly incompatible with natural vision, have been indispensable for constraining the space of mathematical solutions. Early success in solving specific problems then led to the, overly optimistic as one knows today, claim for achieving general-purpose computer vision systems in the future. Aloimonos and Rosenfeld (1991) clearly pointed out in an almost heretical fashion that the belief in this scientific route claiming to yield a better understanding of vision or, respectively, to create more powerful computer vision system has to be considered a fallacy now:

> "The recovery paradigm, which regards vision as a set of low- and middle-level modules that recover the structure of the scene, and that provide input to high level modules which can then reason about the scene, has not led to the design of successful vision systems, that is, systems that robustly perform recognition or navigation by means of vision."

Despite the criticism of reconstructivism (see also Witkin and Tenenbaum, 1983), one has to admit that research on computational vision has been significantly fostered by this early work. Conclusively, it is safe to state that the past international research within the reconstructivism paradigm successfully achieved fundamental insights into the intrinsic problems of modeling vision from an information processing perspective, into mathematical tractability and the nature of algorithmic solutions, into the validity of results and limits of explanatory power of these computational models (see also Neumann and Stiehl, 1995, for a critical review of early visual information processing).

A key deficit in most of these early contributions was the ignorance of facts like (to name a few) i) vision in living things is rather acquired than congenital, qualitative than quantitative as well as holistic than modular and ii) observers are active per se w.r.t. to their environment. It is a by now commonly held view that the visual sense cannot be decoupled from behaviour, since vision is survival-supportive, task-oriented, purpose-directed, and motor-coupled. In short, vision supports basic behaviour: E.g. orientation and navigation in the space-time continuum, exploration of unknown environments, obstacle and enemy avoidance, prey catching, search for reproductive partners. The successful visual real-time performance of an active agent, may it be an animal or a mobile autonomous vehicle, in an environment subject to change is primarily facilitated by an extremely efficient visual system with a tight coupling of structure, function, and behaviour (which is one of the credos of computational neuroscience). Taking perception as an active process implies several aspects: i) alert agents with instinct or, respectively, consciousness and subject to ego-(eye-, head-, neck- and body-)motion, ii) the existence of rich distal visual trigger features in the environment, iii) efficient pre-attentive visual processes within the retino-cortical path acting on e.g. retinotopic, compact, redundancy-free, error-tolerant etc. representations of the visual world, and iv) the capability of selective attention to master the exorbitant amount of visual data (known also as the cocktail party effect in auditory perception). Key abilities which have to be brought forth to ensure an agent's active perception are, for instance, compensation of egomotion to render possible a stable perception of the environment, fovealisation through binocular vergence to synchronically direct the high-resolution foveae to a certain part of the field of view which requires detailed analysis, saccade generation to visually explore the field of view, and smooth pursuit to track moving objects.

As a consequence of the past lamentations about reconstructionist computer vision, parts of the computer vision research community "rediscovered" the early seminal work by the Gestaltists on spontaneous pre-attentive vision (see e.g. Metzger, 1953, for an in-depth treatise), by Gibson (1950) on ecological vision, and by the scientific community working for a long time on eye movement issues (see Findlay et al, 1995, for a description of recent interdisciplinary research) - apart from the "rediscovery" of neurobiology of the visual system since the seminal work of the Nobel prize winners Hubel and Wiesel (see e.g. Hubel, 1988). The contemporary advocates of these schools of thought have enriched the state-of-the-art on both pre-attentive (early) and attentive (active) computational visual processes. A prime example of interdisciplinary and thus biologically adequate modeling seriously taking into account empirical data from both visual neuroscience and psychophysics as related to Gestalt perception is the work by Grossberg and colleagues, who from the very beginning of their endeavour consequently swam against the tide of reconstructivism (see Grossberg, 1994, for a survey). With respect to active vision, it was Bajcsy (1985) who considered perceptual activity as axiomatic for future computer vision systems and thus proposed the active perception paradigm in her milestone paper (see also Bajcsy, 1988). The motto for the post-reconstructivist area, which she recommended to the computer vision community exactly one decade ago, was:

> "Perceptual activity is exploratory, probing, searching; percepts do not simply fall onto sensors as rain falls on the ground. We do not just see, we look."

Since then active vision theory, meant here in the widest sense of perception-to-action cycles, as well as innovative computational architectures resembling intertwined visuomotor capabilities in animals have become a hot topic not only in computational vision (Aloimonos, 1993; Blake and Yuille, 1993; Sood and Wechsler, 1993; Gaussier and Nicoud, 1994; Papathomas et al., 1995) but also in advanced robotics (Brooks, 1991b; Steels, 1995). Given the ease with which animals can successfully and economically as well as (though disputed) non-symbolically perform complex visual tasks as related to e.g. primitive behaviour supporting survival, the basic question was whether findings particularly from theoretical biology, neuroscience, and ethology suffice to model such biological systems. In this context several advanced research programs have been established which are again connected to milestone papers by Ballard (1991) on animate vision, Brooks (1991a,b) on the the concept of a subsumption architecture, and von Seelen and Mallot (1991) on computational neural architectures. In contrast to reconstructivism, the decomposition of a system with visual behaviour (see Martin et al., 1994, for up-to-date results from a workshop) is derived from knowledge about classes of behaviour with increasing complexity. Subsequently, models of complex behaviour can be achieved through composition of, once identified, generic behavioural classes along with their coupled visual capabilities.

Interestingly or non-surprisingly, again according to the reader's point of view, these approaches are also deeply rooted in bio- and neuro-cybernetics as can be grasped from the seminal book by Braitenberg (1984). Moreover, the view of complexity on superior levels of a biological system emerging from local interactions of elements on inferior levels, usually coined emergence principle, is also a key issue in computational neuroscience (Churchland and Sejnowski, 1992, p. 5):

> ".. we need to figure out the interaction principles governing the system, and that although interaction hypotheses should be constrained by microlevel data, their job is to characterize higher-level (emergent) features."

Laxly spoken, the following scientific issue has to be addressed: "How can behaviour computationally emerge from neurons?". In this context, von Seelen and Mallot (1991) introduced the phrasing "search for the neural instruction set", meaning scientific search for neural principles and eventually irreducibles (hence, universalia) related to neural activities on the signal level. Specifically with respect to the visual system, this search has been strikingly successful in the past as demonstrated by paramount discoveries: E.g. local interactions such as excitation and inhibition of signals; signal convergence, divergence, and recurrence in laminated tissue structures; signal representation of visual qualities in retinotopic maps etc. This conception of a neural instruction set has its roots in computer science, since in this discipline the key question of how to bridge the gap between a complex computable problem, formulated in a high-level programming language, and the physical layout of the lowest level of a digital computer, capable of processing signals only, has already been successfully answered. This view is just an analogy solely on the level of computation, which should not be misinterpreted as identity in real structure and function.

Since one premise in computational neuroscience is the strong coupling between structure and function in nervous systems, which again is related to the generation of behaviour, the convergence of computational active vision, computational neuroscience, and advanced robotics will further develop such as to successfully strive for biologically adeqate models of systems with autonomy. Moreover, in the last years a bridge to these research issues has also been built from Artificial Intelligence (AI) researchers theorising on distributed AI, specifically on intelligent autonomous agents and multi-agent cooperative problem solving (Steels, 1995; Castelfranchi and Müller, 1995). Meanwhile one has to witness a substantial advancement of the interdisciplinary grounding as related to active perception, which is also due to paramount contributions from eye movement research, psychophysics, cognitive psychology, and clinical neurology (as demonstrated also in relevant chapters of this book).

Despite the rapid progress made w.r.t. active computational vision, the reality of theory and practice is still sobering in comparison to the performance of even only lower animals than us. Aloimonos and Rosenfeld (1991) touched on sore points by hinting at theoretical deficits to be tackled in the future (some of which are addressed in Chapter 4):

> "However, the paradigm still lacks theoretical foundations, including a formal definition of a visual agent and the dependence of behavior on agent characteristics (size, mobility, and so forth); a formal definition of behavior (as a sequence of perceptual events and actions); and a calculus of behaviors or purposes that can generate new behaviors by combining existing behaviors or by learning and that can provide the basis for controlling the agent; and a corresponding repertoire of visual routines ...".

For a concluding remark on modeling vision from a computational perspective, one cannot do better than Aloimonos and Rosenfeld (1991) did in their critical survey:

> "The theoretical foundations of computer vision are not yet fully developed ...The study of vision in organisms and computers continues to be a rich source of interesting research problems."

2. THE LEVEL APPROACH TO MODELING VISION AND EXEMPLARY RESEARCH

As pointed out above, interdisciplinary and biologically adequate modeling of visual perception, whether pre-attentive or attentive, given the premise of information processing requires a convergence of computational vision and computational neuroscience. Apart from all the neat definitions and catchy objectives on the list of desiderata, some of which have been briefly presented in the previous paragraph, a first key question to be answered is whether there is a methodology for biologically adequate computational modeling. In recent years, a point of view has been adopted within the computational neuroscience community which refers to levels of organisation in the nervous system (Churchland and Sejnowski, 1992, p. 18) nicely related to different kinds of empirical observation. This level approach tacitly assumes decomposability of the visual system, e.g. in mammals, into a hierarchy according to different complexity levels w.r.t. structure, functionality, scale, etc. Since the lowest possible level is connected to Ångstrœm dimensions and the most superior one to behaviour, a second key question is how to relate, for instance, neurons to behaviour. An evident approach, which at the same time can be characterised as a research programme in its own right, is to define levels in such a way that structure and function of consecutive levels are appropriately related, e.g. more complex structure/function derived from less complex structure/function (see also the discussion in the previous paragraph). As Churchland and Sejnowski (1992, p.11) put it:

> "The hallmark of co-evolution of theories is that research at one level provides corrections, constraints, and inspiration for research at a higher and lower level. ... Theorizing at a high level without benefit of lower-level constraints runs at risk of exploring a part of that (solution) space that may be interesting in its own right but remote from where the brain's solution reside. Thus microlevel constraints and testing of hypotheses against microlevel facts are of central importance."

By ignoring here subcellular details (and by concentrating further on structural issues only), the lowest and hence micro-scale levels are neurons and neuron populations with their connectivity patterns for signal transmission and processing in local circuits, primarily accessible through electrophysiology and microscopy of stained cells. The subsequent levels of increasing complexity are related to laminated (sub-)cortical structures and so-called retinotopic maps to be understood as spatial representations of visual qualities, e.g. colour or brightness, typically preserving the topography of distal stimuli in the visual field. These micro-to-meso levels are preferentially approachable through electrophysiological, cytoarchitectural, neuroanatomical, and partly also clinical neurological studies. Next in the level hierarchy are anatomically or functionally significant compartments, e.g. visual areas in our case, and larger-scale connectivity patterns, which basically are subject to observation through the same bulk of empirical techniques plus, due to their meso-scale characteristics, through advanced radiological (functional MRI or PET) imaging and partly also psychophysics. Going further up the hierarchy, eventually the level of the visual system itself along with global interconnections can be analysed, typically lending itself to MRI/PET imaging and psychophysical analysis. Finally, behaviour as associated with the system under consideration can be observed by empirical disciplines such as psychophysics, cognitive psychology, and ethology. In the ideal case, computational neuroscience renders possible modeling at micro-, meso-, and macro-levels in a way that a biologically adequate model at a particular level is derived in such a way that empirical facts from neighbouring levels constrain the space of potential models for that particular level. For instance, research on computational models of pre-attentive vision as described in Grossberg (1994) is a typical example of this approach. These models are rigorously determined in a bottom-up manner by findings from neurosciences at various lower levels and, at the same time, in a top-down fashion by insights from visual psychophysics. Hence they are capable of accounting for empirical data from both psychophysics, a discipline related to upper levels and providing top-down constraints to the model, and relevant neurosciences (see also the discussion on biological adequacy above). Modeling the top-level w.r.t. human problem solving associated with behavioural tasks is eventually the prime domain of Artificial Intelligence and Cognitive Science. Modeling and realisation of e.g. mobility and autonomy of artificial agents/vehicles is typically connected to i) advanced robotics incl. approaches from (neuro-)ethology, computational neuroscience, artificial neural networks, and A.I. (for a

recent survey on some of these issues, see Schöner, Dose and Engels, 1995), as well as to
ii) the classical engineering sciences, e.g. control theory and mechanical engineering.

In the remainder of this paper, the individual contributions to this chapter, spanning the
range from the neuronal level up to active cooperation of autonomous agents, will be
summarised as well as linked to the modeling aspects discussed so far.

Schierwagen (University of Leipzig, Institute of Computer Science) addresses the problem
of modeling on a micro-scale level the synchronous activity of populations of neurons in the
motor map of the superior colliculus, a laminated grey-matter structure in the midbrain being
of fundamental importance for eye movement. The superior colliculus in mammals consists
of superficial layers with stimuli-responsive neurons as well as deep layers with saccade-
triggering neurons, both organised as topographical maps (ergo called motor map for the
latter). His work is based upon electrophysiological, anatomical, as well as behavioural
studies and takes into account the fact that the spatio-temporal dynamics of neural activity
in the motor map triggers neurons controlling eye movement. Having discussed principles of
neural computations in layered systems, he presents a non-feedback model - coined mapped
neural field with Amari dynamics - which is capable of spatially propagating trajectories of
activity hills resembling dynamic neuronal activity in the collicular motor map.

Schwegler (University of Bremen, Institute of Theoretical Neurophysics) reports on ongoing
computational neuroscience research on a variety of hierarchy levels such as to model the
linking of neural principles to animal behaviour . The focus has been set on computational
models of animal optomotor processes, specifically neural control of prey catching, in
tongue-projecting plethodontic salamanders. These cute animals have binocular vision for
fast and precise stereoscopic depth perception but no ability of saccadic eye movements and
are able to even catch flies cruising in space with a speed of approx. 20 cm/sec. The basis of
his endeavour to come up with mathematically stringent models are empirical data derived
from both neurophysiological, neuroanatomical, and behavioural studies. Particular interest
has been given to a deeper understanding of structure and function of retinotopic maps in the
optic tectum (which is functionally equivalent to the primary visual cortex in primates). A
continuous neural field model of activities in the optic tectum as well as a discrete three-
layer neural network model, called simulander, are discussed.

Pahlavan (Royal Institute of Technology Stockholm, Computational Vision and Active
Perception Laboratory) presents the anthropomorphic design and development of one of the
most advanced experimental "artificial head" set-ups in the computational vision community
resembling the prime biomechanics of the primate eye-neck-system. His work is part of
ongoing research on computational active vision principles and has to be considered a key
contribution to modeling active binocular agents. After a review of the basic principles
underlying his design, he thoroughly describes the electro-optico-mechanical engineering
feat. Two high-resolution semiconductor cameras mounted on a baseline rig are fixed to a
neck module. The large number of degrees of optical/mechanical freedom (DOF) are
controlled by small motors. Each camera module has two degrees of mechanical freedom
(pan and tilt, plus a means for compensating movements of the lens center due to focusing
and zooming) and three degrees of optical freedom (focusing, zooming, and aperture
setting). The neck module also has two degrees of mechanical freedom, again pan and tilt as
in the case of the cameras' mechanical DOF. Neither vestibulo-ocular phenomena, such as
the compensation of egomotion, nor elaborate visual processes have been modeled yet. At

the end of his paper, the author also presents impressive data recorded from experiments, e.g. a saccade speed of the camera module of up to 170 deg/sec.

Janßen (Ruhr-University of Bochum, Institute of Computational Neuroscience) focuses on design and realisation of a system primarily modeling stimuli- as well as expectation-guided saccades again on a variety of levels. His research is embedded in a large interdisciplinary computational neuroscience effort and eventually became part of a working experimental vehicle called MARVIN. The system heavily draws upon modeling biological principles such as foveal versus peripheral vision processing, vergence and smooth pursuit, expectation-driven gaze, selective attention driven by visual saliency, incremental learning of objects as well as complex scenes by means of directed fixations, and emergence of behaviour e.g. through competition and cooperation of preattentive and attentive targets. The model has to be considered a blend of computational vision, computational neuroscience, and artificial neural networks, demonstrating that for the time being it is not possible to fully realize biologically adequate models spanning all levels from above within a real-time performing vehicle. The author also reports on realisation and laboratory results of the system equipped with visual behaviour. Moreover he points out that the experimental system is currently the only one realizing the integration of saliency controlled saccadic exploration with fast saccadic recognition in approx. 1 second of cycle time.

Bajcsy (University of Pennsylvania, GRASP Laboratory, University of Pennsylvania) in her essayistic treatise extends the notion of active perception, introduced by her one decade ago, to active cooperation - hence a contribution related to the topmost levels. The focus in her paper is set on autonomous agents (whether human or artificial) which are distributed in space and possibly time and are also interacting with a dynamic, often unpredictably changing environment. She claims that only a proper understanding of cooperation will lead to a foundation of intelligent behaviour and thoroughly discusses cooperative sensing, processing, manipulation, behaviour, and agents. Fundamental issues from a variety of disciplines (such as computational vision, advanced robotics, and distributed Artificial Intelligence) which are conceptually and theoretically connected to active cooperation, are also touched upon, e.g. behaviour modeling, autonomous systems, and multi-agent problem solving. Within this cooperative framework, she elaborates on the utilization of discrete event systems and dynamical systems theory as key building blocks. As a consequence she proposes that proper models of an agent should be based on its dynamics and, moreover, must also include dynamic interaction of the agent with its environment.

ACKNOWLEDGEMENTS

I am grateful to Kai-Oliver Ludwig for critical reading. Thanks also to Walt "The Dolphin" for piecewise polishing my English in the draft version.

REFERENCES

Aloimonos, Y., and A. Rosenfeld, 1991, Computer Vision, Science **253**, 1249.

Aloimonos, Y., ed., 1993, Active Perception (L. Erlbaum Assoc., Hillsdale).

Bajcsy, R., 1985, Active Perception vs. Passive Perception, Proc. IEEE Workshop on Computer Vision, Representation, and Control, October 1985 (IEEE Computer Society Press, Los Alamitos), p 55.

Bajcsy, R., 1988, Active Perception, Proc. of the IEEE **76**, 996.

Ballard, D.H., 1991, Animate Vision, Artificial Intelligence **48**, 57.

Beck, J., B. Hope, and A. Rosenfeld, eds., 1983, (Proceedings of First Workshop) Human and Machine Vision (Academic Press, New York).

Blake, A., and A. Yuille, eds., 1993, Active Vision (The MIT Press, Cambridge, Mass.).

Braitenberg, V., 1984, Vehicles: Experiments in Synthetic Psychology (The MIT Press, Cambridge, Mass.).

Brooks, R.A., 1991a. Intelligence without Reason, in: Proc. 12th Intn. Joint Conference on Artificial Intelligence, Sydney, August 1991, 569 (Academic Press, New York).

Brooks, R.A., 1991b, New Approaches to Robotics, Science **253**, 1227.

Bruce, V., and P.R. Green, 1992, Visual Perception - Physiology, Psychology, and Ecology (L. Erlbaum Assoc., Hillsdale).

Castelfranchi, C., and J. Müller, eds., 1995, From Reaction to Cognition (Springer-Verlag, Berlin).

Christensen, H.I., K.W. Boyer, and H. Bunke, eds., 1993, Active Robot Vision - Camera Heads, Model Based Navigation, and Reactive Control (World Scientific, Singapore).

Churchland, P.S., and T.J. Sejnowski, 1992, The Computational Brain (The MIT Press, Cambridge, Mass.).

Findlay, J. et al., eds., 1995, Eye Movement Research - Mechanisms, Processes, and Applications (North-Holland, Amsterdam).

Gaussier, P., and J.-D. Nicoud, eds., 1994, Proc. Conference From Perception to Action, Lausanne, September 1994 (IEEE Computer Society Press, Los Alamitos).

Gibson, J.J., 1950, The Perception of the Visual World (Houghton Mifflin, Boston).

Grossberg, S., 1994, 3-D Vision and Figure-Ground Seperation by Visual Cortex, Perception & Psychophysics **55**, 48.

Hubel, D., 1988, Eye, Brain, and Vision (Scientific American Library Series No. 22).

Landy, M.S., L.T. Maloney, and M. Pavel, eds., 1996, Exploratory Vision - The Active Eye (Springer-Verlag, Berlin).

Levine, E., 1989, Grand Challenges to Computational Science, Comm. of the ACM **32**, 1456.

McCulloch, W.S., and W. Pitts, 1943, A Logical Calculus of the Ideas Immanent in Nervous Activity, Bulletin of Mathem. Biophysics **5**, 115.

Marr, D., 1982, Vision - A Computational Investigations into the Human Representation and Processing of Visual Information (W.H. Freeman, San Francisco).

Martin, W.N. et al., eds., 1994, Proc. Workshop onVisual Behaviors, Seattle, June 1994 (IEEE Computer Society Press, Los Alamitos).

Metzger, W., 1953, Die Gesetze des Sehens (in German), 2nd edition (W. Kramer, Frankfurt).

Neumann, H., and H.S. Stiehl, 1995, Modelle der frühen visuellen Informations-verarbeitung, in: Einführung in die Künstliche Intelligenz, 2nd edition, ed. G. Görz (Addison Wesley Deutschland GmbH, Bonn), p. 583 (in German).

Newell, A., and H.A. Simon, 1976, Computer Science as Empirical Enquiry: Symbols and Search, Comm. of the ACM **19**, 113.

Orban, G.A., 1991, Visual Neuroscience, in: Cognitive Neuroscience - Research Directions in Cognitive Science, eds. G.A. Orban, W. Singer and N.O. Bernsen (L. Erlbaum Assoc., Hillsdale).

Papathomas, T.V. et al., eds., 1995, Early Vision and Beyond (The MIT Press, Cambridge, Mass.).

Poggio, T., V. Torre and C. Koch, 1985, Computational Vision and Regularization Theory, Nature **317**, 315.

Roth, G., 1994, Das Gehirn und seine Wirklichkeit - Kognitive Neurobiologie und ihre philosophischen Konsequenzen (in German), 1st edition, (Suhrkamp, Frankfurt).

Schwartz, E.L., ed., 1990, Computational Neuroscience (The MIT Press, Cambridge, Mass.)

Schöner, G., M. Dose and C. Engels, 1995, Dynamics of Behavior: Theory and Applications for Autonomous Robot Architectures, Robotics and Autonomous Systems (Special Issue, in press).

Sood, A.K., and H. Wechsler, eds., 1993, Active Perception and Robot Vision (Springer-Verlag, Berlin).

Spillmann, W., and J.S. Werner, eds., 1990, Visual Perception - The Neurophysiological Foundations (Academic Press, San Diego).

Steels, L., ed., 1995, The Biology and Technology of Intelligent Autonomous Agents (NATO ASI Series F Vol. 144, Springer-Verlag, Berlin).

von Neumann, J., 1958, The Computer and the Brain (Yale University Press, New Haven).

von Seelen, W., and H.A. Mallot, 1991, Information Processing in a Neural Architecture, in: Artificial Neural Networks, eds. T. Kohonen et al. (Elsevier Science Publ., Amsterdam), p. 885.

Wiener, N., 1948, Cybernetics or Control and Communication in the Animal and the Machine (John Wiley & Sons, New York).

Witkin, A.P., and J.M. Tenenbaum, 1983, On the Role of Structure in Vision, in: Human and Machine Vision, eds. J. Beck, B. Hope and A. Rosenfeld (Academic Press, New York), p. 481.

Zeki, S., 1993, A Vision of the Brain (Blackwell Scientific Publications, Oxford).

Visual Attention and Cognition
W.H. Zangemeister, H.S. Stiehl and C. Freksa (Editors)
© 1996 Elsevier Science B.V. All rights reserved.

THE COLLICULAR MOTOR MAP AS MODELLED BY A TWO-DIMENSIONAL MAPPED NEURAL FIELD

Andreas Schierwagen
Institut für Informatik, Universität Leipzig, FRG

Abstract

In contrast to traditional methodologies in Artificial Intelligence, the new paradigm of *active vision* argues that vision is more readily studied in the behavioural context of the system. Active vision systems (AVS) have features derived from biology (binocularity, fovealization, high speed gaze control). In this paper, computational strategies of visuomotor control as used in biological vision are analysed with the goal to employ them in artificial AVS. Neural maps, population coding and space-variant processing in layered systems are identified as high-level principles of neural computing underlaying saccadic eye movement control. These principles are applied to formulate a *mapped neural field model* of the spatio-temporal dynamics in the motor map of the superior colliculus, a sensorimotor transformation centre in the brain stem involved in eye movement control. Mapped neural fields embody a general scheme of representation and computation which is especially adapted to the coordinate transformations involved in sensorimotor control.

Keywords: Active vision, saccades, collicular motor map, neural fields, space-variant processing

1   Active vision systems

The performance of living beings is distinctly superior to artificial devices with respect to orienting and exploratory behaviour. The main reason for this situation may be that traditional methodologies in Artificial Intelligence have largely ignored behavioural aspects. In vision, for example, the hitherto most important computational theory developed by Marr (1982) was essentially about passive vision, i.e. the coupling with the perceiver's behaviour was excluded. Likewise not included were special features of human vision such as its elaborate gaze control system that includes fast eye movements (saccades) and the fovea with its greatly enhanced resolution.

The new paradigm of *active vision* (Bajcsy, 1988; Aloimonos, 1993; Ballard and Brown, 1992) argues that vision is more readily understood in the behavioural context of the system. Active vision systems (AVS) have biological features such as binocularity and fovealization. The most important characteristic, which has been seen as one way of defining active vision, is gaze control performing with high speed. Depending on the task, an AVS is able to orient the visual sensor during data sampling. Compared to

Table 1. Summary of primate eye movements

Movement	Description	Latency
Saccades	discrete, high-speed $(300 - 400°/s)$ eye movements to foveate a target; average rate $< 4/s$	$150\,ms$
Pursuit	maintains foveation of a target using retinal slip	$50\,ms$
Vergence	binocular movements to facilitate the computation of target depth	$> 200\,ms$
VOR	eye rotation rate = - head rotation rate	$14\,ms$
OKN	uses visual feedback to move the eyes to stabilize full field motion or protracted head motion	

Latency is the time from target onset to initial response. Different latencies allow identification of different eye movement subsystems (VOR - vestibulo-occular reflex, OKN - optokinetic nystagmus). After Ballard (1987).

passive systems, AVS show that visual computations can be vastly less expensive, when considered in the behavioural context.

The primate eye movement system is capable of five basic kinds of movements (Table 1). At least three of these movement subsystems are modularly structured. That is, these subsystems operate relatively decoupled to correct different sources of error, as indicated by the distinct differences between latencies. The sensor surface in the human eye (the retina) differs from that of current commercial electronic cameras in having a high-resolution area (the fovea) near the optical axis. Over this small region (less than 1% of the retina!) the resolution is better by an order of magnitude than in the periphery. By means of this retinal design, a large part of the visual field is mapped onto the retina, with high acuity only in the fovea. Thus, the primate visual system has to perform saccades in order to direct the fovea to different spatial targets. As discussed in Ballard (1987), several constraints could lead to such a foveal vision system in primates. Once a fovea is present, adaptive gaze control is of fundamental importance.

The principles of neural computations governing gaze control include neural maps, population coding and processing in layered systems. In the present paper, these principles are applied to build a mapped neural field model of the spatio-temporal dynamics observed in the motor map of the superior colliculus (SC), a sensorimotor transformation centre in the brain stem.

2   Eye movement control in biological vision

A major role in eye movement control plays the SC. The SC is a laminated structure consisting of 7 alternating fibre and cell layers. From anatomical, physiological and behavioural investigations, mainly in cats and monkeys, the picture emerged that the SC layers can be separated into two major subdivisions - the superficial and deep layers.

Neurons in the superficial SC layers respond exclusively to visual stimuli. They are distributed over the SC surface in a topographical, map-like format, i.e. the location of a neuron within this map is determined by the position of the centre of its receptive field (RF). This retinotopic representation extends on the SC surface from 0° up to 80° of the contralateral visual hemisphere (Fig. 1).

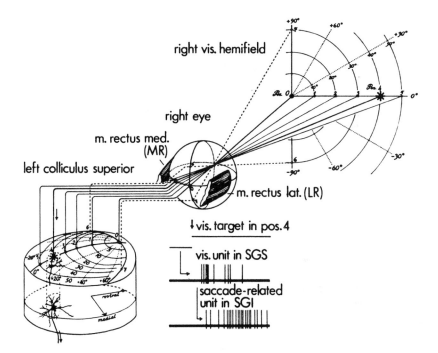

Fig. 1. Schema of the relationships between the visual field, the visual map in the SC, and the motor responses towards a peripheral visual target. A visual signal is generated by neurons of the upper SC and forwarded to projection cells of the deep SC which discharge prior to saccadic eye movement. A spatial to temporal transformation must subsequently take place to ensure coordinated activity of different eye muscles. Reproduced with permission from Grantyn (1988).

Cells in the deep layers discharge high-frequency bursts of spikes before the onset of rapid eye movements. The range of possible saccades prior to which a given neuron discharges defines its movement field (MF). The MF of a saccade neuron has a centre which is related to maximal discharge, and a gradient of response fading away for saccade vectors which deviate from optimal. Thus, one neuron is firing for a specific but large range of movements. Neurons in the deep layers are also organized in topographic order: the MF centres of saccade neurons build a motor map (for review, see Sparks and Mays

(1990)). This means that the location of active neurons represents the motor error which is defined by the vector of eye movement (i.e. amplitude and direction) yet to be made by the eyes in order to reach the target. The topography of the motor map is such that horizontal motor error is encoded mainly along the rostro-caudal axis while vertical motor error is encoded along the medio-lateral axis. The more caudal (medio-lateral) the centre of activity is located, the larger the horizontal (vertical) motor error (Fig. 2).

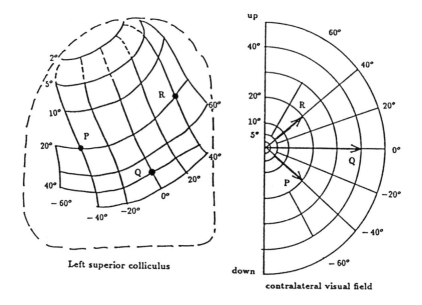

Fig. 2. The motor map formed on the SC. Stimulation at sites P, Q, and R in the left SC evoke corresponding and respective saccades P, Q, and R to the contralateral visual field. After Robinson (1972).

A population of saccade neurons starts firing when a motor error occurs, where the activity distribution within the motor map looks like a bell-shaped hill. The neuronal firing rates encode movement velocity (Berthoz et al., 1987). Saccades to different parts of the visual field are preceded by activity hills in different regions of the map. In recent tracer studies (Grantyn, 1988; Hilbig and Schierwagen, 1994), it was shown that the upper, visual layers are connected to the deep layers in such a way that both maps might be in spatial register. Activity in the visual map then could be conveyed to corresponding areas in the motor map, thus moving the eye from its current fixation point to the target that activates the visual cells.

Recent experimental studies (Munoz and Guitton, 1989; Munoz et al., 1991) showed that in the cat's SC during a saccade the activity hill travels through the motor map from its initial location towards the fixation zone at the rostral pole (a hill-shift effect). The instantaneous hill location on the map specifies the remaining motor error. The saccade is terminated when the travelling activity hill reaches the fixation zone where it ceases. Another recent investigation which aimed at reconciling the apparent species-dependent differences in the collicular dynamics (Munoz and Wurtz, 1992) has identified two types of movement-related cells in the SC of rhesus monkeys, i.e. burst neurons (BNs) and buildup neurons (BUNs). The activity in the BN layer declines during movement as the motor error decreases (a hill-flattening effect), while activity in the BUN layer resembles the hill-shift effect found in the cat's SC. These results show that in both species the hill-shift effect is present although the situation in primates seems to be more complex than in cats. These studies propose how the spatial representation of activity on the motor map is transformed into the temporal code (frequency and duration of discharge) required by motoneurons: by continuous, dynamic collicular control of the eye movement. Thus, the trajectory of activity on the motor map of the cat SC spatially encodes the instantaneous eye movement motor error signal.

Almost all models of biological gaze control are based on a global feedback loop in order to maintain the accuracy of saccades. This idea, however, causes some problems. Any SC model based on global feedback has to explain, how spatial-temporal (downstream) and temporal-spatial (upstream) transformations could be performed, in order to calculate saccades and dynamic motor error. Whereas the coding of saccades in the motor map of the SC is well understood, the idea of back-projections to this map performing the necessary temporal-spatial transformations remains speculativ. Although the projection from brain stem structures to the SC has been anatomically investigated, no definitve evidence could be derived clarifying which mechanisms the gaze control system employs for updating the activity of the saccade neurons.

The present approach instead is based on the both structurally and computationally simpler assumption that collicular dynamic error coding might be realized without global feedback, alone through the nonlinear, spatio-temporal dynamics of neural populations, considered as mapped neural fields.

3 Computing in neural architecture

Artificial neural networks have been occasionally criticized by neurobiologists as poor carricatures of their biological counterparts. When realistic neural networks are to be modelled, a number of higher-level structural principles must be included. One of the most prominent of these architectural features is neural mapping. Omitting entirely the problem of map formation via self-organization, we consider maps as computationally attractive, biologically plausible data structures and their relation to nonlinear, spatio-temporal dynamics in neural layers.

A neural map consists of a layer of neurons, the computational properties of which vary with their spatial position. The position of a neuron in the map largely determines (1) which part of the input it receives, (2) how this input is processed and (3) to what target the result eventually is transferred, see, e.g. Knudsen et al. (1987) and Mallot et al. (1990) for discussion.

The neurons of a receptotopic map represent an array of broadly tuned filters that operate in parallel on the input signal. Their input is instantaneously transformed into a spatially coded distribution of neural activity where values of the mapped parameter are represented as locations and heights of hills of activity. This spatially coded information can be readily accessed by higher-order processors (which might be also maps), using relatively simple connectivity schemes.

From a formal point of view, computation can be defined as any (nontrivial) transformation in the representation of information (Knudsen et al., 1987). Then, biological receptotopic maps are not computational, since they simply map sensory epithelia by preserving spatial relationships in the peripheral sensorium. Computational maps discovered so far are mostly involved in processing sensory information and programming of movements (Knudsen et al., 1987). In motor maps, systematic variations of movement parameters (amplitude and direction) are represented topographically on the neural layer. The computational character of these maps is obvious: the topographically represented movement command must be transformed into spatio-temporal patterns of motoneuron activity, and the centre of activity on the map determines the features of the transformation. This processing principle of computational motor maps has been characterized as reversed to that of computational sensory maps: while sensory maps represent the results of space-variant computations, motor maps represent the source code governing systematically varying computations.

4   Homogeneous neural fields and their dynamics

The synchronous activity of large populations of neurons in the form of, e.g. oscillations and travelling activity waves, is a general property of neural systems in the mammalian brain (Freeman, 1975; Eckhorn et al., 1988; Gray and Singer, 1989; Abeles, 1991; Gray, 1994). On the other side, a common architectural feature of many neural subsystems both in vertebrate and invertebrate brains is layering (Mallot, 1995). Neural layers are characterized by anatomical and physiological parameters which remain more or less constant within the layer, but vary between layers. Therefore, the transition from discrete neural network models to continuous neural field models seems appropriate, especially to neural systems like the SC or the cortex which are organized in layers with connectivity patterns of a particular type.

We consider a 2-dimensional neural field. Let $u(\mathbf{x}, t)$ be the average membrane potential of neurons located at position $\mathbf{x} = (x, y)$ at time t. The average activity (pulse emission rate) of neurons at $\mathbf{x}$ at t is given by $f[u(\mathbf{x}, t)]$, and the average strength of synaptic connections from neurons at position $\mathbf{x}'$ to those at position $\mathbf{x}$ by $w(\mathbf{x}, \mathbf{x}')$. With u_0 the global threshold of the field and $s(\mathbf{x}, t)$ the intensity of applied stimulus from the outside of the field to the neurons at position $\mathbf{x}$, the neural field equation reads:

$$\tau \frac{\partial u(\mathbf{x}, t)}{\partial t} = -u(\mathbf{x}, t) + \iint_{\mathcal{R}^2} w(\mathbf{x}, \mathbf{x}') f[u(\mathbf{x}', t)] d\mathbf{x}' - u_0 + s(\mathbf{x}, t), \qquad (1)$$

which is the 2-dimensional generalization of Amari's (1977) equation.

The linear term in Eqn. (1) defines the time scale, τ, and the integral term represents interaction through local, short-range excitation and lateral, long-range inhibition, cf.

Eqn. (2). The transfer function f is a sigmoid shaped nonlinearity. Eqn. (1) can easily be extended to the case where the field consists of many mutually connected sublayers. For homogeneous fields, $w(\mathbf{x}, \mathbf{x}') = w(\mathbf{x} - \mathbf{x}')$ holds.

For fields of lateral-inhibition type, excitatory connections dominate for proximate neurons and inhibitory connections dominate at greater distances, described e.g. by a radially symmetrical weighting function of on-centre off-surround type modelled by a difference of Gaussians,

$$w(\mathbf{x} - \mathbf{x}') = g_e \cdot \exp\left(-\left(\frac{\mathbf{x} - \mathbf{x}'}{\sigma_e}\right)^2\right) - g_i \cdot exp\left(-\left(\frac{\mathbf{x} - \mathbf{x}'}{\sigma_i}\right)^2\right) \qquad (2)$$

where g_e and σ_e are the height and width of the excitatory centre and g_i and σ_i are the corresponding values for the inhibitory surround.

A categorization of the dynamics of 1-dimensional variants of such fields has been provided by Amari (1977). In single-layer fields, five types of dynamics were proved to exist, which are in general multi-stable. Some fields have the ability of keeping a localized excitation pattern at the position where a stimulus arrived, even after it disappeard. This might be related to short-term memory. Interaction of excitation patterns is also possible: two excited regions may attract each other, combining into one local excitation. In other cases they can repel each other, or coexist independently. Two-layer fields admit oscillatory and travelling wave solutions. Later it was shown that the results derived originally for a step transfer function $f(u)$ remain valid for sigmoidal transfer functions f (Kishimoto and Amari, 1979).

In the case of 2-dimensional neural fields, a similar categorization of the dynamics can be given, but the results are more complex (Amari, 1982). It cannot be expected, however, that the equations do admit solutions which correspond to isolated 1-dimensional trajectories of activity hills, as observed in the motor map of SC. This conclusion can be drawn from general results on the dynamics of active media (of which neural fields are special cases), saying that in continuous active media (AM) propagation of excitation is independent on direction (Keener, 1988; Mikhailov, 1990). Accordingly, in 2-dimensional continuous fields spiral and target waves are the main dynamic activity patterns which have been proved to exist (Ermentrout, 1982; Fohlmeister et al., 1995). For the various stationary patterns which are supported by neural fields, cf. Ermentrout and Cowan (1979), Markus and Schepers (1992), Fohlmeister et al. (1995).

5 Mapped neural field model of SC motor map

In Amari's theory of neural fields, space-invariance or homogeneity of the weighting function is essential. However, there is evidence that, e.g. in the internal cortical cortical processing, space-variance occurs (see Mallot et al.(1990) and the references therein). Likewise, it has been shown that both visual RFs and MFs of collicular neurons typically have a skewed (asymmetrical) sensitivity profile (Ottes et al., 1986).

Space-variance may be due either to a nonuniform afferent mapping where the subsequent intrinsic operations acting on this distorted mapping are space-invariant, or to intrinsic weighting functions depending on both input and output site, rather than on their mere difference. There is experimental evidence that space-variance of the first type is present both in cortical areas 17, 18 (Mallot et al., 1990) and the SC of the cat (Ottes et al., 1986). It can be realized by *mapped filters*, i.e. a cascade composed of a topographic mapping and a subsequent space-invariant filtering (Mallot et al., 1990).

A second line of evidence for introducing space-variant operators comes from analyses of specific AM, i.e. fields of FitzHugh-Nagumo (FHN) neurons (Keener, 1988). The FHN model holds a prominent position in studies of AM because of its simplicity and qualitative corresponence with more complicated models (Schierwagen and Francu, 1989). In the present context, a particularly important result from investigations of 2-dimensional FHN fields is the following: while in a 2-dimensional, continuous field of FHN neurons with any type of weighting functions (space-invariant or not), propagation of excitation does not depend on direction, a discrete field model with space-variant, asymmetrical weighting functions exhibits dynamic behaviour which corresponds to 1-dimensional trajectories of activity hills. That is, these hills fail to spread laterally to excite the adjacent field regions, if the asymmetry of the weighting function is strong enough (Keener, 1988).

Thus, we modelled the collicular motor map by a discrete version of a mapped neural field of the Amari type, i.e. the field model, Eqn. (1), endowed with space-variant weighting functions of the mapped filter type. In contrast to the case of space-invariant, homogeneous neural fields, no analytical results on, e.g. the types of possible dynamic behaviour, or on the stability of the solutions are available for mapped fields. Therefore, we studied the spatio-temporal activity of such fields through computer simulations.

The weighting function was chosen to model the combined effect of the complex logarithmic mapping and subsequent space-invariant processing, as suggested by the experimental and theoretical work of Ottes et al. (1986). Thus, we used a rotationally asymmetric weighting function modelled as a difference of 2-dimensional Gaussian functions, each of which is the product of two orthogonal 1-dimensional Gaussians. The weighting function $w(\mathbf{x}, \mathbf{x}')$, of which the centre and surround regions have elliptical isoefficacy contours, is given in normal form (i.e. for $\mathbf{x}' = \mathbf{0}$ and coincident axes of ellipses and $\mathbf{x}$-coordinates) by

$$w(\mathbf{x}, \mathbf{0}) = g_e \cdot \exp\left(-\left(\frac{x}{\sigma_{e_x}}\right)^2 - \left(\frac{y}{\sigma_{e_y}}\right)^2 \right) - g_i \cdot \exp\left(-\left(\frac{x}{\sigma_{i_x}}\right)^2 - \left(\frac{y}{\sigma_{i_y}}\right)^2 \right) \quad (3)$$

where $\mathbf{x} = (x, y)$. g_e, σ_{e_x} and σ_{e_y} are the height, x-axis width and y-axis width of the excitatory centre, and g_i, σ_{i_x} and σ_{i_y} are the corresponding values for the inhibitory surround. An additional asymmetry shown by mapped filters is induced by space-variant areal magnification of the nonuniform mapping (see Fig. 3c of Mallot et al. (1990)). We modelled this asymmetry as follows: the major semi-axes of the elliptical isoefficacy contours, described by σ_{e_x} and σ_{i_x}, differed for the half-planes $x < 0$ and $x > 0$ which was characterized by the compression factor, κ (Fig. 3A).

The 2-dimensional motor map was modelled by a 30×30 grid, i.e. neurons were represented by grid points. All the neurons of the grid had a step transfer function f. The origin of the map coordinate system corresponding to the fovea region was fixed at point $(15, 15)$ (Fig. 3). To each grid point an asymmetrical weighting function described

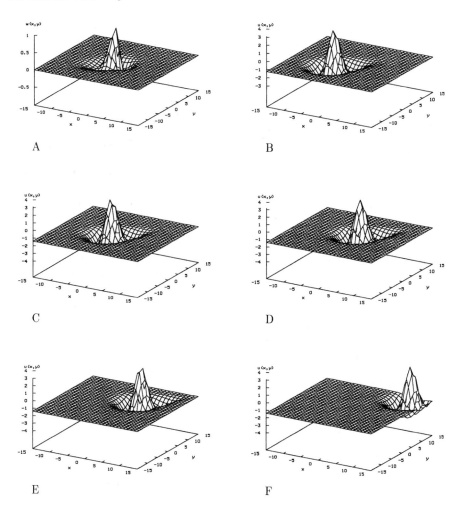

Fig. 3. Simulation of the hill-shift effect with the mapped neural field model. The SC motor map was spatially represented by a 30×30 grid. Eqn. (1) was integrated employing the Euler scheme with a time step of $\Delta t = 0.1$. The 2-dimensional, spatial integral in Eqn. (1) was computed by repeated 1-dimensional integration, using the extended trapezoidal rule with stepsize $\Delta x = \Delta y = 1.0$. **(A)** Asymmetrical weighting function $w(x, y)$ used in the simulations. **(B)-(F)** Example of simulated activity pattern in the neural field model. Starting from initial location $(-5, -5)$, the activity hill moves over the field which is shown at different, consecutive times $t = 2$ **(B)**, $t = 5$ **(C)**, $t = 9$ **(D)**, $t = 13$ **(E)**, $t = 23$ **(F)**. Movement direction is defined by the steeper decaying flank of the weighting function, $w(x, y)$. Parameters used in the simulations are $\tau = 1$, $u_0 = 1.4$, $s(\mathbf{x}, t) = 0$, $g_e = 3.6$, $g_i = 4.0$, $\sigma_{e_x} = 2.8$, $\sigma_{e_y} = 1.4$, $\sigma_{i_x} = 5.7$, $\sigma_{i_y} = 2.8$, $\kappa = 0.5$.

by Eqn.(3) was assigned in such a way that the direction of the major axes of the elliptical centre and surround regions coincided with that of the line through the grid point and the origin of the map coordinate system. That is, space-variant processing in the neural field model has been realized through the asymmetrical centre and surround structure of the weighting function (the dimensions of which are the same for all grid points), and through the radial organization of the weighting functions. The specific spatial organization of the weighting functions was suggested by experimental evidence: RFs in the cat's cortical areas 17, 18 and SC exhibit a radially organized asymmetry (cf. Mallot et al. (1990) and the references given therein), and MFs of collicular neurons show this feature, too (Ottes et al., 1986).

As the initial state we chose a localized excitation on the grid that should eventually develop into a hill of activity on the mapped field. The localized excitation had cubical shape and covered a 2×2 area within which the field potential was set to $u = 1.0$. We run 30 simulations, placing the activity hill in randomly selected locations of the field.

The simulated pattern of activity in the neural field model showed a clear anisotropy, resulting from the space-variant coupling of the neurons. The direction of movement was determined by the orientation of the steeper decaying flank of the weighting function defined by κ (Fig. 3A). In the example shown in Fig. 3, the initial location of the activity hill was at $(-5, -5)$. The asymmetrical, radially oriented weighting functions caused the hill to move towards the origin $(15, 15)$ of the map coordinate system where it stopped, due to the presence of the boundary (Fig. 3B-F).

6   Conclusions

In this paper we proposed a model of the spatio-temporal dynamics in the motor map of the SC. In particular, we studied which qualitative behaviours of the collicular neurons can be obtained if the model is based on some high-level computing principles governing saccadic eye movement control, i.e. neural maps, population coding and space-variant processing in layered systems. A model type that is especially appropriate to incorporate these principles is provided by neural fields.

As pointed out elsewhere (Schierwagen, 1995), neural fields of the Amari type, Eqn. (1), are special cases of AM. Several authors have suggested to consider AM as devices for analog computations, e.g. Mikhailov (1990 and Steels (1990). This is based on the idea of mapping the particular problem onto the dynamics of some AM where the solution can be obained by following the evolution of the AM. Amari fields exhibit rich dynamic behaviour which has been successfully employed to realize this idea. In particular, a spatially 1-dimensional homogeneous neural field model has been proposed, devoted to memorization and target selection in saccadic gaze control (Kopecz et al., 1993). A 2-dimensional, homogeneous field architecture has been considered in the context of target acquisition and obstacle avoidance of a mobile robot (Engels and Schöner, 1995).

We have tried to show in this paper, that the general computational scheme represented by uniform, space-invariant Amari fields must be complemented with space-variant operators. Two lines of evidence exist for this, (1) the recent study on mapped filters (Mallot et al., 1990), and (2) theoretical analyses of specific AM, i.e. fields of FHN neurons (Keener, 1988).

In generalizing Amari's concept of homogeneous, space-invariant fields, we modelled the motor map as a 2-dimensional neural field endowed with space-variant weighting functions. In simulations with a discrete version of the mapped neural field model, we could reproduce Keener's (1988) results obtained with a discrete FHN field model, i.e. our model exhibited 1-dimensional trajectories of activity hills. Although such inhomogeneous neural fields have to be investigated in much more detail, a first conclusion seems appropriate. Mapped neural fields embody a general scheme of representation and computation which is especially adapted to the coordinate transformations involved in sensorimotor control. In particular, our simulation study has presented evidence for the assumption that collicular dynamic error coding can be realized without global feedback. Instead, the nonlinear spatio-temporal dynamics of neural populations, considered as mapped neural fields might suffice for this purpose. Because of this feature, mapped neural fields are proposed as building blocks for future devices controlling gaze in artificial active vision systems.

Acknowledgement

Thanks are due to Herrad Werner who did the simulation work.

7 References

Abeles, M., 1991, Corticonics (Cambridge University Press, Cambridge).

Aloimonos, Y., ed., 1993, Active Perception (L. Erlbaum Assoc., Orlando, FL).

Amari, S., 1977, Biol. Cybern. **27**, 77.

Amari, S., 1982, Competitive and cooperative aspects in dynamics of neural excitation and self-organization, in: Competition and Cooperation in Neural Nets, ed. S. Amari and M.A. Arbib (Springer-Verlag, Berlin) p. 1.

Bajcsy, R., 1988, Proc. IEEE **76**, 996.

Ballard, D.H., 1987, Eye movements and spatial cognition (Technical Report 218, University of Rochester).

Ballard, D.H. and C.M. Brown, 1992, CVGIP: Image Understanding **56**, 3.

Berthoz, A., A. Grantyn and J. Droulez, 1987, Neurosci. Lett. **72**, 289.

Eckhorn, R., R. Bauer, W. Jordan, M. Brosch, W. Kruse, M. Munk and H.J. Reitboeck, 1988, Biol. Cybern. **60**, 121.

Engels, C. and G. Schöner, G., 1995, Robotics and Autonomous Systems **14**, 55.

Ermentrout, G.B., 1982, Asymptotic behavior of stationary homogeneous neuronal nets, in: Competition and Cooperation in Neural Nets, ed. S. Amari and M.A. Arbib (Springer-Verlag, Berlin) p. 57.

Ermentrout, G.B. and J.D. Cowan, 1979, Biol. Cybern. **34**, 137.

Fohlmeister, C., W. Gerstner, R. Ritz and J.L. van Hemmen, 1995, Neural Computation

7, 1046.

Freeman, W.J., 1975, Mass Action in the Nervous System (Academic Press, New York).

Grantyn, R., 1988, Gaze control through superior colliculus: Structure and function, in: Neuroanatomy of the Oculomotor System, ed. J. Büttner-Ennever (Elsevier, New York) p. 273.

Gray, C.M., 1994, J. Computat. Neurosci. **1**, 11.

Gray, C.M. and W. Singer, 1989, Proc. Natl. Acad. Sci. USA **86**, 1698.

Hilbig, H. and A. Schierwagen, 1994, NeuroReport **5**, 477.

Keener, J.P., 1988, J. Math. Biol. **26**, 41.

Kishimoto, K. and S. Amari, 1979, J. Math. Biol. **7**, 303.

Knudsen, E.I., S. du Lac and S.D. Esterly, 1987, Ann. Rev. Neurosci. **10**, 41.

Kopecz, K., C. Engels and G. Schöner, 1993, Proc. ICANN, ed. S. Gielen and H. Kappen (Springer-Verlag, Berlin) p. 96.

Mallot, H.A., 1995, Layered computation in neural networks, in: The Handbook of Brain Theory and Neural Networks, ed. M.A. Arbib (MIT Press, Cambridge, MA) p. 513.

Mallot, H.A., W. von Seelen and F. Giannakopoulos, 1990, Neural Networks **3**, 245.

Markus, M. and H. Schepers, 1992, Pattern formation in neural activator-inhibitor networks, in: Spatio-Temporal Organization in Nonequilibrium Systems, eds. S.C. Müller and T. Plesser (Projekt Verlag, Dortmund) p. 151.

Marr, D., 1982, Vision (Freeman, San Francisco).

Mikhailov, A.S., 1990, Foundations of Synergetics I (Springer-Verlag, Berlin).

Munoz, D.P. and D. Guitton, 1989, Rev. Neurol. (Paris) **145**, 567.

Munoz, D.P. and R.H. Wurtz, 1992, Society for Neuroscience Abstracts, **19**, 787.

Munoz, D.P., D. Pelisson and D. Guitton, 1991, Science **251**, 1358.

Ottes, F.P., J.A.M. Van Gisbergen and J.J. Eggermont, J.J., 1986, Vision Res. **26**, 857.

Robinson, D.A., 1972, Vision Res. **12**, 1795.

Schierwagen, A.K., 1995, Syst.Anal.Model.Simul. **18-19**, 713.

Schierwagen, A.K. and J. Francu, 1989, The continuum approach as applied to wave phenomena in physiological systems, in: Nonlinear Waves in Active Media, ed. J. Engelbrecht, (Springer-Verlag, Berlin Heidelberg New York Tokyo) p. 185.

Steels, L., 1990, Robotics and Autonomous Systems **6**, 71.

Sparks, D.L. and L.E. Mays, 1990, Ann. Rev. Neurosci. **13**, 309.

Visual Attention and Cognition
W.H. Zangemeister, H.S. Stiehl and C. Freksa (Editors)
© 1996 Elsevier Science B.V. All rights reserved.

OPTOMOTOR PROCESSING
IN THE PREY CATCHING OF AMPHIBIA

H. Schwegler

Institute of Theoretical Neurophysics,
Center for Cognitive Sciences,
University of Bremen, D-28334 Bremen,
Germany

ABSTRACT

On the basis of empirical data concerning the behavior and the neurophysiology of tongue-projecting salamanders (Bolitoglossini) mathematical models of the neural control of prey catching are presented. One model uses a continuous "neuron field" to describe the neural processing with respect to the orientation movement as well as to the tongue protraction. There are subroutines for the determination of distance and angle and for the extrapolation of the prey motion. A second family of models uses three-layer neural networks of McCullogh-Pitts neurons with the empirically determined distribution of visual receptive fields. The "Simulander I" simulates the neural processing for the control of the orientation movement, the "Simulander II" the processing for the control of the protraction length in the case of a centrally situated prey object. The models of this family allow for an understanding of the "course coding" of object features by neurons with large receptive fields.

Key words: Neural networks, coarse coding, sensorimotor processing, prey catching control, salamanders.

1. INTRODUCTION

During the last years, many attempts have been made in order to investigate the relations between neural activity and animal behavior. Concerning amphibia emphasis is laid on predator avoidance and prey capture behavior (Grüsser-Cornehls 1984; Ewert 1987; Roth 1987). In contrast to this, only a few models exist which yield a quantitative description based on the available data (House 1989). Here I present two types of neural network models which have been developped in the Bremen research group in Cognitive Sciences. They model the optomotor processes in the brain of tongue-projecting plethodontid salamanders of the tribe Bolitiglossini during prey capture actions.

The first model (Straub 1993; Straub et al. 1993) uses continuous activity fields in two neuron layers of the optic tectum by which the neurons of the motor nuclei are stimulated. It shows the advantage that most calculations can be done analytically. Only a few parameters have to be introduced which can be well determined by empirical data, but at the price that the tectum neurons of the afferent layer are assumed to have all the same receptive field size. It takes into account explicitly the empirically found retinotopy of the afferent layer. The main stages of the prey catching behavior are treated, that is the control of the orientation movement and the processes necessary for a successful projection of the tongue, namely determination of distance and angle of the prey and extrapolation of the prey motion.

The models of the second type called "Simulander" (Eurich 1995; Eurich et al. 1995; Wiggers et al. 1995b) are three-layer neural networks of the perceptron class. They allow being adjusted to all details of the empirically determined distribution of receptive field sizes. The many free parameters (the efficacies of the synapses) have to be fixed by an optimization procedure as which an evolution strategy is used. The "Simulander I" simulates the neural processing for the control of the orientation movement, the "Simulander II" the processing for the distance control of the protraction length in the case of a prey which is situated in the center of the visual field. The angular control of side movements of the tongue in the case of noncentral prey positions has to be added along the same principles which have been used for the orientation movement in Simulander I.

2. SOME EMPIRICAL FACTS

Tongue-projecting salamanders of the tribe Bolitiglossini exhibit a "sit-and-wait" (or ambush) feeding strategy. In many cases, their first reaction to an observed prey is an orientation movement of the head to bring the object into the binocular visual field. Motivation is necessary to do that, and it causes attention. If the motivation is high enough, and the prey comes into the catching distance, by a protraction of the tongue the prey is catched very precisely, that is failures are very seldom. The maximum length of the projected tongue (catching range) of the species Hydromantes italicus, for example, is about 5 cm which is more than half of the body length. The protraction process takes not more than about 5 milliseconds. Typical prey are slugs, mites, and even houseflies flying at high speed (abouit 20 cm/s).

The anatomy of the retina, the brain, and the muscles is known in all details (cf. Roth 1987) and is not reported here. The animals do not show considerable eye movement, there are no saccades. The central processing region of optomotor control is the optic tectum in the midbrain which is functionally equivalent to the primary visual areas in the human cortex. The tectum of the tongue-projecting plethodontid salamanders receives not only contralateral but also strong ipsilateral retinotectal projections in contrast to most other amphibia (Wiggers 1991; Wiggers et al. 1995a), see Figure 1. This allows for a very fast and very precise stereoscopic depth perception. Beside these direct projections there are indirect ipsilateral and contralateral projections via the nucleus isthmi which might be used for an extrapolation of the prey motion.

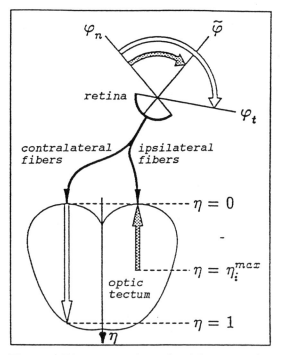

Figure 1. Direct maps from the right eye to the optic tectum. η is a coordinate from rostral to caudal.

All projections preserve the topographical neighbourhood in the following sense: A tectum neuron has a so-called "receptive field" in the angular visual field. Now the neurons of a projection map in the tectum have approximately the same neighbourhood relations as the centers of their receptive fields (the receptive fields are relatively large namely about 15^0 for the retinal afferences, and even larger for the tectum neurons themselves, cf. Figure 9). We speak about topographic or retinotopic maps, and there are at least four different such visual maps on each tectal hemisphere (cf. Figure 6). Some more details of these maps are described in the next paragraph. Beside neurons with monocular afferences we find neurons with binocular afferences in the optic tectum as well; some details about their receptive field distribution are reported below in chapter 6.

The organisation of the direct maps in the optic tectum is sketched in Figure 1. An object moving in the visual field of the right retina from the nasal bounding angle φ_n to the temporal bounding angle φ_t elicits an excitation in the left hemisphere (contralateral map) moving from the rostral edge ($\eta = 0$) to the caudal edge ($\eta = 1$). In the ipsilateral map in the right hemisphere only the more central part of the visual field is represented by the rostral tectum only, in such a way that the described retinal motion from left to right gives rise to a tectal motion opposite to that in the left hemisphere.

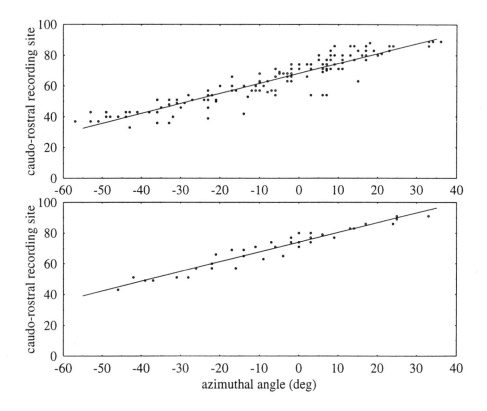

Figure 2. Retinotopic maps of the retinal afferences in Hydromantes italicus (from Wiggers 1991).
Abscissa: Azimuth angle of the receptive field center.
Ordinate: Tectum coordinate from caudal to rostral.
Upper part: Contralateral map.
Lower part: Ipsilateral map.

If we consider in the *same* hemisphere the contralateral and the ipsilateral map which come from the visual field via both eyes, a motion in the visual field is represented by a *parallel* motion in the tectum (e.g. a motion from left to right is represented from rostral to caudal in the left hemisphere, both contralaterally with respect to the right eye, cf. Figure 1, as well as ipsilaterally with respect to the left eye. The same motion is represented from caudal to rostral in the right hemisphere). The empirical data from Wiggers (Wiggers 1991; Wiggers at al. 1995a) for the right hemisphere of the species Hydromantes italicus are shown in Figure 2; instead of η a tectum coordinate is used increasing from caudal to rostral.

Whereas the horizontal angle φ (azimuth) of the visual field is mapped rostro-caudally the vertical angle ϑ (elevation) is mapped orthogonally from medial to lateral in the tectum. In the continuous model we restrict ourselves to events in the horizontal plane (to a "two-dimensional world") and do not consider the elevation.

How the distance of an outer object is represented in the tectum by the different maps? It is a geometrical fact that an object is seen by the two eyes under different angles, and the difference between the two angles called the disparity angle is different for different distances of the object. Considering now the parallel maps in one hemisphere we see that for a given azimuth φ there can be only one distance of an object so that it is represented at the same tectum position both contralaterally and ipsilaterally. In that case we say that the rostro-caudal disparity is zero. Otherwise we have two different positions in both maps with a finite rostro-caudal disparity between. By using the data of Figure 2 we can calculate the points of outer space which are represented with disparity zero, the so-called *horopter* curve. This horopter is shown in Figure 3 for Hydromantes italicus. It is approximately a circle of radius 4.5 cm which is equal to the catching range of the tongue.

3. A MODEL WITH CONTINUOUS "NEURON FIELDS"

In this model the neural activities in the optic tectum are described in terms of continuous "fields" $I(\eta)$, $C(\eta)$, $E(\eta)$ depending on the rostro-caudal tectum coordinate η. The model speaks about two layers with the ipsilateral retinotopic field $I(\eta)$ and the contralateral $C(\eta)$ in an "afferent layer" elicited by the optic nerve coming from the retina, and the field $E(\eta)$ in an "efferent layer" projecting down to the motor nuclei. The second layer is not identified empirically. A recent interpretation of old and new physiological and new morphological data by G. Roth and U. Dicke of the Bremen Institute of Brain Research seems to show that the afferent tectum neurons are the efferent ones at the same time. This would mean that our second layer is not in the tectum, but probably in the premotoric areas of the brainstem. The model is not dependent on such a change.

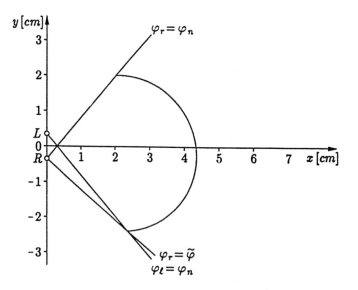

Figure 3. The horopter of Hydromantes italicus. These are
the points of outer space which are represented at the same
tectum locus both contralaterally and ipsilaterally.

3.1 Modelling of the orientation movement

In each tectum hemisphere we have an ipsilateral field $I(\eta)$ and a
contralateral field $C(\eta)$ with a retinotopic organization which according to the
empirical findings can be assumed to be linear in the coordinates, and is
determined from the experimental results by linear regression. The finite sizes of
the receptive fields of tectum neurons are taken into account in the way that a
point-like object gives rise to gaussian excitations $I(\eta)$ and $C(\eta)$ in the afferent
layer; and from that there is another map with Gaussian broadening to the
efferent layer

$$E(\eta) = \int d\eta' K_i(\eta, \eta') I(\eta') + \int d\eta' K_c(\eta, \eta') C(\eta') \tag{1}$$

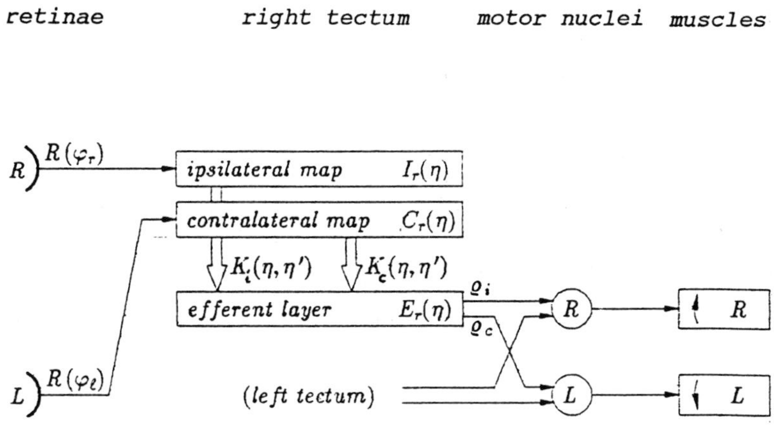

retinae   right tectum   motor nuclei   muscles

Figure 4. Block diagram of the control of the orientation movement in the continuous model. The ipsilateral and contralateral activity fields in a hemisphere are processed to an efferent layer according to eq.(1). By ipsiversive and contraversive projections to the right and left motor nuclei the neck muscles are innervated. Similar diagrams are used for the determination of distance and angle in order to control the tongue projection and for the mechanisms of the extrapolation of the prey's motion.

The output of the efferent layer is interpreted as a population code for the muscle contraction; synaptic densities K_i and K_c describe the connection to the motor nuclei which are involved in the contraversive and ipsiversive movement. The whole procedure is sketched graphically in Figure 4.

Analytical and numerical calculations show a turn of the head to the prey object which is in qualitative agreement with the observed behavior. Also a continuous movement of the head tracking a moving prey is simulated sufficiently. Since the model functions without the ipsilateral map as well it can be used also for other amphibia, frogs and toads included.

Because the model is a "closed-loop" system one can conclude that there is no need for a motor map in the optic tectum (Jordan et al. 1990). Optical stimuli are translated directly into muscle contractions.

3.2 The tongue projection

A successful use of the tongue-projecting apparatus requires knowledge about position (distance and angle) and velocity of the prey. Amphibia have only two mechanisms to determine the distance of an object, namely accomodation and disparity. For frogs and toads (Anura) it is known (Collett 1977; Jordan and Ludhardt 1980; Douglas 1986) that binocular animals use mainly disparity; only monocular animals fall back on accomodation. The same is assumed to be true for salamanders. The existence of the ipsilateral maps enables the plethodontid salamanders to evaluate the disparity very effectively.

The modelling of all mechanisms involved in the tongue projection is performed very similarly to the modelling of the orientation movement. Of course, other muscles have to be taken into consideration. There are two protractor muscles (subarcuales recti) and two retractor muscles (recti cervicis profundi). These muscles should be triggered only if a prey is in the catching range. Their cooperation determines how far the tongue is projected, and this should depend on the exact distance of the prey. In addition, two other, lateral muscles (geniohyoidei laterales) determine the horizontal angle of projection in dependency on the angular position of the prey.

The determination of the distance is performed in the following way. The activity fields $I(\eta)$ and $C(\eta)$ of the afferent tectum layer affect neurons in the efferent layer by synaptic densities K_i and K_c like in eq.(1); however, both terms are essential now in contrast to the angle calculation of 3.1. It is used that (as explained in chapter 2) the rostro-caudal disparity between the two direct maps in the tectum depends on the distance of the object. Therefore the strength of the superposition of the two terms in eq.(1) were maximal for the horopter distance if the two gaussians K were equal. But if one gaussian is shifted against the other appropriately then the maximum of the superposition can be shifted to a much smaller distance so that the decrease of the strength of the superposition can be used as a measure of the distance of the object. This strength triggers the decision to project the tongue by a threshold mechanism which is not released outside the horopter and, moreover, it controls the cooperation of the two muscles, protractor and retractor, so that the tongue projects only up to the distance of the prey.

The determination of the angle follows similar principles as described already in 3.1. But an essential difference is the following. In the case of the orientation movement the motor nuclei control the change of the head direction slowly so that a "closed loop" is realized. The tongue projection is a very fast process for which the angle-controlling muscles geniohyoidei must be adjusted before. This is done by a direct translation of the angle measured by the retinotopic tectum maps to these muscles.

In this context, an extrapolation of the prey's motion is necessary calculating an advanced angle. The processing time from the retinal receptors to the muscle is about 130 milliseconds, mainly due to the first steps in the retina. In this time a fly with a speed of 25 cm/s flies a distance of 3 cm, and even with a speed of 5 cm/s the distance is half a centimeter which is too much for an exact hitting of the fly. The salamander must know in advance where the fly is when the tongue shoots. There are two possible mechanisms allowing for this extrapolation. One is the velocity measurement by velocity dependent retina ganglion cells, the other one is the retardation of the indirect maps via the nucleus isthmi.

First mechanism: Figure 5 shows the activity R of velocity dependent retina ganglion cells at azimuthal positions φ_r on the equator of the right eye for different angular velocities ω of the prey. In all cases the prey is at the same angle φ_r. According to the retinotopy there are similar shifts for tectum neurons. If these shifted curves are used for the setting of the angle-controlling muscles according to eq.(1) appropriately then the projection angle can show the necessary advance. After fitting some parameters in the computation to empirical data the angles are very precise at the horopter distance. They become worse at smaller distances but this does not matter because at small distances the tongue hits the fly anyway.

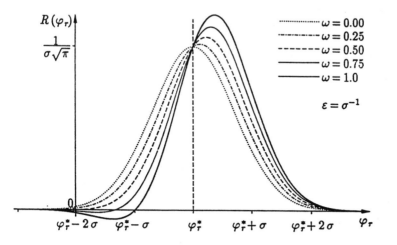

Figure 5. Velocity dependent activities of retina ganglion cells. Similarly shifted peaks in the tectum cause the calculation of a lead by eq.(1).

Second mechanism: Figure 6 shows the four maps on the right tectum hemispere. For the sake of simplicity, in the modelling we use only the direct contralateral map C and the indirect contralateral map D1 which is known to be inhibitory. Because D1 is retarded by 10 milliseconds according to a monosynaptic feedback via the nucleus isthmi it shows the angular position of the pray 10 ms earlier. It is easy to understand that both maps together contain information about the speed of the prey. The neural processing can be realized as a simple superposition. If both maps influence the motor nuclei appropriately then the angle controlling muscles set the same advanced angle as in the case of the first mechanism.

Because both mechanisms produce a successful extrapolation we assume that both are used in parallel by nature. However, the retarded maps might be used to solve other problems,too. Particularly species without the strong direct ipsilateral maps can determine distance by the disparity between the direct contralateral and the indirect ipsilateral map.

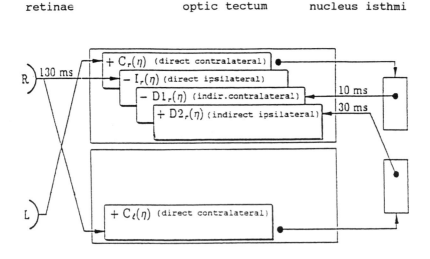

retinae   optic tectum   nucleus isthmi

Figure 6. The four maps in the right tectum hemisphere (the left one is incomplete). The two indirect maps are delayed back projections via the ipsilateral and contralateral nuclei isthmi. In the model only the contralateral direct and indirect maps are used. With the delay the lead is calculated.

3.3 Discussion

The advantage of the continuous model is that it contains only a few parameters which are fairly determined by empirical data. On the other side, however, there are some disadvantages. As relatively harmless the assumption of a strong retinotopy can be seen though it is only true for the centers of the receptive fields because it suffices to be realized functionally and not in real space. But in order to restrict the number of parameters we must assume a strong homogeneity in a sense that all parts of the visual field are processed identically. Moreover, it would be very difficult to introduce into the model the fact that there are neurons of very different receptive field sizes. So, in a sense, the continuous model, particularly in the presented version, has not enough parameters to take into account all empirical data.

Anyway, one must question if the assumed mechanism for the distance determination is compatible with all empirical facts. Remember that it uses the distance between the centers of the ipsilateral and the contralateral activities in the tectum. It seems difficult for the brain to perform the computation of eq.(1) precisely enough because not only the mean angular diameter of the receptive fields are large (about 35^0) but also the tectal position of their *centers* show a standard deviation of 10^0 (as can be seen in Figure 2 for the retinal afferences; it is similar for the tectum neurons themselves).

4. SIMULANDER: MODELS WITH THREE-LAYER NEURAL NETWORKS

In order to overcome the disadvantages of the continuous model we have developped another family of models based on usual discrete neural networks. Their advantages are that we can take into account almost arbitrarily complicated details of the neural connections, and more specifically that we can adjust it to the empirically determined distribution of receptive fields of tectum neurons; we can also introduce feature dependent neurons launching a treatment of object identification and segmentation. We pay by having a huge number of parameters (synaptic efficacies) which can only be fixed by optimization or "training" procedures which need not have any biological adequacy.

In the first approach of Simulander I we have modelled the orientation movement by a network of 300 neurons a third of them being tectum neurons. Their receptive field distribution has been taken from the experiments (Wiggers 1991; Wiggers et al. 1995a). The interesting result was that such a small network performs successfully and, moreover, that this is the case with the use of relatively large receptive fields.

In contrast to the continuous model the orientation movement is modelled in the full three-dimensional world, that is the direction of a prey's position is parameterized by an azimuth φ and an elevation ϑ. The muscles can turn the head correspondingly.

For the control of the tongue projection a determination of direction and distance of the prey is necessary as well as an extrapolation of the prey's motion. Because the angle-dependent control of the tongue muscles geniohyoidei can be formulated along the same *principles* as for the neck muscles in the theory of the orientation movement, for the sake of simplicity in Simulander II we have restricted ourselves to the distance control of the protraction length of the tongue for the case of a prey which is situated in the center of the visual field. Then a complete model should add the angle control of the protraction muscles as well as a neural network processing of the extrapolation of the motion.

Simulander II is a network of 168 neurons, namely 144 binocular tectum neurons, 12 motor neurons and 12 inhibitory interneurons. The tectum neurons are approximated as McCulloch-Pitts ones, they have large binocular receptive fields corresponding to the empirical findings of Wiggers (1991).

5. SIMULANDER I : ANGULAR CONTROL

5.1 The network design

The architecture of the network is shown in Figure 7. In each hemisphere the network consists of 50 tectum neurons, then there are 100 interneurons in the brainstem and four groups of 25 motor neurons each which innervate four muscles. The muscles work antagonistic; whenever one of the neck muscles is activated the corresponding antagonistic muscle is inhibited by interneurons.

There are only feedforward connetions from the tectum neurons to the interneurons and to the motor neurons, and from the interneurons to the motor neurons. Analog neurons are used with the firing rate as state variable n. A neuron in the first layer, the tectum, fires only if the prey is in its receptive field, and with a rate which is sligthly dependent on the angular velocity of the prey. This dependency is taken from experiments (Wiggers 1991) but does not influence the network performance very strongly so that in the tectum we could use McCulloch-Pitts neurons as well. Each neuron reacts to the incoming signals n_i from other neurons in the simplest way:

$$n = F\left(\sum_i w_i n_i\right)$$ (2)

The sum is over all incoming signals, w_i are the corresponding synaptic efficacies. F is a transfer function which is the sigma-shaped Fermi function in the case of firing rates, and a Heaviside step function in the McCulloch-Pitts case.

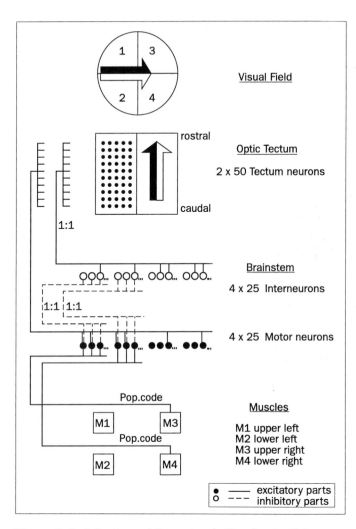

Figure 7. Architecture of the network Simulander I for
the control of the orientation movement.

The receptive field sizes of the tectum neurons and their distribution over the
visual field are taken from the empirical data of Hydromantes italicus (Wiggers
1991; Wiggers et al. 1995a). Figure 8 shows the distribution of the receptive field
centers depending on the azimuth (medio-lateral) angle φ as abszissa and the
elevation (dorso-ventral) angle ϑ as ordinate. Most of the receptive fields are
located in the central part, and less in the lateral part.

Figure 9 shows the distribution of receptive field sizes most of them are relatively large: the mean diameter is about 40⁰, and their are fields up to 180⁰, especially in the lateral visual field. This is in contrast to the angular size of a prey which is typically smaller than 10⁰.

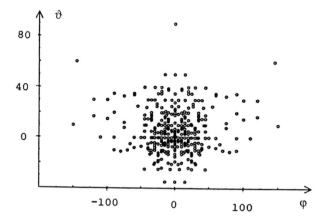

Figure 8. Distribution of receptive field centers in *Hydromantes italicus* (from Wiggers 1991)

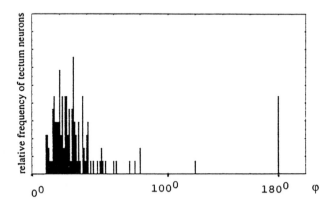

Figure 9. Distribution of receptive field sizes in *Hydromantes italicus* (from Wiggers 1991).

5.2 The scenario of simulation and the "training" of the synaptic efficacies

The scenario of the simulation is shown in Figure 10. We generate a fly of size 0.6 cm in a box of 20 x 10 x 10 cm³ which flies at a speed of 2 ± 0.5 cm/s. After 1.5 ± 0.5 s it changes speed and direction the latter with a mean angular deviation of 20^0. The irregularity is introduced to prevent the salamander from getting used to a particular motion pattern of the fly. With respect to this real time behavior the network dynamics is calculated in discrete time steps assumed to be 0.2 s (which is of the order of magnitude of the processing delay in real salamanders). The considered prey speeds are relatively slow so that advanced angles need not be calculated.

The idea is to choose the synaptic efficacies so that the network performs best that is the axis of the turning head hits the moving prey most of the time. As an optimization procedure a so-called evolution strategy (Rechenberg 1973) was used. In a typical training phase about 10,000 networks are tested out of which about 40 lead to an increase in fitness.

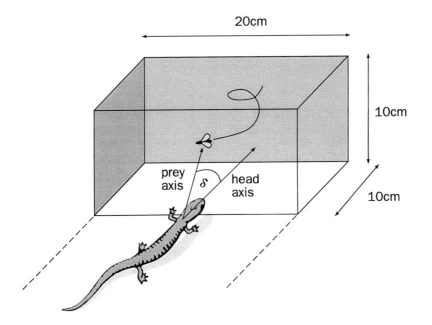

Figure 10. Scenario of the simulation.

5.3 Some results

After training the success rate is about 90%. Probably the real salamander uses some more tectum neurons, and then is even more successful. The high success of about 90% is achieved in the model despite of the receptive fields being large for most neurons (compared with the angular diameter of the prey). This observation is accentuated if we change the receptive field distribution from the empirical one of Figure 9. If we take away neurons with larger receptive fields the network performance decreases drastically, but if we take away neurons with smaller receptive fields the performance does not change significantly as long as not too many of them are taken away. How is this possible?

The angular resolution is not brought forth by single neurons but by the assembly as a whole. In the assembly a fine-graining is realized by the many possibilities of intersections between receptive fields. This strategy called "coarse coding" needs much less neurons than would be necessary if each position would have its own neuron. We have studied this on a more principal level by analytical

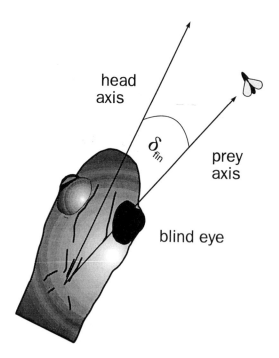

Figure 11. The monocular salamander.

calculations for the case of McCulloch-Pitts neurons (Eurich et al. 1994; Eurich 1995). In the case of a 360⁰ visual field the best resolution would be achieved with receptive fields of 180⁰; for an angular resolution of 0.6⁰ only 300 such neurons are necessary. In case of the salamander's receptive field distribution (Figure 9) 800 neurons accomplish this resolution, whereas not less than 150,000 pixel neurons would be necessary. Even with only 100 neurons the simulander achieves a resolution of about 3⁰.

Another surprising result was the following. If we make our simulander model monocular (by removing a tectum hemisphere) the head axis is not oriented to the prey direction anymore but is declined away from the blind side as shown in Figure 11. This is against our intuitive expectation. But after this result of the model had been found we could confirm it by reading about empirical observations of the same kind (Wiggers 1991).

6. SIMULANDER II: STEREOSCOPIC DEPTH DETERMINATION

In order to extend the model from the orientation movement to a precise control of the tongue projection a mechanism to determine the distance of the prey has to be built in. We bear in mind that in the optic tectum neurons with binocular afferents are found, too (Wiggers 1991; Wiggers et al. 1995b). Their binocular receptive field is the intersection of two monocular receptive fields (both in the frontal binocular visual field) as can be seen in the upper part of Figure 12. Again it has a very wide angular diameter in most cases, and in any case it is extended from a near distance to infinity (or at least to a focal distance of about 30 cm beyond that everything becomes blurred) so that a single neuron cannot have any information about distance.

And again the problem is solved by "coarse coding". The principle can be understood by the following. If one considers three binocular tectum neurons with binocular receptive fields as shown in Figure 12 one can understand how the localization of an object in the small rhombus region is possible because the object stimulates the neuron of the upper part and does not stimulate the two others.

As explained already above the network Simulander II is restricted to the control of the protraction length in the case of a prey which is situated in the center of the visual field.

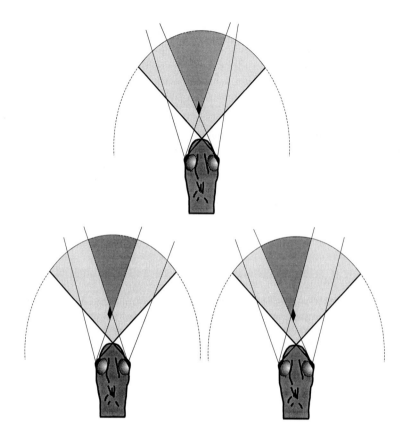

Figure 12. Binocular localization by large receptive fields.
Light grey: Binocular visual field.
Dark grey: Receptive fields of 3 neurons, resp.If the first neuron (upper part) is elicited, and the other two (lower part) are not, then the prey is exactly in the small rhombic area (black).

The network architecture is shown in Figure 13. It has 144 binocular tectum neurons, 12 interneurons and 12 motor neurons which control the muscles rectus cervicis profundus und subarcualis rectus. There are 1884 synaptic efficacies which are trained for 900 positions in an evolution strategy. The training needs 5 days on an Intel pentium. After 75,000 generations and 183 successful descendants.

The result is a success rate of about 90% for object distances between 1 and 5 cm (which is the maximum protraction length. There is no action in the case of larger object distances without the exception trials to catch objects immediately behind 5 cm.

In the near future the Simulander models should be joined, improved and completed, for instance with respect to an extrapolation of the prey's motion. Another important problem to work on are the processes of object identification.

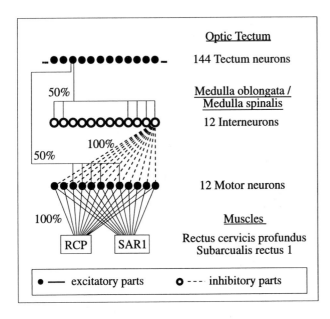

Figure 13. Architecture of the network Simulander II for the control of the tongue protraction.

REFERENCES

Collett, T., 1977, Nature **267**, 349.

Douglas, R.H., T.S. Collett and H.-J. Wagner, 1986, J.Comp. Physiol. **A158**, 133.

Eurich, C., 1995, Objektlokalisation mit neuronalen Netzen, Thesis, Universitaet Bremen (published by Verlag Harri Deutsch, Frankfurt am Main).

Eurich, C., H. Schwegler und M. Strohmeier, 1994, Analytische Betrachtungen zum Problem des "Coarse Coding": Berechnung des Auflösungsvermögens von Ensembles breitbandig abgestimmter McCullogh-Pitts-Neuronen, ZKW-Bericht No. 6/94, Zentrum fuer Kognitionswissenschaften, Universitaet Bremen.

Eurich, C., G. Roth, H. Schwegler and W. Wiggers, 1995, J.Comp. Physiol. **A176**, 379.

Ewert, J.P., 1987, Behav. Brain Sci. **10**, 337.

Grüsser-Cornehls, U., 1984, The Neurophysiology of the Amphibian Optic Tectum, in: H. Vanegas (ed.), Comparative Neurology of the Optic Tectum (Plenum Press, New York and London).

House, D., 1989, Depth Perception in Frogs and Toads (Springer, New York).

Jordan, M., G. Ludhardt, C. Mayer-Naujoks and G. Roth, 1980, Z.Naturforsch. **35c**, 851.

Jordan, M., T. Matsushima and G. Roth, 1990, Does the Toad have a Motor Map? Transformations of Tectal Activities into Motor Patterns, in: N. Elsner and G. Roth (eds.), Brain - Cognition - Perception (Georg Thieme, Stuttgart and New York).

Rechenberg, I., 1973, Evolutionsstrategie (Friedrich Frommann, Stuttgart).

Roth, G., 1987, Visual Behavior in Salamanders, (Springer, Berlin).

Straub, A., 1993, Mathematische Modelle für das visuomotorische Verhalten von Amphibien, Thesis, Universitaet Bremen.

Straub, A., G. Roth, H. Schwegler, and W. Wiggers, 1993, Control of Prey Catching Behavior of Salamanders by a Continuous Neural Network, in: N. Elsner and M. Heisenberg (Eds.), Gene - Brain - Behaviour (Georg Thieme, Stuttgart and New York).

Wiggers, W., 1991, Elektrophysiologische, neuroanatomische und verhaltensphysiologische Untersuchungen zur visuellen Verhaltenssteuerung bei lungenlosen Salamandern, Thesis, Universitaet Bremen.

Wiggers, W., G. Roth, C. Eurich and A. Straub, 1995a, J.Comp. Physiol. **A176**, 365.

Wiggers, W., C. Eurich, G. Roth, und H. Schwegler, 1995b, NeuroForum **1**, 6.

Visual Attention and Cognition
W.H. Zangemeister, H.S. Stiehl and C. Freksa (Editors)
269

DESIGNING AN ANTHROPOMORPHIC HEAD-EYE SYSTEM

Kourosh Pahlavan

Computational Vision and Active Perception Laboratory (CVAP),
Royal Institute of Technology, S-100 44 Stockholm, Sweden.
Email: kourosh@bion.kth.se

ABSTRACT

Computational vision research has its roots in image processing and the field has mainly followed the methodological views from the information processing school of thought. These characteristics have long kept computer vision research in a state of *algorithm* development rather than *system* development.

The introduction of the active vision paradigm in computer vision had several impacts on the field. The major impact was the sudden interest for building robotic heads and investigations into the control issues involved in such systems. The real issues however are not the control schemes, but understanding the dynamism present in vision; active vision research might have to reformalize many classical problems. This paper sketches an introduction to the problem, reveals some basic connections with biological systems and suggests some elementary parameters to be considered in the design of such systems. In the end, the KTH-head, an anthropomorphic head-eye system that is designed following the mentioned design criteria is described.

Key Words: computer vision, active vision, head-eye system, anthropomorphic robots, robotics.

1. Introduction

People often employ *actions* to sense better. Looking at objects from different angles, going around them, touching them, lifting them, knocking on them etc. are examples of these actions. This procedure comprises cue integration on at least two inter-modal and local levels. An example of the inter-modal integration is using the direction information in e.g. the sound emanating from a bell and localizing the bell using vision. An example of the local integration on the modality level is integrating the shading cue with surface markings to recover a surface orientation reliably.

The actions employed are not necessarily *mechanical* movements, but they often are. The idea is to manipulate *all* parameters involved in the vision to sense better and more reliably. That is, an active system *searches* for proper cues, it does not *hope* for them. The active vision paradigm was introduced to the computer vision community through e.g. Bajcsy(1985) and Aloimonos (1987). Soon it was realized that experimental work on active vision is preconditioned by designing and utilizing high performance visual agents that can employ the power of the paradigm. A successful active vision system is a system that is designed for its specific tasks and interests. Although one could entitle human vision as a "general purpose" vision system, due to its flexibility and extensive range of functionality, it is not a "general purpose" system in the real sense of the word. This point is stressed by Aloimonos (1993) and is worth having in mind. Any active vision system that is designed in accordance with the idea of mutual interaction between the agent and its environment should take the set of interesting interactions into consideration... and this is something that affects the design of the system already at the stage of initial sketches.

There is a metaphorical relationship between a system design of this kind and the evolutionary formation of a perceptive being. One could suggest a resemblance between a carefully designed robot and a hypothetical biological being that could have evolved under similar constraints. However, the analogy ends here, because a fabricated system as opposed to a biological species does not experience a number of crucial constraints in its activity and operational life. It does not need to reproduce itself; it does not need to be developed for personal survival or species survival... and a number of similar significant factors that form the natural life.

The brief argument above is an effort to show why it is reasonable to let the inspirations from the biological beings affect our robot design. We are trying to design active vision systems that perform under similar constraints and with similar tasks as human vision. The natural choice is to consider the geometry and structure of human vision as a guideline in our head-eye system design strategy; this is what this paper is about.

2. The human visual parameters

Computer vision research is influenced by anthropomorphic views of perception. In the case of *active vision*, this influence is particularly apparent. The visual system in human beings and many other animals is partially assisted by other sensory organs. Very important is the vestibular system that together with the ocular system stands for the vestibulo-ocular responses. We do not ignore the role of the vestibular information in the control loop of eye movements. However, due to the stationary nature of the design discussed in this work and our preference to study vision in isolation when possible, further discussion on the contribution from the vestibular system is excluded.

Excluding inertial and other extraretinal stimuli leaves illumination as the only source of stimuli that affect movement of the eyes. Accordingly the human visual parameters that are involved in this discussion are geometrical and optical only.

Figure 1 illustrates the *mechanical* degrees of freedom of the human head. These could be considered as axes rather than degrees of freedom, because in their normal binocular operation, there is a clear dependence between some of them. This is, however, not always true.

Each eye in the figure is marked with 3 perpendicular semi-circular arrows to illustrate its rotational abilities. The neck is also given 3 degrees of freedom, but the arrows are not really an abstraction of any physical muscles involved in the same directions as arrows; they are rather resembling the mechanical degrees of freedom that could be distinguished in the neck.

The human eye accommodates by altering the shape of the crystalline lens, i.e. by manipulating the focal length of the lens. The accommodation procedure affects also the

Figure 1. The mechanical degrees of freedom of the human head. The eyes have actually lateral and vertical movements that are not depicted here. The neck movement is abstracted as motion about one single point; this is, however, not the case in reality.

iris size, although to a small extent. The iris is otherwise mainly engaged in regulating the amount of light impinging onto the retina. These two major optical adjustments are entitled as 2 optical degrees of freedom.

Ignoring the dependencies enforced by the particular model of the oculomotor system, the degrees of freedom in the human head can be listed as follows:

Eyes-mechanical DoF:

Each eye has 3 mechanical degrees of freedom → a total of 6 mechanical degrees of freedom which are:
superior-inferior (tilt)
lateral-medial (pan)
cyclotorsion (about the visual axis)

Neck-mechanical DoF:

The neck has 3 degrees of freedom, these are:
neck tilt
neck pan
the lateral tilt movement

Eyes-optical DoF:

Each eye has 2 optical degrees of freedom → a total of 4 optical degrees of freedom which are:
Change of focal length
Change of iris opening

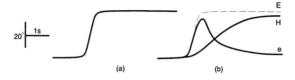

Figure 2. Head and eye movements made when looking at novel objects:
(a) eye movement (saccade) made in fixating an eccentric target with the head fixed.
(b) head "H" and eye "e" movements made under exactly the same conditions, but with
the head free. The sum of "H" and "e" is the gaze (the dotted curve "E"). The abscissa
represents time and the ordinate represents the amplitude of the movement. Redrawn
after Morasso *et al.* (1973).

3. Body movements and eye movements

From a geometrical point of view, there are two classes of movements of the visual
system—body movements and eye movements. From a visual processing point of view,
these two kinds of movements are essentially different and it is crucial to understand their
differences and their role in the process of perceptual sensing.

The interesting body movement here is the movement of the neck. Neck movement *in
man* is actually a special kind of body movement. This is not the case in all animals.
For example, some of the tasks that are performed by eye movements in human beings,
are executed with neck-head movements in other animals. However, before elaborating
on these matters, the difference between eye movements and body movements should be
clarified.

3.1. Neck movements

Neck movements *in man* are external to the *human* visual system. That is, except
for some positioning difficulties for the observer, his visual system would be perfectly
functional even without neck movements. Neck movements are beneficial for:

- Expansion of the total field of view of the *stationary* observer:
  A binocular scan of the scene results in a larger field of view. However, although
  human eyes are very agile, their practical span of rotation is usually limited to 20°.
  Neck movements can be used to extend the span. Besides, neck movements can be
  used to obtain symmetric fixations. This is actually what is happening in Figure 2.
  The eye movements generate an asymmetry in vergence that is compensated by an
  immediate neck movement. The neck movements can in this manner guarantee the
  observer to obtain as similar left and right views as possible.

- Introducing motion parallax to the *stationary* observer:
  Neck movements while fixating generate motion parallax. For the sake of maximizing

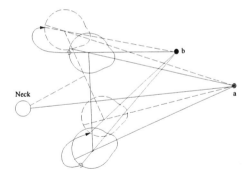

Figure 3. The position of the neck behind the baseline causes motion parallax due to neck movements. In this figure, the solid line represents the geometry of the system at time t and the dashed line represents the system at time $t + \Delta t$. the Point **a** is the fixation point. The fixation is preserved on point **a** during the time the neck is moved and the image of **b** has moved on the retina along a distance which is a function of the relative depth of the two points. That is, the retinal distance between the points **a** and **b** change in both eyes, since the points are at different distances relative to the observer.

the effect of motion parallax, it is desirable to have the neck joints as far as possible behind the baseline. So is the case in primate heads. Figure 3 illustrates the position of the center of rotation of the top of the spine in relation to the eye orbits. The real effect of motion parallax is indeed achieved when the observer is in motion. However, the parallax motion due to the neck movements should not be overlooked.

- Speeding up gaze movements:
  The movements due to gaze shiftings or gaze holdings or a combination of them, is normally a sum of the neck and eye movements.

- Minimizing the distortion due to image stabilization. This phenomenon should be studied in conjunction with the other items mentioned above. Figure 4 illustrates an observer moving forward. During a movement on an uneven ground, the direction of the gaze is changed very little along the gaze direction. Although this image stabilization effect is better adapted to e.g. a camel (vertical neck movements) or a pigeon (longitudinal neck movements), it suggests a potential need for a neck mechanism.

The first and second items above can be performed by other kinds of body movements, assuming that the observer is not *stationary*. However, the third and fourth items cannot be substituted by body movements. Nevertheless, these last items are not *functionally* necessary in man.

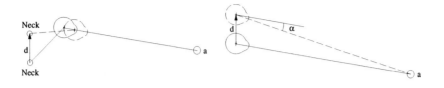

Figure 4. The effect of stabilization by neck movements. If the observer is translated an amount of d, pure stabilization by eyes would generate a shift by α. The same stabilization by neck would result only in an posterior-inferior movement of the eye which has second order effects on the image.

3.2. Eye movements

Eye movements, contrary to neck movements, do not affect the geometry of the view markedly. Eye movements are classified in the following categories (Carpenter 1988):

Gaze-shifting movements :

fast: saccades
      microsaccades
      quick phase of nystagmus

slow: smooth pursuit
      vergence

Gaze-holding movements :
      vestibular
      optokinetic

Fixational movements :
      tremor
      drift

Fixational movements are the small movements that are observed during fixation on a point. In this work we will not address fixational movements. The reason is mainly that the effect of the movements on vision is subject to discussion.

Movement of the eyes help the visual agent in different ways. They are present in all vertebrates although sometimes only to a small extent. They are used for different goals and fulfill different functions in different animals.

In primates, eye movements show a very complex behavior in terms of frequency, amplitude and variety. An interesting characteristic of eye movements is their connection to the behavior, i.e. to the intensions and actions of the observer.

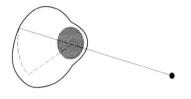

Figure 5. A ramp retina and the so-called 'static accommodation' in vertebrates using eye movements (or in some cases even neck movements) to focus on objects. The ramp shape of the retina makes it possible to focus by rotating the eye ball. Flatfishes, skates, rays and even horses use this mechanism. Some vertebrates use a combination of this technique with accommodation by the crystalline lens. For detailed information, see Ali and Klyne (1985).

4. Eye movements and the stable perception of the world

An amazing point about our visual sense is its perceptual stability, although everything in the scene, including our eyes, is continuously moving, jumping, flying etc., it perceives the environment in a very stable manner. On the contrary, our visual perception fails when everything, including our eyes, stands perfectly still.

We need eye movements not only to direct our gaze towards specific directions or objects. Prior to that, we need them to have a stable perception of the world. Understanding eye movements from an engineering point of view is preconditioned by understanding their functions and the underlying mechanisms.

In general, one could observe three major reasons behind eye movements:

- limited field of sharp view due to foveal perception

- velocity blur and image stabilization

- binocular fixation

It is evident that the movement of the eyes are partly due to the foveal-peripheral distribution in the retinal structure. The species having fovea use often large eye movements. Some other vertebrates use eye movements to compensate for other kinds of non-uniform retinal structures, e.g. as depicted in Figure 5. The geometric shape of the retina in the figure in conjunction with eye movements perform accommodation! This kind of accommodation which is e.g. present in the horse eye, is usually called static or inactive accommodation (although it is certainly very active!)

Some eye movements are only present due to the existence of fovea centralis. Vergence is such a movement. However, there are yet some other reasons behind the movement of the eyes. These reasons have already been mentioned as three items in the beginning of this section. Since the present semiconductor camera systems are not yet capable of

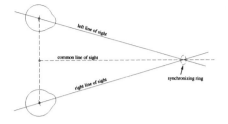

Figure 6. The two eyes move normally as if their lines of sight go through a ring that can control their common fixation point. A common line of sight, also going through the ring can be imagined as the common coordinator of the movements of the eyes.

foveal vision and the present efforts toward such a design are yet to succeed (see e.g. the foveal CCD chip described by Spiegel *et al.*, 1989), the current work is mainly focused on the three mentioned items.

4.1. Limited foveal field of view

A very small portion of our static view is sharp and the field of view of the sharp area, the foveal field of view, is hardly 2° in extent. Movements of the eyes expand this tiny foveal field of view and makes the world appear to us so with overall clarity and sharpness. Those vertebrates who do not employ foveal vision do not perform corresponding movements either.

4.1.1. Convergence and divergence of the visual axes

Among the vertebrates who use binocular fixation, the two eyes are synchronized by a fictitious axis and ring as depicted in Figure 6. The ring can be imagined to travel along the fictitious axis. The movement of the ring represents the synchronization of the movements of the left and right lines of sight.

The movement of the lines of sight of the two eyes in this manner is called *vergence* (the common name for convergence and divergence of the eyes). The position of the origin of the axis on the baseline denotes the level of dominance of the two eyes in the common movement and sighting.

Vergence movements are generated by opposite slow movements of the eyes and are accompanied by common accommodation of the two eyes.

4.1.2. Saccades in man

Saccades are point to point ballistic movements of the eyes, i.e. their trajectories are not affected by the image during the motion. As point to point movements they are purely position controlled and require exact position of the target beforehand.

Saccades can be performed voluntarily without any training; at the same time they are also very markedly combined with other involuntary movements like smooth pursuit. The voluntary component of saccades reveals that the movement is actually controlled both actively and reactively.

The frequency of saccades and the latency prior to the movement is a part of the mystery about saccades. The frequency is about 4-5 Hz in man and the latency can be from 150-350 ms. For detailed data about the duration and latency see e.g. Yarbus (1967) or Carpenter (1988)). Saccades are very fast movements. They can typically accelerate to speeds like $700°/s$ for larger amplitudes. In the fixational movements with small discontinuities in depth, saccades stand for the largest portion of the movement. The high velocity of saccades, which is normally much higher than the delay in the visual feedback loop (in engineering terms the time between two image transfers), is the reason why we do not notice these movements that are repeated several times in a second.

In the binocular case, when fixating from one stationary point to another, the so-called Hering's principle of 'equal innervation' states that saccades are equal for both eyes in speed and amplitude[1]. The binocular saccade movement is described by Figure 6. In the same way that the movement of the ring along the common line of sight resulted in vergence, the movement along the circle going through the notional center of rotation of the two eyes (the so-called Vieth-Müller circle) describes a saccade. It should, however, be noted that the two movements are totally different in terms of speed characteristics and control scheme.

4.2. Velocity blur and image stabilization

It is essential to an observer to perceive the visual world as stable as possible. However, the objects in the visual world are temporally undergoing spatial and physical changes. This dynamism includes the observer too. The result is two types of movements that have their own special compensation mechanisms. These mechanisms are common to many animals and are actually developed also at very low stages of evolution of the visuomotoric system.

The two kinds of movements discussed here are due to the locomotion of the observer, and the motion of the observed objects in the world.

The classification criterion is based on the portion of the image that contains the consistent optic flow. Movement of a large portion of the image in a certain direction is presumed to be due to ego-motion. Local movements in a stable background are perceived as moving objects. There are clear difficulties in defining what "large" or "consistent" movements are. However, this assumption seems to simplify a major problem in passive navigation.

4.2.1. Ego-motion and optokinesis

The movement due to ego-motion is called optokinesis. This movement together with the earlier discussed vestibular movement and smooth pursuit build a class of eye movements entitled *gaze-holding*. The vestibular information assures the visual system about its judgement on ego-motion. A major limitation of optokinesis is its slow speed, with a response time of 200 ms (Carpenter (1988)). From a technical and image processing point of view, the slow nature of the movement could be speculated to be due to the global processing needed for a proper reaction. In any case, it turns out that some animals with

---

[1]This is not exactly true; Collewijn (1991) has shown that one can arrange situations in which Hering's law is not exactly valid.

Figure 7. Birds, among many other vertebrates with lateral vision, stabilize their retinal image by their special neck movements.

flexible necks and light heads like birds choose to keep their heads stable (as depicted in Figure 7), some others, like humans, use the inertial information from the semicircular canals of the vestibular system to predict the direction of the motion and cause a faster response to it.

Optokinesis constitutes a distinguished class of movements for the *eyes*. This is something that a designer of an active head-eye system should take into careful consideration. Despite this, we saw that animals like birds perform similar motion compensations by the neck movements. A decisive point here is the direction of movements and the position of the eyes in the head. This is actually what Figure 7 illustrates. The head of the bird is staying stable in front of the lateral field of view, while a system with frontal vision should stabilize the image in the directions that have first order effects on the retinal image and ignore the second order effects generated by front-ward movement. That is, the choice of what areas should be stabilized in a system is strongly dictated by the position of the eyes with respect to the body.

4.2.2. Tracking dynamic objects and smooth pursuit

The static fixation procedure mentioned earlier in this chapter was meant to realize the process of looking at different objects in the scene. The optokinetic movement could thereby compensate for the movements of the observer. The question is what happens if the point of fixation, the target, starts moving around. We already know the answer; our eyes will track them.

Tracking a target comprises movements composed of small saccades to correct retinal errors and smooth pursuit to correct the retinal slip. The combination of the two movements results in a rather fast dynamic fixation of the target on the foveal area[2]. Although smooth pursuit and optokinesis are basically different mechanisms, many computational steps in them are similar. Hence, they could have many common sub-modules.

The maximum velocity of smooth pursuit in man is estimated to be $80 - 160°/s$. The velocity characteristics depend on the species. Naturally, one would expect better head cooperation and less eye activity in the animals with lighter heads and less flexible eyes.

---

[2] Actually we are even capable of pursuing targets that do not lie on the fovea; parafoveal tracking is also feasible, see e.g. Collewijn and Tamminga (1986).

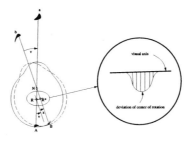

Figure 8. The position of the notional nodal point and the center of rotation, the sighting center, do not agree. The figure gives an account for how the systematic lateral movements of the eyes can solve this problem. A rotation about the center of the eye ball is the same as a rotation about the notional nodal point (angle v) and a translation (vector x). The size of x can become as large as 0.4 mm that explains why we do not need to do correction saccades for angles up to $15° - 20°$.

Smooth pursuit has a strongly predictive nature. These predictions are both present during the motion and at the initial phase of the motion. The initial phase of the movement is actually predicted and is not dependent on the target speed and position.

4.3. Eye movements and the locus of the rotation center

Instead of ordinary rotations in the orbit, human eyes follow a very complicated pattern of movements. Human eyes rotate coarsely about a point (the cross-point of the three roll, pitch and yaw axes) in the *eyes*, but rather precisely about a point in the *head*. The visual axis of an eye goes through this fixed point when the eye points at different directions.

On the one hand, the source of this deviation of the eyes in the orbit, and on the other hand the confusion raised by the disagreement of optical and visual axes and the line of sight, has been subject of discussion among physiologists. To solve the former confusion, Alpern (1969) suggested a point of rotation in about 13.5 mm from the cornea (i.e. almost the center of the eye ball). The suggestion could not however explain the deviation of the center of rotation.

Shipley and Rawlings (1970a; 1970b), gave an explanation for the deviation by pointing at the disagreement between the notional nodal point of the eye and its center of rotation. They suggested that the deviations help compensate for distortions introduced in near vision by the difference between the center of the eyeball and the notional nodal point.

Figure 8 attempts to explain how a lateral translation of the eye ball (vector x) added to the equivalent rotation suggested by the stimulus (the angle v) solves the problem of the disagreement between the notional nodal point and the center of rotation. One could ask how come the crosspoint of the visual axes in the head is preserved and is not affected by all these deviations. The answer is suggested to be the observed small rotations of the

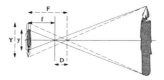

Figure 9. The magnification effect of focusing/defocusing in the sharpness by lens translation strategy that is used in man-made lenses and even by some other vertebrates. A change of focal length to compensate for this error helps also keep the optical center in place.

crystalline lens about the vertical axis that makes the difference between the optical and visual axes vary[3]: This results in small adjustments of the visual axis depending on the amount of rotation of the eye.

5. The impact on the design of the KTH-head

Like Krotkov (1989) , Ballard (1991) and others, we have chosen to design a binocular head-eye system. In our particular design, we have also applied the described biological inspirations, as far as technological constraints have permitted.

Briefly, one could state that biological vision in general and the anthropomorphic elements of vision in particular have affected the design of the KTH-head on both the physical and the behavioral level. While the physical aspect is realized in the mechanics and electronics of the system, the behavioral characteristics are represented by the control and visual processes embodied in simple competing-cooperating primary processes and their integration. The cooperating processes and the control architecture is discussed in Pahlavan et al. (1992) and Pahlavan (1993).

In the following, it will be shown, how the mechanics, hardware and software of the system are designed and integrated to serve this idea. The design was also constrained by the desire to keep the level of complexity and cost within reasonable limits for a research group (i.e. a cost of about $30.000 and complexity of a PhD project). The requirement to purchase off the shelf products as much as possible, was fulfilled. Hence, from the point of view of state of the art in robotics, the components used in the design are not exotic or tailored to the system. However, limited tailored solutions have been employed for the sake of removing major bottlenecks which appear due to the speed limitations or interface incompatibility of the off the shelf products. Figure 11 depicts the KTH-head.

---

[3]See Crane and Steel (1985), but preferably the whole discussion in Carpenter (1988) pp. 139-147, that covers other aspects and views too.

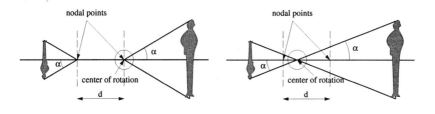

Figure 10. Two approaches in modelling an optical center for the objective. Left: rotations can be performed about the first nodal point. In this approach, the position of the nodal points must be known, or achieved by calibration. Right: choosing a fictitious point as if the lens is a thin lens; the method simplifies the mathematical computations that often assume a pinhole camera geometry, but needs intensive position measurments for different focal lengths and focusing distances.

6. The degrees of freedom in the KTH-head

An account of the degrees of freedom in the human head and his visual parameters was given earlier. The same procedure will be repeated here for the KTH-head[4]. These degrees of freedom are listed here in the same manner:

Eyes-mechanical DoF:

Each eye module has 2 mechanical degrees of freedom → a total of 4 mechanical degrees of freedom which are:
tilt or elevation
pan or azimuth

Neck-mechanical DoF:

The neck module has 2 degrees of freedom, these are:
neck tilt
neck pan

Eyes-optical DoF:

Each eye module has 3 optical degrees of freedom → a total of 6 optical degrees of freedom which are:
focusing
zooming

---

[4]The earlier work on head-eye systems in other laboratories is often based on a 4 degrees of freedom solution with common tilt, pan and vergence (with two actuators). The Pennsylvania head (see Krotkov(1986)) had two more degrees of freedom for vertical and horizontal transformations.

Figure 11. The KTH head-eye system.

iris manipulation

We also have a compensation movement in each eye module for keeping the optical center of each lens at the crosspoint of pan and tilt axes of the eyes. They are not considered as 2 degrees of freedom; although the movement can also be freely adjusted and does not associate with any other kind of movement. The reason why they are not considered as degrees of freedom is that the corresponding movements in human eyes are not modelled as degrees of freedom either. The corresponding movements are the small lateral anterior-posterior movements of the eye ball.

The relationship between the left and right eyes is very complex . This complexity can be observed in e.g. the relative dominance of one of the two eyes. Hence, it is logical to model and realize our head-eye system as having completely independent eye modules and then create the dependency between the modules by means of the control architecture in software. This is exactly the case in biological vision; each vertebrate eye is mechanically a separate unit. Hence, it can be influenced by the stimuli from both its own visual input and the input to the other eye.

7. The mechanical structure

The KTH-head is designed to be able to carry high resolution CCD cameras (756×581 elements) including their control units with motorized zoom lenses up to $1 : 1.2/12mm - 75mm$. The reason is that there is a desire to solve the issue of foveal vision with obtaining higher resolution in the center of the image rather than decreasing the resolution in the periphery, i.e. the resolution in the center of the CCD chip should become higher with respect to the currently available technology. The desired resolution could be changed on the chip by zooming in, and the peripheral information is achieved by zooming out. Depending on the desired range, one has the possibility to mount different lenses that can physically be mounted on the eye modules.

The mechanical structure of the head can be divided into three modules:

The neck module: The module is also the base of the head. It contains pan and tilt motors of the neck and the proper attachment facilities to be connected to the other modules from top and bottom.

The baseline rig: A cage-like slide with two parallel rails for the slide and a couple of ballscrews attached to a motor between them, for dynamic and static adjustment of the length of the baseline. From the bottom it is connected to the neck module or a robot arm and on the slide at the top, it carries the eye modules.

The eye modules: Separate (normally two) modules that are mounted on the described slides described in the baseline rig. They are also attached to the ballscrew mechanism mounted in the rig, so that their position can be manipulated by the baseline adjustment mechanism. Each module has three motors for pan, tilt and optical center compensation.

Figure 12 illustrates the outline drawings of the KTH-head where these different modules are marked.

It should be noticed that although the KTH-head is a real-time machine and mainly used as such in e.g. the experiments accounted for in Pahlavan et al.(1992, 1993), the effort in the design has been to find an optimal compromise between its performance, abilities, flexibility and cost so that it can also be used in other contexts e.g. as a measuring instrument, with small technical losses.

7.1. The eye/camera modules

In the KTH-head, the eye modules are separate units, capable of doing their own tilt and pan rotations. Each module is capable of moving the camera along the optical axis as to compensate for movements of the lens center due to focusing and zooming. Thus it is able to maintain camera rotations about the lens center or any other desired point along the 90 mm long stroke of the mechanism. The mechanics allow a maximum compensational movement of 90 mm. This is an essential feature of the design which allows for eye movements in the true sense, i.e. without parallax, no matter what focal length or focus distance is used. It might be necessary to underline that the important point here is the ability to rotate about a certain point and the actuation capacity for changing the position of this point according to the parameter changes that necessitate such a movement.

When changing the accommodation distance in a camera, the image of the viewed object undergoes a magnification effect. By changing the focal length accordingly (zooming a little bit), not only the image size is compensated for, but also the lens center remains in its original position. The magnification μ due to defocusing is[5] Y/y. The defocusing causes a drift of the optical center denoted with D. The change of the focal length that can compensate for the magnification is $F - f$. At the same time $D = F - f$ is also the

---

[5]Note that $\mu > 1$ for defocusing to a nearer distance, and $\mu < 1$ for defocusing further away from the object in question.

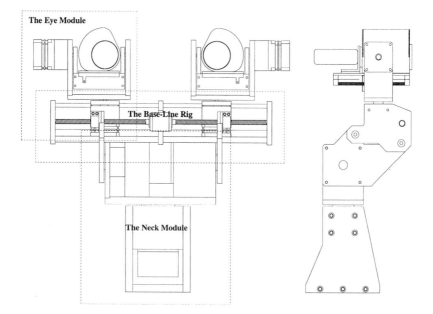

Figure 12. An outline drawing of the front and side views of KTH-head. Different modules are segmented.

displacement of the optical center due to the change of focal length from F to f. Figure 9 illustrates this trivial argument.

This means that two methods can be used to compensate for the dislocation of the optical center of the lens with respect to the crosspoint of the actuator axes of the eye module. The first method moves the whole camera unit including the lens in the computed direction. This method can not only compensate for the dislocations of the optical center, but also positions the center of rotation wherever needed, to the extent mentioned above. The second approach is actually a side-effect of the focal length compensation needed for demagnification of the image that undergoes focusing.

In any case, the compensation mechanism can also be used for deliberately generated deviation of the optical center from the center of rotation.

Figure 10 illustrates two different approaches to model the problem of rotation about the lens center. The first model suggests rotations about a point somewhere between the object and the image plane. The formula for calculating the position of this point can be determined experimentally. The approach has the advantage that the motion computations that often assume the pinhole model can directly use the geometry of the lens. The drawback is the intensive work of finding the formula or an equivalent look up

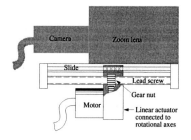

Figure 13. The mechanism used to adjust the position of the optical center. Any change of the optical parameters is translated into the number of steps needed to position the tray properly.

table.

The other approach is to use the lens formula for a thick lens in tracing the rays; let the rotation happen about the first nodal point and take the distance between the principal planes into consideration. This approach is especially attractive when the data about the principal planes are known.

In any case, the displacement of the optical center is a result of changes in optical parameters like focal length, focusing distance and even the iris opening and such a displacement should be activated due to changes in these parameters.

The mechanical implementation of the compensation mechanism is schematically illustrated in Figure 13. The mechanism is based on a tray mounted on a slide. The translational movement of the slide is caused by a screw connected to the shaft of a 4-phase stepper motor via a reduction gear-box. The compensation is performed in parallel with the change of optical parameters. The speed of the mechanism is compatible with the speed of the lens motors. However the positioning accuracy is compatible with the positioning accuracy on the mechanical degrees of freedom.

In a simple system with fixed short focal length, the compensation may be overlooked. It is, however, rather easy to compensate for the displacement of the optical center for most of the lenses with fix focal length.

7.1.1. Muscles vs. motors

The muscle structure in the human eyes can be modelled to comprise at least 3 mechanical degrees of freedom: superior-inferior rotation (tilt), lateral-medial rotation (pan) and superior-inferior oblique rotation (cyclotorsion). This model would not cover the small translational movements observed in human eyes. However, the major movements, i.e. rotational movements are well represented by the model.

Apart from these small translational movements, the eye modules in a head-eye system should be specified to perform the basic rotations illustrated in the figure[6]. The approach

---

[6]In the KTH-head, these translational movements can actually be performed by two mechanisms: the

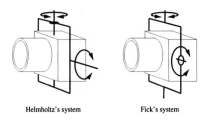

Helmholtz's system   Fick's system

Figure 14. Helmholtz's system (left) and Fick's model (right). In Helmholtz's system, if the tilt axes of left and right cameras are connected to each other, one single motor is enough. The approach not chosen in this work, since the design cannot become compact and the common tilt motor would be a bulky one with its following inertial consequences.

in this work has been to postpone the implementation of the cyclotorsion movement. It should be pointed out that a future enhancement by adding cyclotorsion is planned in the mechanical design and is easy to accomplish.

The remaining movements are elevation and azimuth that are local tilt and pan movements (local to each eye). There are two mechanically feasible (i.e. utilizing rigid construction elements) approaches to implement these rotational movements: Helmholtz's system or Fick's system. Figure 14 illustrates the two systems. The two systems are almost equivalent although the kinematics of Helmholtz's system is a bit simpler. However, the change of the baseline was a desired function of the head, and taking this factor into account, Fick's system resulted in a compact and dynamically better design. Therefore Fick's system was chosen, although the kinematic chain was slightly more complex.

In this context, it should be underlined that the real benefit of Helmholtz's system, namely the possibility to use one single motor for tilting both eyes, could in practice be an improper approach, because the dependence of the eyes on each other is hardwired and cannot easily be subject to on-line calibrations. Besides, unless the lenses are small and light, two small motors with favorable dynamic characteristics are always better than one bulky motor with higher rotor inertia. However, this issue should be considered as design dependent and such a simplification is acceptable in small and light heads.

Figure 15 illustrates an eye/camera module in the KTH-head. Two of these modules make the head binocular. Although the human oculomotor system constrains the motion of the two eyes, the eye modules in the KTH-head can move totally independently. Hence, the control system implemented in software handles the coordination of the two eyes.

7.2. The neck module

As mentioned earlier, the major difference between an eye movement and a neck movement is that the movement of the eyes does not change the geometry in the image, while neck movements do. Hence parallax information can be extracted by neck movements.

---

one that changes the length of the baseline and the compensation mechanism for the position of the lens center

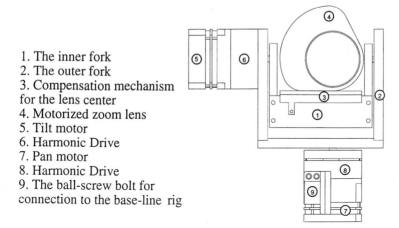

1. The inner fork
2. The outer fork
3. Compensation mechanism for the lens center
4. Motorized zoom lens
5. Tilt motor
6. Harmonic Drive
7. Pan motor
8. Harmonic Drive
9. The ball-screw bolt for connection to the base-line rig

Figure 15. An eye module in the KTH-head.

The primate neck could be modelled as having three degrees of freedom. However, the flexible spine mechanism makes the situation more complicated. This construction was considered to be too elaborate to model and the effort was concentrated on implementing those kinematic properties of the human neck that are most important for vision. Hence we have contented ourselves with two degrees of freedom here, pan and tilt, much in line with what other systems have, i.e. tilt and pan. However, it is important to note that this particular design allows eccentric motions with a constant geometry and hence a proper study of kinetic depth, at least to some extent.

7.3. The baseline rig

The ability of changing the size of the baseline is a special feature of the KTH-head. Unlike animals, the head can change the length of the baseline. This is an experimental feature of the head and is designed to allow a flexible approach to the study of stereopsis.

It is important to point out that the rotation of the eyes about the optical centers guarantees that changing the length of the baseline does not generate any side effects. The baseline is defined as the line between the two optical centers. If the eyes do not rotate about their optical centers, their rotations result in a foreshortening or extension of the baseline.

7.4. The visual processing unit

The visual processing unit and the motor controllers are heavily integrated so that the visual processes have easy access to all motor control abilities[7]. In spite of this, they are physically and electrically in two different environments; therefore they are described as separate units.

Figure 16 illustrates the transputer network in which the visual processing is performed.

[7] A description of these units is outside the scope of this article. For more information on these issues see Pahlavan (1993)Pahlavan93thesis).

There are 3 marked areas or partitions in the figure. The "left" area takes care of the flow of the image data coming from the left camera; so does the the "right" area for the right camera.

The part of the network labeled "cyclopean" is where the common representation of the left and right images is generated, stored and processed. Consequently, all common actions are also commanded from this unit. It should be noted that the partitioning here between left, right and cyclopean is decided by the programs and there are no hardware obstacles for choosing partitions in another way. Even the configuration can be altered softly and the only limitation would then be the number of links and transputers.

The left/right partitions are each gathered around a transputer-based frame-grabber. That is, the system has two frame-grabbers; each of these uses an 18Ms/s digitizer 4MB RAM accessible for the transputer on board and 1MB VRAM accessible for both the digitizer and the transputer.

The transputer modules are mounted on a number of mother boards in a VME rack. A Sun SPARC-station 10 that is hosting the VME arrangement can also be directly involved in the computations and/or sending commands to the controllers.

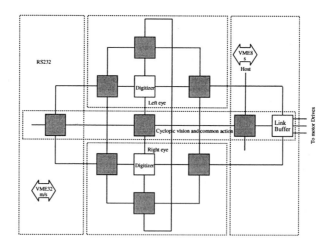

Figure 16. The processor configuration in the KTH-head. Each node is a T8 transputer.

8. Performance

The KTH-head has 7 mechanical and 6 optical degrees of freedom. However, these are not literally independent of each other. Physically each degree of freedom has its own motor and power drive, but the control scheme enforces the appropriate dependency

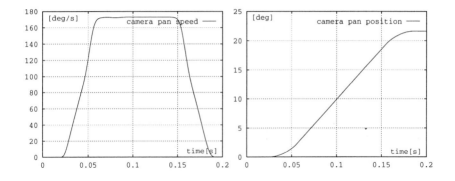

Figure 17. Left: the speed characteristics of an eye module in the KTH-head. The curve depicts the motion characteristics of a large saccade stimulated by a flash lamp. Right: a large saccade (22°) and its step response in an eye module. Since the smallest possible focal length is used here, the bulk of the lens is hanging on one side of the lens center which is the rotation axis, resulting in a large inertial torque.

between these degrees of freedom. In our laboratory we have mainly applied human-like oculomotor models to the head and thereby the two eyes are coordinated in their tilt and pan movements resulting in saccades and vergence movements synchronized with accommodation. In parallel to accommodation, the focal length is changed so that the displacement of the lens center is compensated for and at the same time the magnification effect due to focusing is avoided. The iris movements and their adaptation to changes in the illumination should actually also affect the focal length and/or the accommodation distance, but presently, this has not been addressed; mainly because the effect seems to be small enough to neglect in the lab environment.

The neck movement can be totally independent of the eyes, but in our experiments on generating reactive behavior in the KTH-head (see e.g. Pahlavan et al. (1992,1993) or Pahlavan (1993)), the neck joints try to achieve the best possible angle of view by minimizing the asymmetry of the fixation triangle. This is the scheme observed in human beings and has two major benefits. The first one is that the speed of the neck is added to the speed of the eyes and the other benefit is that the object of interest is always observed as frontal as possible.

Figure 17 left, depicts the speed response of the eye module. The data here is recorded from a saccade to the position of a flash lamp and as it is seen here, the speed of the movement approaches the top speed. The same is true about Figure 17 right; the acceleration, constant speed and deceleration can be observed from the curve which is recorded for a step response of about 22°.

Figure 18 is an example of recorded data when the movements from the tilt joint of the

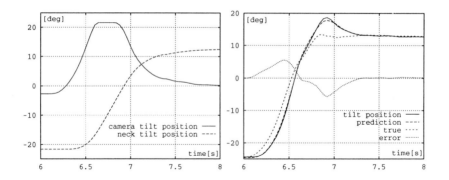

Figure 18. Left: the combination of neck and eye movements in the KTH-head. This movement is very similar to the human case. Movements of the eyes passing a certain threshold, initiate neck movements as demonstrated in the figure. The neck movement is totally independent of the eye movement apart from the initial triggering. Right: the figure demonstrates tracking a real object and the quality of the tracking procedure. As depicted here, the motor response to the predicted speed is very precise. However, the agreement between the predictor and the real speed is not equally good and depends on whether the movement is linear or not (the predictor used here is a linear one).

neck and the tilt joint of an eye are combined. As it is seen in the figure, the eye module accelerates faster and when the neck module has followed its motion well enough, the eye moves back to almost the original position.

In practice, most of the movements are controlled in some predictive manner. Figure 18 shows the effect of prediction on the motion and the agreement between the motor response to the prediction input. The predictive filter is an α-β tracker (see Deriche and Faugeras (1990)), i.e. a steady-state Kalman filter, and thus a linear one. As it is seen in the figure, the motor position agrees very well with the predicted one. The prediction, however, is not in full agreement with the "true" motion of the object.

9. Acknowledgement

The preparation of this document was due to Oliver Ludwig's endless enthusiasm for active vision and his effort to introduce this work to the German computer vision community; I am very grateful to him. Furthermore, this work would not be realized without significant contributions by Tomas Uhlin and Prof. Jan-Olof Eklundh. The work has been sponsored by The Swedish Research Council for Engineering Science, TFR, with additional support from the basic research program in computer vision by The Swedish National Board for Industrial and Technical Development, NUTEK. These supports and assistances are gratefully acknowledged.

REFERENCES

1. M.A.Ali and M.A.Klyne, Vision in Vertebrates, Plenum Press, New York, 1985
2. Y.Aloimonos, I. Weiss and A. Bandyopadhyay, Active Vision, Proc. 1st ICCV, London, June 1987, pp. 35-54
3. Y.Aloimonos, Personal communication, 1993
4. R.Bajcsy, Active Perception vs. Passive Perception, Proceedings Third IEEE Workshop on Computer Vision, Bellair, MI, October 1985, pp. 55-59
5. M.Alpern, Kinematics of the Eye, in The Eye (H.Davson ed.), Academic Press Inc, 1969, vol.3, Chapter 3.1
6. D.H.Ballard. Animate Vision, Artificial Intelligence, 48, 1991, pp. 57-86
7. R.H.S.Carpenter, Movements of the Eyes, Pion Press, London, 1988
8. H.Collewijn, E.P.Tamminga Human Fixation and Pursuit in Normal and Open-Loop Conditions: Effects of Central and Peripheral Retinal Targets, Journal of Physiology, London, 1986, 379, pp. 109-129
9. H.Collewijn Binocular Coordination of Saccadic Gaze Shifts: Plasticity in Time and Space, Sixth European Conference on Eye Movements, Leuven, Belgium, August 1991
10. H.D.Crane, C.M.Steele, Generation V Dual-Purkinje-Image Eye-Tracker, Applied Optics, 1985, 24, pp. 527-537
11. R.Deriche, O.Faugeras. Tracking Line Segments, Proc. 1st ECCV, Antibes, April 1988, pp. 259-268
12. E.P. Krotkov, J.F. Summers and F. Fuma, The Pennsylvania Active Camera System, University of Pennsylvania TR-CIS-86-22, 1986
13. E.P.Krotkov, Active Computer Vision by Cooperative Focus and Stereo, Springer Verlag, 1989
14. P.Morasso, E.Bizzi and J.Dichgans, Adjustment of Saccade Characteristics During Head Movements, Experimental Brain Research, 1973
15. K.Pahlavan, T.Uhlin and J.O.Eklundh, Integrating Primary Ocular Processes, Proc. 2nd ECCV, Santa Margherita Ligure, Italy, May 1992, pp. 526-541
16. K.Pahlavan and J.O.Eklundh, A Head-Eye System–Analysis and Design, CVGIP: Image Understanding, Special Issue on Active Vision (Y.Aloimonos ed.) 56:1, July 1992, pp. 41-56
17. K.Pahlavan, T.Uhlin and J-O.Eklundh, Active Vision as A Methodology, Active Vision (Y.Aloimonos ed.), Advances in Computer Science, Lawrence Erlbaum, Hillsdale, NJ, 1993, pp. 19-46
18. K.Pahlavan, T.Uhlin and J.O.Eklundh, Dynamic Fixation, Proc. 4th ICCV, Berlin, Germany, May 1993, pp. 412-419
19. K.Pahlavan, Active Robot Vision and Primary Ocular Processes, PhD Thesis, TRITA-NA-P9316, Royal Institute of Technology, Computational Vision and Active Perception Laboratory, Stockholm, 1993
20. T.Shipley, S.C.Rawlings, The Nonius Horopter. I. History and Theory, Vision Research, 1970, 10, pp. 1225-1262
21. T.Shipley, S.C.Rawlings, The Nonius Horopter. II. An Experimental Report, Vision

Research, 10, 1970, pp. 1263-1299
22. J.van der Spiegel, G.Kreider, C.Claeys, I.Debusschere, G.Sandini, P.Dario, F.Fantini, P.Bellutti and G.Soncini, A Foveated Retina-Like Sensor Using CCD Technology, Analog VLSI Implementations of Neural Systems, Kluwer, 1989, Editors C.Mead and M.Ismail
23. A.Yarbus. Eye Movements and Vision, Plenum Press, New York, 1967

Visual Attention and Cognition
W.H. Zangemeister, H.S. Stiehl and C. Freksa (Editors)
© 1996 Elsevier Science B.V. All rights reserved.

SACCADIC CAMERA CONTROL FOR SCENE RECOGNITION ON AN AUTONOMOUS VEHICLE

Herbert Janßen

Institut für Neuroinformatik
Ruhr–Universität Bochum
44780 Bochum, Germany

heja@neuroinformatik.ruhr-uni-bochum.de

ABSTRACT

A system for visually as well as expectation guided saccades is proposed which is part of an architecture for basic visual behavior of an autonomous vehicle[1]
The saccadic control is achieved by independent processing pathways for both foveal and peripheral images. Goal is the learning and recognition of complex scenes or objects by means of directed fixations.
Different types of mathematical models for saccadic recognition are examined. Hopfield type dynamical neural networks and Markov models are show to have interesting properties, but - even in extended form - lack robustness. Scene recognition is obtained by classification of the foveal images and temporal integration of the classification results with respect to their relative positions. Hypotheses about a scene are "tested" by the recognition system by trying to find expected but yet unfoveated parts of the scene. Expectations generate a tendency to gaze at a specific position as well as look for a specific feature, the latter by using selective masking of salient peripheral features.
The system tends to emergently generate object specific scanpaths but does not rely on them for recognition. Integration of visually and expectation guided saccades is achieved by an interest map which implements competition and cooperation between different target demands.
This saccadic control and recognition subsystem is embedded in a control system for basic camera behavior including vergence, focus control and tracking and additionally providing segmentation, classification, distance and depth information as its output.

Keywords: saccades, attention, autonomous behavior, scene recognition

Introduction

Saccades, i.e. fast "jumps" of the eyes, are the most common kind of eye movement. The ability for fast shifts of our eyes corresponds to the space dependent receptor density of our retina with a small high resolution fovea (2–3 deg.) and a low resolution periphery

---

[1]Part of this work has been carried out together with Gerd–Jürgen Giefing, see [9, 4]

(cone density approximately 1 : 10). Therefore, the computationally expensive processing of visual information can be selectively directed to arbitrary locations *(saccadic scanpath)*, using the environment as a kind of external buffer for visual information [1].

Several influences on the selection of fixation targets have been reported. In general, the following basic distinction[20] may be made:

- *Preattentive* saccades are made to moving patterns in the scene (a very strong effect) or to simple outstanding image features like color blobs or texture discontinuities. In those cases latency time does not depend on the complexity of the image - thus suggesting parallel processing in the brain.

- For *attentive* saccades however, some kind of sequential attentional process selects the targets *(overt attention)*, and eventually cognitive tasks determine the scanpath [24].

While quantitative properties of preattentive gaze selection are known [20, 10], for the higher level "cognitive" phenomena so far only phenomenological models exist ([22] for critical discussion). One effect found is that human scanpaths tend to be cyclic [14], however models like the one by Noton and Stark represent cyclic scanpaths explicitly and therefore have problems with deviations and moreover fail completely to explain why the reproduction of the learning scanpath is not *necessary* for a successful recognition.

Another crucial question is the interaction of different levels of saccadic control: specifically, how can preattentive and attentive/cognitive fixation demands be integrated ?

Our general solution here is an emergent model; in our case, the model produces emergent behavior through competition and cooperation of preattentive and attentive targets and through the recognition mechanism, which does not rely on explicit cyclic scanpaths, but produces them in the limit of ideal conditions.

Methodological Background   Many approaches to model visual attention in cognitive science are phenomenological and describe or predict the performance of a subject exposed to stimuli of very reduced complexity.

On the other hand the most important function of visual attention is to support the selective perception of important aspects in a visually rich and often messy environment. Here attention is a primary concern of behavioral control, with the purpose to utilize the limited senory abilities, processing resources and effector potentialities to a maximum extent.

In this general sense attentional control is not done by *one* specific mechanism, but probably uses a variety of allocation schemes appropriate to the respective resources. So it is crucial to narrow the investigation to specific attentional mechanisms[12].

While experimental data supporting a functional view of visual attention in the saccadic system is still rare and fragmentary, the task to model behavioral control for systems in the technical domain becomes more and more urgent.

The demand for this is relatively recent but obviously leads to a quite different impact on modelling. On the other hand, a constructive approach may well be more successful to answer central questions about attentional control.

For this work, the learning and recognition of scenes or objects by means of multiple fixations was defined as the behavioral goal, having in mind problems like orientation in a natural environment or, more specifically, navigation of an autonomous robot vehicle equipped with a mobile stereo camera system. In this case the question which parts of the environment shall be attended to, becomes a rather well defined problem and helps to define versatile terms like *saliency* for this context.

Following the paradigm of saccadic recognition[13, 14], scene resp. object recognition is discussed as the problem of learning and recognizing objects or scenes in a complex visual environment by means of local foveal views. Thus the model has to specify how to scan an unknown scene, how to "learn" its relevant properties and how to recognize known scenes in an otherwise unfamiliar environment via saccadic movements.

Visual Saliency

In general visual saliency is an ill–defined term. A useful definition should include properties like *local distinctness* and *invariance* [6] but also temporal change and task–dependent clues. Our approach is to use a very simple saliency definition based on nonlinear filtering of the peripheral image to be able to find features in a reproducible way.

First we will discuss how a measure for local distinctness can be found for the greyvalue image function $I(x, y)$. In differential geometry the Gaussian curvature K is defined as the product of the minimal and maximal curvature of a surface $K = k_1 k_2$. Thus K is zero for any points laying in a plane or on an edge, while it is large for local peaks. The absolute of Gaussian curvature $|K|$ therefore would be an optimal measure for local distinctness since it quantifies how much "curved" a surface is[2].

However since it is defined as a property of a surface, i.e. for a function $f(x, y, z)$ and not as an operation on a function $f(x, y)$ it would be computationally rather awkward to compute for an actual image. The solution is to use a similar measure, that is very simple to compute:

$$s_k = \left| \frac{\partial I(x, y)}{\partial x} \frac{\partial I(x, y)}{\partial y} + \frac{\partial I(x, y)}{\partial (x + y)} \frac{\partial I(x, y)}{\partial (x - y)} \right|$$

which is a good approximation to the absolute of Gaussian curvature[3].

While this saliency measure may already yield good results, it can be improved further: White noise - as it is present in real camera images - would limit the use of s_k considerably. Therefore we compute s_k on a number of different scales of the image, each computed by lowpass filtering and subsampling with a factor of two. The modified saliency measure s_p is now computed as the sum of the absolute Gaussian curvatures of the n single scales

$$s_p = \sum_{i=1}^{n} s_k^{(i)}.$$

This leads to a saliency measure that is especially sensitive for broader image structures which also means that it is more stable under differing viewing conditions.

To implement selective attention, i.e. to define saliency as a matching process to a specific feature, a somewhat different approach is required. There are of course several algorithms for feature matching available, but what is required in our case is a selective feature detector that is simple, works with a high number of templates and should be adaptive to cope with different environment conditions.

For feature–specific saliency we thus use an adaptive principal–component expansion of the image $I(x, y)$ into n vectors $\mathbf{v}_i$ [17] and compare this to a vector of required coefficients l_i. This defines an additional selective saliency term as

$$s_e(x, y, t) = \sum_{i=0}^{n} \|l_i(t) - (I(x, y, t) * \mathbf{v}_i(x', y'))\| \tag{1}$$

For an adaptation of a feature channel mapping, an adaptive principal components analysis (PCA) can be utilized. Let $\mathbf{x} \in \mathbb{R}^N$ be the M input vectors, $C \in \mathbb{R}^{M \times N}$ the matrix to be evaluated and $\mathbf{y} = C\mathbf{x}$ with $\mathbf{y} \in \mathbb{R}^M$ the output vector to be calculated. Then the PCA network is defined by:

$$V_i = \sum_j w_{ij}\xi_j = \mathbf{w}_i^T \boldsymbol{\xi} = \boldsymbol{\xi}^T \mathbf{w}_i \tag{2}$$

and a learning rule

$$\Delta w_{ij} = \eta V_i(\xi_j - \sum_{k=1}^{i} V_k w_{kj}). \tag{3}$$

Pattern Recognition

Concerning the system behavior the pattern recognition method used is only relevant with respect to its overall performance. We use a linear classifier based on higher–order–autocorrelation features (for details see [11]), which yields a *similarity vector* $\mathbf{c}$ between the actual foveal image and all stored foveal patterns. Its maximum value $c_{i'}(t) = \max_i(c_i(t))$ determines the actual recognized pattern i' at time t.

Models for Saccadic Recognition

In the following, the term *view* or *pattern* will be used for a single (foveal) image or its representation, while the term *object* or *scene* stands for the physical item that can possibly be recognized by integration over several views or patterns. Furthermore, a *sequence* shall stand for a number of patterns ordered in time, while a *set* simply stands for a number of unordered patterns that belong to an object.

Adopting the paradigm of saccadic recognition, i.e. a framework in which scene or objects are recognized as a sequence of local foveal views plus their relative position resp. the saccadic motor commands needed to proceed between subsequent views, there are different types of mathematical models that may be used.

Neural Network Models for Temporal Sequences   One well known type are *neural network sequence recognition* models, which have been described for various kinds of network architectures. These networks are able recognize and generate temporal sequences of patterns. They are most easily understood as a dynamical system with several limit

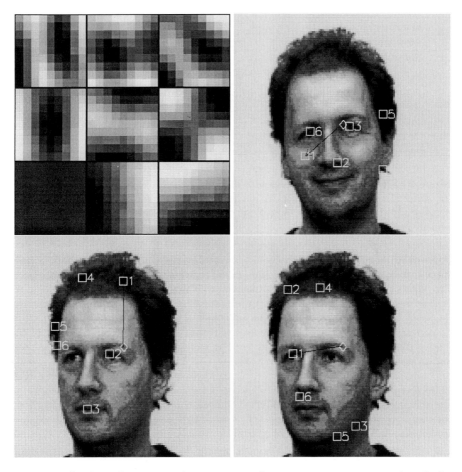

Figure 1: a) The 9 first principal components of an image series, computed with the adaptive PCA algorithm (Sanger) as discussed in the text,
b) image A with sensor–driven saliency priority, the 6 highest saliency values are marked,
c) image B with sensor–driven saliency priority,
d) image B with *selective saliency*, the "left–eye feature" (mark no. 6) of image A was used to define the l_i in eq.2 and thus the saliency measure was made selective to a certain part of the face.

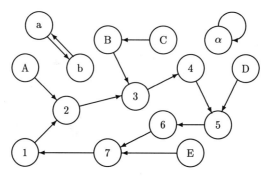

Figure 2: Schematic trajecory map of a discrete dynamical system. For convenience, the states are denoted by numbers or letters: states 1 to 7 and a and b are part of two dynamically stable limit cycles, A to E are transient and will lead onto the cycle 1 to 7, while α is a stable fixpoint.

cycles as its attractors. The patterns to be recognized resp. produced are points in state space that lie on the limit cycle. For the - most interesting - case of a discrete state space Fig. shows the principal schema with the relevant structures. Starting from any point on or close to such a limit cycle, the system will proceed governed by its implicit dynamics, i.e. it will oscillate, visiting a number of patterns in a predetermined order.

A very nice network for temporal sequences can be achived by an extension of the original Hopfield model, which we will describe as a typical formulation of a dynamical system which is able to display limit cycles.

The Extended Hopfield Model   Consider a network of n formal neurons where the state of each neuron is described as $S_i(t) \in \{-1, +1\}$. For the original Hopfield model[7, 8], the task is to store p random patterns $\{\xi_i^\mu\} \in \{-1, +1\}^p$, so that the network will respond to the presentation of a new pattern ζ_i^μ with the most similar stored pattern ξ_i^ν. Synaptic connections are modelled via weights

$$J_{ij} = \frac{1}{N} \sum_\mu \xi_i^\mu \xi_j^\mu \tag{4}$$

and each neurons is affected by a "local field" $h(t) = h_e(t) + h_i(t)$, that describes the external input and the influence of the other neurons via the respective weights, thus

$$h_i(t) = \sum_j J_{ij} S_j \tag{5}$$

The state of each neuron is determined by a threshold function of the local field

$$S_i(t) = \text{sign}(h_i(t)) \tag{6}$$

With low memory loading, a pattern μ is correctly recognized if the overlap

$$m^\mu = \frac{1}{N} \sum_j \xi_j^\mu S_j \tag{7}$$

between the stored pattern and the input pattern is maximal.

For temporal sequence recognition and generation, one has to extend the model by allowing unsymmetrical connection matrices[2]

$$J_{ij}^t = \frac{\lambda}{N} \sum_{\mu=1}^{q} \xi_i^{\mu+1} \xi_j^\mu \tag{8}$$

such that the local field becomes

$$h_i(t + \delta t) = \sum_{\mu=1}^{p} \xi_i^\mu m^\mu(t) + \lambda \sum_{\mu=1}^{q} \xi_i^{\mu+1} m^\mu(t - \tau) \tag{9}$$

There are however several problems with this approach:

- Any pattern (or point in state space) may be visited by only one sequence, hence including one pattern in two sequences involves blowing up the state space e.g. by introducing additional time delayed synapses. However this only reduces the problem for limited length sequences at the cost of introducing many additional memory variables.

- There is no possibility to output the sequence identification itself. Rather only the relation between the patterns themselfes are stored. To overcome this, one would need a second network, that tracks the pattern/object relationship.

- The order of patterns in the sequence is determined. This may be appropriate for many tasks, but introduces problems in the case of saccadic scanpaths. Not only are scanpaths varying to a certain extent, but also changes in the scene - especially occlusions - would cause the whole recognition mechanism to break down. Adopting additional synapses as described above will again reduce but not solve these problems.

To extend this model for explicit sequence recognition, we introduce auxiliary variables x amd y

$$\xi_i = \begin{cases} x_i & : & i \le u \\ y_j & : & i > u \quad (j = i - u) \end{cases} \tag{10}$$

that distinguish between u x–neurons and $n - u$ y–neurons and set

$$J_{ij}^t = 0 \quad \text{for all } i > u \text{ or } j > u. \tag{11}$$

Thus we have a network that consists of two interconnected subnets. Now consider an input pattern sequence ν is stored into this network with the input patterns defining $x^{(\mu\nu)}$ but with the same random pattern y^ν for any input pattern in the sequence. This will result in a network that will recognize and generate a sequence of patterns where the x– part is changing over time, while the y–part will be stable and may be used to recognize

---

[2]For stability with asynchronous updates of the network, further extensions need to be made, see [18, 5].

the sequence identity. An additional advantage of this type of network is that sequences that consist of one or more equal pattern steps (in the x–part) result in dynamically stable limit cycles. Actually this network is even able to react to an input that consists of a stored y–part and a random x–part with the correct sequencing behavior.

This approach solves any of the discussed problems with exception of the still predetermined pattern order in a sequence.

Markov Models   A second possible approach uses statistical models, in particular *Markov models*.

First oder Markov models are a very fundamental type of statistical models describing a process that can be in one of n discrete states S_n at any time, and that undergoes state changes only at discrete timesteps. These transitions can be described by a probability $P(q_t|q_{t-1}, q_{t-2}, \ldots) = P(q_t|q_{t-1})$, i.e. the probability of a state $P(q_t)$ depends only on the state $P(q_{t-1})$ one timestep ago.

A particular instance of a Markov model can therefore be described with only the transition matrix $A = (a)_{ji}$, where $\sum_{i=1}^{n} a_{ji} = 1$.

The advantages of Markov models - besides their simplicity - are that

- any transition from state q_j to state q_i is possible as long as $a_{ji} > 0$ holds, i.e. variations in the scanpath are easy to obtain,

- and that learning a scanpath can be easily done by averaging over all transition probabilities.

There are also major disadvantages though:

- To store more than one "scene", one either gets the same problems for shared patterns as with sequence networks, or - as Rimey and Brown suggested[15] - one needs to use a different transition matrix for every stored scene.

- As with deterministic sequence networks, one also runs into the problem of sequence identification.

String Editing   Stark and Ellis[19] propose another method, which overcomes the limitation of sequence order by using string editing techniques, i.e. they use a similarity measure for pattern sequences that is based on the number of string editing operations needed to transform one sequence into another. While the introduction of such a measure obviously reduces the order problem for recognition, it nevertheless is based on an explicit storage of an ordered sequence and does not provide cyclic scanpaths as the *emergent* result of an continuous interaction with the environment.

A Model for Visual Attention and Saccadic Recognition

In the following we will propose another approach based on a recurrent hierarchical model utilizing a *Bayes network*. A Bayes network consists of a matrix $P = (p)_{ij}$ containing the conditional probabilities for object j under the condition of pattern i, i.e. the evidence that object j is present if pattern i is recognized. Given this matrix and a vector $\mathbf{c} =$

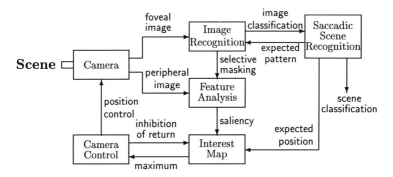

Figure 3: Overview of the saccadic recognition system

$(\mathbf{c})_i$ containing the probability of any pattern i at a given time, one can compute the probabilities $\mathbf{a} = (\mathbf{a})_j$ for all objects by the simple multiplication $\mathbf{a} = \mathbf{Pc}$. Therefore Bayes networks recently have been incorporated in saccadic recognition systems[9, 4, 16].

The complete system (Fig.) consists of the following parts:

- A preattentive peripheral feature detection extracts "salient" points in the periphery of the actually sensed image - based on either simple image measures or on "selective attention" for specific image features, see section .

- A multi–resolution foveal image recognition classifies the actual input image based on higher order autocorrelation features in scale space[11].

- A scene recognition module classifies by means of temporal integration of foveal pre-classifications. The underlying scene definition is a set of foveal views plus their spatial relationship (saccadic shifts). The output is a "saliency–map" defining expected locations for other relevant parts of the scene; thus the scene recognition tries to verify its scene hypothesis by generating saccades to specific positions. Another output contains the expected pattern to be gazed at next and may be used for selective attention by the saliency module.

- An egocentered interest map integrates the two types of fixation demands and selects the next fixation position.

Generation of object hypotheses

Scene recognition is performed as transsaccadic integration of the pattern recognition information. The evidence of the known u foveal patterns for the v objects is stored in the pattern–object relation matrix $\mathbf{Q} \in \mathbb{R}^{u \times v}$. This can be interpreted as a Bayes matrix that defines conditional probabilities for the different scenes or objects. $\mathbf{Q}$ constitutes the associative "what"–memory[21]. While the position of the foveal patterns of an object is stored in the "where"–memory $\mathbf{R} \in \mathbb{C}^{u \times v}$. The matrix $\mathbf{R}$ is complex to accommodate horizontal and vertical angles as the real and imaginary parts of one matrix element. $\mathbf{Q}$ and $\mathbf{R}$ are sparse for large numbers of foveal patterns and objects.

The object recognition process temporally integrates this information in a vector $\mathbf{a}(t)$:

$$\frac{d\mathbf{a}(t)}{dt} = - \underbrace{\tau_a \mathbf{a}(t)}_{\text{relaxation}} + \underbrace{\mathbf{Q}\mathbf{c}(t)}_{\text{input}} - \underbrace{\mathbf{d}(t) \cdot \mathbf{a}(t)}_{\substack{\text{position} \\ \text{error}}} \tag{12}$$

An internal object hypothesis for object j' is generated if the condition $a_{j'} = \max_j(a_j) \wedge a_{j'} > \theta$ is valid, where θ is a threshold to suppress "weak" hypotheses.

The *input term* is a vector containing the evidence of the current foveal image for the v learned objects. All position vectors are complex, thus expressing horizontal angles as real parts and vertical angles as imaginary parts. The *position error term* reduces the value of the actual object hypothesis. It quadratically depends on the spatial difference between the most recently executed saccade (position $r'(t_{k-1})$ to $r'(t_k)$) and the last saccadic shift according to the "where"–memory (position $r_{i'(t_{k-1})j'(t_k)}$ to $r_{i'(t_k)j'(t_k)}$):

The *relaxation term* enables the system to "forget" acquired information.

This *emergent saccadic model* uses a very efficient and robust representation avoiding memory consuming "fully connected graph" representations or explicit scan path storage[15].

The positional error can be neglected completely if the system is not stating an hypothesis, and is small if there is no significant spatial disturbance between the patterns. In this case Equ. (12) becomes linear and the stability of a hypothesis is given if $(\mathbf{Q}\mathbf{c}(t))_k \geq \tau_a\theta$ where k denotes the index of the considered object. For $(\mathbf{Q}\mathbf{c}(t))_k > \tau_a\theta$ the object k will become a hypothesis if there is no other stronger evidence.

Learning of relevant patterns and objects is easily achieved by using the explorative saccadic scanning behavior.

Generation of Cognitive Targets

A *pattern accumulator* $\mathbf{b}$ is used to generate the cognitive target demands. The relative size of the values in $\mathbf{b}$ denotes the urgency to foveate a pattern to verify the current hypothesis, while trying to avoid patterns that have been gazed at lately:

$$\frac{d\mathbf{b}(t)}{dt} = - \underbrace{\tau_b \mathbf{b}(t)}_{\text{relaxation}} - \underbrace{\mathbf{c}(t)}_{\text{recognition}} + \underbrace{\mathbf{Q}^T \mathbf{a}'(t)}_{\text{verification}} \tag{13}$$

$$\text{where} \quad a'_j(t) = \begin{cases} a_j(t) & \text{for } j = j' \\ 0 & \text{for } j \neq j'. \end{cases} \tag{14}$$

A *recognition term* reduces all values b_i by the certainty they have already been assigned. The *verification term* is calculated by the back–projection of the current object hypothesis j' according to the matrix $\mathbf{Q}$, and contains the evidence of the foveal views belonging to the object hypothesis. Note that this uses the Bayes matrix in an "inverse" direction and thus the results would have to be renormalized to be interpreted as probabilities. Values of $\mathbf{b}$ are decreased over time by temporal *relaxation* to enable return to recognized patterns again. By using the "where"–memory, the system generates a weighted list of discrete top–down target positions, which is transformed into a smooth excitation distribution s_o for the interest map. The most urgent target also defines the selective saliency computation.

Interest Map

Input to the interest map are the three 2-dimensional excitation distributions supplied by the "preattentive" (saliency) and "cognitive" (scene recognition) target demands. The goal is to define the simplest possible model with the following properties:

- A cooperation/competition mechanism between the different possible gaze targets must be installed selecting the location with maximal accumulated evidence.

- "Inhibition of return" must be incorporated, i.e. it must be assured, that the scan-path for a given scene does not simply oscillate between the two most salient positions.

- While it is questionable if the human saccadic system with its angle of view of nearly 180 degree uses any buffering, most of the current technical systems are limited to about 1/4 of that. With our hardware being limited to less than 30 degrees for the image diagonal, we definitely need some kind of "saliency memory" to be able to scan the environment.

- If one takes the accumulating error of saccadic shifts relative to a fixed (head centered) coordinate system into account, some kind of positional forgetting will inhibit false fixations.

The interest map is defined as a system of two linear differential equations:

- A *target map* $\psi(\mathbf{x}, t)$ sums the inputs[3] and defines a "leaky memory" function by a relaxation term. Diffusion compensates for the accumulating position error over time and models "positional forgetting".

- An *inhibition map* $\rho(\mathbf{x}, t)$ memorizes the locations already gazed at. Again relaxation and diffusion allow for effects of memory limitations.

$$\frac{d\psi(\mathbf{x}, t)}{dt} = -\tau_\psi \psi(\mathbf{x}, t) + D_\psi \Delta \psi(\mathbf{x}, t) + s_p(\mathbf{x}, t) + s_e(\mathbf{x}, t) + s_o(\mathbf{x}, t) \quad (15)$$

$$\frac{d\rho(\mathbf{x}, t)}{dt} = -\tau_\rho \rho(\mathbf{x}, t) + D_\rho \Delta \rho(\mathbf{x}, t) + I_f(\mathbf{x}, t) \quad (16)$$

$\psi(\mathbf{x}, t), \rho(\mathbf{x}, t)$	target map, inhibition map
$s_p(\mathbf{x}, t), s_e(\mathbf{x}, t)$	input from saliency module
$s_o(\mathbf{x}, t)$	input from scene recognition
$I_f(\mathbf{x}, t)$	input from camera control (actual fixation)

---

[3]Note that $\mathbf{x}$ denotes a coordinate on a spherical surface. To model the human saccadic system, Listing coordinates would be most appropriate.

Note that $s_p(\mathbf{x}, t)$ and $s_e(\mathbf{x}, t)$ are unequal zero only in the relatively small area of the image, while the maps and eventually $I_f(\mathbf{x}, t)$ are defined for the whole scene i.e. the area the sensors can be shifted to.

The next fixation position is determined by the position of maximum activity in the difference of the maps: $\mathbf{x}_{t_n} = \max_{\mathbf{x}} \left(\psi(\mathbf{x}, t_n) - \rho(\mathbf{x}, t_n) \right)$.

Given a completely static scene and therefore constant input to the maps, the system will generate a cyclic scanpath dependent on the excitation distribution of the input: Relatively high preattentive input over the whole scene will generate longer periodic sequences. The relaxation parameters τ_ψ and τ_ρ determine the "buffer function" for targets resp./ the tendency to avoid already fixated positions. The ratios of D_ψ and D_ρ relative to the fixation time adjust the interaction radius of different inputs resp. the minimal target distance.

Some Results In a first run the system was started "dumb" in the hall of our institute and explored the environment with ca. 50 saccades. This scene information (foveal patterns and saccadic shifts) were learned into memory. A typical intermediate state of the interest map during this exploration is shown in Fig. 4.

In the main run, we put MARVIN with this learned representation into the hall again but changed one part of the scene rather drastically (objects were shifted etc.). The starting behavior was of course exploration again, but after finding some already known foveal views a hypothesis was formed, and the scene was classified as the one seen before. However, after continuing with this hypothesis, saccades to the changed parts of the scene correctly falsified the hypothesis again. The time course of recognition in the main run shows all principal shifts of behavior: sole exploration, scene hypothesis verification and falsification.

Conclusion

The results on our robot vehicle MARVIN have shown that it is possible to implement a saccadic recognition system that runs fast (approximately 1 second cycle time) and efficiently. Furthermore the system described is the only implemented system that integrates saliency controlled saccadic exploration with saccadic recognition to yield a flexible behavior that is useful under different environment conditions. In fact the fixation control achieved has been combined with other behavioral modules for vergence control, depth reconstruction and tracking of moving objects [23]. Further investigations of saccadic control and recognition have to show how providing this basic behavior can be utilized for diverse applications in autonomous systems.

One fundamental problem still to be addressed is to find a useful adaptive learning process for saccadic recognition. This leads to the question which objects in the environment are worth recognizing and which properties can be used to segment those from the surroundings.

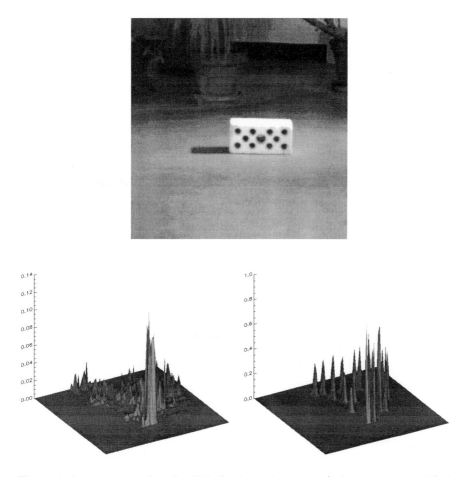

Figure 4: Interest map after the 20th fixation: shown are a) the input image, b) the neural maps for target selection and c) the inhibition of return map. The time course of fixations can be easily seen from the inhibition map (starting in the middle, then going from top to bottom in a curve). In the target map the high contrast brick generates high priority saccade targets.

References

[1] D. H. Ballard. Eye movements and spatial cognition. Technical Report TR218, Computer Science Department, University of Rochester, 1987.

[2] E. Barth. unpublished talk given at the Symposion Präattentive und attentive Prozesse bei der visuellen Wahrnehmung, Göttingen, 1994.

[3] T.-J. Fan, G. Medioni, and R. Nevatia. Segmented descriptions of 3-d surfaces. *IEEE Journal of Robotics and Automation*, 3:527 – 538, 1987.

[4] G. Giefing and H. Janßen. Saccadic object recognition with an active vision system. In *Proceedings of the 10th European Conference on Artificial Intelligence (ECAI 92)*, pages 803 – 805. ECAI, Wiley and Sons, 1992.

[5] H. Gutfreund and M. Mezard. Processing of temporal sequences in neural networks. *Physical Review Letters*, 61:235 – 238, 1988.

[6] R. M. Haralick and L. G. Shapiro. *Computer and Robot Vision, Vol. 2*. Addison–Wesley, 1993.

[7] J. J. Hopfield. Neural networks and physical systems with emergent collective computational abilities. *Proc. Nat. Acad. Sci. USA*, 79:2554 – 2558, 1982.

[8] J. J. Hopfield. Neurons with graded responses have collective computational properties like those of two–state neurons. *Proc. Nat. Acad. Sci. USA*, 81:3088 – 3092, 1984.

[9] H. Janßen, G. Giefing, and H. A. Mallot. A saccadic camera movement system for object recognition. In *Artificial Neural Networks*, pages I–63 – 68. Elsevier North–Holland, 1991.

[10] B. Julesz and J. R. Bergen. Textons, the fundamental elements in preattentive vision and the perception of textures. *Bell System Technical Journal*, 62:1619 – 1644, 1983.

[11] M. Kreutz, B. Völpel, and H. Janßen. Scale–invariant image recognition based on higher–order autocorrelation features. Internal Report 94-07, 1994.

[12] O. Neumann. Theorien der Aufmerksamkeit. *Psychologische Rundschau*, 43:83 – 101, 1992.

[13] D. Noton. A theory of visual pattern perception. *IEEE Transactions on Systems Science and Cybernetics*, SSC-6:349 – 357, 1970.

[14] D. Noton and L. Stark. Scanpaths in saccadic eyemovements while viewing and recognizing patterns. *Vision Research*, 11:929 – 942, 1971.

[15] R. D. Rimey and C. M. Brown. Selective attention as sequential behavior: Modeling eye movements with an augmented hidden markov model. Technical Report TR327, Computer Science Department, University of Rochester, 1990.

[16] R. D. Rimey and C. M. Brown. Where to look next using a bayes net: Incorporating geometric relations. In *Proceedings of the ECCV*, 1992.

[17] T. Sanger. Optimal unsupervised learning in a single layer linear feedforward neural network. *Neural Networks*, 2:459–473, 1989.

[18] H. Sompolinsky and I. Kanter. Temporal association in asymmetric neural networks. *Physical Review Letters*, 57:2861 – 2864, 1986.

[19] L. Stark and S. Ellis. *Scanpaths Revisited: Cognitive Models Direct Active Looking*. Erlbaum Press, 1981.

[20] A. Treisman. Preattentive processing in vision. *Computer Graphics and Image Processing*, 31:156 – 177, 1985.

[21] L. Ungerleider and M. Mishkin. Two cortical visual systems. In *The Analysis of Visual Behavior*. D.J. Ingle et al. (ed.), The MIT Press, 1982.

[22] P. Vivani. Eye movements in visual search: cognitive, perceptual and motor control aspects. In E. Kowler, editor, *Eye movements and their role in visual and cognitive processes*. Elsevier Science Publishers BV, 1990.

[23] von Seelen et al. (ed.). Neural architecture for an autonomous mobile robot. to be published, 1995.

[24] A. Yarbus. *Eye Movements and Vision*. Plenum Press, New York, 1967.

Visual Attention and Cognition
W.H. Zangemeister, H.S. Stiehl and C. Freksa (Editors)

FROM ACTIVE PERCEPTION TO ACTIVE COOPERATION — FUNDAMENTAL PROCESSES OF INTELLIGENT BEHAVIOR

Ruzena Bajcsy*

General Robotics and Active Sensory Perception Laboratory
Department of Computer and Information Science
University of Pennsylvania
Philadelphia, PA 19104, USA

ABSTRACT

In the ten years since we put forward the idea of *active perception* (Bajcsy 1985, Bajcsy 1988) we have found that cooperative processes of various kinds and at various levels are often called for. In this paper we suggest that a proper understanding of cooperative processes will lead to a foundation for intelligent behavior and demonstrate the feasibility of this approach for some of the difficult and open problems in the understanding of intelligent behaviors.

Keywords: cooperation, hybrid systems, modeling agents, perception-action cycle, signal-to-symbol transformation.

1. INTRODUCTION

Approximately ten years ago we put forward the idea of *active perception* (Bajcsy 1985, Bajcsy 1988), which, contrary to the widely held views of the time, argued that the problem of perception was not necessarily one of signal processing but of control of data acquisition. There were three points to our argument:

1. The agent (human or artificial) not only sees and feels but looks and touches, i.e. perception is an active process of seeking information from the environment. This idea finds its origins in human psychology, especially as formulated by Gibson (1950).

2. If one accepts the first premise, then the next question is this: What are the strategies for selecting the *next* or the *best* view?

3. If one takes several views or other measurements, then another question follows. Namely, how does one combine these different views or measurements? That is, how does one integrate or fuse this information into a coherent representation?

* I would like to thank my colleagues Profs. Vijay Kumar, Max Mintz, Richard Paul and Xiaoping Yun for their unlimited support and valuable discussions that led to the issues presented in this article. The students involved in the multi-agent project, Julie Adams, Jana Košecká, Robert Mandelbaum, Chau-Chang Wang and Yoshio Yamamoto, were also critical to the evolution of the ideas presented here. I also want to thank Dr. Yasuo Kuniyoshi and his colleagues at Electrotechnical Laboratory for giving me the peaceful and stimulating environment to pull together this paper. Finally, it is difficult for me to find the right words of thanks to Craig Reynolds, GRASP Lab Administrator, for everything he does. This research has been supported by the following grants: ARO grant DAAL03-89-C-0031, ARPA grant N00014-92-J-1647, and NSF grants STC SBR89-20230, CISE CDA88-22719, and IRI93-07126.

Once formulated, several others set to work on this new paradigm, such as Aloimonos (Aloimonos et al. 1987, Aloimonos 1993), Ballard (1991) on animate vision, and Blake (Blake and Yuille 1992) on dynamic shape.

During the period 1985 through 1988, as we proceeded to follow through with this research program, we found that cooperative processes of various kinds and at various levels were called for. For example, in Krotkov's work (1989) we found that cooperative processes are needed to integrate the two different behaviors of focus and control of vergence for the recovery of robust three dimensional information. Later we employed the same cooperative philosophy to integration of multimodal sensory information, such as vision and touch (Stansfield 1986, Allen 1987). Since then, we have embarked on studies of cooperation between different manipulators and different agents (Bajcsy et al. 1992, Adams et al. 1995). We have found that cooperation is a fundamental process in organisms both artificial and biological. In this paper, we wish to elaborate on this problem and suggest that a proper understanding of cooperation will lead to a foundation for intelligent behavior.

2. A DEFINITION OF COOPERATION

Cooperation is the process of taking different observations and *a priori* information from the *shared world* (our world includes the agents) and combining it in such a way that the process achieves a *common task*.

Note that there are two critical assumptions in our definition of a cooperative behavior:

1. The shared world and/or knowledge do not have to be identical, but there must be sufficient overlap such that the participating agents have a common understanding/interpretation of the input information and the task.

2. Agents agree on what the common task is, even if the means to accomplish it differ from agent to agent.

Another obvious implication of the cooperative process is that individual agents are distributed in space and/or in time. In this regard, there has been a great deal of work done in the area of Distributed Artificial Intelligence, as witnessed by several workshops and books. Examples include (Gasser and Huhns 1989, Brauer and Hernandez 1991, IJCAI 1991, von Martial 1992).

What, then, are the problems associated with cooperative processes? There are several:

1. Design of individual agents, including such questions as: (a) Should agents be homogeneous or heterogeneous? (b) What degree of autonomy should each agent have? (c) What communication abilities should each agent have? (d) What architecture should be selected for each agent?

2. Control of the cooperative process, including such questions as: (a) Should control be centralized or decentralized? (b) How should tasks be distributed? (c) What should be the means of communication?

3. Modeling agents and their cooperative behaviors.

4. Design of a task specification language and its compiler.

The study of cooperative processes is not new. Operation researchers interested in modeling organization have attempted to do so for the last 25 years, but due to computational limitations they were only able to consider a small number of players, as is the case with the prisoner's dilemma and its like. Recent computer technologies, however, have rekindled the scientific community's interest in this area. It is an interest motivated by two different forces: on the one hand, multidistributed computer networks, and on the other hand, the possibilities of distributed robotics systems in various applications. These two motivations impose different requirements when formulating the problem of cooperative processes. The former leads to software agents, whereas the latter leads to physical agents that interact with a dynamic world often unpredictable in its changes.

As mentioned in the introduction, cooperation takes place on many levels, namely: cooperative sensing, cooperative processing, cooperative manipulation, cooperative behaviors, and cooperative agents. We shall discuss each of these cases below.

3. COOPERATION ON DIFFERENT LEVELS

3.1. Cooperative sensing

Cooperative sensing occurs when one has distributed sensing, meaning either sensors of a single type that are distributed in space, (e.g. several cameras spatially distributed around a scene or object), or several different types of sensors that make observations from the same vantage point or again are spatially distributed (e.g. a camera, laser, ultrasound, and infrared scans taken from the same or different positions in space). The literature is full of such examples: Draper et al. (1989) describe a system for image interpretation by a distributed cooperative process; in the GRASP Laboratory, Mandelbaum (Mandelbaum and Mintz 1994, Mandelbaum 1995) employs ultrasound, a light striper and stereo for map recovery of the laboratory space, and Bogoni (Bogoni and Bajcsy 1994, Bogoni 1995) makes sequential observations of visual tracking, position encoding and force measurements, and integrates them into one coherent framework in order to asses whether a tool is penetrating an object. The operative principle of all these efforts is that in order for cooperative sensing to work the following must hold:

- In the case of homogeneous sensors, there must be a common shared framework and/or coordinate system.

- In the case of heterogeneous sensors, measurements must be converted into a common representation.

- Different observations must overlap so that continuity is preserved.

3.2. Cooperative processing

The whole field of cooperative processing was initiated by the distributed operating systems community, which confronts the problem of coordinating multiprocessing tasks and the issues of deadlocks, conflicts (i.e. when the same process is concurrently assigned two different jobs), scheduling, synchrony versus asynchrony, and so on. A good text on this subject is (Peterson and Silberschatz 1985). We shall not discuss these related works, but only mention that some of their formal tools and approaches such as petri nets, temporal logic and constraint nets are in fact useful in our domain as well.

3.3. Cooperative manipulation

The need for cooperative manipulation comes from the desire to improve the performance of robotic systems in areas such as dexterity, payload capacity, grasping, and so on. In principle, there are two types of cooperation, one when manipulators cooperate without the interaction of forces, i.e. manipulators do not hold the same object at the same time, and the other when they cooperate with interaction of forces, i.e. manipulators hold the same object. In the first case, the task of planning is the most important technical issue, while in the second case control of the two robot system is most critical. Historically, Tarn, Bejczy and Yun first dealt with this latter problem in the mid-80's (Bejczy et al. 1986, Tarn et al. 1987a, b). Later several other researchers designed different dynamical controllers to control a nonlinear redundant chain of mechanisms, such as (Dauchez and Uchiyama 1987, Arai and Osumi 1991, Hashimoto 1993, Yamamoto 1994). Cooperation here takes place through physical coupling of the manipulated object, when the manipulators communicate through state variables, i.e. position and forces.

3.4. Cooperative behaviors

In his seminal paper Brooks (1986) challenged the prevailing wisdom regarding architectures for building intelligent agents. The old paradigm considered separate functional units where the information flow was strictly horizontal (the output of one functional unit was the input to another) and the external feedback loop was closed through the environment (Moravec 1983, Nilsson 1984). The functional units included sensing, mapping the sensor readings into the world representation, planning, task execution and motor control (see Figure 1a).

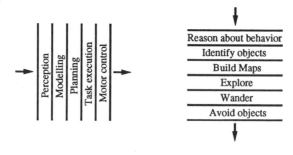

Figure 1. Architectures for robotics control: (a) horizontal (b) vertical.

Even though this kind of horizontal decomposition provides a nice modular partitioning of the problem, it fails to produce robust working systems. An alternative bottom-up approach was motivated by the process of natural evolution. Several researchers observed that a seemingly intelligent behavior can emerge from many simple ones and the interactions between them (Braitenberg 1984, Arbib and House 1987, Arkin 1987, Reynolds 1987, Brooks 1991, Levy 1993). The key idea of Brooks' approach (1986) was to make the loop between perception and action through the world much tighter by developing perception-action processes with different levels of competence ranging from simple to complex. Decomposition of the design of autonomous agents is done in a vertical fashion (see Figure 1b) where the component behaviors are activated in parallel, issuing appropriate commands to the agents' actuators. The main characteristics of this approach are the simplicity, modularity and independence of elementary behaviors.

It is this independence, however, that is not always guaranteed when dealing with cooperative behaviors. For example, consider two simple behaviors: one of avoiding obstacles, the other of tracking a target. In both cases, different perceptual stimuli control the same actuators, i.e. the steering wheel. The problem arises when the two stimuli direct the motion in opposite directions! The cooperative process turns here into a prioritization process in which one behavior must give priority to the other in order to avoid conflict. Hence, the cooperative process must turn into an arbiter or supervisor that properly schedules the sequence of behavior execution (i.e. enables and disables the right behavior at the right time). There are many instances of this kind of conflict whenever two or more perceptual events direct the same actuator or actuators in conflicting directions, such as reaching for an object while keeping the body balanced.

3.5. Cooperative agents

Here we shall consider autonomous agents that are not physically coupled, for the simple reason that if agents are physically coupled then it is a case of cooperative manipulation as discussed in Section 3.3. There are several issues one must address: communication, autonomy, and cooperative task specification. We shall discuss them in turn.

3.5.1. Communication

In biological systems, it is well known that animals can communicate many different ways. We shall not, however, review biological systems, but rather take an engineering point of view in the hope that it will give insight into one plausible solution to this problem. For communication to occur there must be a sender and a receiver. In principle we can distinguish between an active and passive sender/source. In the case of an active source, the agent sends messages with given meanings (e.g. alarm, hunger, sexual desire, etc.); this act is under its control. In the case of a passive source, the agent does not send any messages except indirectly, i.e. by existing in an environment in which other agents can detect its existence. The communication channels cover the whole spectrum of sensory capabilities, from smell, touch, temperature, sonar/audio to vision. The open problems in the communication of distributed networking systems are throughput, bandwidth, delays, packet losses, and congestion. The common term encompassing all these parameters is *quality of service*. The question is, for a given application, how to guarantee the quality of service such that it will minimize communication in the distributed robotic system and thereby enable the system to perform the given task. The new challenge in robotic applications is guaranteeing quality of service in order to meet the stringent requirements for delivery of sensory feedback and force feedback in particular (Nahrstedt and Smith 1995). These issues are discussed in many variations in (Asama et al. 1994).

3.5.2. Autonomy

In our definition, autonomy is directly proportional to the number and variety of elementary behaviors available to an agent. Remember that an elementary behavior is defined as the connection between perception and action. It is instructional to consider the extreme cases. One extreme is when an agent has no autonomy whatsoever; it receives all inputs as commands from another agent. In this case, the agent's communication is only one sided, i.e. the agent only receives messages and has no control over them. The other extreme is when an agent is completely autonomous; it has complete control over its input and output messages and hence acts independently. This agent, with such a degree of autonomy, typically does not cooperate with other agents except by accident. Unlike either extreme case, the cooperative agent will give up some of its autonomy for the good of the group!

3.5.3. Cooperative task specification language

The problem at hand is how to encode and/or communicate to the agents the cooperative task. Again, it is instructive to consider extreme cases. One extreme is when cooperation is defined or specified through a common goal. This is the situation, for example, when agents are told meet at a common location. Here, each agent is autonomous regarding how it carries out the task, as long as it reaches the *goal* state. The other extreme is when agents are coupled very tightly and must share every step along the way. The language that describes these cooperative tasks must be expressive enough to encode the degrees of coupling. We have so far observed that most systems do not possess this expressiveness in the task description language, rather the degree of coupling is encoded in the supervisor or coordinating architecture. This is a challenge for the future.

4. MODELING AGENTS AND THEIR BEHAVIORS

In the previous section we discussed cooperative processes as they occur at different levels. We also defined what we mean by behavior and considered what problems may arise when one has two simultaneous behaviors, even though cooperating, with conflicting actions. In order to make some predictions, we need a theory of behaviors. What, then, is the problem? The connection of perception to action in its simplest form is the classical control theoretic loop. The typical example is the standard automatic control of temperature or pressure, that is of a single parameter (scalar or vector) control. The mathematical model is a linear differential first order, or sometimes second order, equation. In the context of robotics, the typical scenario is motion control, the mechanism being either a manipulator or a vehicle.

The motion equations are derived from Lagrangian mechanics, which formulates the problem as follows: the Lagrangian $L = K - P$, where K is the kinetic energy and P is the potential energy of the system. The kinetic and potential energy of the system may be expressed in *any* convenient coordinate system, not necessarily in Cartesian coordinates. We call this system *generalized coordinates*, denoted by q_i. In his classic text, Paul (1981) gives a detailed derivation of the motion equations for a robotic manipulator. The dynamics equations relate forces and torques to position, velocities and acceleration. These equations represent six coupled non-linear differential equations which are impossible to solve except in the most trivial cases. We are interested in *effective inertias* at each joint and the inertial couplings between them and the acceleration at a joint, the relationship between torque and acceleration at a joint, and the relationship between torque at a joint and accelerations at other joints. If the coupling inertias are small with regard to the effective joint inertias then we can treat the manipulator as a series of independent mechanical systems. This is the goal!

The goal, then, of the designer and/or modeler of an agent is to decouple individual mechanism/actuators and their corresponding sensors in such a way that they can be described, preferably by linear transformation or simple computable functions. As Paul (1981) points out, a multilink manipulator can be considered as a series of weakly coupled independent servo mechanisms. The coupling effects are reduced by the actuator inertia and by ensuring that the outer joints have greater servo bandwidth than the inner joints. The servo bandwidth is determined by friction and gravity load effects. In order to compensate for gravity loading and to calculate the effective inertia of the joints, the mass and moments of any load must be known. This, of course, is possible by a wrist force sensor that measures all six forces and torques. Thus, given the number of links, one can model and control the dynamics motion of such manipulators, including rigid load, in one continuous fashion.

However, the moment the manipulator is connected to another nonrigid object, such as another manipulator, the whole model *changes* and subsequently the control changes! Hence, we come to the problem of how to structure the agent-environment, where the environment includes different agents, so that one can systematically synthesize a model and controller of the dynamic motions of agents. This is the classical dilemma of the division between *continuous* models versus *discrete* models. In Artificial Intelligence terminology, this is the problem of *signal-to-symbol* transformation and vice versa.

Why do we need discrete, symbolic representations? Symbols are not only a simplified shorthand of the signal for communication purposes, but they are also economic for representation purposes. They are necessary as part of a language that describes the task and in general enables communication amongst agents and humans. The open question still remains, however, of determining at which level of the signal one should attach the labels/symbols.

Traditionally, AI researchers have described the agent by an agent function from percept sequences to actions (Agre and Chapman 1987, Geneserth and Nilsson 1987, Brooks 1986). This is coupled with Rosenschein and Kaelbling's theory of situated automata (1986) and the indexical-functional aspects of the reactive planner *Pengi* proposed by Agre and Chapman (1987). All these approaches partition perception-action (behaviors) with respect to situations that are recognized based on perceptual observations. Indexicalization is a winner in terms of space only if the number of situation referents and object referents (indexical-functional aspects) is much smaller than the total number of situations and objects described in the theory T in the situation calculus (Subramanian and Woodfill 1989). In fact, this is at the heart of our question. In the past we modeled elementary behaviors, such as the behaviors GOTO (with some given heading and assuming a free path) and AVOID obstacles for a mobile base (Košecká and Bajcsy 1994). This approach, however, is too granular! We now have a *fundamental process* for a mobile base that includes three different control laws or strategies:

1. GoTo. This control strategy is implemented by a procedure that, given a goal and information about obstacles in the vicinity, generates the desired linear and turning velocity commands.

2. GoToHead. This basic strategy is a pure rotation in order for the mobile platform to reach a desired heading. This mode is needed since the GoTo strategy cannot guarantee the desired heading of the mobile base, due to the fact that final goal configuration is specified only in terms of position and the orientation of the mobile base must obey the nonholonomic constraints.

3. GoToMarch. This control law generates commands for the mobile base while marching in parallel formation with another base and keeping the distance between them constant.

The fundamental process is modeled in the language of Discrete Event Systems, where each of the strategies is a different state (in addition to the states Initialize and Wait/Ready).

The question before us now is this: should the fundamental process be one continuous dynamic model? That is, should behaviors be partitioned based on the dynamics of the system? It is the dynamics motion equations that change as the mechanisms' degrees of freedom change. We can envision a supervisor that recognizes the new couplings and automatically generates a new dynamics model of motion and its control. In this way, we have for the same structural mechanism (manipulator or vehicle or mobile mechanism) the same dynamic equations of motion provided that the degrees of freedom do not change. Even if the load changes, as long as it is rigid and one can measure the forces and torques the same equations hold for their control. One can make similar arguments for mobile agents. Yamamoto (1994) models the dynamics of a mobile agent/vehicle with three degrees of freedom and derives both holonomic and non-holonomic constraints. His dynamic equations reflect the masses of the vehicle and inertial forces. This model is adequate if the vehicle moves on a flat surface, i.e. one assumes there are no rolling or slipping forces between the vehicle and the road. On the other hand if the road surface is inclined, then the dynamical system again changes. (Intuitively, if one drives a vehicle then one shifts gears in this situation!) Similarly, the tractor trailer configuration imposes a new dynamical model (DeSantos 1994), as does a unicycle (Sheng and Yamafugi 1994).

Hence, we have established that for any change in the degrees of freedom of the agent/environment interaction, the dynamical model changes. This is reflected in the dynamical equation. Consider that the agent interacts with its environment through visual stimulus. Schöner (1991) studies the perception-action cycle under the following assumptions:

1. The state of the postural control system can be described by position x of the eye measured in a forward-backward direction.

2. Without vision (i.e. eyes closed), the posture control system generates a fixed point $x = 0$ (by the choice of the coordinate system); the dynamics of x without vision is the *intrinsic* dynamics and is assumed to be a second order linear system.

3. The visual information couples additively into the dynamics through the *expansion* rate $e(x, t)$ of the visual surround.

Expressed mathematically:

$$\ddot{x} + \alpha\dot{x} + \omega_0^2 - \sqrt{Q_x}\xi_t = -c_{env}e(x, t), \tag{1}$$

where the left hand side of the equation is the *intrinsic* dynamics, i.e. a linear damped harmonic oscillator. After Dijkstra (1994), the expansion rate can be modeled as:

$$e(x,t) = \frac{\dot{x} - \dot{D}(t)}{x - D(t)},$$

where $D(t)$ is the movement of the visual surround as it projects on the optic array of the subject. The expansion rate depends on the velocity of the subject as well as on the velocity of the surround. Now consider that this optic flow is also modeled by a harmonic oscillator:

$$D(t) = D_0 + D_r \sin(\omega_D t).$$

We can then rewrite the previous equation as:

$$\ddot{x} + \tilde{\alpha}\dot{x} + \omega_0^2 x - \sqrt{Q_x}\xi_t = c' \cos(\omega_D t),$$

which has an asymptotic solution:

$$x(t) = r_0 \sin(\omega_D t + \phi_0).$$

The dynamics of the perception-action cycle can be studied more generally by investigating the function:

$$x(t) = r(t) \sin(\omega_D t + \phi(t)).$$

The important component here is the relative *phase* between the posture sway and the visual motion. Transforming Equation 1 into polar coordinates and using an averaging method we obtain:

$$\dot{\phi} = \tilde{a} + \tilde{b}\sin(\phi(t) - \phi_0) + \sqrt{\tilde{Q}}\xi_t. \tag{2}$$

The important parameters are $\tilde{a}$ and $\tilde{b}$. If $abs(a) < abs(b)$ then these two oscillators are phase locked. Hence, we can speak of *absolute coordination*. If $abs(a) > abs(b)$ then there is no fixed phase relationship, and hence we can speak of *uncoordinated behavior*. Lastly, if $abs(a) \sim abs(b)$ then we have *relative coordination*.

In summary, the model of the agent should be based on its dynamics. We have the following equation:

$$M(q)\ddot{q} + D(q,\dot{q})\dot{q} + Uq + G(q) = -c_{env}e(q,t),$$

where the left side represents the agent's dynamics and contact with its environment and the right side represents the coupling of the agent with the environment via non-contact sensing. If either side of the equation changes, then the *model changes*; hence, we have a *new symbol* and/or *new state*.

Now we can offer a new definition of behavior: behavior is the *harmony/coordination*, or *lack* thereof, of an agent with its environment modulo the given *task*. If an agent and its environment filtered by the task can each be modeled as an *active* (non-linear) oscillator, then the interaction between the agent and its environment in carrying out the task can be measured by the *phase* relationship between these two oscillators. Abrupt changes in the parameters a and b detected by some "edge measure" imply a new *symbol*. Note that in this manner the symbols are *situated* and *embedded*. This new perspective on behavior has, of course, implications on how we can describe the task. We discuss them below.

5. TASK DESCRIPTION LANGUAGE

The idea of representing tasks and plans as networks of processes was originally proposed by Lyons (1989) in his *RS* (Robot Schema) model. The RS model is essentially a robot programming language with the basic unit schema representing a single locus of computation.

What should such a task specification contain? First, the task must specify the agent's capabilities (the left side of Equation 2). Second, the task must specify the environment (the right side of Equation 2). Third, the task must specify the interaction between the agent and its environment, which will imply the granularity or the sensitivity of the perception and action in carrying out the task. The task specification must also recognize the difference in spaces, i.e. the difference between the task or environment space and the agent's space.

6. CONCLUSION

We have put forward the premise that cooperation is a process fundamental to both biological and artificial intelligent systems. In Section 2 we defined the necessary conditions for a cooperative process, namely that agents must share a common task or goal, and agents must share some common knowledge and its representation. We also argued that cooperation takes place on several levels internal to the agent: sensation, manipulation (two-handed), locomotion, and behavior, e.g. when two or more behaviors must cooperate because they share the same resources within the agent. Finally, cooperation also takes place on a level external to the agent, specifically, when there are several agents cooperating in a society of agents.

Why is cooperation so fundamental? The chief reason is that the alternative is chaos or disorder. Disorder leads to inefficient use of resources/energy and ultimately degrades performance and impedes achievement of goals.

In our study of appropriate models of agents and their behaviors (see Section 4), we have concluded that the proper models must include *dynamic* interaction of the agent and its environment, which in turn allows the agent to *actively control* its behaviors and thereby achieve its performance goals. We have shown inductively that the models and their respective control modes are discrete with respect to the degrees of freedom of the system. Furthermore, we have shown that as the system is coupled with its environment it must be in *harmony* with and *cooperate* with its environment in order to perform its task efficiently. Hence, we can extend our definition of cooperation from agent-to-agent cooperative behavior to agent-environment cooperative behavior. This perspective unifies the process of interaction of agents with their environment in the same *cooperative framework*. This insight into models of dynamic interaction of agents and their environment also offers a *systematic* approach to understanding signal-to-symbol transformation anchored in physical principles because each control mode can be viewed as a different symbol. The open question that remains, however, is how to deal with the discretization of the environment that does not follow from dynamic agent interaction yet is useful for *task* description.

We believe that the basis for understanding intelligent agents lies in understanding the representations/models of these agents and their interaction with their environment during task execution. This interaction is dynamic and hence must be modeled as such. Different degrees of freedom of the system (agents and environment) imply different discrete models, i.e. symbols. Efficient performance demands that agents and their subsystems (sensors, actuators, and elementary behaviors) cooperate with the environment. Thus, the journey continues — from active perception to active cooperation.

REFERENCES

Adams, J., R. Bajcsy, J. Košecká, V. Kumar, R. Mandelbaum, M. Mintz, R. Paul, C. C. Wang, Y. Yamamoto and X. Yun, 1995, Cooperative Material Handling by Human and Robotic Agents: Module Development and System Synthesis, in: Proc. International Robotics and Systems Conference, Pittsburgh, PA, Aug. 1995.

Agre, P., and D. Chapman, 1987, Pengi: An implementation of a theory of activity, in: Proc. of the AAAI, (Lawrence Erlbaum, Hillsdale, NJ), 1987.

Allen, P.K., 1987, Robotic Object Recognition Using Vision and Touch (Kluwer).

Aloimonos, Y., 1993, Active Perception (Lawrence Erlbaum, Hillsdale, NJ).

Aloimonos, Y., I. Weiss and A. Bandyopadhyay, 1987, Active vision, in: Proc. DARPA Image Understanding Workshop, p. 552-573.

Arai, T., and H. Osumi, 1991, Heavy Work Handling by the Cooperative Control of a Crane and a Robot, in: Jrnl. Japan Society of Precision Engineering, **57**, 3, p. 467.

Arbib, M.A., and D.H. House, 1987, Depth and Detours: An Essay on Visually Guided Behavior, in: Vision, Brain and Cooperative Computation (MIT Press, Cambridge, MA).

Arkin, R.C., 1987, Motor schema based navigation for a mobile robot, in: Proc. IEEE International Conference on Robotics and Automation.

Asama, H., T. Fukuda, T. Arai and I. Endo, 1994, Cooperative Operation, in: Distributed Autonomous Robotic Systems (Springer-Verlag, Tokyo).

Bajcsy, R., 1985, Active perception vs. passive perception, in: Proc. 3rd Workshop on Computer Vision: Representation and Control, Bellair, MI, Oct. 1985, p. 55-59.

Bajcsy, R., 1988, Active perception, in: Proc. of the IEEE, **76**, 8, p. 996-1005.

Bajcsy, R., V. Kumar, M. Mintz, R. Paul and X. Yun, 1992, A small-team architecture for multiagent robotic systems, in: Workshop on Intelligent Robotic Systems, Design and Applications, SPIE Intelligent Robotics Symposium, Boston, MA, Nov. 1992.

Ballard, D.H., 1991, Animate vision, in: Artificial Intelligence, **48**, 1, p. 57-86.

Beeer, R.D., H.J. Chiel and L.S. Sterling, 1990, A biological perspective on autonomous agent design, in: Designing Autonomous Agents, ed. Pattie Maes (MIT Press, Cambridge, MA).

Bejczy, A.K., T.J. Tarn and X. Yun, 1986, Coordinated Control of Two Robot Arms, in: Proc. IEEE International Conference on Robotics and Automation, San Francisco, CA, Apr. 1986.

Blake, A., and A. Yuille, eds., 1992, Active Vision (MIT Press, Cambridge, MA).

Bogoni, L., 1995, Functionality Recovery through Observations and Interaction, Dissertation Proposal, GRASP Laboratory, Computer and Information Science Dept., Univ. of Pennsylvania, Philadelphia, PA.

Bogoni, L., and R. Bajcsy, 1994, Active Investigation of Functionality, in: Proc. Workshop on the Role of Functionality in Object Recognition, IEEE Computer Vision and Pattern Recognition Conference, Seattle, WA, June 1994.

Braitenberg, V., 1984, Vehicles, Experiments in Synthetic Psychology, (MIT Press, Cambridge, MA).

Brauer, W., and D. Hernandez, eds., 1991, Distributed AI and Cooperative Working, Proc. 4th International GI-Congress (Springer-Verlag).

Brooks, R.A., 1986, A robust layered control system for a mobile robot, in: IEEE Journal of Robotics and Automation, 2, 1, p. 14-23.

Brooks, R.A., 1991, Intelligence without reason, in: A.I. Memo, Apr. 1991.

Dauchez, P., and M. Uchiyama, 1987, Kinematic Formulation for Two Force Controlled Cooperative Robots, in: 3rd International Conference of Advanced Robotics, Versailles, France, Oct. 1987.

DeSantos, R.M., 1994, Path-Tracking for a Tractor-Trailer like Robot, in: International Journal of Robotics Research, 13, 6, Dec. 1994, p. 533-544.

Dijkstra, T., 1994, Visual Control of Posture and Visual Perception of Shape, Ph.D. dissertation, Katholieke Universiteit Nijmegen, College van Decannen, CIP-Gegevens Koninklijke Bibliotheek, Den Haag, Nederlands.

Draper, B.A., R.T. Collins, J. Brolio, A.R. Hansen and E.M. Riseman, 1989, The Schema System, in: International Journal of Computer Vision, 2, 3, Jan. 1989.

Gasser, L., and M.N. Huhns, eds., 1989, Distributed AI (Pitman/Morgan Kaufman).

Geneserth, M.R., and N.J. Nilsson, 1987, Logical Foundations of Artificial Intelligence (Morgan Kaufman).

Gibson, J.J., 1950, The Perception of the Visual World (Houghton Mifflin, Boston, MA).

Guckenheimer, J., and P. Holmes, 1982, Nonlinear Oscillations, Dynamical Systems and Bifurcations of Vector Fields (Springer-Verlag, New York).

Hashimoto, K., ed., 1993, Visual Servoing: Real Time Control of Robot Manipulators Based on Visual Sensory Feedback, World Scientific Series in Robotics and Automated Systems, 7 (World Scientific Press, Singapore).

von Holst, E., 1937/1973, On the nature of order in the nervous system, in: The behavioral physiology of animals and man, R. Martin, trans., 1 (Methuen, London).

Hooman, J., 1992, Top-Down Design of Embedded Real Time Systems, in: IFAC AI in Real-Time Control, Delft, The Netherlands, p. 453-458.

Huhns, M., ed., 1990, Proc. 10th Workshop on Distributed AI, Technical Report ACT-AI-355-90, MCC, Austin, TX.

IJCAI (International Joint Conference on Artificial Intelligence), 1991, Workshop on Intelligent and Cooperative Information Systems, Sydney, Australia, Aug. 1991.

Jeannerod, M., 1994, The representing brain: Neural correlates of motor intention and imagery, in: Behavioral and Brain Sciences, 17, p. 187-245.

Khatib, O., 1995, Inertial Properties in Robotic Manipulation: An Object Level Framework, in: International Journal of Robotics Research, 14, 1, Feb. 1995, p. 19-36.

Košecká, J., and R. Bajcsy, 1994, Discrete Event Systems for Autonomous Mobile Agents, in: Journal of Robotics and Autonomous Systems, 12, p. 187-198.

Krotkov, E.P., 1989, Active Computer Vision by Cooperative Focus and Stereo (Springer-Verlag).

Levy, S., 1993, Artificial Life (Pantheon Books).

Lyons, D.M., 1989, A formal model of computation for sensory-based robotics, in: IEEE Transactions of Robotics and Automation, 5, 3, p. 280-293.

Mandelbaum, R., 1995, Sensor Processing for Mobile Robot Localization, Exploration and Navigation, Dissertation Proposal, GRASP Laboratory, Computer and Information Science Dept., Univ. of Pennsylvania, Philadelphia, PA.

Mandelbaum, R., and M. Mintz, 1994, Sonar signal processing using tangent clusters, in: Proc. OCEANS'94, Special session on automated unmanned vehicles, **2**, Brest, France, Sept. 1994, p. 544-549.

von Martial, F., 1992, Coordinating Plans of Autonomous Agents, Lecture Notes in AI (Springer-Verlag).

Moravec, H.P., 1983, The Stanford cart and the CMU rover, in: Proc. of the IEEE, **71**, p. 872-884.

Nahrstedt, K., and J.M. Smith, 1995, The QoS Broker, to appear in: IEEE Multimedia Magazine.

Nilsson, N.J., 1984, Shakey the robot, Technical Report 323, SRI AI Center.

Paul, R.P., 1981, Robot Manipulators – Mathematics, Programming and Control (MIT Press, Cambridge, MA).

Peterson, J.L., and A. Silberschatz, 1985, Operating systems (Addison Wesley).

Reynolds, C.W., 1987, Flocks, herds and schools: A distributed behavioral model, in: SIGGRAPH, 1987, p. 25-33.

Rosenschein, S.J., and L.P. Kaelbling, 1986, The synthesis of machines with provably epistemic properties, in: Proc. Conference on Theoretical Aspects of Reasoning about Knowledge, 1986.

Schöner, G., 1991, Dynamic theory of action-perception patters: the "moving room" paradigm, in: Biological Cybernetics, **64**, p. 455-462.

Sheng, Z., and K. Yamafugi, 1994, Stability and Motion Control of a Unicycle, in: Journal of Robotics and Mechanotrics, **6**, 2, p. 175-182.

Stansfield, S., 1986, Primitives, Features and Exploratory Features: Building a Robot Tactile Perception System, in: Proc. IEEE International Conference on Robotics and Automation, Apr. 1986.

Subramanian, D., and J. Woodfill, 1989, Making Situation Calculus Indexical, in: Proc. of Knowledge Representation, 1989.

Sun, J., T. Nagato and K. Kurosu, 1994, Cooperative Behavior of a Schedule-Based Distributed Autonomous Robotic System, in: Journal of Robotics and Mechanotrics, **6**, 2, p. 162-168.

Tarn, T.J., A.K. Bejczy and X. Yun, 1987a, Nonlinear Feedback Control of Multiple Robot Arms, in: JPL 1987 Telerobotics Workshop, Jet Propulsion Laboratory, Pasadena, CA.

Tarn, T.J., A.K. Bejczy and X. Yun, 1987b, Design of Dynamic Control of Two Cooperating Robot Arms: Closed Chain Formulation, in: CRA87, Raleigh, NC, Mar. 1987, p. 7-13.

Toro, M., and J. Aracil, 1988, Qualitative Analysis of System Dynamic Ecological Models, in: System Dynamic Review, **4**, p. 56-60.

Wilson, E.O., 1971, The Insect Societies (The Belknap Press of Harvard Univ. Press, Cambridge, MA).

Yamamoto, Y., 1994, Control and Coordination of Locomotion and Manipulation of a Wheeled Mobile Manipulator, Ph.D. thesis MS-CIS-94-39, GRASP Laboratory, Computer and Information Science Dept., Univ. of Pennsylvania, Philadelphia, PA.

CHAPTER 5

APPLICATION ASPECTS

Visual Attention and Cognition
W.H. Zangemeister, H.S. Stiehl and C. Freksa (Editors)

ORIENTATION AND VISUAL ATTENTION IN THE REAL WORLD: A SYNOPSIS

Andrew H. Clarke

Vestibular Research Lab
Department of Otolyryngology
Universitätsklinikun Benjamin Franklin
Freie Universität Berlin

Abstract

The study of human orientation in space has been evolving rapidly in recent years, both in terms of basic research into sensorimotor mechanisms and applications such as improving man-machine interfacing. An important precondition for the performance of such studies has been the development of adequate measurement techniques. The contributions to this chapter deal with recent research into the complexity of man-machine interfacing and the use of novel approaches to the measurement of situational behaviour in humans.

The study of human orientation in space has been evolving rapidly in recent years, both in terms of basic research into sensorimotor mechanisms and applications such as improving man-machine interfacing. An important precondition for the performance of such studies has been the development of adequate measurement techniques. The contributions to this chapter deal with recent research into the complexity of man-machine interfacing and the use of novel approaches to the measurement of situational behaviour in humans. The focus of attention in the first paper by Gauthier et al is directed at task performance in the telemanipulation environment, an area where operator proficiency is of increasing importance. They point to our lack of knowledge on the process of visuomotor adaptation associated with task learning in this situation. The object of their study is the classical telemanipulation task of controlling a robotic arm with the aid of a remote two-dimensional video display. Here the operator has to adapt to to spatiotemporal transformation between his own arm movements and the resulting motion of the robot arm. In order to examine the dynamics of the visuomotor co-ordination involved in this task, they employ the adaptive modification paradigm, perhaps best known from the studies involving sensorimotor adaptation while wearing reversing prisms or magnifying lenses in a real environment. This paradigm lends itself conveniently to the virtual environment of telerobotics, where either the optical relationships or motor control parameters can be altered systematically. The authors concentrate on the proficiency of motor control and its adaptation to changes in the sensitivity of the motion detectors for either horizontal or vertical translation of the operator's hand. Non-invasive measurement of hand movements was employed for data acquisition. The authors point out that although similar dynamics are observed in the telemanipulation situation and during real-world visuo-manual behaviour, it is important to recognise the differences in the internal processing of the two situations. This is argued on the basis of models involving neural plasticity in the internal CNS representations rather than peripheral recalibration. Besides the relevance to man-machine engineering, this research also contributes to our understanding of limb movement control.

In his review of eye movement measurement techniques Clarke points out the essential role of such technological advances in many fields of human research. The contribution covers the development, including some mention of earlier approaches and a more detailed description of the current technology. The increasing number of video-based techniques that have evolved in more recent years is dealt with more extensively. As an innovator in this field himself, Clarke maintains that the exploitation of optoelectronic and digital processing devices will increasingly dominate this field in coming years. The video-based measurement technique, designated as video-oculography (VOG) was developed by the author's research group for clinical and research studies of eye movements related to the vestibular and oculomotor systems. By way of digital image processing, this technique permits recording and measurement of the three - horizontal, vertical and torsional - components of eye movements and the concomitant movements of the head. The current development of similar video-based techniques in other laboratories indicates the importance of this approach. The continuous improvement in imaging and processing technology should enable such systems to fulfil the requirements of most areas of application. The author also describes the application of videooculography in research in acute situations such as the clinical bedside examination and under microgravity conditions during spaceflight.

The contribution by Fleischer & Becker is concerned with the higher-order mechanisms of visual attention and cognitive capacity during man-machine interaction. This is of critical importance in an increasing number of industrial applications where supervision intervention during complex, machine-controlled processes is largely supported by graphic dsplays. Good design of the graphic representation of the complex informational flow is often crucial to the safety and efficiency of such industrial plants. With reference to this problem, Fleischer & Becker describe their experimental study into the structure of scanpaths during multiple-task performance at a graphics workstation. Insight into the interaction of multiple-task, visual workload and cognitive capacity was thus obtained. They point out the importance of including the contextual structure of the controlled plant, in order to determine the underlying principles of the visual information processing, and of defining criteria for the ergonomic design of such visual display layouts. The test subject's were seated at a workstation, which displayed graphical information for four simultaneous subsystems. Given the task of controlling these processes, the test subjects developed strategies for scanning and processing the ongoing visual information.

Here again, the employment of an adequate eye-movement measurement technique is essential to the quality of the results. The authors describe a binocular video-based pupil tracker and an ultrasonic movement sensor system for head movement. These were employed to measure head-in-space and eye-in head, yielding a continuous measure of the test subject's gaze direction. The resulting scanpaths were further analysed to determine the distribution and structure of scanpaths. The authors hypothesise that the test subjects incorporated the display of graphical information into their own visual memory. This is argued on the observation of repetitive scanning of particularly informative areas of the display, which the authors interpret as a preference for re-scanning the information rather than utilising their own memory to hold information, which in an ongoing process may rapidly become obsolete.

Visual Attention and Cognition
W.H. Zangemeister, H.S. Stiehl and C. Freksa (Editors)

ADAPTIVE CONTROL OF TELEOPERATORS IN RESPONSE TO VISUO-MANUAL RELATIONSHIP ALTERATION

Gabriel M. Gauthier, Olivier Guédon, Rolandas Purtulis and Jean-Louis Vercher

Laboratoire de Contrôles Sensorimoteurs, Université de Provence, Marseille, France[*]

ABSTRACT

In telemanipulation tasks, such as steering a robot arm using remote video display, training is essential because it allows the operator to learn the spatial and temporal transformations between joystick and robot motions. This adaptive control is similar to the adaptive control that develops when an observer is fitted with an optical system which alters the relationship between the actual arm motion and the visually perceived arm motion. We have investigated the adaptive changes which occur in observers submitted to target tracking on a screen when the relationship between hand motion and target motion is suddenly changed. We recorded changes in the observers' visuo-manual tracking performance and collected the observers' verbal reports of cognitive sensing after the imposition of visuo-manual changes. The adaptive perturbation consisted of a sudden increase in the hand motion detector sensitivity by 2.5 in either or both the horizontal or vertical directions. The target trajectory was predictive (circles). The adaptive change time course was determined by testing the observers' performance in open-loop condition. Adaptation was observed in all observers through both progressive horizontal and vertical gain changes, during open-loop tracking, and a concomitant decrease of instantaneous tracking errors during the closed-loop condition. The time course of the adaptive changes were similar to the ones commonly observed in experiments involving optical alteration of the visuo-manual relationship (prisms or magnifying lenses). Our results could be used to design adaptive man-machine interfaces that would allow new operators to learn more quickly teleoperation tasks. They should also lead to further understanding of human arm movement control.

Keywords: Adaptive control -Visuomanual relationship adaptation - Visuo-manual tracking -Telemanipulation- Man/machine interface

---

[*] This work was supported by a grant from the Cogniscience/Cognisud CNRS program. R. Purtulis was a visiting scholar from Kaunas University in Siauliai, Lituania.

1. INTRODUCTION

Numerous actions of our everyday life concern handling, moving or transforming objects in our external environment. For these actions, we often use tools which require motor behavior adjustment to satisfy metrical and directional transformations between motor activity and resulting action as sensed through visual or other sensory channels. As an example, steering a robot arm through the video display of a remote robot and its working environment is becoming a fairly common task. The operator must learn the spatial and temporal transformations between the motion of his own arm and the resulting motion of the robot. Of interest is whether these learning processes develop automatically or are conditioned by attention and cognitive control. To understand how an operator learns such transformations and compensates for incidental alterations of visuo-motor relationships in Man-Machine interaction, it is worth considering the basic aspects of adaptive control in human visuo-motor systems.

1.1 Visuo-motor adaptation

When the normal visuo-manual relationship is modified as with a microscope, refraction corrective spectacles or telescopic lenses (or any optical system), sensorial, motor and cognitive performance of the hand motor system is at first degraded, then progressively recovers normal function through adaptation. Here, adaptation is defined as the process by which the performance of the operator returns progressively towards normal in spite of the persistence of the alteration (Welch 1974; Eskridge, 1988). The observations derived from experiments carried out on visuo-motor adaptation over the past several decades, which constitute a basis for the interpretation of telemanipulation experiment data, involve various optical alterations such as those resulting from prisms (Harris, 1963) or magnifying lenses (Gauthier et al., 1987). In these studies, the observers usually performed in tasks which required the localization of objects in visual space. Specially designed protocols identify the various levels of the visuo-motor system which are first affected by the alteration and subsequently undergo adaptive changes. In particular, the protocols attempt to separate the contribution of the visual information, which is used to program a pointing movement, from the information which can be used on-line to correct for error during the execution of the movement. For example, the adaptive control of the visuo-manual system in response to a visuo-manual relationship alteration by prisms is studied in tasks where the observer points at visual targets, with or without visual on-line control of the arm. The condition without vision of the limb is named visual open-loop as opposed to the closed-loop condition where the visual feedback loop operates and continuously corrects for the error between the intended and the actual motion. The performance of the visual localization function in these two conditions is compared in terms of hand movement accuracy. The adaptive changes may then be recorded through time and particularly after a period during which the observer is allowed to see his limb during the pointing movement. This condition allows the brain to be informed of the mismatch between intended and executed motion and to initiate progressive and appropriate changes in the ongoing and ensuing pointings.

1.2 Example of adaptation to prisms

A typical adaptation experiment features series of pointings at visual targets executed in visual open-loop or closed-loop conditions with or without the optical alteration in a sequence which permits adaptive change quantification. The adaptive control of the visuo-manual system can be studied using the experimental arrangement shown in Fig. 1. The observer, seated behind a table, is presented targets. The observer then indicates with his unseen hand the perceived position of the targets. Typically, the observer first executes a series of control trials where he indicates with his unseen hand the perceived position of targets. The average pointing error observed in this series is considered as systematic and characterizes the operator's ability to locate a target without visual control of the hand motion. Following this, the observer is fitted with an optical system selected to induce an alteration of the visuo-manual relationship and a series of target localization trials is immediately executed (still in visual open-loop condition). The error observed between the previous control trials and these trials is a measure of the alteration produced by the optical system. For example, if the observer is fitted with right deviating wedge prisms, he will indicate a perceived position of targets as being shifted to the right by an angle equal to the optical deviation of the prisms (Fig. 1A).

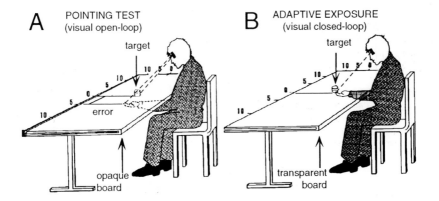

Figure 1. Experimental arrangement to study adaptation following visuo-manual relationship alteration with prisms. A: Adaptive changes are measured in pointing tests executed in the absence of visual control (open-loop condition). B: During the adaptive procedure the observer points towards the targets with full view of his arm (closed-loop condition). Adaptive changes are evaluated in terms of error between the actual and perceived target position indicated by the limb.

The pointing error will persist as long as the observer does not evaluate his pointing error by simultaneously seeing his limb and the target. Access to the error is provided during a given period, usually referred to as the "exposure period", during which the observer is pointing at objects under full visual control of both the hand and the targets (Fig. 1B). To determine the extent of the adaptive changes of the visuo-manual relationship, a series of open-loop pointings is run immediately after the end of the adaptive exposure while the observer is still viewing through the optical system. The adaptive changes are determined from the comparison of the pointing accuracy before and after the exposure period.

The adaptive changes observed as a result of a long period of visuo-manual relationship alteration may last way beyond the exposure period. Indeed, normal performance does not resume immediately upon return to normal viewing. The pointing error then observed in open-loop condition is opposite in direction to the error resulting immediately after the setting of the alteration. For instance, immediately after removing right wedge prisms, the observer will indicate the position of a target as being shifted to the left of the actual target position.

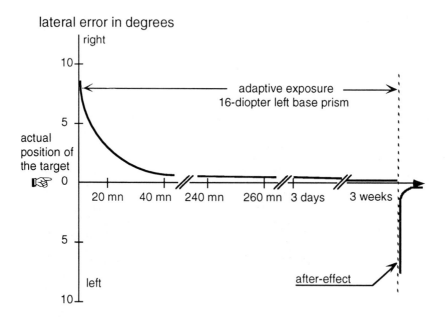

Figure 2. Time course of the adaptive changes observed during exposure to 16-diopter base-left wedge prisms. At the beginning of exposure, the pointing error is equal to the perceptual prism-induced shift. As the exposure proceeds (closed-loop), the error decreases. After about 40 minutes, pointing is fairly accurate. Immediately after removing the prisms, the pointing accuracy is poor as demonstrated by the large pointing error in the direction opposite to the one induced by the prisms, but the deadaptation time course is fairly short.

Figure 2 shows the time course of adaptive changes resulting from visuo-manual relationship alteration by 16-diopter base-out prisms. The curve represents the target pointing error measured in the condition where the observer was not allowed to see his hand. The data were collected every 5 minutes. Between tests, the observer was repeatedly pointing with full vision of his limb, at targets randomly positioned in front of him. After 40 minutes, the observer was almost fully adapted to the prismatic alteration, as indicated by the small error in the perceived target position. For a short period of time following the return to the normal viewing condition, the observer made large errors in locating the targets. The error was in the opposite direction of the initial error recorded while the observer viewed the targets through the prisms. This effect, known as the after-effect, is a further cue indicating that plastic changes developed in the visuo-manual system as the result of exposure to the wedge prisms. After-effects are short lasting as compared to the duration of development of adaptation.

Protocols involving the alteration of the visuo-oculo-manual relationship through optical systems such as prisms have been largely exploited to study the psychophysical and physiological aspects of the phenomenon and also determine the role of peripheral (muscular proprioception) and central information (efference copy of the motor command) in adaptive changes. Further knowledge regarding the central nervous system structures involved and the cellular processes handling adaptive control are currently gathered from experiments with animals (Lisberger and Sejnowski, 1992; Gauthier et al., 1995).

1.3 Visuo-motor adaptation in teleoperation

While a fairly large body of data is available regarding adaptive control in the visuo-manual system as a response to optical alterations, little is known about learning in the visuo-manual relationship of teleoperated tools and the operator reaction to alteration that affect this learnt relationship. When first exposed to a telemanipulation task, such as moving an index on a video display screen through mouse displacements, an observer must learn the metrical and directional relationship relating hand and cursor displacements. Daily observations show that the motor performance of the operator increases as learning progresses to finally reach an optimal level. If suddenly the visuo-manual relationship changes as a result of some mechanical alteration, i.e. the sensitivity to displacement along the horizontal direction is increased by 2 while the sensitivity along the vertical direction remains unchanged, the operator performance will first be strongly affected but with practice, the operator will modify (adaptively) his behavior and recover normal motor performance.

More complex adaptations typically arise in telemanipulation tasks involving mobile machines such as robots whose static (metrical) and dynamic (inertial) characteristics sensed by the observer will combine with those of the steering device. One may also predict that the rate, amplitude and nature of the adaptation observed during a period of exposure to the visuo-manual relationship alteration will depend on the nature of the target trajectories (random or predictive).

While studies have addressed the question of hand movement accuracy in 2-dimensional space (Bedford, 1994) and of cognitive sensing (Droulez and Cornilleau, 1986; Ross et al., 1970), no study has addressed the question of sensorimotor adaptation developing as a result of visuo-motor alteration in task involving hand tracking of visual targets evolving in 2- or 3-dimensional space. Still some data are available such as those by Bedford (1994) dealing with mouse control of a cursor on a computer screen. Although these data apply to pointing motions, they can also be used as a basis for the design of experiments involving tracking tasks.

The following section describes the adaptive changes which developed in observers submitted to sudden alteration of the relationship between their hand motion and the motion of a steered cursor on a screen. The observers were requested to closely follow the motion of a visual target with the cursor. The tracking performance was evaluated in terms of position and velocity errors, as well as in terms of tracking gain in vertical and horizontal directions. We studied the adaptive control which occurred in the observers as a result of sudden changes to the relationship between the arm motion and the cursor moving on the screen. In telemanipulation tasks where the robot working space is video-monitored, changes to the visuo-manual relationship can often occur as a result of a shift from one camera position to another. The ensuing effect may be a perspective or a magnification change of the image.

2. METHODS

2.1 Protocols

The observers performed adaptive protocols where the visuo-manual relationship between the steering device (the hand motion) and the remote system (a cursor on the screen) was suddenly changed. Figure 3 illustrates the experimental arrangement. Through hand motion, the observer actuated a cursor in order to track a target moving on the screen. We measured the static (metrical) and dynamic (delay and lag) properties of each observer's adaptive control by following the changes of their visuo-manual tracking performance. The experimental protocol involved series of closed-loop (the observer was visually aware of the tracking error) and open-loop (the observer tracked the target through appropriate motion of the arm without vision of the cursor) tracking trials. In the closed-loop condition, the observer was instructed to accurately follow the target with the cursor by moving his hand. In the open-loop condition, the observer imagined the cursor on the screen and follow the target with the imaginary cursor, using hand motion. The observer was never allowed to see his arm and hand so that forelimb motion sensing in the open-loop tracking condition had to be derived from forelimb kinesthetic information only. The hand motion occurred in the vertical plane and the observer's control performance was determined in a condition where the arm motion within the vertical plane induced a homomorphic motion of the cursor on the screen. The target moved through a 15x15 cm area on the screen and the corresponding cursor motion occurred as a result of hand motion through the same size area. The adaptive alteration was achieved by suddenly changing the metrical relationship between arm motion and resulting cursor motion. We typically increased the hand motion detector sensitivity by 2.5 in either the horizontal or vertical direction, or concomitantly in both directions. The target trajectory was predictable (circle) and we used either low tangential velocity (a full trajectory in 5 s) which allowed for tracking through on-line position and velocity corrections, or higher velocity (trajectory in 2 s) which allowed for trial to trial tracking performance adjustment but not for on-line corrections.

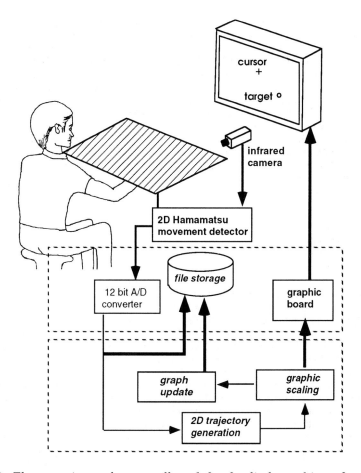

Figure 3. The experimental setup allowed for forelimb tracking of targets presented on a graphic screen. The observer was seated, facing the screen. The height of the stand was adjusted to be just above shoulder level which allowed free forelimb motion and prevented vision of the arm (and entire body). The screen was positioned vertically in front of the observer. The target was a green dot, while the tracking cursor was a white cross. The observer's hand steering motion (with the forelimb extended as in blackboard drawing) occurred in a vertical plane. The 2-dimensional hand motion was monitored with an infrared device whose sensitivity insured a one-to-one metrical relationship between hand motion and the resulting cursor motion. Adaptive changes in observer's visuo-manual tracking system were studied in response to alterations of the visuo-manual relationship (X2.5 changes to the hand-to-cursor sensitivity).

Vertical and horizontal components of both the target and the hand trajectories were stored on disk for off-line analysis. The observers' tracking performance was analysed in quantitative terms by computing the spatio-temporal error as the cumulated distance, over the recorded samples (100 samples per second), between target position and cursor position, expressed in mm. The overall global adaptation was described by a factor that we named the gain. The gain was calculated by comparing the size (horizontal and vertical extent) of the envelop containing the tracking response with the envelop containing the target trajectory. The observer's tracking gain changes were thus represented on a time scale as vertical and horizontal components. Further spatial and temporal aspects of the performance were derived from the tracking velocity and position errors in the vertical and horizontal directions.

2.2 Adaptation procedure

An adaptive session consisted of series of tracking trials (one trial = one trajectory) beginning with 20 closed-loop trials followed by a series of 10 trials in open-loop condition. Following these series, and without instructing the observer, the horizontal, vertical or both horizontal and vertical visuo-manual relationship was changed, and a series of 50 tracking trials was initiated (adaptive exposure). At the end of this adaptation series, 10 open-loop trials were completed to measure the effect of the training. Since the adaptive changes were observed to be fairly labile, and in order to follow the time course of recovery, the observers were submitted to 10 trials of closed-loop tracking in the altered condition to restore an adaptation level similar to the one attained at the end of the initial 50 adaptive trials. The process of deadaptation was recorded by running a series of 10 trials with a normal visuo-manual relationship. Throughout the session, the observer was verbally encouraged to minimize the tracking error and keep alert so as to respond with constancy both in reaction time and overall tracking performance.

The observers were submitted to three changes of the visuo-manual relationship in three different sessions, executed on different days, one by which the sensitivity of the hand position monitor was increased by 2.5 (one cm displacement of the hand along the horizontal direction resulted in a 2.5 cm displacement of the cursor on the screen, while the hand to screen motion relationship remained unchanged in the vertical direction), one affecting the vertical direction only by the same amount and a final one where both directions were affected. The adaptive changes were determined after the full exposure period. During the exposure period we followed the changes of the tracking performance of both the vertical and horizontal gain components and the tracking error. In other experiments, the time course of the adaptive changes was determined by testing the observer's tracking performance in open-loop condition at regular intervals during the adaptation period.

Tracking performance changes in the open-loop condition resulting from exposure to visuo-manual relationship alterations were compared to a control condition where the observer performed the same number of tracking trials executed during an adaptation session. This allowed us to verify the stability of the observer's performance over time in both open- and closed-loop conditions.

3. RESULTS

3.1 Adaptation to visuo-manual alteration with predictive, slowly moving trajectories

Cognitive aspects: In the control condition, all observers reported to feel a good sense of correspondence between their hand motion and the ensuing motion of the cursor on the screen, in terms of both parallax and amplitude. When the visuo-manual relationship was changed, all observers immediately sensed the change and reacted to it by modifying the amplitude of their arm motion in the appropriate direction. However, this change in hand trajectory was not a cognitively computed change but a reaction of the visuo-manual system to reduce the current tracking error. None of the observers were able determine the nature and amplitude of the alteration. The observers' reaction to compensate for the visuo-manual relationship alteration was somehow "automatic". In fact, in one control experiment where one observer was engaged in a cognitive task (counting backward by steps of 7 from a three-digit number) the observed adaptive response of the observer was the same as that recorded in the sessions where the task was limited to tracking. When questioned after the experiment, the observers reported that the alteration in either vertical or horizontal direction only was more distressful than the change applied simultaneously to both directions. In the latter condition, all observers realized that they managed the task by making a "smaller" hand motion. In contrast, when only one hand motion direction sensitivity was altered only a few observers reported that they had to perform an elliptic hand motion to compensate for the alteration. Following adaptation to simultaneous vertical and horizontal change, restoration of normal visuo-manual relationship was correctly reported by all observers. In contrast, restoration to normal following either vertical or horizontal alteration was almost systematically sensed as an illusory decrease in the sensitivity of the non-affected direction. Some observers reported a feeling of "heaviness" in their hand motion, instead of a decrease of sensitivity, in the direction where normal sensitivity was newly restored.

Sensorimotor aspects: All the observers progressively adapted to either horizontal, vertical or simultaneous alteration of the visuo-manual relationship as demonstrated by a decrease of instantaneous tracking errors while in closed-loop condition and directional gain changes during open-loop tracking trials. Figure 4 illustrates the hand tracking performance of an observer during an experimental session involving a sudden change of the visuo-manual relationship in the horizontal direction. The target trajectory was a circular path executed in 5 s. The trials selected along the various phases of the session summarize the results from all the tested observers. During the first set of normal visuo-manual trials executed in the open-loop tracking condition, the response of this observer was fairly accurate except for a minor shift of the entire trajectory to the right. During the first series of trials executed in the visual closed-loop condition, the hand tracking was also accurate (Fig. 4A), owing to on-line control of the error between target and cursor position. During the subsequent set of open-loop condition trials with a normal visuo-manual relationship, the response of the observer continued to be fairly accurate (Fig. 4B) except for a minor error affecting the final part of the path (the observer movement did not systematically end on the starting point).

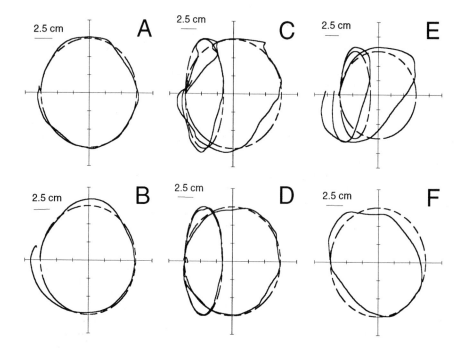

Figure 4. Selected tracking responses to illustrate adaptive changes. Superimposition of target and hand-steered cursor trajectories emphasizes the spatial tracking error. The target described a circular path in 5 s. Observer's cursor trajectory in the normal unaltered visuo-manual relationship, with full visual control of the cursor (A) and without visual control (B). The first trial following a sudden increase in the hand-to-target motion relationship by 2.5 in the horizontal direction, resulted in a large tracking error (C). The superimposed ellipse represents the requested hand motion and the slightly warped ellipse is the actual hand trajectory in space. After 50 adaptive trials under visual control of the tracking error, tracking accuracy was close to pre-exposure level (D). When the observer was obliged to track the target in the absence of visual control, his performance during the first trials (Fig. E) was close to the one observed at the end of the training period. In spite of visual control, the tracking accuracy was severely affected in the first trial after returning to normal hand-to-cursor sensitivity (F).

When the visuo-manual relationship alteration was introduced, a large error appeared in the horizontal direction. Because of the unpredicted change in the hand motion detector sensitivity, the direction of the initial hand motion was inappropriate. This error was corrected after some delay, but the hand motion was still not appropriate since large errors occurred at some intervals along the final part of the trajectory (Fig. 4C). As the adaptive period proceeded, the performance improved, marked by a progressive adjustment of the early hand motion direction and a decrease in the tracking error along the overall trajectory. At the end of the adaptive period during which the observer executed 50 trials under visual control, the tracking performance was close to that observed in the control trials executed in the closed-loop condition at the beginning of the experiment. Figure 4D shows the last trial of the adaptive exposure series. The observer adaptively modified the motion of his hand in the horizontal direction to compensate for the artificial sensitivity increase in the hand movement detector. The tracking trials executed immediately after the end of the adaptive period, in the open-loop condition, confirmed the above observation. Figure 4E illustrates the first trial following the end of the adaptive exposure. The hand trajectory was closely related to the target trajectory, in spite of the alteration still affecting the horizontal hand motion and the absence of visual control of the cursor motion.

As the visuo-manual relationship was suddenly returned to normal, the observer's tracking performance was severely affected in a predictive way (Fig. 4F). Indeed, the direction of the early vertical hand movement was exaggerated, before the visual feedback loop addressed an appropriate corrective command to the hand. However, deadaptation occurred more rapidly (in 3 to 5 trials), than the adaptation process which, on average took 20 to 30 trials to stabilize.

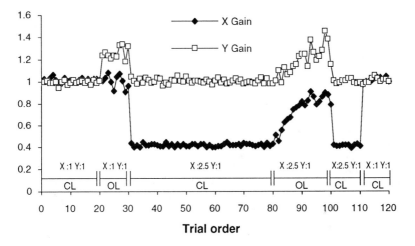

Figure 5. Time course of performance changes during the adaptive exposure. The tracking performance change is quantified in terms of horizontal and vertical gain changes resulting from a 2.5 increase in the hand-to-target sensitivity (one trial = one circular trajectory in 5 s). The horizontal or vertical gain is defined as the ratio between the horizontal or vertical size of the observer's "circular" trajectory and the diameter of the target circle. During the closed-loop adaptive exposure the horizontal gain decreased to match the alteration. When the normal condition was restored, the visuo-manual tracking performance recovered only after 2 to 3 trials demonstrating the robustness of the adaptive changes. CL and OL refer to open-loop and closed-loop tracking, respectively. The hand-to-cursor sensitivity for each series of trials is shown on the bottom of the graph.

Figure 5 shows the time course of vertical and horizontal gain changes in one observer during an experimental session involving alteration of the horizontal visuo-manual relationship. In the first closed-loop series of trials, the performance was very good as demonstrated by stable vertical and horizontal gains, close to unity. During the subsequent series of trials, in open-loop, vertical and horizontal gains were slightly different from each other but still close to unity. During the all adaptive exposure in open-loop the tracking gains were as expected close to 1 and 0.4 for the vertical and horizontal directions, respectively. After the adaptive exposure the horizontal gain was strongly reduced (approximately 0.5 for the first 2 trials) while the vertical component of gain remained close to 1. As this closed-loop sequence proceeded, the horizontal gain increased continuously towards about 0.8. In the meantime, the vertical gain returned slowly to its pre-exposure level. The corresponding tracking spatio-temporal error curve is shown in Fig. 6. The average error in the first series of closed-loop condition trials was around 2000 mm. In the course of the adaptive exposure, the tracking error which was first large (around 7000 mm), decreased slowly and stabilized to around 2500 mm after 5 to 6 trials. The error level was about the same during the second exposure period. The first trial following return to a normal visuo-manual relationship had a tracking error close to 6500 mm in spite of available visual control. Subsequently, the tracking error decreased rapidly towards pre-exposure level.

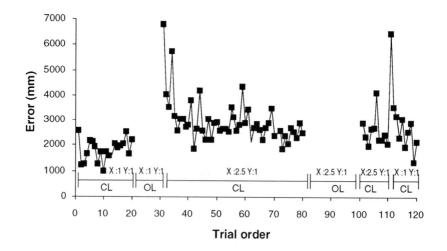

Figure 6. Time course of the spatio-temporal tracking error during the adaptive session illustrated in Fig. 5. The error is the cumulated sum of error vectors which join, at the same sampling time, target position and cursor position. During the adaptive periods the tracking error decreased rapidly to stabilize around a value close to the closed-loop error and normal hand-to-cursor sensitivity.

Figure 7 illustrates a typical time course of the adaptation which developed as a result of suddenly increasing the sensitivity of the visuo-manual relationship in the horizontal direction, similar to the experiment described above and illustrated by Figs. 4 A-F, 5 and 6. However, in this experiment, the adaptive exposure was interrupted every 5 trials by an open-loop condition trial in order to follow the progressive changes in vertical and horizontal gains. While before the adaptive exposure the gain of the hand tracking system was close to 1 in both the vertical and horizontal directions, after 5 to 10 trials in the closed-loop condition (filled symbols) with the alteration applied to the horizontal direction, the horizontal tracking gain decreased to about 0.5 (open symbols). Subsequently, this gain remained around 0.5 until the end of the exposure period. In the meantime, the vertical gain decreased slightly. This later change affecting the vertical gain was commonly observed in our experiment and has already been reported in the literature (Bedford, 1994). Further experiments addressing this effect should clarify the nature of cross directional changes which seem to have a paradoxical appearance. Following the exposure period, the normal visuo-manual relationship was restored and further closed-loop trials were executed. As noted earlier, the deadaptation process was more rapid than the adaptive process. Vertical and horizontal tracking gains returned to pre-adaptation level within 3 to 4 trials.

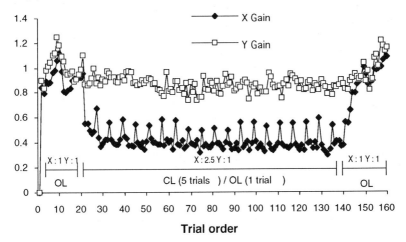

Figure 7. Typical time course of adaptive changes to vertical and horizontal gains caused by sudden increase of the visuo-manual relationship sensitivity in the horizontal direction. The adaptive exposure was interrupted every 5 trials by an open-loop trial in order to follow the progressive changes in vertical and horizontal gains. At the end of the adaptive exposure, the gain components matched the hand-to-cursor sensitivity.

Similar results were observed in experiments involving changes to the visuo-manual relationship in the vertical direction only and in both the vertical and horizontal direction, simultaneously. While experiments involving changes in the vertical or horizontal direction were basically similar the adaptive changes following simultaneous vertical and horizontal visuo-manual relationship alteration occurred much faster and yielded more accurate tracking trajectories. Likewise, the deadaptation process was faster than the one observed in the single alteration experiments reported above.

Another series of experiments was carried out to evaluate the ability to adapt to visuo-manual alteration when the current tracking error cannot be corrected on-line (as with 5-s circular trajectories) but where the sensorimotor adjustments of the motor command can improve the following trial. A trajectory executed in 2 s allowed us to investigate these aspects. Figures 8 through 10 show that the overall amount of adaptation reached after a 50 trial exposure period and the adaptation/deadaptation time course were basically the same in both 5-s and 2-s trajectory experiments. Still, gross analysis of the trajectories uncovers a main difference between the two in that, during the 2-s trajectories, the movement was made without periodical corrections. It follows that 2D-drawings of the hand trajectories have smoother shapes with the faster trajectories. In addition, the average initial error, resulting from the hand movement reaction time, was greater with the 2-s than the 5-s trajectory.

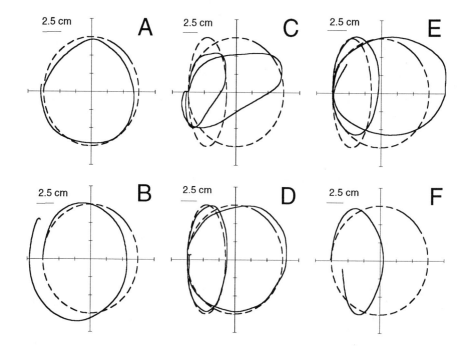

Figure 8. Selected tracking responses to illustrate adaptive changes resulting from a sudden X2.5 change in the horizontal hand-to-cursor sensitivity. The experiment applies to 2-s trajectories. The represented trials were recorded in the same order as the ones shown in Fig. 4. Compared to slow trajectory (5-s) response, the hand tracking trajectory was smooth, mainly due to the absence of on-line visually induced corrections.

Figure 8 A illustrates the tracking performance of an observer in the closed-loop condition before any alteration of the visuo-manual relationship. The vertical and horizontal hand tracking gains were fairly close to unity and the trajectory was smooth and circular. When visual control was not allowed, the response was still smooth and fairly circular but because on-line visual control of the cursor was absent, the response trajectory was sometimes shifted to the left (as in Fig. 8B) or to the right. When the alteration was applied to the horizontal direction (X2.5 increase of the hand-to-cursor sensitivity), the hand response in the initial 1 to 3 trials was markedly different from the one requested to have the cursor describe a circular trajectory. Figure 8C reproduces the first trial of the adaptive exposure period, and shows that the cursor trajectory was far beyond the requested circle. After approximately 20 trials, the hand motion trajectory changed to resemble the target trajectory. Figure 8D illustrates the high hand accuracy recorded during the last trial. The hand motion was then an ellipse with a ratio between vertical and horizontal axes equal to 2.5. The operator was fairly well adapted to the alteration as shown in Fig. 8E which applies to the first open-loop trial following the exposure. The hand movement trajectory was similar to that recorded near the end of the exposure period (Fig. 8D). As observed in the previous series of experiments with 5-s trajectories, the adaptive changes, although short lasting, did not vanish immediately after returning to the original visuo-manual relationship. Indeed, Fig. 8F which illustrates the first trial in the closed-loop condition with a one-to-one hand to cursor relationship, definitely shows the effects of the plastic changes to the visuo-manual relationship. The hand motion trajectory was an ellipse, identical to the ones executed in the altered condition (instead of a circle). About three to four trials later, the hand tracking performance had returned to normal.

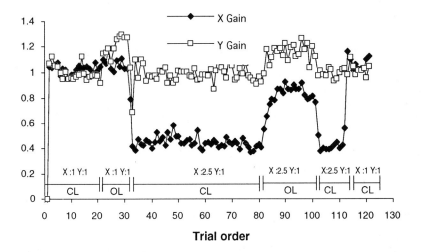

Figure 9. Time course of performance changes during adaptive exposure to a X2.5 increase in the horizontal hand-to-target sensitivity (one trial = one circular trajectory in 2 s). Conventions are the same as in Fig. 5.

Figures 9 and 10 illustrate the changes of the time course of vertical and horizontal gains and the spatio-temporal error during the full experimental session. These figures show the same basic features as the 5-s trajectories (Figs. 5 and 6). This observation raises an interpretation problem which will be examined later since the tracking control was different with the two trajectories.

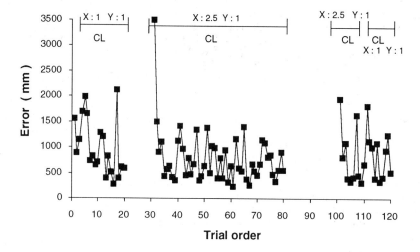

Figure 10. Time course of the spatio-temporal tracking error during the adaptive session illustrated in Fig. 9 (2-s trajectories). Observations and representation are the same as in Fig. 6.

A global analysis of our data shows that the degree of adaptation reached after visuo-manual relationship alteration, as well as the time course of the adaptation process, varied between observers. Nonetheless, all observers showed systematic adaptation which was close to complete by the end of a 50-trial exposure period. There was a cross direction effect so that an adaptive decrease of gain of the horizontal hand motion resulting from a sudden instrumental increase of sensitivity of the visuo-manual relationship in that direction, usually resulted in a concomitant decrease of gain in the vertical direction as well. This cross directional effect occurred equally in both directions. The observers' adaptive response was more rapid and more efficient after simultaneous vertical and horizontal alteration than to an uni-directional alteration.

4. DISCUSSION

4.1 Visual manual adaptation

Visuo-manual adaptation in telemanipulation and hand pointing at visual target through prisms or magnifying lenses (uni-dimensional space), share characteristic features. In particular, the profile, the amount of adaptation reached after similar adaptive periods, and to some extent the adaptation and deadaptation time course scales are similar. This observation does not allow an extrapolation of the large body of knowledge regarding adaptation processes resulting from visuo-manual relationship alteration in hand pointing to oculo-manual tracking. Indeed, when dealing with manual tracking, one must consider further aspects related to the shape and dynamics of the trajectory. For example, if the angular velocity is low, the visuo-manual feedback control efficiency may alone insure high tracking accuracy in spite of major alterations to the visuo-manual relationship, and the adaptive mechanism may not be activated or its intervention may be delayed. To the contrary, if the target moves rapidly along a predictable trajectory, the hand motor system will rely on predictive control. This control may react on-line if the trajectory is not too fast, or in a trial-to-trial manner. The two target trajectories we used were selected so that they both induced predictive control. A sudden alteration of the visuo-manual relationship resulted in large alteration of the tracking performance and the activation of adaptive processes. The time course and extent of adaptation appeared fairly similar with both the 5-s and 2-s trajectories. Still, the adaptation in the two conditions have different characteristics and probably involved different central nervous system structures. Indeed, comparative detailed analysis of the data derived from the target trajectories allow to further investigate the nature and characteristics of the adaptive response to visuo-manual relationship alteration. When related to a general model describing hand control in visuo-manual tracking of targets, such as the model represented Fig. 11, our data allow to identify the element(s) of the visuo-manual tracking system which develop plastic changes.

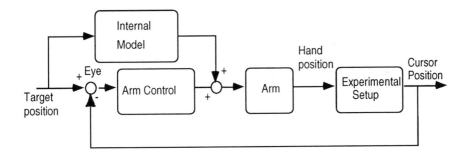

Figure 11. Model of the visuo-manual tracking system featuring a main feedforward path, a classical visual feedback loop and a secondary feedforward path containing an internal model of the target trajectory. The arm receives a command from the central nervous system and provides a hand position output. The observer's visual system elaborates position and velocity error signals processed by the controller to produce the arm command. The additional internal model branch works in conjunction with the visual feedback loop. For fast predictable targets the overall system is driven by the internal model in a feedforward manner (with respect to the visual input). A global error signal becomes available at the end of the trajectory through comparison of the target and the actual cursor trajectories.

Our model of the visuo-manual tracking system features, as in Bullock et al.'s model (1986), a main path that handles the spatial-to-motor and directional-to-rotation transformation which is needed to carry out a spatially defined trajectory. It also features, as in Hollerbach's model (1982), a classical feedback loop (here the main sensor is visual), and a secondary feedforward path containing an internal model of the target trajectory, as in Kawato et al.'s model (1988). The observer's visual system provides an error signal as the distance between the target position and the cursor position. A velocity error signal is also elaborated out of the difference between target and cursor trajectory velocities. The arm controller processes these signals to produce an arm command to reduce the tracking error. The internal model additional branch works in conjunction with the visual feedback loop if the target is slow. For fast predictable targets the overall system is driven by the internal model in a feedforward manner (with respect to the visual input), since the visual feedback does not operate on-line. The error signal is elaborated out of the difference between expected and current cursor motions. A global cognitive error signal becomes available at the end of the trajectory through the comparison of the target and the actual cursor trajectories.

When the normal visual manual relationship was altered as in our protocol, adaptation must have developed in the internal structure of the system since the performance was slowly restored. Indeed, after adaptive exposure the hand movement accuracy without visual feedback showed that, in response to an input identical to that presented to the non-altered system, a new command had been produced by the arm control system to yield appropriate output. It is as if the system had created an inverse static characteristic element exactly matching the imposed alteration. Where in the model do these plastic changes develop? Hollerbach's model (1982) does not contain a learning component as opposed to Kawato et al.'s model (1988) which features an "iterative learning memory of transformation" element (sensory association cortex, areas 2, 5 and 7). Our model (Fig. 11) does not explicitly situate the plastic changes in a particular element because we hypothesize that plastic changes may develop in different parts of the system depending upon the nature of the task (tracking, pointing, centering) and the trajectory (predictable, unpredictable, rapid, slow). The protocol arrangements and target trajectories used during our tests and exposure periods were designed to determine where, in the system, the plastic changes developed. Since the plastic changes were evaluated during open-loop tracking trials, thus preventing direct visual feedback, it follows that the plastic changes must have developed elsewhere in the system. One may assume that most of the adaptive changes do not occur in the peripheral apparatus (the arm), but rather in the controller and/or in the internal model of the trajectory. To determine whether the controller or the internal model handles the plastic changes, future experiments should selectively and differentially test the involvement of these two central structures. Such experiments would test the observers in a tracking task involving unpredictable trajectories after adaptive training with circular trajectories. Accurate tracking would. suggest that the adaptive changes occur in the controller. A control experiment would involve test trials with predictive trajectories different from those used during the adaptive training. Preliminary results from a study in progress, involving these protocols, suggest that the controller and the internal model share the adaptive changes.

4.2 Possible implications of these findings in telerobotics

Let us consider a situation where the working environment is viewed first from a particular point, hence providing a given visuo-manual relationship to the interface linking the operator to the manipulated machine. If the view point suddenly comes from another camera situated closer to the operated machine (for higher resolution) or from a side-shifted camera (to observe another feature) the apparent gain will change. The first case is equivalent to a horizontal and vertical gain increase while in the second case, the gain change will be equivalent to altering the horizontal gain while maintaining constant the vertical gain. Our experiments simulated the latter condition, in a simplified way, since we only considered single dot targets and predictive trajectories. Still, the tracking performance of the observers was poor for several trials before the adaptive control became efficient. Larger decreases in accuracy are expected in teleoperation where the operator controls, for example, a robot with several degrees of freedom. To compensate for this effect, the visuo-manual relationship could be automatically modified to maintain visuo-manual constancy, for example by changing joystick sensitivity with changes viewing camera distance. Welch et al. (1993) have shown that repeatedly adapting and readapting to two mutually conflicting sensory environments leads to a separate adaptation to each condition, as well as an enhancement of the capacity to adapt to other alterations. Further experiments should be designed to evaluate the benefit to the operator of automatically maintaining the visuo-manual constancy, compared to letting the operator learn new visuo-manual relationships.

Another practical implication of our study relates machine maintenance. In case of slow degradation of the visuo-manual relationship caused by progressive instrumental failure (mechanical wear, electronic alteration etc.), the operator will slowly compensate for the alteration through adaptive control. With an interface designed to compensate for its own degradation, severe problems may arise if the time constant of the operator and machine corrective actions are not appropriate and counteract each other. Further studies like the one described in the present paper should allow to choose, in one field of implications between, for example, an automatic adjustment of the visual monitoring point of view and the interface gain, and in another field of implications, between various maintenance devices. Such studies would also complement previous regarding visuo-manual control and help define the properties and features of the internal model which, in spite of the efforts, over the past few years (Bullock et al. 1993; 1986; Flash and Hogan 1985; Moray, 1986; Kawato et al. 1988), has not yet provided an unified representation.

REFERENCES

Bedford, F.L., 1994, Cahiers de Psychologie Cognitive/Current Psychology of Cognition, **13**, 405.

Bullock, D., S. Grossberg and F. H. Guenther, 1993, J. Cognitive Neuroscience, **5**, 408.

Droulez, J., and V. Cornilleau, 1986, Vision Res., **26**, 1783.

Eskridge, J.B., 1988, Am. J. Optometry & Physiological Optics, **65**, 371.

Flash, T., and N. Hogan, 1985, J. Neurosci., **5**, 1688.

Gauthier, G.M., C. de'Sperati, F. Tempia, E. Marchetti, and P. Strata, 1995, Exp. Brain Res., **103**, 393.

Gauthier, G.M., J-M. Hofferer, W. F. Hoyt, and L. Stark, 1979, Arch. Neurol., **36,** 155.

Gauthier G.M., P. Mandelbrojt, J-L. Vercher, E. Marchetti, and G. Obrecht, 1987, in: Presbiopia, eds L. Stark and G. Obrecht, (New York: Professional Press Book) p 167.

Harris, C.S., 1963, Science, **140**, 812.

Hollerbach, J. M., 1982, TINS, **June**, 189.

Kawato, M., Y. Uno, M. Isobe, and R. Suzuki, 1988, IEEE Control Systems Magazine, **April**, 8.

Lisberger, S.G., and T. J. Sejnowski, 1992, Nature, **360**, 159.

Moray, N., 1986, NATO ASI Series. Vol F21. In: Intelligent Decision Support in Process Environments, eds E. Hollnagel et al. (Berlin Heidelberg: Spring-Verlag) p 273.

Ross, H.E., S. S. Franklin, G. Weltman, and P. Lennie, 1970, Br. J. Physiol., **61**, 365.

Welch, R.B., 1974, Perception, **3**, 367.

Welch, R.B., B. Bridgeman, S. Anand, and K. E. Browman, 1993, Perception & Psychophysics, **54**, 195.

Visual Attention and Cognition
W.H. Zangemeister, H.S. Stiehl and C. Freksa (Editors)
347

Current trends in eye movement measurement techniques

Andrew H. Clarke

Vestibular Research Lab, Dept of Otorhinolaryngology,
Klinikum Benjamin Franklin, FU Berlin.

ABSTRACT

The measurement of eye movements represents an essential major tool for physiologists, neuroscientists, psychologists and clinicians working in the most diverse fields. Accordingly, the development and improvement of techniques for comprehensive, high resolution measurement remain of central interest. The contribution covers the development, including some mention of earlier approaches and a more detailed description of the current technology.

In recent years an increasing number of video-based techniques have been implemented and are being more extensively used. It is maintained that the exploitation of optoelectronic and digital processing devices will increasingly dominate this field in coming years.

The video-based measurement technique, designated as video-oculography (VOG) was developed by the author's research group for clinical and research studies of eye movements related to the vestibular and oculomotor systems. By way of digital image processing, this technique permits recording and measurement of the three - horizontal, vertical and torsional - components of eye movements and the concomitant movements of the head. The current development of similar video-based techniques in other laboratories indicates the importance of this approach. The continuous improvement in imaging and processing technology should enable such systems to fulfil the requirements of most areas of application.

1. INTRODUCTION

Eye movements mean different things to different people. Accordingly, the manner in which they are recorded and the precision with which they are analysed can vary widely among disciplines. The importance of eye movement measurement in applications ranging from the social psychology of gaze contact, through cognitive processes involving examination of scanpaths and the like, to investigation of oculomotor function in neurological disease and the more exact neurophysiological studies of saccade behaviour illustrate this point. In view of the disparate requirements of eye movement research , it can be foreseen that a number of measurement techniques will remain necessary. This contribution will concentrate on image-based evaluation of eye movement, an approach which is gaining momentum due to the ongoing refinement in image sensors and processing hard- and software. The reader is referred to the earlier review by Young & Sheena (1975) and the more recent critical appraisal by Carpenter(1988) of the divers techniques employed for measuring eye movements.

2. HISTORICAL BACKGROUND

Around fifty years ago the first reports of the employment of image-based techniques for oculometric measurement were published. These involved   photographic   and cinematographic   recording of the eye for pupillometric analysis (Machemer, 1933; Lowenstein & Friedman, 1942).

Lowenstein & Lowenfeld, 1957	**Electronic pupillography**
Stark & Sandberg ,1961	**A simple instrument for measuring eye movements.**
Green & Maaseidvaag, 1967	**Closed circuit television pupillometer**
Ishikawa et al, 1970	**A new videopupillography**
Merchant et al, 1974	**Remote measurement of eye direction allowing subject motion over one cubic foot.**
Barbur et al,1987	**A new system for the simultaneous measurement of pupil size and two-dimensional eye movements.**

Table 1: Exemplary approaches using video and image-scanning techniques in oculometry.

Some 25 years later, with the establishment of electronic techniques for image scanning and reproduction, what may be termed "the image processing approach" to oculometric measurements was introduced by such researchers as Lowenstein & Lowenfeld (1957). These authors reported the use of mechano-optical image scanning, as adapted from classic television camera principles. This seminal report was succeeded by a number of refinements by e.g. Asano et al (1962), who employed purely electronic techniques, all based on the television image-scanning principle. Subsequent developments by Green & Maaseidvaag (1967) and O'Neill & Stark (1968) employed more sophisticated exploitation of vidicon imaging tubes and the resulting video signals. This historical development is illustrated by the exemplary publications listed in Table 1.

A particularly novel approach to the measurement of eye position by way of video techniques was published by Merchant et al. (1974). This permitted the evaluation of the horizontal and vertical position of eye in head. This device was unique in that it not only measured eye position, but performed this task remotely, allowing the test subject completely non-invasive freedom of head movement within a space of one cubic foot. The measurement accuracy of this system was reported to be one degree. Refined versions of this technique are employed in currently available, commercial eye-tracking equipment from a number of manufacturers.

In addition to these remote systems, a variety of head-fixed, state-of-the-art video eye trackers perform measurement of horizontal and vertical eye position with accuracies specified between 1.0 deg and 0.1 deg, typically over a range of +/- 2 degs. Discrete sampling rates range from standard video frame frequency of 25 Hz /30 Hz, with multiples of up to 200/240 Hz, whereby the higher sampling rates usually involve a corresponding loss in spatial resolution.

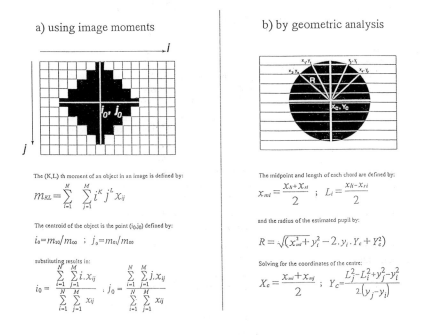

Fig. 1 Principles of pupil tracking. A) Centre of pupil is estimated from low-order image moments. b) Centre and radius of best-fit circle are estimated by geometric analysis, using chord pairs. Both methods allow for estimate improvement by subpixel interpolation (see text).

With only a few exceptions, these devices operate on the principle of tracking the pupil centre, as an indicator of eye position. The estimation of centre of pupil can be performed in a number of ways. The first step, common to almost all techniques, is the binarisation of the eye image. This is performed by thresholding the monochrome video signal (luminance component) of the eye, to separate the 'black pupil' from all other areas of the image. The centre of the 'black pupil' is then calculated on the basis of the binarised image. This can be performed by estimating the centroid of the 'black pupil' using low-order image moments (e.g. Rosenfeld & Kak, 1982). Thus, the image can be regarded as a matrix of point masses, the "mass" of each image pixel being defined by its grey level (cf Fig. 1a). A variation of this approach involves tracing the pupil boundary of the 'black pupil' and averaging the x and y co-ordinates of the boundary points (Hatamian & Anderson, 1983).

Manual evaluation

Graybiel &Woellner 1959	**A new and objective method for measuring ocular torsion**
Melvill Jones , 1963	**Ocular nystagmus recorded simultaneously in three orthogonal planes.**

2D Correlation

Edelmann & Oman, 1981	**Video measurement of torsional eye movement using a soft contact lens technique.**
Parker JA et al, 1985	**Measurement of torsion from multitemporal images of the eye using digital signal processing techniques.**

Polar correlation

Hatamian & Anderson, 1983	**Design considerations for a realtime ocular counterroll instrument.**
Viéville & Masse, 1987	**Ocular counterrolling during active head tilting in humans.**
Peterka, R, 1989	**Response characteristics of the human torsional VOR.**
Clarke AH et al, 1989	**Video-oculography - an alternative method for measurement of three-dimensional eye movements.**
Bucher U et al, 1990	**A novel automatic procedure for measuring ocular counterrolling.**
Moore ST et al, 1991	**VTM - an image processing system for measuring ocular torsion.**

Table 2. Image-processing techniques for measurement of ocular torsion resp. all hree components of eye movement.

Alternatively, after the initial binarisation, the centre of pupil can be estimated by geometric analysis of the boundary points (cf. Fig. 1b). Thus, the centre of that circle, which best fits each pair of identified pupillary 'chords' can be calculated (Barbur et al. 1987). To their advantage, these approaches inherently include averaging procedures, which yield subpixel resolution, i.e. higher spatial resolution than the original pixel resolution of the imaging device.

3. VIDEOOCULOGRAPHY

In recent years, there has been an increasing awareness and interest in the importance of simultaneous measurement of all three degrees of freedom of eye movement - that is, not only the horizontal and vertical, but also the cyclorotational, or torsional component. Recently, systematic research into the three-dimensional aspects of the anatomy and neurophysiology of the vestibular and oculomotor systems (e.g. Cohen & Henn, 1988) has been initiated. This approach has indicated clearly the relevance of the three-dimensional nature of these systems for an adequate understanding of spatial orientation and perception in the natural world. It is beyond doubt that a major precondition for such work was provided by the introduction of the scleral search coil technique by Robinson (1963) and its subsequent refinement by Collewijn et al (1985).

As far as image processing techniques are concerned, an interesting pioneering attempt to record all three degrees of freedom of eye movement responses to visual-vestibular stimulation was reported by Melvill-Jones (1963), who was interested in the eye movements of pilots during aircraft spin manoeuvres. He employed a specially modified head-mounted 16mm film camera for this purpose. After filming, the material was analysed manually on a frame by frame basis on a calibrated projection surface.

Over the last decade a variety of digital image processing approaches to the problem of measuring all three eye movement components has been reported. An illustrative selection is listed in Table 2. Apart from the earlier photographic and cinematographic approaches requiring manual evaluation, the more recent techniques are all based on digital image processing.

2D Correlation techniques

The so-called 2D correlation techniques involve the manual recognition resp. selection of at least two landmarks on the iris of the eye (optimally 180 degs apart). The translation of each landmark can be estimated by calculating the normalised cross-correlation function as a similarity measure on a frame-by-frame basis. The rotation of the image can then be estimated from the distance between the two landmarks and their respective translations from the centre of the image (e.g. Parker et al, 1985).

Polar correlation techniques

This approach exploits the fact that the relevant information for determining ocular torsion is contained in the natural landmarks of the iris. More specifically, in terms of polar co-ordinates, it is premised that this information is reflected by the angular (rather than the radial) component of the iris image. Thus, in addition to accurate determination of centre of pupil this concept requires the extraction of a natural luminance profile derived from circular sampling around the iris1.

This approach was first described by Hatamian & Anderson (1983) for the evaluation of eye movements. To date, it has been employed successfully in various laboratories (cf Table 2).

In our current implementation of the videooculography system, frame-by-frame detection of centre of pupil is performed by geometric analysis of the binarised image as described above. This provides an extremely good estimation of the horizontal and vertical co-ordinates of eye position. Experience has demonstrated that this geometric analysis approach is least sensitive to artefacts such as partial lid closure and shadow effects caused by illumination.

Based on the current centre of pupil, the co-ordinates of the circular sample around the iris are calculated. This amounts to a Cartesian-to-polar transformation. In a second sampling procedure the corresponding luminance profile around the iris is extracted. This circular sample is defined uniquely by its radius and centre. An additional parameter is the width of the sampled annulus, which can be set according to the structure of the available landmarks in the eye to be analysed.

During an initial set-up procedure, the radius and width of the annulus are selected interactively by the operator for one, or more, reference frames with the eye in primary position, i.e. with zero torsion2. These reference frames are employed to establish the zero reference for the subsequent correlation processing.

During the frame-by-frame acquisition, the corresponding subset of pixels are addressed and their luminance (grey-level) value extracted. The luminance profiles thus extracted from the video images are stored in memory for final off-line processing, each profile containing the necessary information to uniquely define the degree of ocular torsion.

Estimation of the ocular torsion is then performed by one-dimensional correlation of the current circular sample against the predetermined zero- reference.

---

[1]This method has the advantage that it exploits the contrast profiles yielded by natural iral landmarks, an is thus completely non-invasive. However, in at least one case (cf. Viéville & Masse, 1987) an optically neutral contact lens with clear infrared markings was attached to the measured eye to enhance the "signal-to-noise ratio".

[2] For present purposes it is sufficient to assume primary position coincides with the subject's head positioned such that head and eye are aligned to fixate a clear target at infinity. The objective is rather to obtain a 'zero-reference' for ocular torsion.

The concept of 'zero' torsion can of course also be challenged, given that torsional instability typically amounts to +/- 30 arc min (Ferman et al, 1987; Diamond & Markham, 1988).

4. VOG MEASUREMENT PROCEDURE

The video images of the eye are acquired by a miniaturised CCD video sensor mounted in a light-occluding mask; infrared LED sources mounted concentrically with the sensor lens

provides the necessary lighting. This assembly was originally designed for use during standard vestibular testing where it is required to exclude voluntary fixation. Alternatively, for those tests requiring freedom of visual field, a head-fixed, dichroic lens arrangement is employed.

The resultant eye image is either input directly to the image processing system or recorded for later off-tape3 processing. The image processing algorithms are implemented on IBM-AT compatible hardware. The current image processing boards operate with the CCIR (European) video norm (25 frames/s resp. 50 fields/s). The hardware permits the acquisition of each video frame into a storage matrix with 768 x 512 square pixels of 8-bit depth (256 discrete grey levels). As mentioned above, realtime operations are restricted to non-critical calculations. These are the calculation of the pupil centroid coordinates (centre of rotation) and extraction of those image data required for calculation of eye torsion (Fig. 2).

European standard video has a frame repetition rate of 25/s; as each frame is divided spatiotemporally into two video fields, the first field being composed of the odd-numbered video lines and the second of the even-numbered lines, two distinct temporal samples of the recorded image (i.e. video fields) are obtained. Eye movement can thus be sampled discretely at a rate of by fifty per second (using the European standard[4]). The image processing algorithms permit evaluation either on a frame-by-frame basis, or on a field-by-field basis. The former yields optimal spatial resolution at the cost of temporal resolution (i.e. 25 samples/s), while the latter renders the twofold sampling rate (50/s) but with a reduced spatial (vertical) resolution. At present, evaluation of ocular torsion is performed at the frame rate of 25/s.

The first stage of image processing identifies the dark pupil area by thresholding the incoming video image, so that all pixels with luminance level below the predefined level are identified, and a binary, or single-bitplane projection is obtained. Thus, the object of interest is demarcated against the background. However, a number of artefacts, reflections, and shadow effects often lead to wrongly identified image elements. These first order errors are corrected by heuristically defined validity checks in the algorithm. In principle, those video lines on the bitplane projection, which transect the black pupil area are selected by this process. The centre of pupil is estimated for each consecutive frame.

---

[3] The term 'off-tape' is employed in order to differentiate between the possible video signal sources. The online VOG acquisition software operates identically regardless of whether the video source is the 'live' camera, or the videotape. In practice, videotape recording of the test sequence has the advantage that during actual testing, the operator need only concentrate on image quality, and possibly observation of the behaviour of the eye. The recorded video material can then be reviewed, edited and evaluated as the question in hand requires.

[4]The current version of the VOG software automatically recognises either CCIR (European) and EIA (US American) video norms. The software then evaluates the video frame rate of 25 /s resp. 30/s.

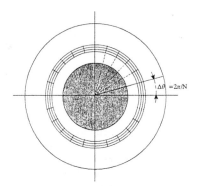

A. Schematic representation of centre-of-pupil definition and polar sampling.

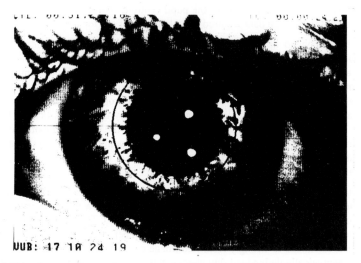

B. Video image with superimposed centre-of-pupil crosshair, fitted pupil boundary and polar sampling ring.

Fig. 2 Illustration of circular sampling in iris image. The schematic diagram in the upper panel (A) indicates how, after determination of centre of pupil, the co-ordinates of the circular sample are calculated and extracted for each frame. The example shows an annulus with a width of four pixels. In the lower panel (B), a still video is shown with superimposed crosshair on the centre of pupil, and the circular sampling path, set-up to extract clear landmarks in the iris.

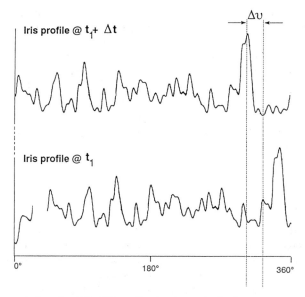

A. Angular shift of iris profile due to ocular torsion.

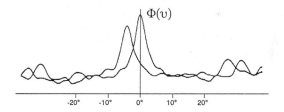

B. Corresponding correlation functions.

Fig. 3 Offline processing operations for determining ocular torsion. After filtering and cross-correlation of each current profile against the zero reference, the maximum of the cross-correlation function is detected; the correlation shift corresponds to the magnitude of ocular torsion. For each profile(see upper panel A) the grey-scale intensity, or luminance (0% - 100%) is plotted against angle (0 to 360 deg). In the lower panel the correlation functions are shown for the autocorrelated zero-reference profile (centred on zero) and for a second profile cross-correlated with the zero-reference. For the illustrated example the ocular torsion amounts to approximately 6 degrees.

The algorithm thus outputs the vertical and horizontal coordinates of pupil position during the sync interval immediately after each video frame. The point defined by these coordinates is constant with reference to the bulbus and coincident with the optic axis of the eye. In this way, realtime frame-by-frame measurement yields a two-dimensional sampled time series representing the horizontal and vertical coordinates of eye position. In addition to the position coordinates, the algorithm also yields a discretely sampled measure of pupil diameter.

The degree of ocular torsion is derived solely from the natural luminance structure of the iris pigmentation; in this way the use of marker contact-lenses and the related slippage problem is eliminated (cf. Lichtenberg et al., 1982).

Addressed in polar coordinates, as described above, an annulus within the iris is defined uniquely by its radius, width and centre. The centre is defined by the estimated centre-of-pupil coordinates. The radius and width are specified as parameters by the operator during the initial set-up, or 'teaching', procedure.

In this manner, the horizontal and vertical coordinates of the pupil centre, the pupil diameter, and the definitive iris profile are acquired in video realtime . These realtime operations reduce the image data stream from the nominal 384 Kbytes (corresponding to the spatial sampling of a video frame of 768 x 512 pixels) to approximately 3 Kbytes per frame. This subset of image data can be stored comfortably on standard mass storage devices and eliminates the problems involved in storing excessive quantities of image data.

Optics[*] (mm)	Eye movement component	Range (deg)	Resolution	
			direct (arc min)	subpixel (arc min)
	vertical	+/-20	14	3
17	horizontal	+/-30	9	2
	torsional	+/-30	18	4
	vertical	+/-34	24	5
10	horizontal	+/-50	15	4
	torsional	+/-30	30	6

[*] Using a sensor of 2/3 inch diagonal, and an object distance of 34 mm.

Table 3. Specification of dynamic range and measurement resolution for three orthogonal components. Measurement resolution is specified for direct, and for subpixel calculation mode. Values are specified for two focal lengths.

Final processing of ocular torsion is performed off-line (Fig. 3) using correlation and approximation techniques. The software interface prompts the user to select the angular range over which the correlation is performed, i.e. after inspection of the acquired iris profiles (0 to 360 degrees), a smaller range - typically 40 - 50 degrees around a clear landmark - is specified. The final cross-correlation estimation routine is performed using the sampled data over this range only. This landmark, or range selection enables optimisation of the effective signal-to-noise ratio of the signals employed for the cross-correlation, which for each eye is uniquely dependent on the contrast characteristics of the natural iris pigmentation.

The degree of ocular torsion is estimated for each successive iris profile by correlating to the predefined zero-reference. The measured shift, or lag, of the correlation peak is directly proportional to the degree of ocular torsion. Measurement resolution is improved by additional subpixel calculations (Table 3). This is performed by least-square-fitting a quadratic function to the resultant cross-correlation function.

5. SYSTEM PERFORMANCE

The effective spatial resolution and dynamic range for the recorded eye movements is determined essentially by the focal length of the lens, and the dimensions and imaging resolution of the CCD sensor and image acquisition hardware. Measurement resolution and range can be modified easily by changing the focal length of the sensor optics. At present, two lenses are in routine use in our laboratory. A 17mm lens is employed when a higher spatial resolution is desirable, e.g. for ocular counterrolling measurements. This involves a smaller measurement range for the horizontal and vertical components. A 10mm lens might be used when a wider measurement range is required. Other focal lengths may be employed, for example, with higher magnification for pupillometric or other ophthalmological measurements.

The measurement bandwidth defined by the sampling rate of 50/s is adequate for measuring those eye movements that occur in routine vestibular testing (smooth pursuit, caloric, rotatory, optokinetic nystagmus activity). It does not however permit detailed analysis of the time course of saccades or of high frequency tremor or miniature eye movements with higher frequency components.

The measurement range and resolution for horizontal and vertical components is better than with EOG and most photoelectric and infrared reflection techniques.

Quantitative measurement of system accuracy and linearity was performed using an artificial eye mounted on a three-degree-of-freedom micro-manipulator. This permitted setting of 'eye position' to better than 0.01 deg. The accuracy and linearity of the VOG system, as determined with this test set-up are presented in Fig 4.

These results demonstrate a system accuracy of better than 0.02 deg, 0.01 deg and 0.025 deg for the vertical, horizontal and torsional components respectively. The linearity, over the measurement range of +/-30 deg was found to be 0.34 +/- 0.24 deg, 0.18 +/- 0.15 deg, and 0.38 +/- 0.28 deg for the vertical, horizontal and torsional planes respectively.

The linearity and validity of the system was also examined using human subjects. Each subject performed a fixation task, which required direction of gaze at a randomised point target sequence. The targets used for this test were red LEDs, situated at 1.0 metres from the subject and arranged in an x-y matrix in the visual field. The LEDs were spaced at 5 deg intervals over a +/-25 deg range. The results of this fixation test, as obtained from a sample of 5 subjects are shown in Fig. 5.

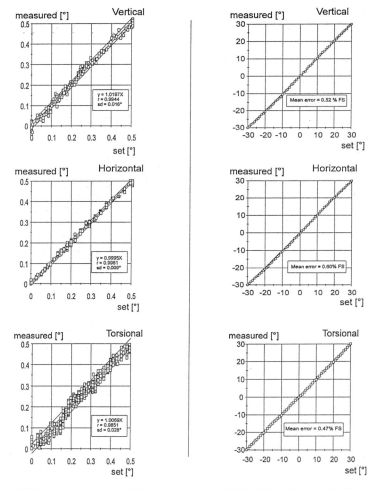

A. VOG accuracy (0 - 0.5°)   **B. VOG linearity (+/- 30°)**

Fig. 4 Measurement of VOG performance in the three orthogonal planes. The accuracy of the system was examined over the range from 0 degrees to 0.5 degrees rotation, and the linearity over the range from +30 degrees to -30 degrees rotation. All measurements were performed using artificial eye mounted on a triaxial micromanipulator (from *Teiwes, 1991*).

Vertical coordinate [°]

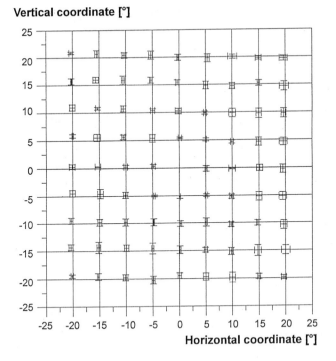

Horizontal coordinate [°]

Fig. 5 The validity was checked using measurements on a group (N=5) of human subjects. The horizontal and vertical co-ordinates were measured using a LED matrix positioned in the frontal plane of the human test subject. Each subject was instructed to fixate the diodes as they were randomly illuminated. The geometry of the diode spacing was corrected to provide equiangular intervals at a radius of curvature of 1 metre (from *Teiwes, 1991*).

In practice, the VOG technique behave robustly over an angular range of up to +/- 25 degrees of horizontal and vertical movement. The ellipticity of the pupil image caused by the projection of the eyeball onto the image sensor plane scarcely effects the accuracy of the algorithms (see Fig. 4B) over this range.

Rather, this phenomenon of ellipticity can be exploited to discriminate eye rotation from pure translation (either of physiological nature, or due to camera-to-head movement). Thus, by approximating an ellipse to the pupil image, the ratio of the principal axes correspond to the actual amount of rotation undergone by the eyeball. Deviation from the expected ellipticity yields a measure of translation. This analysis can equally be performed by two-dimensional Fourier transformation of the pupillary object. Accordingly, any object rotation, is represented by a rotation of equal magnitude and phase in the frequency plane.

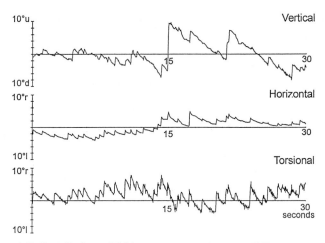

A. Patient: Fr. S, rec. 8.1.94, spontaneous nystagmus activity.

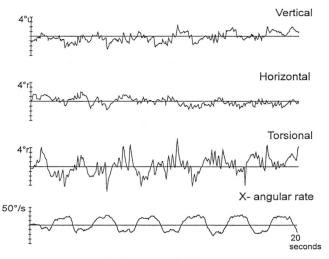

B. Normal: active head roll at approx. 0.3 Hz.

Fig. 6 Examples of VOG recordings of vertical, horizontal and torsional eye components. In the upper panel (A) an excerpt from a record of spontaneous eye movements in a patient suffering from acute peripheral disorder is shown. The patient was seated upright with head stationary.

In the lower panel (B), the complex eye movement response during active head roll (tilt) is illustrated. The subject was cued by a modulated tone. The head angular movement around the naso-occipital (X) was recorded by a rate sensor (see lower trace). The amplitude of head movement was of the order of +/- 15 degrees.

However, if a translatory component of the object is involved, a phase shift occurs in the Fourier transform, while the magnitude remains unaffected.

A comparative study between videooculography and the scleral search coil technique has recently been completed (Teiwes et al. in preparation). The results indicate that the error between the two systems is better than 1% for slow phases of nystagmus and smooth pursuit. As to be expected from the limited VOG sampling rate, the performance of the VOG technique is poorer for eye movements with high frequency content, such as fast phases or saccades. On the other hand, the findings also demonstrate that the VOG technique is immune to the problem of coil slippage, which can be particularly troublesome measurement of ocular torsion. Coil slippage is also known to occur during eye blinks, leading to unpredictable signal drift after the eyes are re-opened. Whilst eye blinks obviously represent loss of data for the VOG technique, such events are clearly marked by the ongoing measure of pupil radius and can be clearly demarcated; further, no signal drift is encountered after the image is regained.

In addition, appropriate matrix transformations have recently been developed, which yield the eye position as a three-dimensional vector, either in Fick or Helmholtz coordinates. This representation also permits correction for the error caused by projection of the eye onto the image plane of the sensor (Moore et al, 1994).

6. APPLICATIONS

A variety of system implementations can be assembled from the currently available sensor elements, recording media and processing units. A minimal solution includes only the VOG assembly together with a small, high quality VTR unit. Such a configuration is presently in use in our clinic as a portable system for the collection of transient eye movement disorders during bedside examination and in other clinical situations where it is important to record transient conditions quickly and in an uncomplicated manner. These recordings can subsequently be analysed off-tape with the laboratory VOG workstation.

The essential role of the vestibulo-ocular system in the stabilisation of the eye during head movement is put to use for the study and functional diagnosis of the vestibular system per se. For this reason, the basic VOG eye movement measurement system is complemented by a head movement sensor system, consisting of triaxial linear accelerometers and angular velocity transducers. With this implementation, comprehensive measurement of head and eye movement in all six, resp. three degrees of freedom is enabled. In the currently available systems, the eye image and head sensor signals are recorded onto a single videotape; thus all data are synchronised for subsequent analysis.

Such an integration has been developed for research applications in extreme environments such as during spaceflight. In this case, several supplementary experimental data signals (triaxial linear acceleration, triaxial angular velocity, visual target position, system status data) are recorded as PCM data synchronously onto a longitudinal track of the video tape.

The resulting video and data records can likewise be analysed off-tape with the laboratory workstation.

A more comprehensive solution for employment in the space environment would include a portable PC workstation, thus providing "local intelligence" and enabling on-line monitoring or telescience applications via downlink communication.

In this sense, the use of modern workstation architectures should facilitate the flexibility required by the individual scientist, and permits both standalone solutions and interfacing to communications and data transmission standards.

7. CONCLUSION

Over the last decade the developments in digital image processing have advanced sufficiently to allow the practical realisation of three-dimensional oculometric measurement systems. Of considerable advantage is the facility for simultaneous video-monitoring of the eye image and realtime eye position measurement during the entire test procedure. This improves the investigator's insight and control during the experiment, increases data quality and permits additional qualitative observations to be made.

This is of particular importance to the clinician, who can exploit these features to improve the classical Frenzel lens examination - a procedure that has remained essential to the preliminary diagnosis of vestibular and oculomotor disorders. The holistic impression obtained from Frenzel lens screening cannot be replaced by even the most precise measurement system (Clarke & Scherer, 1987). Nevertheless, the diagnostic procedure can be substantially improved by supplementing the "hands-on" Frenzel examination of pathological, VOR-related eye movements with video monitoring and on-line quantitative measurement. Moreover, eye movements can be recorded onto videotape for documentation or education purposes, and, if desirable, further detailed measurement can be performed off tape.

The performance and limitations of video-oculometric systems have been outlined in this contribution. At present, the main drawback of such video-based systems remains the limited effective sampling rate, which is usually defined by the timing of the video norm employed (50Hz CCIR, 60Hz EIA). An additional problem is the geometric distortion introduced by the projection of the quasi-spherical eyeball onto a two-dimensional image plane.

In order to attain a higher sampling rate it will be necessary to abandon the standard video conventions, using image sensing and processing architectures that permit flexible, pixel-oriented operations. Such devices are becoming available. Preliminary trials indicate considerable increase in sampling rate (>100-200 /s), without compormising on high spatial resolution (< 6 min arc). The flexible pixel-oriented architecture of such devices also frees up valuable processor time, enabling real-time geometric compensation and other refinements. It is likely that such techniques wil become state-of-the-art in the foreseeable future.

REFERENCES

Asano J, Finnila CA, Sever G, Stanten S, Stark L Willis P (1962) Pupillometry. Quart Prog Rep, 66: 404-412, Res Lab Electronics, MIT Cambridge.

Barbur J, Thomson WD, Forsyth PM (1987) A new system for the simultaneous measurement of pupil size and two-dimensional eye movements. Clin Vision Sci 2(2): 131-142.

Bucher U, Heitger F, Mast F, N(1990) A novel automatic procedure for measuring ocular counterrolling. Beh Res Meth Instr Comp 22(5): 433-439.

Clarke AH, Scherer H (1987) Video meliora proboque - Eine Verbesserung der Frenzelbrille ? Proc. Jahreskongreß Deutscher HNO Gesellschaft.

Clarke AH, Teiwes W, Scherer H (1991) Videooculography - an alternative method for measurement of three-dimensional eye movements. In: Schmid R & Zambarbieri D (eds): Oculomotor Control and Cognitive Processes. Elsevier, Amsterdam.

Cohen B, Henn V (1988) Representations of Three-Dimensional Space In the Vestibular, Oculomotor and Visual Systems. Ann NY Acad Sci Vol 545.

Collewijn H, van der Steen, AV Ferman L, Jansen TC (1985) Human ocular counterroll: assessment of static and dynamic properties from electromagnetic scleral coil recordings. Exp Brain Res 59: 185-196.

Diamond SG, Markham CH (1988) Ocular torsion in upright and tilted positions during hypo- and hypergravity of parabolic flight. Aviat Space Environ Med 1158-1161.

Edelmann ER, Oman CM, Cavallerano AA, Schluter PS (1981) Video measurement of torsional eye movement using a soft contact lens technique. Proc. Conf OMS-81 on the Oculomotor System, Caltech.

Ferman L, Collewijn H, Jansen TC, Berg van der AV (1987) Human gaze stability in the horizontal, vertical and torsional direction during voluntary head movements. Vision Res 27, 939-951.

Graybiel A, Woellner RC (1959) A new and objective method for measuring ocular torsion. J Ophthalmol 47: 349-352.

Green DG, Maaseidvaag F (1967) Closed circuit television pupillometer. J Opt Soc Am 57: 830.

Hatamian M, Anderson DJ (1983) Design considerations for a realtime ocular counterroll instrument. IEEE Trans Biomed Engg BME-13(2): 65-70.

Ishikawa S, Naito M, Inaba K (1970) A new videopupillography. Ophthamologica 160: 248-259.

Lichtenberg BK, Young LR, Arrott AP (1982) Human ocular counterrolling induced by varying linear acceleration. Exp Brain Res 48: 127-136.

Lowenstein O, Friedman ED (1942) Pupillographic studies. I. The present state of pupillography, its method and diagnostic significance. Arch Ophthalmol (NY) 27: 969-993.

Lowenstein O, Lowenfeld IE (1958) Electronic Pupillography Arch Ophthalmol 59: 352-363.

Machemer H (1933) Eine kinematographische Methode zur Pupillenmessung und Registrierung der Irisbewegung. Klin Monatsbl Augenheilkd 19: 302-316.

Melvill Jones G (1963) Ocular nystagmus recorded simultaneously in three orthogonal planes. Acta Otolaryngol (Stockh) 56: 619-631.

Merchant J, Morrissette R, Porterfield JL (1974) Remote measurement of eye movement allowing subject motion over one cubic foot. IEEE Trans Biomed Engg BME-21, 309-317.

Moore ST, Curthoys IS, McCoy SG (1991) VTM - an image processing system for measuring ocular torsion. Comp Meth Progs Biomed 35: 219-230.

Moore ST, Haslwanter T, Curthoys IS, Smith ST (1994) A geometric basis for measurement of three dimensional eye position using image processing. (submitted to Vision Res).

O'Neill GD, Stark L (1968) Triple function ocular monitor. J Opt Soc. AM 58: 570.

Parker JA, Kenyon RV, Young LR (1985) Measurement of ocular torsion from multitemporal images of the eye using digital signal processing techniques. IEEE Trans Biomed Engg BME-32 (1): 28-36.

Peterka R (1991) Response characteristics of the human torsional VOR. Ann NY Acad Sci 656: 877-879.

Robinson DA (1963) A method of measuring eye movement using a scleral search coil in a magnetic field. IEEE Trans Biomed Engg BME-10: 137-145.

Rosenfeld A, Kak A (1982) Digital Picture Processing. Vol II Academic Press, NY.

Stark L, Sandberg A (1961) A simple instrument for measuring eye movements. Quart Prog Rep, 62: 268, Res Lab Electronics, MIT Cambridge.

Teiwes W (1991) Video-Okulografie Registrierung von Augenbewegungen in drei Freiheitsgraden. Doctoral Dissertation, TU Brlin.

Viéville T, Masse M (1987) Ocular counterrolling during active head tilting in humans. Acta Otolaryngol (Stockh) 103: 280-290.

Visual Attention and Cognition
W.H. Zangemeister, H.S. Stiehl and C. Freksa (Editors)
© 1996 Elsevier Science B.V. All rights reserved.

Selective visual attention during multiple-process control

Andreas G. Fleischer and Günther Becker

AB Arbeitswissenschaft/Biokybernetik,
Universität Hamburg, FRG

Abstract

During supervisory control eye movements are central for the performance of aimed actions and the development of working strategies. In order to investigate visual and informational workload the behavioural pattern has been analysed. The presented results provide evidence, that the contextual structure of the task determines the uptake of specific visual informations. The amount of visual workload affecting the subject during the control of four simulated processes is determined by their kinetics. This effect is due to the limited capacity of the subject to deal with more than one process state within a certain time interval. The subject is forced to devide his or her visual attention between different processes. With respect to the amount of information processed by the subject characteristics of the scanpath are described on the basis of the state space in order to obtain criteria which show, that the analysis of eye movements provides an appropriate tool for the evaluation of visual workload during multiple-task performance.

Key words: action theory, visual information processing, scanpath, process control, mental workload

1. Introduction

Man-computer interaction becomes increasingly important for industrial process control since it allows a large flexibility on managing a complex information flow at a single workstation. In general, graphic process information is presented on a screen and has to be visually analysed in order to achieve a decision on the actions to be performed. Normally peripheral vision and the knowledge of the displayed optical structure is used to select the next position of fixation (Fleischer 1986, 1989). The resulting scanpath is determined by the context and the dynamics of the processes to be controlled. However, the demands of multiple process control force the subjects to apply a time-sharing strategy, i. e. to devide visual attention between different processes and keep them in a stable state.

Scanning different homogeneous scenes or searching for a small target in a pattern, results in very similar distributions of fixation duration and saccade magnitude. These observations lead to the hypothesis that saccades are triggered at random (Harris 1989). However, from a cognitive point of view one has to assume that during scanning fixation durations are determined by information load. For instance, during steady keying at a text processor touch typists scan copy and display in a repetitive way (Fleischer 1986). During the first phase they read a certain amount of text from the clipboard and subsequently check the typed characters on the display. On the basis of the memorized text positions saccades larger than 35° were performed without any correction saccades. The landing points of the saccades lie precisely within the area for continuing the reading or the checking process.

The fixation duration depends clearly on the amount of text processed during a single reading and checking cycle and the scanning pattern is determined by the requirements of the information flow. Similar results can be obtained when visually organizing sequences of different hand movements (Fleischer 1989). Ellis and Stark 1986 showed that there are statistical dependencies in the visual scanning behaviour of subjects viewing dynamic displays of air traffic.

The contextual structure of the control task forces the subject to perform sequences of actions on the basis of processing definite elements of visual information in the environment. The uptake of a certain information element requires a specific fixation duration and the subsequent saccade is determined by the task demands as well. The synthesis of these information-related distributions of the fixation durations represents the basis of the overall distribution. These considerations make clear that these specific distributions should be much more sensitive to changes in the structure of the visual target or in the strategy of information uptake than the superimposition of all these distributions. Therefore, the question arises how the performance and the visual information uptake changes as the difficulties, i. e. the kinetics of the process, increase.

2. Methods

In order to test this approach an experimental set-up (Figure 1) was designed which allowed to record the gaze positions of a subject on a screen during the performance of a complex control task. During the experimental session the subject sat at a workstation for computer-aided design and moved a hand-held cursor on a horizontal graphic tablet. The current position of the hand cursor was displayed on the screen in the form of a crosshair cursor consisting of a vertical and a horizontal line, each 5 mm long. In parallel with the actions on the graphic tablet, the head position in space and the eye positon with respect to the head were recorded to gain information about the gaze position on the screen.

The device for measuring eye and head movements was especially developed for this experiment. Eye movements were recorded by means of two infrared reflecting glasses (mir1 and mir2) mounted in front of the eyes and by two cameras (C1 and C2) mounted on the left and right side of the head, respectively. The head movements were recorded by measuring the transmission time of ultrasonic pulses emitted from three sources E1, E2 and E3, mounted on top of the head, to four microphones M1, M2, M3 and M4 above the test table. From these data the X,Y,Z-coordinates of the sources could be computed. Eye movements were sampled every 20 ms and head movements eyery 40 ms. Applying an artifical pupil for computing the line of sight a resolution better than 0.2° could be achieved. Nonlinearities caused by imaging the pupil on the surface of the optical sensor area of the camera and interpolation between calibration points deteriorate the resolution up to ±0.5°. At the beginning of the experiment the subject sitting in an upright body posture was positioned at a viewing distance from the screen of about 50 cm. After this initial adjustment the subject was allowed to behave freely.

During the experimental sessions trained subjects were asked to control a complex process simulation by means of cursor movements. This simulation displayed on a high resolution colour screen (noninterlaced, 60 Hz), consisted of four process units, subsystem SS I to SS IV (Figure 2). It was designed similar to the waterbath paradigm developed by Crossman & Cooke (1974) and Moray & Rotenberg (1989). Each subsystem consisted of a fluid type selector, input valve, recycling valve, output valve and a heater underneath the tank. Temperature and fluid level represent the control variables for each process unit. The settings of the valves and the heater could be changed by positioning the cursor in the valve symbol (square) and activating the corresponding up or down key on the hand cursor (Figure 2: SS I: input 3, output 5, recycling 0, heater +4). The settings of the valves ranged from 0 to 9 and the settings of the heater from -9 (- cooling) to +9 (+ heating). Fluid level and temperature readout of each subsystem were represented by an analogue and by a digital (0-100) display, respectively (SS I: temperature 85°, fluid level 25). At the analogue display of the thermometer the set point of the temperature was displayed (arrow). The cycle time of the simulation amounts to 16.6 ms.

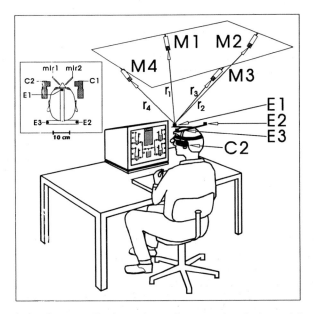

Figure 1. Experimental set-up. The inset shows the measuring device. mir1, mir2: infrared reflecting glasses; C1, C2: CCD-cameras; E1, E2, E3: ultrasonic emitters; M1, M2, M3, M4: microphones; r_1, r_2, r_3, r_4: distances from the ultrasonic emitter E1 to the mircrophones M1, M2, M3 and M4.

According to the recipe given in the upper middle part of the process diagram the subject was asked to mix four different fluids with a specific temperature in the large blending tank shown in the lower middle part of this diagram. These fluids were of different viscosities. This means that the rising velocity of the fluid level ranged in terms of relative units from 1 - that is slow - to 16 - that is fast. Choosing the maximal input setting a tank could be filled within 80 s by applying the slow kinetics and within 5 s by applying the fast kinetics. One recipe contained only fluids of the same kinetics.

At the beginning of the experiment the subject had to choose a certain fluid type and to try to reach the given set points of fluid level and temperature. By positioning the cursor within the corresponding setting symbol and pressing the up-key on the hand cursor the subject had to open the input valve and let a selected fluid rise up to a certain level. Underneath each tank a heater is installed which allows to reach a certain temperature of the fluid. Fluid level and temperature readout of each subsystem were represented by an analogue and a digital readout, respectively. The experimental sessions lasted two hours. The visual scanpath and all actions on the graphic tablet were recorded continuously during the experimental sessions.

Twelve subjects (students with professional training) were tested. During three pre-sessions they were introduced to the task and carefully trained. Each experimental session lasted two hours. During this time the subjects had to handle as many recipes as they could. A moderate time pressure was applied. For statistical evaluation of the presented results the standard deviation of the mean *s* has been plotted in some of the following figures.

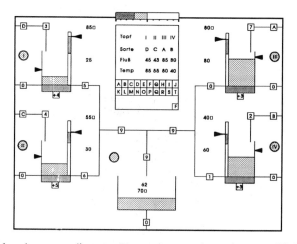

Figure 2. Displayed process diagram. Four process units, subsystem SS I to SS IV are shown. Each subsystem consists of a tank, a fluid type selector, input valve, recycling valve, output valve and a heater underneath the tank; SS I: fluid type D, input 3, recycling 0, output 5, heater +4, fluid level 25, temperature 85°. Arrows mark the set points. The width of the upper middle area which shows the recipe amounts to 7.8 cm.

3. Results and Discussion

An example of the action pattern during the final adjustment of the fluid levels of all four tanks is given in Figure 3. For instance, in order to reach the required set point of subsystem SS I, the subject has opened the input valve to setting 7 and then increases its setting to level 8. The fluid level slowly reaches the set point. The input setting is reduced to setting 4 and then to setting 0. The set point is reached. During the final control phase one can observe an overshoot of subsystem SS II and SS III. The second part of this figure shows the horizontal and the vertical scanpath on the screen; l: left, r: right, u: up, d:down. This is possible since the gaze position on the screen could be computed from the recorded eye- and head-data. The third part presents the cursor positions. The last part presents the actions on the keys of the hand-held cursor. According to the state of the process saccades precede or run in parallel with cursor moves, as can be seen in Figure 3, arrow 2. The target is fixated until the cursor move comes to an end and the required setting is adjusted.

A typical spatial distribution of the gaze positions on the screen during managing a whole recipe is presented on Figure 4a. The gaze positions are marked by black dots. The plotted time interval amounts to 4.5 min. Target areas, i. e. input and output valves as well as display areas, are marked by squares, 3 cm large.

With respect to Figure 4a the allocation of attention is shown on Figure 4b. If the distribution of the gaze position on the screen is considered a three-dimensional probability distribution, contour lines can be computed. For instance, 95% of the gaze positions lie within the shaded areas, 50% lie within the darker shaded areas and 5 % within the darker dotted areas. From this picture it becomes clear that most of the attention is focused on input and temperature settings and on fluid level and temperature readout. This approach provides an efficient criteria for improving display organization. For instance, the operators need a specific display arrangement in order to find the desired information as accurately and quickly as possible (link analysis).

However, if we want to learn more about the underlying principles of visual information flow, we have to investigate sequences of visual information uptake with respect to the contextual structure of the working process. Therefore, two levels of analysis, the action pattern with the hand cursor and the visual information processing have to be considered. First the action pattern of the subjects will be discussed, since the end of an action provides a well defined process status within the contextual structure of task performance.

The operator had to control four subsystems at the same time. However, he or she is only provided with a limited information processing capacity and develops certain strategies during multiple task performance. If the operator is allowed to behave freely, it is assumed that he or she chooses with respect to visual workload an optimal action pattern (strategy) to control the multiple task. He or she tries to avoid underload and overload, respectively.

Slow kinetics should allow the operator to control several processes in parallel, that means the minimal time interval between two required subsequent actions to control a single process is large enough to allow a shift of attention to control other processes in the meantime. In contrast, fast kinetics only allow the operator to focus his or her attention on the desired process until the set point is reached. The operator is forced to work in a serial manner. Due to limited resources for dealing with a task a shift from parallel to serial control of several processes is determined by the amount of mental workload. The operator tries to reach a balance between mental workload and the available amount of resources. Figure 5 (curve consisting of filled circles) shows that with increasing kinetics the subject shifts clearly his or her strategy from parallel to serial performance. 100% serial work means that the subject only concentrates on a single subsystem until it is adjusted without performing any additional control actions concerning other subsystems. The application of a more parallel strategy saves time. Theoretically, controlling four processes fully in a parallel manner would reduce the required time to 25%. Additionally, Figure 5 (curve consisting of squares) shows that the different kinetics of the fluids do hardly affect the strategy in controlling the temperature of the fluids. The thermal capacity of the fluids remains constant throughout the experiment and close to the set point temperature changes are relatively slow.

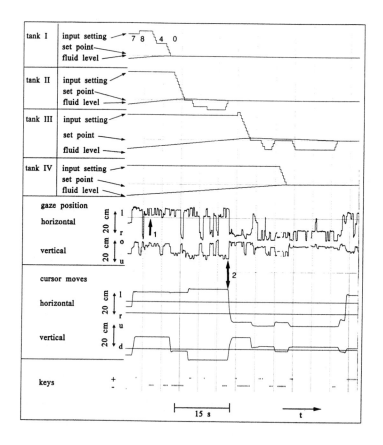

Figure 3. Action pattern during the final control phase.

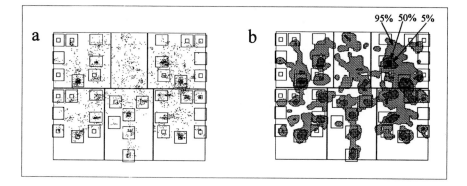

Figure 4. Distributions of gaze positions. (a) Typical spatial distribution of the gaze positions (dots) on the screen during managing a whole recipe. (b) Allocation of attention. 95% of the gaze positions lie within the shaded areas, 50% lie within the darker shaded areas and 5 % within the darker dotted areas.

Increasing kinetics of the fluids cause the subject to shift his or her control strategy from a more parallel to a more serial action pattern. This observation leads to the question up to what extent the available amount of time for the performance of control actions changes with increasing kinetics. According to the settings of the valves fluid and temperature levels reach within certain time intervals the set points, respectively. This buffer time represents the time interval between a valid action on the hand cursor by pressing the up or down key and the time until the set point of the corresponding subsystem would be reached. The buffer time represents the amount of time available to react without exceeding the set point. Depending on this buffer time the subject is forced to shift his or her attention appropriately in order to avoid an overshoot of one or more subsystems. However, one has to take into consideration that the subject is allowed to choose the effective buffer time in a wide range. The relationship between the average buffer time ABT and increasing kinetics is shown in Figure 6a. Additionaly, the average final control time FCT was introduced. During the control of a single subsystem a sequence of actions has to be performed. Finally, if the control level is close to the set point the cursor is positioned within the corresponding valve setting area and will not be moved out of this area until the set point is reached and the valve is closed. This time interval was called final control time FCT and was as well as the buffer time averaged for all experiments. The relationship between the average final control time FCT and increasing kinetics is shown in Figure 6b. From Figure 6 it becomes evident that with increasing kinetics the amount of time to deal with the control task decreases clearly. This effect leads to the assumption that the increase of the kinetics should affect the scanning behaviour of the eyes.

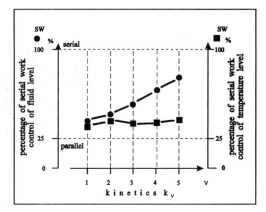

Figure 5. Shift of control strategies caused by different kinetics of the fluids; ●: control of fluid level, ■: control of temperatur.

The contextual structure of the task determines the scanning behaviour of the eyes. It consists of saccades and fixations. The analysis of the distributions of saccade magnitude and of fixation duration should provide insight in the principles of visual information uptake. Figure 6 shows that the available buffer time and the required time for the final adjustment of a tank decreases with increasing kinetics. The time interval for the final control phase becomes shorter and the chance to shift attention or gaze position to another subsystem without overshoot of the current process becomes small for fast kinetics. Therefore, further discussion is focused mainly on eye movements during the final control phase.

Figure 3 (arrow 1) shows, that during the final adjustment of the fluid level repetitive eye movements between different target areas, i. e. valve setting and fluid level readout, are performed. It could be shown by time series analysis that repetitive eye movements are a general feature of the scanning behaviour. In Figure 7a a typical distribution of the magnitude of consecutive saccades (saccade definition with respect to the screen surface: magnitude >3 cm, velocity >40 cm/s) is plotted. This result was obtained from a single experiment. The magnitude of saccades SC_{j+1} were plotted with respect to the magnitude of the preceding saccades SC_j. The distribution is not homogeneous but shows a clear increase of density in the range of the bisector. This means that repetitive saccades of the same size are more likely to occur. Restricting the time series analysis to the final control phase FCT results in the distribution shown in Figure 7b with a high density of the events in the range of the bisector as well.

Further analysis of saccades revealed that the contextual structure of the task and the process layout displayed on the screen determines largely the distributions obtained. Computing the distributions of saccades SC_{j+1} by restricting the height of the preceding saccades SC_j to be within a certain range, leads to the results shown in Figure 8. Under these conditions the frequency distributions of saccade magnitude revealed to be different to what one expects from literature. The distributions do not decrase continuously but show several maxima which are determined by repetitive eye movement characteristics and the layout of the process diagram (Figure 8c,d). During repetitive eye movements the subjects look again and again at an area with unchanged information, i. e. the valve setting remains the same. It is not understood why the subjects shows this repetitive scanning behaviour. It is our favoured hypothesis, that on the one hand the subject uses repetitive eye movements to refresh the sensory memory and that on the other hand the subject avoids to load the displayed information in the working memory. The subject knows where the required information is presented. Why should he or she store the visual information in a more costly way in the working memory.

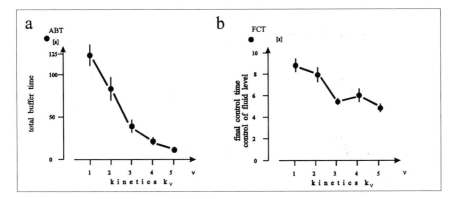

Figure 6. Relationship between buffer time and increasing kinetics, a) average buffer time ABT, b) final control time FCT.

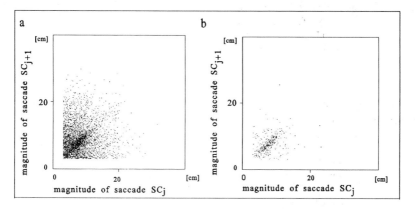

Figure 7. Time series analysis of the magnititude of consecutive saccades. a) Typical distribution of 5095 consecutive saccades obtained from a single experimental session. b) Typical distribution of 434 consecutive saccades from the same experimental session, but restricted to the final control time FCT.

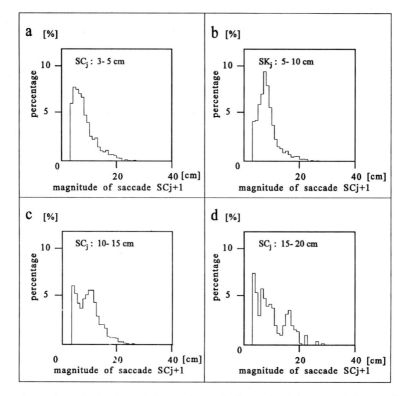

Figure 8. Typical distribution of time series analysis obtained from a whole experiment; SC_j: magnitude of the reference saccade, SC_{j+1}: following saccade. **a)** SC_j: 3-5 cm, **b)** SC_j: 5-10 cm, **c)** SC_j: 10-15 cm, high probability of repetitive saccades between two targets about 10-15 cm apart. **d)** SC_j: 15-20 cm.

During the final control phase a complex behavioural pattern emerges from the individual control strategies and the requirements of information flow. The link between task demands and eye movements is essential to control the processes. Therefore, changes in task demands should affect the distribution of fixation duration (definition of fixation phase with respect to the screen surface: stable within 0.8 cm). From our point of view, the typical shape of the overall distribution of fixation duration (Figure 9d) is composed of specific time intervals required for the uptake of certain but not yet fully identified units of visual information.

Figure 9a shows the distribution of fixation duration during checking the valve setting. The average amounts to 320 ms and the variance is small. Figure 9b shows the distribution of fixation duration during reading the fluid level readout. The average amounts to 1000 ms and the variance is large. Figure 9c shows the distribution (average 564 ms) one obtains only considering the final control phase as a total. The obtained distribution is similar to the overall distribution shown in Figure 9d (average 455 ms). With respect to valve setting and fluid level readout the obtained distributions in Figure 9a and 9b differ enormously. This result lead us to the conclusion, that two different structures of visual information uptake underlie these distributions. In order to test this hypothesis, we investigated whether during the final control phase the average fixation duration of fluid level readout and of valve setting area is affected by the kinetics of the selected fluids, respectively.

The average fixation duration FDA obtained from all recorded fixations (Figure 10, filled triangles) and the average fixation duration FDV of the valve setting display (filled circles) remain nearly constant with respect to increasing kinetics. However, the average fixation duration FDF of the fluid level readout increases steadily (filled squares). We assume that this effect is caused by the limited capacity of the subject to process more visual information. A minimal time interval is required to change the gaze position, to read another part of the display and to return to the previous gaze position. If the subject has to deal with fast kinetics and if the control state is close to the set point it is likely that during this time interval of switching gaze position the corresponding system overshoots the set point. Probably, that is why the subject avoids to change the gaze position. This observation fits to our everyday experience. For instance, during car driving we dare not change the gaze position within a critical moment.

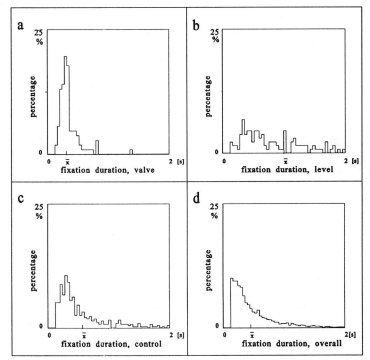

Figure 9. Distributions of fixation duration during the uptake of different visual informations: **a)** checking the valve setting, average 320 ms, **b)** reading the fluid level readout, average 1s, **c)** final control phase, average 564 ms, **d)** full experimental session, average 455 ms.

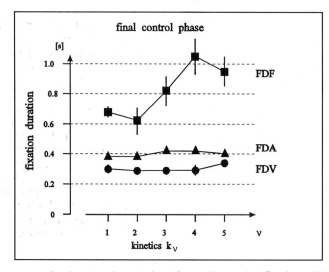

Figure 10. Average fixation duration obtained from all recorded fixations (FDA) , average fixation duration of the valve setting area (FDV) and the fluid level readout (FDF) in relation to increasing kinetics of the fluids.

The presented observations are based on specific scanning strategies and cannot provide evidence for a random execution of saccades. We claim that the context of looking is most important for achieving a better explanation of the described distributions. If, in conjunction with the kinetics of the processes to be controlled, a certain amount of time is required for the uptake of specific information elements, it should be possible to evaluate a paradigm like 'visual workload'. The presented results support the hypothesis, that a link between fixation duration and visual workload can only be expected by considering the fixation duration of specified target informations within the contextual structure of the action pattern. An effect on the overall fixation duration can hardly been expected. This is consistent with the findings during text processing (Fleischer 1986). The subjects have to devide visual attention between different processes in order to keep them in a stable state. Therfore, visual information has to be processed by sequentially fixating different targets. A minimal time interval is required to glance at another display area. During the control of a fast process this time lack may lead to instabilities of the system state. In order to avoid these instabilities the fixation duration of the state readout is increased by the subject.

4. References

Crossman, E. R. R. W., and Cooke, S. E. ,1974, Manual control of slow response systems, in: The Human Operator in Process Control, eds. E. Edwards and F. Leeds, (Taylor & Francis, London) p. 51.

Ellis, S. R. and Stark, L. ,1986, Statistical dependency in visual Scanning, Human Factors **28**, 421.

Fleischer, A. G., 1986, Control of eye movements by working memory load, Biol. Cybern. **55**, 227.

Fleischer, A. G., 1989, Planning and execution of hand movements, Biol. Cybern. **60**, 311.

Fleischer, A. G., Becker, G., 1992, Eye movements during supervisory control, in: Visual Search, ed. A. G. Gale (Taylor & Francis, London) in press.

Harris, C. M., 1989, The ethology of saccades: a non-cognitive model, Biol. Cybern. **60**, 401.

Moray, N. and Rotenberg, I., 1989, Fault management in process control: eye movements and action, Ergonomics **32**, 1319.

Acknowledgements

Supported by the Federal Institution of Occupational Safety and Health, Dortmund, FRG.

CLOSING COMMENT

Elimination of imagery inherited from previous generations of philosophers has always meant progress in science. The idea of a unidirectional flow of events from sensation through perception to motor planning and final execution may have been a stroke of genius in the mind of the philosopher who first thought of it as an ordering principle in psychology, but its (nearly) universal acceptance did not do much for our understanding of the brain. The recent emphasis on the cognitive level as a filter interposed between the sensory inflow and the motor output only stresses the point, and can hardly hide the embarrassment which springs from the confrontation of our simplistic schemes with the psychological reality.

However, over the years, there had always been some who did not succumb to the temptation of unidirectional causal analysis in the style of traditional physics, and instead proposed such ideas as circular causation, feedback, sensory-motor integration, or brains as models of reality. Within the orthodox community, these writers were easily put aside as extravagant, if amusing mavericks, and most of the groundwork in physiology, being limited to restricted segments of the global picture, could well do without their contributions. Some philosophers of the constructivist school saw the point and scolded the neurophysiologists (and computer engineers) for their narrow-mindedness, but they did not speak the language of the laboratory and therefore had little resonance in scientific circles.

As the Italian saying goes, every snarl eventually gets to the comb (*tutti i nodi vengono al pettine*). The intriguing phenomena of attention, unilateral neglect, stability of the perception of space, constancy of object size, form and colour, could no longer be relegated to the realm of psychic oddities when very similar problems were seen to lurk in robotics and artificial intelligence. As it had happened before, for instance with the acceptance of Shannonian information as a conceptual tool in brain theory, or with the idea of neuronal "computation", again it was the synthetic approach of engineering which was instrumental in opening up new vistas in brain science. And suddenly, the ones who had been the mavericks of brain science before, appear to have been the pioneers of a new era which promises to come much closer to the solutions that truly interest us.

V. Braitenberg

Tübingen,
February 1996

Contributors

Ruzena Bajcsy

General Robotics and Active Sensory Perception Lab, Department of Computer and Information Science, University of Pennsylvania, Philadelphia, PA 19104, USA
Fax: +1-215-573-2048
Email: bajcsy@cis.upenn.edu

G. Becker

FB Biokybernetik & Arbeitswissenschaft, Universität Hamburg, Vogt-Kölln-Str. 30, D-22527 Hamburg, Germany
Fax: +49-40-54715-385

V. Braitenberg

Max-Planck-Institut Biologische Kybernetik, Spemannstr. 38, D-72076 Tübingen, Germany
Fax: +49-7071-601575

Y. Choi

Telerobotics & Neurology Units, School of Optometry, University of California at Berkeley, 481 Minor Hall, Berkeley, CA 94720-2020, USA
Fax: +1-510-642-7196
Email: yun@milo.berkeley.edu

A.G.M. Canavan

Institute for Health Science Research, University of Luton, 24th Crazley Green Rd., Luton Bedfordshire LV1 3LF, UK
Fax: +44-1582-45-9787
Email: tcanavan@vax2.luton.ac.uk

A.H. Clarke

Vestibular Research Lab, ENT Clinic, Klinikum der Benjamin Franklin Universität Berlin, Hindenburgdamm 30, D-12200 Berlin, Germany
Fax: +49-30-834-2116
Email: clarke@zedat.fu-berlin.de

J. Findlay

Department of Psychology, University of Durham, Durham DH1 3LE, UK
Fax: +44-191-374-7474
Email: j.m.findlay@durham.ac.uk

A.G. Fleischer

FB Biokybernetik & Arbeitswissenschaft, Universität Hamburg, Vogt-Kölln-Str. 30, D-22527 Hamburg, Germany
Fax: +49-40-54715-385

Linda Free

School of Psychology, University of Birmingham, Edgbaston, Birmingham B15 2TT, UK
Fax: +44-21-414-4897

C. Freksa

Universität Hamburg, FB Informatik, AB Wissens- und Sprachverarbeitung, Vogt-Kölln-Str. 30, D-22527 Hamburg, Germany
Fax: +49-40-54715-385
Email: freksa@informatik.uni-hamburg.de

G. Gauthier

Lab. de Contrôles Sensorimoteurs, Université de Provence, Avenue Niémen, 13397 Marseille Cedex 20, France,
Fax: +33-91-02-05-50
Email: labocsm@vmesa11.u-3.fr

I. Gilchrist

School of Psychology, University of Birmingham, Edgbaston, Birmingham B15 2TT, UK
Fax: +44-21-414-4897

O. Gudon

Lab. de Contrôles Sensorimoteurs, Université de Provence, Avenue Niémen, 13397 Marseille Cedex 20, France,
Fax: +33-91-02-05-50
Email: labocsm@vmesa11.u-3.fr

Hilary Haeske-Dewick

Neurologisches Therapie Centrum, Hohensandweg 37, D-40591 Düsseldorf, Germany
Fax: +49-211-784-353

V. Hoemberg

Neurologisches Therapie Centrum, Hohensandweg 37, D-40591 Düsseldorf, Germany
Fax: +49-211-784-353
Email: hoemberg@ze8.rz.uni-duesseldorf.de

G. Humphreys

School of Psychology, University of Birmingham, Edgbaston, Birmingham B15 2TT, UK
Fax: +44-21-414-4897
Email: g.w.humphreys@bham.ac.uk

M. Husain

Academic Unit of Neuroscience, Charing Cross Hospital, London W6 8RF, UK
Fax: +44-81-846-7715

H. Janßen

Institut für Neuro-Informatik, Ruhr-Universität Bochum, ND 04, Postfach 102148, D-44780 Bochum, Germany
Fax: +49-234-709-4209
Email: heja@neuroinformatik.ruhr-uni-bochum.de

C. Kennard
Academic Unit of Neuroscience, Charing Cross Hospital, London W6 8RF, UK
Fax: +44-81-846-7715
Email: c.kennard@cxwms.ac.uk

U. Oechsner
Neurology Clinic, University of Hamburg, Martinistr. 52, D-20251 Hamburg, Germany
Fax: +49-40-4717-5086
Email: oechsner@uke.uni-hamburg.de

K. Pahlavan
Royal Institute of Technology, Department of Numerical Analysis and Computing Science, Computer Vision & Active Perception Laboratory, S-10044 Stockholm, Sweden
Fax: +46-8-732-0302
Email: kourosh@bion.kth.se

M. Pomplun
Fakultät für Linguistik, Universität Bielefeld, PF 10 01 31, D-33501 Bielefeld, Germany
Fax: +49-521-106-2996
Email: pomplun@hrz.uni-bielefeld.de

R. Purtulis
Lab. de Contrôles Sensorimoteurs, Université de Provence, Avenue Niémen, 13397 Marseille Cedex 20, France,
Fax: +33-91-02-05-50
Email: labocsm@vmesa11.u-3.fr

J. Rieser
Fakultät für Linguistik, Universität Bielefeld, PF 10 01 31, D-33501 Bielefeld, Germany
Fax: +49-521-106-2996
Email: rieser@hrz.uni-bielefeld.de

A. Schierwagen
Universität Leipzig, Institut für Informatik, Augustusplatz 10/11, D-04109 Leipzig, Germany
Fax: +49-341-97-32-209

H. Schwegler
Institut für theoretische Neurophysik, Zentrum für Kognitionswissenschaften, Universität Bremen, D-28334 Bremen, Germany
Fax: +49-421-218-4869
schwegle@theo.physik.uni-bremen.de

R.J. Seitz

Neurologische Klinik, Heinrich-Heine-University Düsseldorf, Moorenstr. 5, Postfach 10 10 07, D-40001 Düsseldorf, Germany
Fax: +49-211-311-8469
Email: seitz@leukos.neurologie.uni-duesseldorf.de

L.W. Stark

Telerobotics & Neurology Units, School of Optometry, University of California at Berkeley, 481 Minor Hall, Berkeley, CA 94720-2020, USA
Fax: +1-510-642-7196
Email: stark@pupil.berkeley.edu

H.S. Stiehl

Universität Hamburg, FB Informatik, AB Kognitive Systeme, Vogt-Kölln-Str. 30, D-22527 Hamburg, Germany
Fax: +49-40-54715-572
Email: stiehl@informatik.uni-hamburg.de

B.M. Velichkovsky

Fakultät Naturwissenschaften und Mathematik, Institut für Psychologie III, Technische Universität Dresden, D-01062 Dresden, Germany
Fax: +49-351-463-3589
Email: velich@psy1:psych.tu-dresden.de

J. Vercher

Lab. de Contrôles Sensorimoteurs, Université de Provence, Avenue Niémen, 13397 Marseille Cedex 20, France,
Fax: +33-91-02-05-50
Email: labocsm@vmesa11.u-3.fr

R. Walker

Department of Psychology, University of Durham, Durham DH1 3LE, UK
Fax: +44-191-374-7474

W.H. Zangemeister

Neurology Clinic, University of Hamburg, Martinistr. 52, D-20251 Hamburg, Germany
Fax: +49-40-4717-5086
Email: zangemeister@uke.uni-hamburg.de

S. Zeki

Department of Anatomy and Developmental Biology, University College London, Gower Street, London WC 1 E6BT
Fax: +44-1-71-380-7316
Email: s.zeki@ucl.ac.uk

Index